RETRIEVER FIELD TRIALS

1967 – 1972

Performances

in

Championship

and

Open and Amateur All-Age Stakes

Published 1973

by

RETRIEVER FIELD TRIAL NEWS

and

LABRADOR RETRIEVER CLUB

Compiled by

AUGUST BELMONT and MRS. TONI REYNOLDS

WILDSIDE PRESS

Thomas W. Merritt

DEDICATION

Thomas W. Merritt, at the time of his death on June 24, 1971 was serving as President and Editor-in-Chief of Retriever Field Trial News, having held that post ever since the acquisition of the News by National Retriever Club and National Amateur Retriever Club.

Tom's interest in retriever field trials was all encompassing. He judged more than 50 trials including four National Championships and the first National Amateur Championship. He was a National Gunner, had starting dogs in eight National Championships and was an interested breeder.

Retriever trials as we know them owe much of their character to Tom, who in his own quiet way did so much to mold and shape this fine sport. One of the original incorporators of the National Retriever Club, he served as its president for three terms. He was a past president of the Labrador Retriever Club. As a director of the American Kennel Club, he acted as chairman of the Retriever Advisory Committee, developing the principles and language by which trials should be conducted, and assured retrievers a strong place in the eyes of the American Kennel Club.

Nothing could be more appropriate than the dedication to Tom's memory of this book, which for the first time combines under one cover the records previously, separately compiled by National Retriever Club, National Amateur Retriever Club and Labrador Retriever Club.

IN APPRECIATION

National Retriever Club and National Amateur Retriever Club wish to express their thanks and sincere appreciation to Retriever Field Trial News for taking over the task of publishing on their behalf the records which previously each Club had to undertake on its own. Thanks are due also to Labrador Retriever Club, which has joined with Retriever Field Trial News as a publisher of this work and permitted the inclusion of the records of open all-age stakes which for previous periods had been published separately by Labrador Retriever Club since the beginning of retriever field trials.

Not only has Retriever Field Trial News undertaken to be a publisher of this book, but its editor, Mrs. Toni Reynolds has spent many hours in compiling information from her files, working with the printer and supplying many of the photographs without which the completion of the task would have been impossible.

August Belmont is not only the author of this book, but his initiative is to be credited for the compilation under one cover of all the information on retriever trials for the period under review, which material had previously been available in three separate volumes only.

The comprehensive information which it contains will make this book a "must" for the book-shelf of every retriever enthusiast.

TABLE OF CONTENTS

FOREWORD

This book for the period 1967 through 1972 for the first time contains in one volume records and information concerning National Retriever Club and the National Championship Stakes; National Amateur Retriever Club and the National Amateur Championship Stakes; Open All-Age Stakes; Amateur All-Age Stakes, and The Double Headers. We have tried to compile a document complete enough to stand on its own feet as a modern reference work.

With respect to the portions of this book concerning Open All-Age and Amateur All-Age Stakes and performance therein, for the first time there are included the total records of all retrievers of all breeds which have placed during the period, 1967-1972, in such stakes. We have included a listing of each parent and grandparent of the dogs so qualifying for inclusion herein. In addition there are listed in alphabetical order the parents of each dog which placed in either of subject stakes showing with respect to each such parent all of his or her first and second generation progeny placing in subject stakes during the period.

Because of limitations of space and the more comprehensive inclusion of data herein, and because substantially similar data can readily be obtained from The American Kennel Club Gazette and Retriever Field Trial News, the usual chronological listings of trials held during the period showing the recipients of first, second, third and fourth places have been omitted.

Supplementary and parallel information to that contained herein is available with respect to earlier Open All-Age stakes in the original 25th Anniversary edition (1931-1955), plus the first Supplement (1956-1961) and the second Supplement (1962-1966), of The Labrador Retriever Club Book. Similarly, information relating to Amateur All-Age stakes since the inception of these stakes is available in The Handbook of Amateur Retriever Trials (1951-1966) and the Supplement thereto covering the period 1962-1966. Similarly also, information with respect to National Championship Stakes for periods prior to 1967 is contained in "The National Retriever Field Trial Club, Inc." and "The National Retriever Field Trial Club, Inc. 1961-1966 Supplement," and information with respect to National Amateur Championship Stakes is contained in the above publications of The National Amateur Retriever Club.

It is impossible that a work of this kind can be prepared and printed without errors and omissions. However, effort has been expended to render this compilation authoritative. Retriever Field Trial News will appreciate hearing from readers concerning any correction which should be filed for use in the next edition.

Much of the basic information in this book was obtained from Retriever Field Trial News through the invaluable help of Mrs. Toni Reynolds, its Editor and Mrs. Theodore E. Fajen, President. Much of the pedigree information with respect to dogs which placed in such trials during the period was obtained with the help of the American Kennel Club. John W. McAssey prepared the portion of this book concerning the Double Headers, and compiled the basic information for the portion concerning Judges.

—August Belmont

PART I

NATIONAL RETRIEVER CLUB

NATIONAL RETRIEVER CLUB

Presidents, Secretary-Treasurers and Chairmen of the Field Trial Committee

Presidents

Alfred Ely	1941, 1942, 1943
John K. Wallace	1944
J. Gould Remick	1945
T. W. Merritt	1946, 1947, 1948
Howes Burton	1949
F. Robert Noonan	1950
Claude Bekins	1951
Paul Bakewell III	1952
C. A. Griscom III	1953
Dr. G. H. Gardner	1954
Chapin Henry	1955
George W. Holmes	1956
W. K. Laughlin	1957
M. B. Wallace, Jr.	1958
Herbert Fleishhacker, Jr.	1959
John Romadka	1960
B. Brannan Reath II	1961
John M. Olin	1962
A. A. Jones	1963
Bing Grunwald	1964
James B. Jackson	1965
Theodore E. Fajen, Jr.	1966
George D. Alt	1967
John Van Bloom	1968
A. Nelson Sills	1969
Hugh I. Klaren	1970
Richard H. Hecker	1971
John W. McAssey	1972

Chairmen of the Field Trial Committee

Morgan Belmont	1941
Ben L. Boalt	1942
M. B. Wallace, Jr.	1943, 1954
C. C. Buehler	1944
Howes Burton	1945, 1953
B. F. Genty	1946
Wes. W. McCain	1947, 1948
L. E. Pierson, Jr.	1949
John Romadka	1950
A. A. Jones	1951, 1959
Dr. G. H. Gardner	1952
Herbert Fleishhacker, Jr.	1955
A. Wells Wilbor	1956
B. Brannan Reath II	1957
W. W. Holes	1958
John M. Olin	1960
James B. Jackson	1961
Bing Grunwald	1962
A. W. Agnew	1963
Theodore E. Fajen, Jr.	1964
A. Nelson Sills	1965
John Van Bloom	1966
John A. Love, Jr.	1967
Hugh I. Klaren	1968
August Belmont	1969
Thomas J. Reames	1970
Gus F. Rathert	1971
Oscar S. Brewer	1972

Secretary-Treasurers

Morgan Belmont	1941
Ben L. Boalt	1942, 1943
Russell G. Lindsay	1944, 1945, 1946
George W. Holmes	1947, 1948, 1949, 1950, 1951, 1952, 1953
Thomas W. Merritt	1954, 1955, 1956, 1957
Dr. George H. Gardner	1958, 1959, 1960, 1961, 1962, 1963 1964, 1965, 1966, 1967, 1968
August Belmont	1969, 1970, 1971, 1972

NATIONAL RETRIEVER CLUB
HISTORICAL HIGHLIGHTS 1967 - 1972

On February 28, 1968, by vote of the member-Clubs, and pursuant to appropriate filings in the State of its incorporation, the name of National Retriever Field Trial Club, Inc. was changed to National Retriever Club, Inc.

At the "Special Called" meeting of member-Clubs on November 12, 1968, the division of the country into three time zones for the conduct of the Championship Stake, with the Stake returning to the Midwest every other year, was revised so that in the future the country would be divided into four newly defined areas, to be known respectively as the PACIFIC ZONE, the WEST CENTRAL ZONE, the EAST CENTRAL ZONE and the ATLANTIC ZONE, with the Stake to be held on a four year rotation basis.

In 1970, The National Championship Stake continued for five days, thus utilizing the extra day (Sunday) anticipated in 1961, when the starting day was moved from Thursday to Wednesday. In 1971, taking advantage of a change in the American Kennel Club's "Standard Procedure" which provided more flexibility in accepting entries of dogs qualifying during the week-end before the commencement of the Stake, the starting date was moved from Wednesday to Tuesday. In 1972, the Stake again lasted five days, ending on a Saturday.

Throughout the period, no changes in qualification requirements were made and they remain:

(a) The winner of the preceding National Championship Stake.

(b) The winner of the preceding National Amateur Championship Stake (must be handled by an amateur)

(c) Those dogs winning a first place and a total of 7 points in an Open or Limited All-Age stakes and during the current year.

During the period the number of Open or Limited All-Age Stakes held, and the number of qualifiers and starters in the National Championship Stakes have been:

	Open or Limited Stakes Held	National Qualifiers	National Starters
1967	125	59	54
1968	127	59	50
1969	130	54	46
1970	134	67	63
1971	138	66	65
1972	140	66	63

Elimination of Contestants by Series

Starters	'67	'68	'69	'70	'71	'72
1st Series	54	50	46	63	65	63
2nd Series	52	45	46	63	62	61
3rd Series	49	41	45	60	53	57
4th Series	37	33	37	50	51	54
5th Series	33	23	31	39	39	38
6th Series	25	23	28	35	29	30
7th Series	17	15	17	22	23	27
8th Series	17	12	11	17	21	19
9th Series	11	11	7	13	16	10
10th Series	11	10	7	11	9	8

Certain Statistics on Starting Dogs and Handlers — 1967-1972

Starters	Dogs	Bitches	Total
Labradors	277	51	328
Goldens	8	—	8
Chesapeakes	3	2	5
Total	288	53	341

Starters Handled by	Amateurs	Professionals	Total
Men	93	227	320
Women	21	—	21
Total	114	227	341

1967 NATIONAL CHAMPIONSHIP STAKE

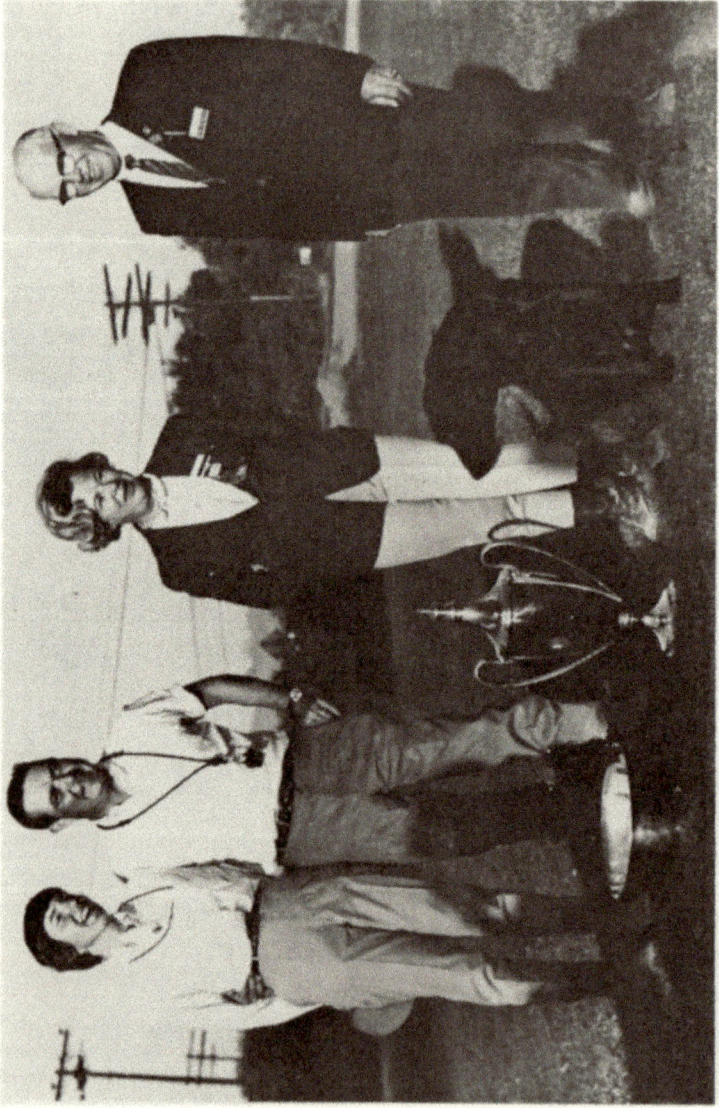

Mohave Valley, California: Winner—Field Champion and Amateur Field Champion Butte Blue Moon (L to R): Ann Walters, D. L. Walters (handler), Brownie Grunwald, Bing Grunwald (owners).

NATIONAL CHAMPIONSHIP STAKE

Mohave Valley, Arizona — November 15-18, 1967

Judges: Harold Mack, Jr., A. Nelson Sills, Dr. Gene B. Starkloff

Starting Dog — Owner	Handler	Series
FC-AFC Butte Blue Moon, L.M. Mr. and Mrs. B. Grunwald	D. L. Walters	WINNER
FC V. Jay's Black Paddle, L.M. J. S. and V. Simpson	Joe Simpson	10
FC Cimaroc Tang, L.M. Wm. K. Laughlin	Ray Staudinger	10
Tar Dessa Venture, L.M. John M. Preston	Ed Minoggie	10
AFC Floodbay's Baron O'Glengarven, L.M. A. B. Mason, Jr.	J. J. Sweezey	10
FC-AFC Guy's Bitterroot Lucky, L.M. Guy P. Burnett	Owner (A)	10
FC-AFC Lord Bomar, L.M. John A. Love, Jr.	D. L. Walters	10
FC Canuck-Crest Cutty Sark, L.F. Mrs. A. P. Loening	J. J. Sweezey	10
FC Mr. Mac's Billy Boy, L.M. Mrs. Geo. Murnane	Joe Riser	10
FC-AFC Flood Bay's Boomerang, L.M. Lewis S. Greenleaf, Jr.	Ray Staudinger	10
FC-'65 NAFC Rebel Chief of Heber, L.M. G. and V. Rathert	Gus Rathert (A)	10
'65 NFC Martens' Little Smoky, L.M. J. M. Olin	T. W. Pershall	8
FC-AFC Jetstone Muscles of Claymar, L.M. C. and M. Johnson	Margie Johnson (A)	8
FC Brazil's Black Jaguar, L.M. Mrs. R. S. Humphrey	Ray Staudinger	8
FC Cedar Haven Matador, L.M. Mrs. Wm. P. Roth	Ed Minoggie	8
FC-AFC Rill Shannon's Dark Del, L.F. M. R. Flannery	Owner (A)	8
FC Sheba's Westmoor Contessa, L.F. S. G. B. Tennant	W. W. Higgs Sr.	8
FC Martens' Scrubby Giant, L.M. L. R. Martens	Owner (A)	6
FC-'67 NAFC Super Chief, L.M. August Belmont	Owner (A)	6
FC Ace of Garfield, L.M. J. M. Olin	T. W. Pershall	6
FC Royal's Moose's Moe, L.M. Dr. E. J. Clayton	C. J. Schomer	6
FC Martens' Stormy, L.M. J. M. Olin	T. W. Pershall	6
FC-AFC Fisherman Bill of Delaware, L.M. Mr. and Mrs. M. B. Wallace, Jr.	T. L. Sorenson	6
FC-AFC Stonegate's Arrow, L.M. Mr. and Mrs. B. Grunwald	D. L. Walters	6
FC-AFC Hoss of Palm Grove, L.M. G. J. Gray	Owner (A)	6
FC-AFC Shawnee Ace of Spades, L.M. P. and L. Lewis	Perle Lewis (A)	5

FC-AFC Jet's Target of Claymar, L.M. Mr. and Mrs. B. Grunwald	D. L. Walters	5
FC-AFC Torque of Daingerfield, L.M. Joan H. Watkins	Owner (A)	5
FC-AFC Sand Gold Kim, L.F. J. D. Bernstein	Owner (A)	5
Dual Ch. Happy Playboy, L.M. Mrs. G. L. Lambert	Wm. Wunderlich	5
FC Gun Thunder Oly, L.M. Mrs. Wm. P. Roth	Ed Minoggie	5
FC Choc of San Juan, L.M. R. C. Cook	Bert Carlson	5
FC Duxbak Scooter, L.M. Mrs. G. L. Lambert	Wm. Wunderlich	5
FC Cinderfeller of Stonesthrow, L.M. J. M. Olin	T. W. Pershall	4
FC-AFC Dessa Rae, L.F. A. J. Scharwat	Owner (A)	4
FC-AFC Balsom's Mandy, L.F. Dr. Ben B. Baker	Owner (A)	4
Dual-AFC Baron's Tule Tiger, C.M. Mrs. W. S. Heller	Owner (A)	4
'66 NFC Whygin Cork's Coot, L.M. Mrs. Geo. Murnane	Joe Riser	3
FC-AFC Tarblood of Absaraka, L.M. John A. Love, Jr.	Ray Olson	3
FC Michelle, L.F. C. R. Tobin	Ed Minoggie	3
FC Del-Tone Buck, L.M. A. M. Stoll	T. L. Sorenson	3
FC Misty of Otter Creek, L.F. R. H. Rovelstad	D. Huffstutter	3
FC-AFC Sazerac Mac, L.M. Dr. J. J. Fertitta	W. W. Higgs, Sr.	3
FC-AFC Glengarven's Mik, L.M. R. Vasselais	Owner (A)	3
I Love Lucy of Audlon, L.F. T. Treadwell III	T. L. Sorenson	3
FC Medlin's Otto of Toothache, L.M. Dr. C. T. Clemm	F. Hayes	3
FC-'66 NAFC Captain of Lomac, L.M. R. R. Deering	Owner (A)	3
FC Double Play of Audlon, L.M. Mrs. H. G. Keeler, Jr.	T. L. Sorenson	3
FC-AFC Grady's Shadee Ladee, L.F. W. K. Chilcott, Jr.	Owner (A)	3
FC Anzac of Zenith, L.M. Carnation Farm Kennels	Doug Orr	2
FC Caliph Obsidian Hobii, L.M. J. G. Odell and A. Ebeling	Ed Carey	2
FC-AFC Paha Sapa Warpath, L.M. Mr. and Mrs. B. Grunwald	D. L. Walters	2
FC Nethercroft Nemo of Nascopie, L.M. Mrs. G. L. Lambert	Wm. Wunderlich	1
FC-AFC Cougar's Rocket, L.M. J. L. Casey	Owner (A)	1

(A) Denotes Amateur Handler

Dogs Which Qualified But Did Not Run

	Owner
FC-AFC Col-Tam of Craignook, L.M.	Mr. and Mrs. R. O. Bateman
FC Cream City Coed, L.F.	Charles H. Morgan
FC-AFC Lucifer's Lady, L.F.	Dr. Richard L. Ellis
AFC Mallard of Devil's Garden, L.M.	Richard H. Johnson
FC Van's Pride Ebony Shadow, L.F.	William E. Van Sickle

Statistics

Starters	Dogs	Bitches	Total
Labradors	43	10	53
Goldens	—	—	—
Chesapeakes	—	1	1
Total	43	11	54

Starters Handled by	Amateurs	Professionals	Total
Men	14	37	51
Women	3	—	3
Total	17	37	54

The 1967 stake was held at McKellip's Ranch, Mohave Valley, Bullhead City, Arizona. Throughout the trial the lack of wind demanded very exact marking and precise handling. Following the precedent set in 1966, most of the handling and throwing of birds was done by volunteer help.

The Field Trial Committee consisted of: John A. Love, Jr. (chairman), George D. Alt, Robert E. Eckis, George H. Gardner (Field Trial secretary), Hugh I. Klaren and John Van Bloom.

First Series

Judges
(L to R): R. Nelson Sills, Dr. Gene B. Starkloff, Harold Mack, Jr.

16

Field Trial Committee

(L to R): Hugh I. Klaren, John A. Love, Jr. (chairman), George D. Alt, Dr. George H. Gardner (F.T. secretary), John Van Bloom.

Test Dog

Herbert Fleishhacker, Jr. and Cha Cha Dancer of District Ten.

Marshals

(Back L to R): Dr. J. J. Fortitta, Mrs. A. W. Wilbor, A. A. Jones, Sandy F. Mackay, C. A. Rice, W. K. Laughlin, (Front L to R): S.G.B. Tennant, S. H. Eliason, Jr. (chief), B. Grunwald, R. Olson, J. W. McAssey, Dr. R. C. Greenleaf.

Traffic Committee

(L to R): P. E. Pound (chairman), S. Nomer, W. Engel, G. W. Faulhaber, W. Wessel, R. Bates, Dr. A. L. Ryan.

1968

NATIONAL CHAMPIONSHIP

STAKE

The Winner
Weldon Spring, Missouri: Winner—Field Champion and 1967 and 1968 National
Amateur Champion Super Chief.
August Belmont, owner and handler.

NATIONAL CHAMPIONSHIP STAKE

Weldon Spring, Missouri — November 13-16, 1968

Judges: Theodore E. Fajen, Jr., James B. Jackson, Dr. John C. Lundy

Starting Dog — Owner	Handler	Series
FC '67-'68 NAFC Super Chief, L.M. August Belmont	Owner (A)	WINNER
'67 NFC-AFC Butte Blue Moon, L.M. Mr. and Mrs. B. Grunwald	D. L. Walters	10
FC-AFC Guy's Bitterroot Lucky, L.M. Guy P. Burnett	Owner (A)	10
AFC Rover of Ramsey Place, L.M. G. R. Pidgeon	T. L. Sorenson	10
FC-AFC Cimaroc Tang, L.M. Wm. K. Laughlin	Ray Staudinger	10
FC Nethercroft Nemo of Nascopie, L.M. Mrs. G. L. Lambert	Wm. Wunderlich	10
FC Brazil's Black Jaguar, L.M. Mrs. R. S. Humphrey	Ray Staudinger	10
FC-AFC Lord Bomar, L.M. J. A. Love, Jr.	Ray Olson	10
FC Tar-Dessa Venture, L.M. J. M. Preston	Ed Minoggie	10
FC-AFC Carr-Lab Penrod, L.M. August Belmont	Louise Belmont (A)	10
FC-AFC Torque of Daingerfield, L.M. Mrs. Joan H. Watkins	Owner (A)	9
Mi-Cris Sailor, L.M. Mrs. Geo. Murnane	Joe Riser	8
FC-AFC Glengarven's Mik, L.M. Roger Vasselais	Owner (A)	7
FC-AFC Hoss of Palm Grove, L.M. Geo. J. Gray	Owner (A)	7
FC Dusty's Doctari, L.M. Mr. and Mrs. R. M. Smith	M. L. Darling	7
FC-AFC Jetstone Muscles of Claymar, L.M. Mr. and Mrs. C. P. Johnson	Margie Johnson (A)	6
FC Duke of Crookston, L.M. John M. Olin	T. W. Pershall	6
Carnation Butter Boy, L.M. Carnation Farm Kennels	Doug Orr	6
FC-AFC Royal's Moose's Moe, L.M. W. D. Connor	C. J. Schomer	6
FC Peg of Turkey Run, L.F. G. P. Schafer, Jr.	Cal Barry	6
FC-AFC Floodbay's Baron O'Glengarven, L.M. A. B. Mason, Jr.	J. J. Sweezey	6
FC Win-Toba's Black High Point, L.M. Mrs. Geo. Murnane	Joe Riser	6
FC Jo Do's Jet Fire, L.M. Dr. F. O. Wright	C. J. Schomer	6
FC Ace of Garfield, L.M. John M. Olin	T. W. Pershall	4
FC Caliph Obsidian Hobbii, L.M. J. G. Odell and A. Ebeling	Ed Carey	4
FC-AFC Creole Sister, L.F. Donald P. Weiss	Owner (A)	4

FC My Rebel, L.M.		
A. Wells Wilbor	R. Reopelle	4
FC-AFC Flood Bay's Boomerang, L.M.		
L. S. Greenleaf, Jr.	Ray Staudinger	4
FC Cedar Haven Matador, L.M.		
Mrs. Wm. P. Roth	Ed Minoggie	4
FC-AFC Nodrog Penny, L.F.		
Gordon B. Olinger	Owner (A)	4
FC-AFC Rosehill's Little Dutch Boots, L.F.		
M. R. Flannery	Owner (A)	4
Lad Crowder's Ranger, L.M.		
B. A. Richardson	Jim Swan	4
FC Van's Pride Ebony Shadow, L.F.		
W. E. Van Sickle	C. J. Schomer	4
FC Michelle, L.F.		
C. R. Tobin	Ed Minoggie	3
FC-AFC Ripp'n Ready, G.M.		
W. D. Connor	C. J. Schomer	3
FC Canuck-Crest Cutty Sark, L.F.		
Mrs. A. P. Loening	J. J. Sweezey	3
'66 NFC Whygin Cork's Coot, L.M.		
Mrs. Geo. Murnane	Joe Riser	3
Dual Ch. Happy Playboy, L.M.		
Mrs. G. L. Lambert	Wm. Wunderlich	3
FC-AFC Jupiter's Hi-Laurel, L.M.		
Cliff Tennant	Owner (A)	3
Luka of Casey's Rocket, L.F.		
Wayne Crook	Owner	3
FC-AFC Fisherman Bill of Delaware, L.M.		
Mr. and Mrs. M. B. Wallace, Jr.	T. L. Sorenson	3
Mr. Lucky of Oak Hill, L.M.		
P. and J. Van Bloom	John Honore	2
FC-AFC Samson's George of Glenspey, L.M.		
Mrs. W. L. Atkins	D. L. Walters	2
FC Warpath Rip, L.M.		
O. S. Brewer	D. L. Walters	2
FC Harrowby Wheeler Dealer, L.M.		
C. L. Weyerhauser	T. L. Sorenson	2
FC Mr. Mac's Billy Boy, L.M.		
Mrs. Geo. Murnane	Joe Riser	1
FC-AFC Mount Joy's Bit O'Ginger, C.F.		
E. C. Fleischmann	Mrs. Fleischmann (A)	1
FC-AFC Tarblood of Absaraka, L.M.		
J. A. Love, Jr.	Owner (A)	1
FC-AFC Rill Shannon's Dark Del, L.F.		
M. R. Flannery	Owner (A)	1
FC-AFC Cougar's Rocket, L.M.		
J. L. Casey	W. Crook	1

(A) Denotes Amateur Handler

Dogs Which Qualified But Did Not Run

	Owner
FC Anzac of Zenith, L.M.	Carnation Farm Kennels
Dual-AFC Baron's Tule Tiger, C.M.	Mrs. Walter S. Heller
FC-AFC Dobe's Desdemona, L.F.	Rupert A. Dobesh
FC Gun Thunder Oly, L.M.	Mrs. Wm. P. Roth
FC Knight's Noel, L.F.	Louise M. Hook
AFC Misty's Sungold Lad, G.F.	K. P. and Valerie D. Fisher
FC-'65 NAFC Rebel Chief of Heber, L.M.	Gus F. and Virginia Rathert
FC Sage's Saskeram Pete, L.M.	Joan and Richard Keskey
Ch-AFC Shamrock Acres Simmer Down, L.F.	Jean and James Marth

Statistics

Starters	Dogs	Bitches	Total
Labradors	40	8	48
Goldens	1	—	1
Chesapeakes	—	1	1
Total	41	9	50

Starters Handled by	Amateurs	Professionals	Total
Men	10	36	46
Women	4	—	4
Total	14	36	50

The 1968 stake was held at the August A. Busch Memorial Wildlife Area, Weldon Spring, Missouri. It will go down as the wet National. The four days of dog work were characterized by some of the most exquisitely uncomfortable weather imaginable. The winner, having won the two preceding National Amateur Championships, became the first National Double Header.

The Field Trial Committee consisted of: Hugh I. Klaren (chairman), John Van Bloom, A. Nelson Sills, John A. Love, Jr., August Belmont, Dr. George H. Gardner (Field Trial secretary).

Judges
(L to R): James B. Jackson, Theodore E. Fajen, Jr., Dr. John C. Lundy.

Field Trial Committee
(L to R): John Van Bloom, John A. Love, Jr., Dr. George H. Gardner (F.T. Secretary), August Belmont, Hugh I. Klaren (chairman). (Not shown): A. Nelson Sills.

Hostess Committee

(L to R) Mrs. Leonard Aldridge, Mrs. Hugh I. Klaren, Chairman; Mrs. John Van Bloom, Mrs. Thomas J. Reames; Mrs. Henry Keeler, Jr., Mrs. Bing Grunwald, Mrs. Mahlon B. Wallace, Jr., Pat Lucas, Retriever Field Trial News Reporter; Mrs. A. Wells Wilbor, Alternate Chairman. (not shown): Mrs. John A. Love, Jr.; Mrs. Helen Pierson; Mrs. Chuck Weyerhaeuser, Mrs. Perry Pound, Mrs. Charles C. B. Stevens.

Grounds Committee

(L to R): Myland Muse, Donald DeZurik (chairman), Donald Bradford, Thomas J. Lucas.

Stewards

(L to R): C. C. B. Stevens (chief), D. Kincaid, Geo. Stebbins, Lee Broussard. (Not shown): E. F. Kitchen, W. Krause, R. M. Smith.

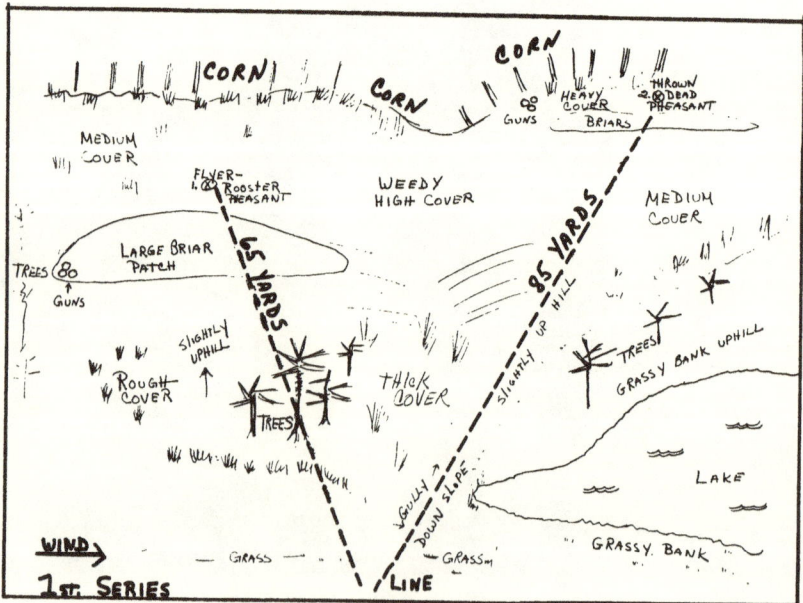

Test No. 1 — Double Mark

1969

NATIONAL CHAMPIONSHIP

STAKE

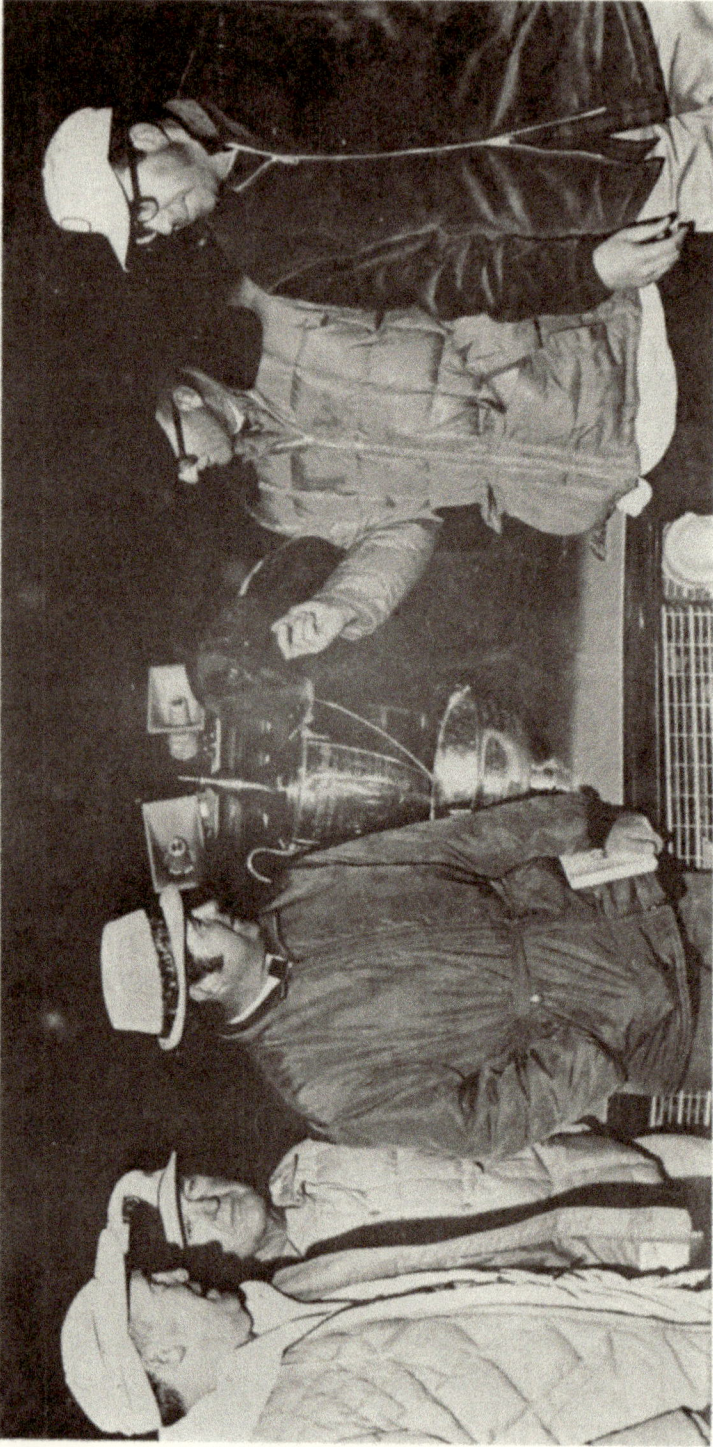

1969 National Champion

Smyrna, Delaware: Winner—National Retriever Champion of 1966 Whygin Cork's Coot.
August Belmont, chairman; Gus F. Rathert, Sid H. Eliason, judges; Joe Riser, handler; S. Alan Williams, judge.

NATIONAL CHAMPIONSHIP STAKE

Smyrna, Delaware — November 12-15, 1969

Judges: Gus F. Rathert, Sid H. Eliason, Jr., S. Alan Williams

Starting Dog — Owner	Handler	Series
'66 NFC Whygin Cork's Coot, L.M. Mrs. Geo. Murnane	Joe Riser	WINNER
FC Dessa's Little Tar Baby, L.M. Douglas David	Ed Minoggie	10
'68 NFC-'67 & '68 NAFC Super Chief, L.M. August Belmont	Owner (A)	10
FC-AFC Misty's Sungold Lad. G.M. K. P. and Valerie D. Fisher	Valerie Fisher (A)	10
FC-'69 NAFC Guy's Bitterroot Lucky, L.M. Guy P. Burnett	Owner (A)	10
FC Ace of Southwood, L.M. John M. Olin	T. W. Pershall	10
FC Shadow of Rocky Lane, L.M. John F. White	T. L. Sorenson	10
FC-AFC Creole Sister, L.F. Donald P. Weiss	Owner (A)	8
FC-AFC Carr-Lab Penrod, L.M. August Belmont	Louise Belmont (A)	8
FC-AFC Royal's Moose's Moe, L.M. W. D. Connor	Owner (A)	8
'67 NFC-AFC Butte Blue Moon, L.M. Mr. and Mrs. B. Grunwald	D. L. Walters	8
FC-AFC Orion's Sirius, L.M. John W. Martin	Owner (A)	7
Sheba's Westmoor Cleopatra, L.F. Mrs. W. K. Laughlin	Ray Staudinger	7
FC-AFC Warpath Tuff, L.M. Dr. R. R. Pfister	D. L. Walters	7
FC-AFC Mount Joy's Bit O'Ginger, C.F. Mrs. E. C. Fleischmann	Owner (A)	7
Carbo Computer, L.M. Mrs. C. V. Brokaw, Jr.	C. Kostrewski	7
FC-AFC Floodbay's Baron O'Glengarven, L.M. A. B. Mason, Jr.	J. J. Sweezey	7
FC-AFC Cimaroc Tang, L.M. Wm. K. Laughlin	Ray Staudinger	6
FC Mr. Mac's Billy Boy, L.M. Mrs. Geo. Murnane	Joe Riser	6
FC Cascade Charade, L.F. Mrs. R. M. Lewis	Vance Morris	6
FC-AFC Rover of Ramsey Place, L.M. G. R. Pidgeon	T. L. Sorenson	6
FC-AFC Serrana Sootana of Genesee, L.F. R. E. and J. Bly	Ray Bly (A)	6
FC Canuck-Crest Cutty Sark, L.F. Mrs. A. P. Loening	J. J. Sweezey	6
FC-AFC Torque of Daingerfield, L.M. Mrs. Joan H. Watkins	Owner (A)	6
FC Tar-Dessa Venture, L.M. John M. Preston	Ed Minoggie	6
FC Nethercroft Nemo of Nascopie, L.M. Mrs. G. L. Lambert	Wm. Wunderlich	6

FC-AFC Glengarven's Mik, L.M.		
Roger Vasselais	Owner (A)	6
FC Dusty's Doctari, L.M.		
R. M. and B. E. Smith	Ralph Smith (A)	6
FC Bigstone Flint, L.M.		
Mr. and Mrs. W. B. Cary	C. J. Schomer	5
FC Misty of Otter Creek, L.F.		
R. H. Rovelstad	D. Huffstutter	5
FC-AFC River Oaks Corky, L.M.		
M. R. Flannery	Owner (A)	5
FC-AFC Smokey of Park Avenue, L.F.		
R. D. and D. C. Borden	Richard Borden (A)	4
Dual Ch. Happy Playboy, L.M.		
Mrs. G. L. Lambert	Wm. Wunderlich	4
FC-AFC Black Rocky, L.M.		
Dr. Roy Hutchinson	M. Logue	4
FC Warpath Rip, L.M.		
Oscar S. Brewer	D. L. Walters	4
Riskin, L.M.		
R. B. Schwyn	W. Crook	4
FC-AFC Lord Bomar, L.M.		
J. A. Love, Jr.	Ray Olson	4
FC-AFC Rowdy's Sean of the Corkies, L.M.		
S. C. Shea	Billy Voigt	3
FC My Rebel, L.M.		
A. Wells Wilbor	R. Reopelle	3
FC Swing Tarzan Swing, L.M.		
J. J. Heneghan	Ed Minoggie	3
FC John's Minnie, L.F.		
G. N. Stewart	J. A. Honore	3
FC-AFC Andy's Partner Pete, L.M.		
Mrs. C. V. Brokaw, Jr.	Owner (A)	3
FC Michelle, L.F.		
C. R. Tobin	Ed Minoggie	3
FC Brazil's Black Jaguar, L.M.		
Mrs. R. S. Humphrey	Ray Staudinger	3
FC Julie Cole of Menomin, L.F.		
Clyde Foster	Jim Weitzel	3
FC Carnation Butter Boy, L.M.		
Carnation Farm Kennels	Doug Orr	2

(A) Denotes Amateur Handler

Dogs Which Qualified But Did Not Run

	Owner
AFC Carnmoney Brigadier, L.M.	R. H. & Dorothea D. Goodrich
FC-AFC Jupiter's Hi-Laurel, L.M.	Cliff Tennant
FC Mi-Cris Sailor, L.M.	Mrs. George Murnane
FC-AFC Mitch of Bitterroot, L.M.	Carl F. Allen
FC-AFC Nodrog Penny, L.F.	Gordon B. Olinger
FC-AFC Samson's George of Glenspey, L.M.	Mrs. Warner L. Atkins
FC Sheba's Westmoor Contessa, L.F.	S. G. Borden Tennant
FC-AFC Velvet's Jezebel, L.F.	Dr. Frank L. Fletcher

Statistics

Starters	Dogs	Bitches	Total
Labradors	35	9	44
Goldens	1	—	1
Chesapeakes	—	1	1
Total	36	10	46

Starters Handled by	Amateurs	Professionals	Total
Men	10	32	42
Women	4	—	4
Total	14	32	46

The 1969 stake was held at the Bombay Hook National Wildlife Refuge, Smyrna, Delaware. The weather started relatively cool and worked down to a chill factor of zero on the last day of the trial. Because of extremely high winds the original 7th series, a water blind, was canceled.

The Field Trial Committee consisted of: A. Nelson Sills, August Belmont (chairman and Field Trial secretary), Hugh I. Klaren, Thomas J. Reames, John W. McAssey and Richard H. Hecker.

Field Trial Committee
(L to R): A. N. Sills, Hugh I. Klaren, J. W. McAssey, T. J. Reames, R. H. Hecker, A. Belmont (chairman and F.T. secretary).

Test Dog
Mrs. Alanson C. Brown III and FC-AFC Tigathoe's Mainliner Mariah.

Setting up for Sixth Series

Traffic Committee

(L. to R): John C. Gibbons, Clinton Swingle, Kenneth Krueger, Col. Wallace Twichell, Dr. Howard A. Priestley (deputy), W. B. Chandlee, Hugh I. Klaren, John F. Nash, Bully Bush, Benjamin Chew, Mrs. Thomas E. Lynch, Jr., Stephen V. Gardner (chairman), C. W. Tyler.

Hostess Committee

(Standing L to R): Mrs. R. G. Metcalf, Mrs. H. Fisher, Mrs. C. W. Tyler, Mrs. M. Stroud, Mrs. W. K. Laughlin, Mrs. G. H. Flinn, Jr., Mrs. J. F. Nash, Mrs. A. N. Sills, Mrs. A. Belmont, Mrs. H. I. Klaren, Mrs. R. M. Lewis. (Kneeling L to R): Mrs. C. V. Brokaw, Jr., Mrs. H. A. Frederick, Mrs. J. J. Mitchell, Mrs. T. J. Reames, Mrs. R. Vasselais.

Marshals

(L to R): Dr. P. C. Kiernan, W. K. Laughlin, R. C. Beach, G. G. Miller, H. C. Potter, W. J. Carrion, D. H. Gearheart, Mrs. B. B. Reath, J. J. Mitchell (chairman), J. E. Lofland, Mrs. R. C. Beach, M. Paterno, J. D. Ryon.

34

1970

NATIONAL CHAMPIONSHIP

STAKE

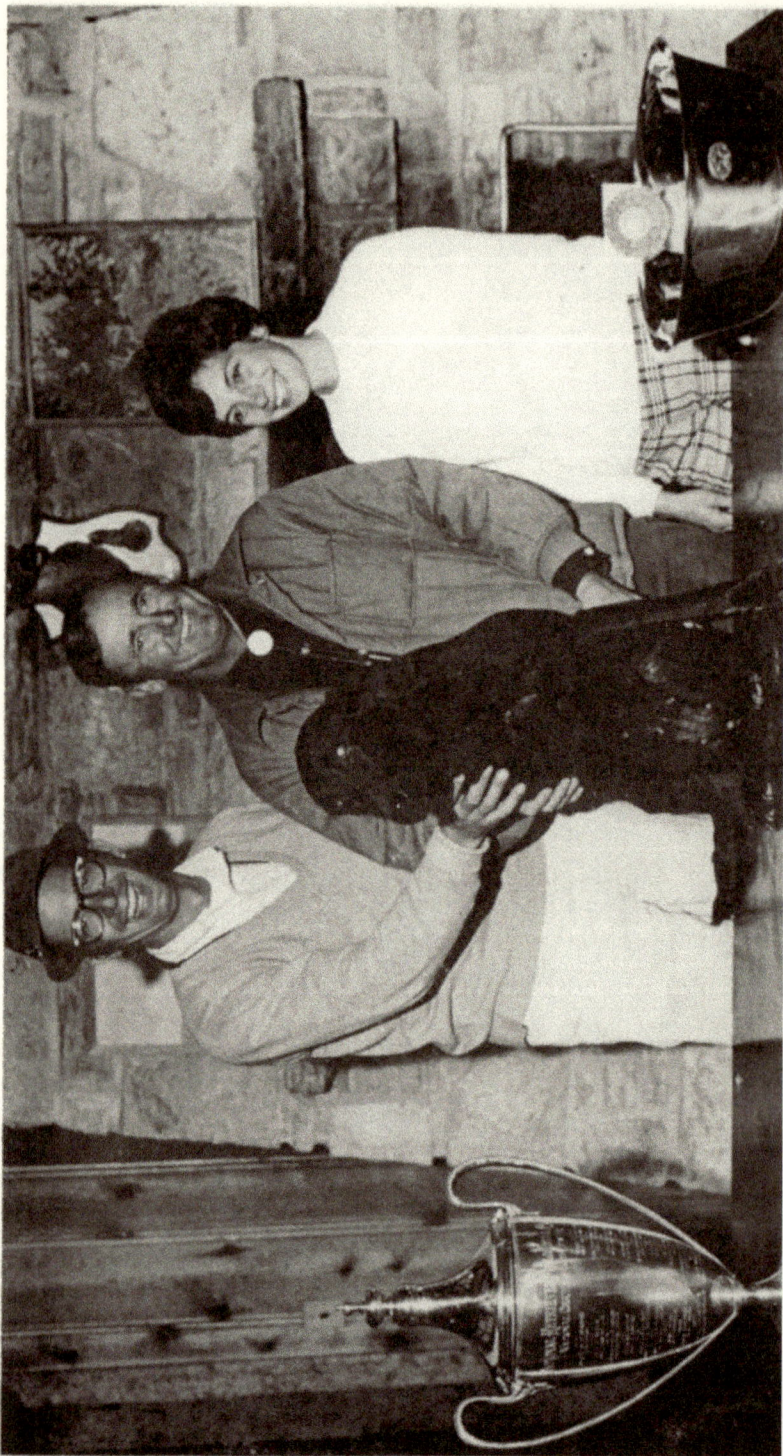

Weldon Spring, Missouri: Winner—Field Champion and Amateur Field Champion Creole Sister. (L to R): Donald P. Weiss (owner-handler), Floyd Hayes, Marion Weiss.

NATIONAL CHAMPIONSHIP STAKE

Weldon Spring, Missouri — November 18-22, 1970

Judges: Dr. Jesse W. Henderson, Edward H. Brown, Marshall Simonds

Starting Dog — Owner	Handler	Series
FC-AFC Creole Sister, L.F. Donald P. Weiss	Owner (A)	WINNER
'66, '69 NFC Whygin Cork's Coot, L.M. Mrs. Geo. Murnane	Joe Riser	10
FC Zipper Dee Do, L.M. Timber Town Kennels	J. J. Sweezey	10
FC Bigstone Flint, L.M. Mr. and Mrs. David Crow	C. J. Schomer	10
FC-AFC Ray's Rascal, L.M. R. H. and D. D. Goodrich	Ray Goodrich	10
FC Nethercroft Nemo of Nascopie, L.M. Mrs. G. L. Lambert	Wm. Wunderlich	10
FC-AFC River Oaks Corky, L.M. M. R. Flannery	Owner (A)	10
Smoky's Black Jet, L.M. John M. Olin	T. W. Pershall	10
'68 NFC-'67, '68 NAFC Super Chief, L.M. August Belmont	Owner (A)	10
FC Mi-Cris Sailor, L.M. Mrs. Geo. Murnane	Joe Riser	10
FC Canuck-Crest Cutty Sark, L.F. Mrs. A. P. Loening	J. J. Sweezey	10
AFC Alamo Black Jack, L.M. N. M. Romano, Jr.	Owner (A)	9
FC Ace of Southwood, L.M. John M. Olin	T. W. Pershall	9
FC Martens' Black Powder Kate, L.F. J. J. Doherty	Ed Minoggie	8
FC Mr. Mac's Billy Boy, L.M. Mrs. Geo. Murnane	Joe Riser	8
FC Carnation Butter Boy, L.M. Carnation Farm Kennels	Doug Orr	8
FC-AFC Tigathoe's Mainliner Mariah, L.F. A. C. Brown III	Owner (A)	8
FC-AFC Randy Mayhall of Tina, L.M. G. Glenn Miller	Joe Riser	7
FC-AFC Beau of Blair House, L.M. Mr. and Mrs. D. Gearheart	Bud Hedges	7
Nascopie Cinder of Lucifer, L.F. Dr. and Mrs. W. N. Bernhard	J. J. Sweezey	7
FC-AFC Misty's Sungold Lad, G.M. K. P. and V. D. Fisher	Valerie Fisher (A)	7
FC-AFC Smokey of Park Avenue, L.F. R. D. and D. C. Borden	R. D. Borden (A)	7
Nilo Brian Boru, L.M. John M. Olin	T. W. Pershall	6
'67 NFC-AFC Butte Blue Moon, L.M. Mr. and Mrs. B. Grunwald	D. L. Walters	6
FC-AFC Clickety Click, G.M. L. P. Floberg and M. Smith	L. P. Floberg (A)	6
FC-AFC Carr-Lab Penrod, L.M. August Belmont	Louise Belmont (A)	6

FC-AF Dee's Dandy Dude, L.M.
M. Paterno .... Owner (A) 6
FC Nilo Staindrop Charger, L.M.
John M. Olin .... T. W. Pershall 6
FC Dusty's Doctari, L.M.
R. M. and B. E. Smith .... R. M. Smith (A) 6
FC Dessa's Little Tar Baby, L.M.
Douglas David .... Ed Minoggie 6
Dual-AFC Koolwaters Colt of Tricrown, C.M.
M. Paterno .... Owner (A) 6
FC Franklin's Tall Timber, L.M.
Mr. and Mrs. R. Magnusson .... R. Magnusson (A) 6
FC Invail's Cavalier Carom, L.M.
Mrs. C. V. Brokaw, Jr. .... C. Kostrewski 6
FC Luka of Casey's Rocket, L.F.
R. J. Doyle, Jr. .... W. Crook 6
FC Warpath Rip, L.M.
Oscar S. Brewer .... D. L. Walters 6
FC Julie Cole of Menonim, L.F.
Dr. P. Hanahan .... J. Weitzel 5
FC Pelican Lake Boo Boo, L.M.
Cal Barry .... Owner 5
FC Bonnie Brooks Tuff & A Half, G.M.
Jane Cooney .... J. Weitzel 5
FC-AFC Sandy of Sourdough, L.M.
C. E. Bunn, Jr. .... Owner (A) 5
Buck's Hobo, L.M.
H. A. Bronner .... F. Hayes 4
FC-AFC Rover of Ramsey Place, L.M.
G. R. Pidgeon .... T. L. Sorenson 4
FC-AFC Royal's Moose's Moe, L.M.
W. D. Connor .... Owner (A) 4
FC Van's Pride Ebony Shadow, L.F.
W. E. Van Sickle .... C. J. Schomer 4
FC Michelle, L.F.
Ed Minoggie .... Owner 4
FC-'69 NAFC Guy's Bitterroot Lucky, L.M.
G. P. Burnett .... Owner (A) 4
AFC Bob's Black Rebel, L.M.
R. and M. L. Chance .... R. Chance (A) 4
FC-AFC Marelvan Mike of Twin Oaks, L.M.
John F. Nash .... J. Weitzel 4
FC-AFC Serrana Sootana of Genesee, L.F.
R. E. and J. M. Bly .... R. E. Bly (A) 4
FC-'70 NAFC Andy's Partner Pete, L.M.
Mrs. C. V. Brokaw, Jr. .... Owner (A) 4
FC Tweet's Bebe, L.M.
Oscar S. Brewer .... J. Rogers 4
Dual Ch. Sherwood's Maid Marion, L.F.
Bill Keyes .... H. Loop 3
FC-AFC Carnmoney Brigadier, L.M.
R. H. and D. D. Goodrich .... R. H. Goodrich (A) ... 3
FC Tar-Dessa Venture, L.M.
John M. Preston .... Ed Minoggie 3
Dual Ch. Happy Playboy, L.M.
Mrs. G. L. Lambert .... Wm. Wunderlich 3
FC Caliph Obsidian Hobii, L.M.
J. Odell and A. Ebeling .... Ed Carey 3
FC My Rebel, L.M.
A. W. Wilbor .... R. Reopelle 3

FC-AFC Samson's George of Glenspey, L.M.		
Mrs. W. L. Atkins	D. L. Walters	3
FC-AFC Floodbay's Baron O'Glengarven, L.M.		
A. B. Mason, Jr.	J. J. Sweezey	3
FC Jo Do's Jet Fire, L.M.		
Dr. F. O. Wright	C. J. Schomer	3
FC Larry's Lasser, L.M.		
G. and N. Roberts	V. C. Morgan	3
FC Baird's Centerville Sam, L.M.		
Mr. and Mrs. M. B. Wallace	T. L. Sorenson	2
FC-AFC Monster Mike, L.M.		
W. B. Stone	C. J. Schomer	2
FC Nassau's Nar of Minnewaska, L.M.		
Mrs. G. L. Lambert	Wm. Wunderlich	2

(A) Denotes Amateur Handler

Dogs Which Qualified But Did Not Run

	Owner
AFC Dent's Midnight Rick, L.M.	Jack Madsen
FC-AFC Grady's Shadee Ladee, L.F.	William K. Chilcott, Jr.
FC-AFC Mollybru Butch of Barmond, L.M.	Rudy R. Deering
FC-AFC Paha's Pow Wow, L.M.	Dr. W. E. Peltzer

Statistics

Starters	Dogs	Bitches	Total
Labradors	47	12	59
Goldens	3	—	3
Chesapeakes	1	—	1
Total	51	12	63

Starters Handled by	Amateurs	Professionals	Total
Men	19	41	60
Women	3	—	3
Total	22	41	63

The 1970 Stake was held at the August A. Busch Memorial Wildlife Area, Weldon Spring, Missouri. The weather, though cool to downright chilly, remained rainless throughout. The Stake lasted five days, finishing on Saturday.

The Field Trial Committee consisted of: Thomas J. Reames (chairman), August Belmont (Field Trial secretary), Richard H. Hecker, Hugh I. Klaren, John W. McAssey, Jesse J. Mitchell, and Gus F. Rathert.

Judges
(L to R): Dr. Jesse W. Henderson, Marshall Simonds, E. H. Brown.

Field Trial Committee
(Top L to R): Hugh I. Klaren, J. W. McAssey, A. Belmont (F.T. secretary), T. J. Reames. (Bottom L to R): R. H. Hecker, Gus F. Rathert. (Not shown): J. J. Mitchell.

Traffic Committee
(L to R): J. F. Nash, Mrs. Chas. Allen, W. R. Burton, Mrs. D. Kamphaus, Jr., C. C. B. Stevens, Mary Howley, R. Magnusson, Mrs. S. B. McCarthy.

Stewards
(Standing L to R): W. C. Rasberry, Jr., G. Poppendorf, S. Vilagi, Dr. Wm. Solberg, L. Broussard (chief). (Kneeling L to R): Dr. J. L. Koch, E. Kitchen, Dr. N. Bone, J. D. Ottley.

Grounds Committee
(L to R): J. W. Dalrymple (chairman), Dr. John DeGarmo, Charles Allen.

Bird Throwers
(Standing L to R): E. M. Carey, R. Mesch, J. A. Love, Jr. (chief), D. Michael.
(Kneeling L to R): W. Frank, T. Hubbard, D. Kamphaus, Jr., J. Trzepacz.

1971

NATIONAL CHAMPIONSHIP

STAKE

Santa Maria, California: Winner—Field Champion Mi-Cris Sailor.
(L to R): Richard H. Hecker (president), Gus F. Rathert (F.T. chairman), Joe Riser (handler).

NATIONAL CHAMPIONSHIP STAKE

Santa Maria, California — November 16-19, 1971

Judges: Warren W. Clarity, Lee C. Broussard, Charles R. York

Starting Dog — Owner	Handler	Series
FC Mi-Cris Sailor, L.M. Mrs. Geo. Murnane	Joe Riser	WINNER
FC Nilo Staindron Charger, L.M. John M. Olin	T. W. Pershall	10
FC-AFC Carnmoney Brigadier, L.M. R. H. and D. D. Goodrich	R. H. Goodrich (A)	10
FC Zipper Dee Do, L.M. Timber Town Kennels	J. J. Sweezey	10
FC Ace of Southwood, L.M. John M. Olin	T. W. Pershall	10
FC-'71 NAFC Dee's Dandy Dude, L.M. M. Paterno	M. Paterno (A)	10
FC-AFC Paha Sapa Warpaint, L.M. Mrs. A. C. Brown III	Owner (A)	10
FC-AFC Carr-Lab Penrod, L.M. August Belmont	Louise Belmont (A)	10
FC Magic Marker of Timber Town, L.M. Marshall Simonds	J. J. Sweezey	10
FC-AFC River Oaks Corky, L.M. M. R. Flannery	Owner (A)	9
FC Smoky's Black Jet, L.M. John M. Olin	T. W. Pershall	9
FC Nassau's Nar of Minnewaska, L.M. Mrs. G. L. Lambert	Wm. Wunderlich	9
FC-AFC Jetstone Muscles of Claymar, L.M. Mrs. M. D. Johnson	Owner	9
FC-AFC Dusty's Doctari, L.M. R. M. and B. E. Smith	M. L. Darling	9
Winrock's Ripper, L.M. Dr. J. H. Anderson	Owner (A)	9
FC-AFC Shadow of Rocky Lane, L.M. John F. White	T. L. Sorenson	9
FC Canuck-Crest Cutty Sark, L.F. Mrs. A. P. Loening	J. J. Sweezey	8
'67 NFC-AFC Butte Blue Moon, L.M. Mr. and Mrs. B. Grunwald	D. L. Walters	8
FC-AFC Warpath Rip, L.M. Oscar S. Brewer	D. L. Walters	8
FC-AFC Bigstone Flint, L.M. Mr. and Mrs. David Crow	C. J. Schomer	8
FC-AFC Midge of Greenwood, L.F. J. Boatright	Owner (A)	8
FC Flint's Nifty Arrow, L.M. Mrs. G. L. Lambert	Wm. Wunderlich	7
V and C Chip, L.M. Dr. A. Jaques	A. N. duTreil	7
Lady of Wake, L.F. W. R. Grimsby	P. McCormick	6
FC Baird's Centerville Sam, L.M. Mr. and Mrs. M. B. Wallace, Jr.	T. L. Sorenson	6
FC-AFC Ray's Rascal, L.M. R. H. and D. D. Goodrich	R. H. Goodrich (A)	6

FC-AFC Pirate's Gold, L.M. W. and A. Murff	Wm. Murff (A)	6
FC-AFC Misty's Sungold Lad, G.M. K. P. Fisher and V. F. Walker	Valerie Walker (A)	6
FC-AFC Orion's Sirius, L.M. John W. Martin	Owner (A)	6
Dual Ch. Happy Playboy, L.M. Mrs. G. L. Lambert	Wm. Wunderlich	5
'68 NFC-'67, '68 NAFC Super Chief, L.M. August Belmont	Owner (A)	5
FC Larry's Lasser, L.M. G. and N. Roberts	V. C. Morgan	5
FC-AFC Beau of Blair House, L.M. Mr. and Mrs. D. H. Gearheart	Bud Hedges	5
FC Bel Aire Lucky Boy, L.M. Mrs. G. L. Lambert	Wm. Wunderlich	5
FC Caliph Obsidian Hobii, L.M. J. Odell and A. Ebeling	Ed Carey	5
FC-AFC Shamrock Acres Drake, L.M. K. Anderson and J. Hogue	Jack Hogue (A)	5
FC-AFC Royal's Moose's Moe, L.M. W. D. Connor	Owner (A)	5
FC-AFC Radar Rip, L.M. R. S. Humphrey	Joan Shoemaker (A)	5
FC Your Shot Minnesota Fats, L.M. G. and D. Anderson	Jim Swan	5
FC Dessa's Little Tar Baby, L.M. Douglas David	Ed Minoggie	4
Black Duke of Sherwood, L.M. Dr. L. M. Roberts	D. L. Walters	4
FC Moby Dick, L.M. Carnation Farm Kennels	Doug Orr	4
FC Randy Dandy of Holly Hill, L.M. Mrs. Wm. Swanland	Hal Loop	4
AFC Candlewood's Little Lou, L.M. Mary C. Howley	Owner (A)	4
FC-AFC Rocky Road of Zenith, L.M. Andrew D. Pruit	C. J. Schomer	4
Carnation Rain Star, L.M. Carnation Farm Kennels	Doug Orr	4
FC Skookum Dale's Nike Mark X, L.M. Mrs. L. S. Greenleaf, Jr.	Ray Staudinger	4
FC Sindbad IV, L.M. R. H. Newbury	Ed Carey	4
FC Bigstone Scout, L.M. Mr. and Mrs. T. E. Fajen, Jr.	J. Weitzel	4
'70 NFC-AFC Creole Sister, L.F. Donald P. Weiss	Owner (A)	4
FC Carnation Butter Boy, L.M. Carnation Farm Kennels	Doug Orr	4
FC Nodrog Punkie, L.M. W. L. Buxton	John Honore	3
FC Hank's Spook, L.M. J. J. Doherty	P. McCormick	3
FC Mr. Mac's Billy Boy, L.M. Mrs. Geo. Murnane	Joe Riser	2
FC My Rebel, L.M. A. W. Wilbor	R. Reopelle	2
FC Bonnie Brooks Tuff & A Half, G.M. C. E. Cooney	J. Weitzel	2

FC Shamrock Acres Super Value, L.M. J. J. Heneghan	Ed Minoggie	2
FC-AFC Harang's Grumpy Express, L.M. J. W. Harang	T. L. Sorenson	2
FC-AFC Tweet's Bebe, L.M. Oscar S. Brewer	D. L. Walters	2
FC-AFC Paha Sapa Warpath, II, L.M. A. J. Robinson	Owner (A)	2
Dual Ch. Danny's Cole Black Slate, L.M. Mrs. G. L. Lambert	Wm. Wunderlich	2
FC-AFC Hiwood's Stormy of Alaska, L.M. R. and J. McFall	Roy McFall (A)	2
FC-AFC Martens' Castaway, L.M. P. R. Fitzgerald	Owner (A)	1
FC-AFC Rodney's Mister M. L. Coon, L.M. G. Cassel and J. Bogrett	Jere Bogrett (A)	1
FC-AFC Ern-Bar's Twinkle Boots, L.M. J. T. Walker II	Owner (A)	1

(A) Denotes Amateur Handler

Dogs Which Qualified But Did Not Run

	Owner
FC Invail's Cavalier Carom, L.M.	Mrs. C. V. Brokaw, Jr.
FC Michelle, L.F.	Edward L. Minoggie
FC Pelican Lake Boo Boo, L.M.	Cal Barry

Statistics

Starters	Dogs	Bitches	Total
Labradors	58	5	63
Goldens	2	—	2
Chesapeakes	—	—	—
Total	60	5	65

Starters Handled by	Amateurs	Professionals	Total
Men	17	42	59
Women	5	1	6
Total	22	43	65

The 1971 Stake was held at Vandenberg Air Force Base, Santa Maria, Calif. The excellent grounds, the tremendous cooperation of Base personnel, particularly in the handling of traffic, and good weather combined to allow the Stake to be completed in four days in spite of the largest number of starters in the history of the National.

The Field Trial Committee consisted of: Gus F. Rathert (chairman), Richard H. Hecker, J. W. McAssey, August Belmont (Field Trial secretary), Oscar S. Brewer, Marshall Simonds and Thomas J. Reames.

Judges
(L to R): Charles R. York, Warren W. Carity, Lee C. Broussard.

Field Trial Committee
(L to R): T. J. Reames, G. F. Rathert (chairman), A. Belmont (F.T. secretary), R. H. Hecker, J. W. McAssey, O. S. Brewer.

Handlers watching test dog — 3rd Series

Hostess Committee
(L to R): Mrs. B. Grunwald, Mrs. E. Cullen, Mrs. W. Saunders, Mrs. R. H. Goodrich, Mrs. R. H. Hecker, Miss G. Rivers, Mrs. E. Corona, Mrs. W. S. Heller (chairman), Mrs. W. Murff Mrs. R. M. Smith. (Not Shown): Mrs. C. Tunnell.

Official Guns

(Standing L to R): W. Gutke, A. W. Agnew, W. Wilson, P. Fulmor, J. Columbo, T. J. Reames, C. S. Ostenberg, E. Piers. (Kneeling L to R): H. Breton (capt.), C. C. Woodson, J. W. McAssey, K. McNeill, R. Harkcom, K. Liddicoat.

Marshals

(Standing L to R): L. E. Pasley, J. D. Ott, E. Craine, Dr. R. L. Ellis (chief), J. T. Walker II, A. Pauley. (Kneeling L to R): Mrs. A. W. Agnew, Mrs. A. A. Jones, Mrs. H. Shidler, Mrs. S. B. MaCarthy.

1972

NATIONAL CHAMPIONSHIP

STAKE

Bosque Del Apache National Wildlife Refuge, San Antonio, New Mexico: Winner—Field Champion & Amateur Field Champion Royal's Moose's Moe. William D. Connor, owner and handler.

NATIONAL CHAMPIONSHIP STAKE

San Antonio, New Mexico — November 14-18, 1972

Judges: Dr. Richard L. Ellis, Richard H. Johnson, Dale Lundstrom

Starting Dog — Owner	Handler	Series
FC-AFC Royal's Moose's Moe, L.M. W. D. Connor	Owner (A)	WINNER
FC Ace of Southwood, L.M. John M. Olin	T. W. Pershall	10
FC Zipper Dee Do, L.M. Timber Town Kennels	J. J. Sweezey	10
LeRoy III, L.M. C. R. Tobin	Ed Minoggie	10
FC-AFC Ray's Rascal, L.M. R. H. and D. D. Goodrich	R. H. Goodrich (A)	10
FC Willowmount El Diablo, L.M. C. E. Cooney	J. Weitzel	10
FC-'71 NAFC Dee's Dandy Dude, L.M. M. Paterno	Owner (A)	10
FC-AFC Baird's Centerville Sam, L.M. Mr. and Mrs. M. B. Wallace, Jr.	T. L. Sorenson	10
AFC Wanapum Dart's Dandy, L.F. Charles L. Hill	Owner (A)	9
FC-AFC Dairy Hill's Michikiniquia, L.F. A. A. Jones	Owner (A)	9
FC Shamrock Acres Super Value, L.M. J. J. Heneghan	Ed Minoggie	8
FC Patsy's Thunder Chief, L.M. R. R. Johnson, Jr.	J. Weitzel	8
FC Round Valley's Lucky Tigger, L.M. Dr. David Collon	Billy Voigt	8
Dual Ch. Happy Playboy, L.M. Mrs. G. L. Lambert	Wm. Wunderlich	8
FC-AFC Carr-Lab Penrod, L.M. August Belmont	Louise Belmont (A)	8
FC-AFC Tigathoe's Mainliner Mariah, L.F. A. C. Brown III	Owner (A)	8
Dual Ch. Danny's Cole Black Slate, L.M. Mrs. G. L. Lambert	Wm. Wunderlich	8
FC-AFC Nemo's Spyder of Round Valley, L.M. Chip Ammarell	Owner (A)	8
FC-'72 NAFC River Oaks Corky, L.M. M. R. Flannery	Owner (A)	8
FC-AFC River Oaks Rascal, L.M. J. M. Pilar	Owner (A)	7
FC-AFC Shadow of Provincetown, L.M. Mrs. J. T. Reeve	W. Crook	7
FC-AFC Warpath Tuff, L.M. O. J. Matthews, Jr.	Owner (A)	7
FC Carnation Butter Boy, L.M. Carnation Farm Kennels	Doug Orr	7
FC-AFC Randy Mayhall of Tina, L.M. G. Glenn Miller	Owner (A)	7
FC-AFC Rocky Road of Zenith, L.M. A. D. Pruitt	Owner (A)	7
FC Cub's Kobi King, C.M. Dan Hartley	C. Crook	7

Shamrock Acres Super Drive, L.M.
Wm. K. Laughlin   Ray Staudinger   7
Angelique, L.F.
J. D. Patopea   C. J. Schomer   6
'71 NFC Mi-Cris Sailor, L.M.
Mrs. Geo. Murnane   Joe Riser   6
FC-AFC Shadow of Rocky Lane, L.M.
John F. White   T. L. Sorenson   6
FC Sauk Trail Senator, L.M.
Oscar S. Brewer   D. L. Walters   5
Country's Delight Caesar, L.M.
Dr. and Mrs. M. Stroud   J. Weitzel   5
FC Nodrog Punkie, L.M.
W. L. Buxton   Owner (A)   5
FC-AFC Ottley's Jazzbo, L.M.
J. D. Ottley   J. J. Sweezey   5
FC-AFC Candlewood's Beau of Beaumont, L.M.
Dr. Joe L. Koch   Owner (A)   5
FC Copy Cat Del Norte, L.F.
M. F. Murray   Jim Swan   5
'68 NFC-'67, '68 NAFC Super Chief, L.M.
August Belmont   Owner (A)   5
FC-AFC Sauk Trail Deepwell "Doc", L.M.
J. N. Boettcher   Owner (A)   5
FC Buck's Hobo, L.M.
H. A. Bronner   Owner (A)   4
FC Hanky's Spook, L.M.
J. J. Doherty   P. McCormick   4
FC-AFC Beau of Blair House, L.M.
Mr. and Mrs. D. H. Gearheart   W. Crook   4
FC Jamie's Little Tigger, L.M.
M. H. Bailey   LeRoy Croshaw   4
FC Your Shot Minnesota Fats, L.M.
T. J. Tracy   Jim Swan   4
FC Nilo Staindrop Charger, L.M.
John M. Olin   T. W. Pershall   4
FC Flint's Nifty Arrow, L.M.
Mrs. G. L. Lambert   Wm. Wunderlich   4
FC Dink's Ginger Guiness Stout, L.F.
Dr. J. D. Ramsey   R. Deskins   4
FC Toni's Blaine Child, L.M.
E. R. Leatherbury   T. L. Sorenson   4
FC-AFC Tioga Joe, G.M.
Vern Weber   Owner (A)   4
FC Smoky's Black Jet, L.M.
John M. Olin   T. W. Pershall   4
FC Lasser's Captain Hook, L.M.
W. D. Swancutt   V. C. Morgan   4
'67 NFC-AFC Butte Blue Moon, L.M.
Mr. and Mrs. B. Grunwald   D. L. Walters   4
FC-AFC Dessa's Black Angel, L.M.
Dr. and Mrs. M. Stroud   Billy Voigt   4
FC-AFC Magic Marker of Timber Town, L.M.
M. Simonds   Owner (A)   4
FC-'70 NAFC Andy's Partner Pete, L.M.
Mrs. C. V. Brokaw, Jr.   C. Kostrewski   4
FC Invail's Cavalier Carom, L.M.
Mrs. C. V. Brokaw, Jr.   C. Kostrewski   3
FC-AFC Deerwood Shantoo, L.F.
D. M. Mahoney   J. Rogers   3

FC Swing Tarzan Swing, L.M.		
J. J. Heneghan	Owner (A)	3
FC-AFC Carnmoney Brigadier, L.M.		
R. H. and D. D. Goodrich	R. H. Goodrich (A)	2
FC-AFC Bigstone Flint, L.M.		
Mr. and Mrs. David Crow	David Crow (A)	2
FC Nassau's Nar of Minnewaska, L.M.		
Mrs. G. L. Lambert	Wm. Wunderlich	2
FC Cody of Wanapum, L.M.		
Mrs. W. K. Laughlin	Ray Staudinger	2
Sills' Black Bandit, L.M.		
Mr. and Mrs. David Crow	John Honore	1
FC-AFC Rimrock's Duke of Orleans, L.M.		
Pete Roussos	Owner (A)	1

(A) Denotes Amateur Handler

Dogs Which Qualified But Did Not Run

Owner

FC Larry's Lasser, L.M.	Gale and Noreen Roberts
FC-AFC Misty's Sungold Lad, G.M.	K. P. Fisher & Valerie F. Walker
Dual and AFC Ronakers Novato Cain, G.M.	Desmond S. MacTavish, Jr.

Statistics

Starters	Dogs	Bitches	Total
Labradors	54	7	61
Goldens	1	—	1
Chesapeakes	1	—	1
Total	56	7	63

Starters Handled by	Amateurs	Professionals	Total
Men	23	39	62
Women	1	—	1
Total	24	39	63

The 1972 Stake was held at the Bosque Del Apache National Wildlife Refuge, San Antonio, New Mexico, and was the first Championship conducted by the recently created West Central Zone. The weather was cool and although rain threatened, it held off except after dark. A wind squall caused the scrubbing of the third series and contributed to the trial being extended into the fifth day.

The Field Trial Committee consisted of: Oscar S. Brewer (chairman), J. W. McAssey, Marshall Simonds, August Belmont (Field Trial secretary), Thomas J. Reames, Gus F. Rathert and Armin C. Frank.

Judges
(L to R): Dr. Richard L. Ellis, Richard H. Johnson, Dale Lundstrom.

Field Trial Committee
(Back row L to R): Marshall Simonds, Armin C. Frank, Jr., August Belmont (F.T. secretary). (Front row L to R): Thomas J. Reames, John W. McAssey, Gus F. Rathert, Oscar S. Brewer (chairman).

Area used in Second and Ninth Series

Hostess Committee

(In door L to R): Mrs. B. B. Grunwald, Mrs. O. S. Brewer (co-chairmen). (Back row L to R): Mrs. G. Johnson, Mrs. R. A. Ellis, Mrs. E. Goppert, Jr., Mrs. W. Buxton, Mrs. J. De Garmo, Mrs. M. Paterno, Mrs. J. Nicholson. to Front row (L to R): Mrs. D. Mahoney, Mrs. C. A. Rice, Mrs. M. Flannery Mrs. T. Reames. (Not shown): Mrs. J. Benson.

Bird Throwers
(L to R): R. Gettys, D. L. Kamphaus, G. Smith, Jay Hokenstrom, J. A. Love, Jr. (chairman), R. Thorson, W. D. Connor.

Traffic Committee
(L to R): H. Ruth, D. Clucas, A. Starke Taylor III, J. Shenar, E. J. Goppert, Jr. (chairman), E. Tautfest, H. A. Jacobs, Dr. I. Brown, C. Burger.

PART II

NATIONAL AMATEUR

RETRIEVER CLUB

NATIONAL AMATEUR RETRIEVER CLUB
FORMER OFFICERS
Presidents

W. W. Holes	1957
Edward R. Spaulding	1958
John Romadka	1959
John F. Nash	1960
Bing Grunwald	1961
Rolland G. Watt	1962
John W. McAssey	1963
Mrs. George H. Flinn, Jr.	1964
Mahlon B. Wallace, Jr.	1965
George D. Alt	1966
John C. Lundy	1967
August Belmont	1968
S. Alan Williams	1969
Richard C. Greenleaf	1970
Sid H. Eliason, Jr.	1971
Michael R. Flannery	1972

Vice-Presidents

Edward R. Spaulding	1957
Lewis S. Greenleaf, Jr.	1957
John M. Olin	1957
Guthrie Bicknell	1958
John Romadka	1958
Joseph W. Smith	1958
John F. Nash	1959
Guy H. Cherry	1959, 1960
Bing Grunwald	1959, 1960
Mrs. George H. Flinn, Jr.	1960, 1961, 1962, 1963
Rolland G. Watt	1961
Charles C. Cook	1961, 1962
John W. McAssey	1961, 1962
Mahlon B. Wallace, Jr.	1962, 1963, 1964
George D. Alt	1962, 1963, 1964, 1965
John C. Lundy	1963, 1964, 1965, 1966
August Belmont	1964, 1965, 1966, 1967
S. Alan Williams	1965, 1966, 1967, 1968
Forrest Flashman	1966, 1967, 1968
Sid H. Eliason, Jr.	1967, 1968, 1969, 1970
Michael R. Flannery	1968, 1969, 1970, 1971
S. G. Borden Tennant	1969, 1970, 1971, 1972
Mrs. Walter S. Heller	1970, 1971, 1972
Guy P. Burnett	1971, 1972
Richard H. Johnson	1972

Secretary-Treasurers

Mahlon B. Wallace, Jr.	1957, 1958, 1959, 1960
K. K. Williams	1961, 1962, 1963, 1964, 1965
John Romadka	1966, 1967, 1968, 1969
John F. Nash	1970, 1971, 1972

NATIONAL AMATEUR RETRIEVER CLUB
HISTORICAL HIGHLIGHTS 1967-1972

During the six year period under review, although a committee appointed for the purpose in 1970 made an in depth review of the Club's By Laws and a number of clarifying changes in these were adopted at the 1971 annual meeting, no basic changes were made in the form of organization of the Club.

Throughout the period, no changes in qualification requirements were made and they remain:

(A) Winner of the previous National Amateur Championship Stake, or

(B) Winner of the National Championship Stake provided the dog was handled by an Amateur in that stake, or

(C) Retrievers which when handled by an Amateur win a first place carrying five championship points, plus two additional championship points in Open, Limited or Amateur All-Age Stakes in American Kennel Club Member Club Trials or trials licensed by the American Kennel Club which begin during the twelve months immediately preceding the first day of June of the year when the Stake is held.

During the period the number of Amateur All-Age Stakes held and the number of qualifiers and starters in the National Amateur Championship Stake have been:

Year	Amateur Stakes Held	National Amateur Qualifiers	National Amateur Starters
1967	120	73	60
1968	126	69	42
1969	128	71	58
1970	132	73	62
1971	135	77	68
1972	138	81	66

Elimination of Contestants by Series

Starters	'67	'68	'69	'70	'71	'72
1st Series	60	42	58	62	68	66
2nd Series	55	41	58	56	67	65
3rd Series	42	38	49	46	62	61
4th Series	31	36	41	34	51	49
5th Series	27	31	37	28	44	36
6th Series	23	27	31	20	30	32
7th Series	16	23	28	20	22	26
8th Series	14	19	27	18	15	19
9th Series	12	15	13	13	12	14
10th Series	9	12	10	10	12	10

Certain Statistics on Starting Dogs and Handlers — 1967-1972

Starters	Dogs	Bitches	Total
Labradors	253	66	319
Goldens	20	7	27
Chesapeakes	9	1	10
Total	283	74	356

Starters Handled By	Men	Women	Total
	294	62	356

1967 NATIONAL AMATEUR
CHAMPIONSHIP STAKE

· The Winner
McCall, Idaho: Winner—Field Champion and Amateur Field Champion Super Chief.
August Belmont (owner and handler).

NATIONAL AMATEUR CHAMPIONSHIP STAKE

McCall, Idaho — June 21-24, 1967

Judges: Edward H. Brown, Hugh I. Klaren, M.D. Orowitz

Starting Dog — Owner	Handler	Series
FC-AFC Super Chief, L.M. August Belmont	Owner	WINNER
FC-AFC Sir Mike of Orchard View, L.M. R. Vasselais	Owner	10
AFC Col-Tam of Craignook, L.M. R. O. Bateman	Owner	10
AFC Guy's Bitterroot Lucky, L.M. G. P. Burnett	Owner	10
FC-AFC Dairy Hill's Mike, L.M. Harold Mack, Jr.	Owner	10
Dual-AFC Baron's Tule Tiger, C.M. Mrs. W. S. Heller	Owner	10
FC-AFC Glengarven's Mik, L.M. R. Vasselais	Owner	10
FC-AFC Lord Bomar, L.M. J. A. Love, Jr.	Owner	10
Rim Rock Roscoe, L.M. Dr. and Mrs. G. B. Starkloff	Dr. Starkloff	10
AFC Hoss of Palm Grove, L.M. G. J. Gray	Owner	9
AFC Caesar of Swinomish, L.M. G. H. Hill	Owner	9
FC-AFC Sam Frizel of Glenspey, L.M. Mrs. W. L. Atkins	Owner	9
FC-AFC Ripp'n Ready, G.M. W. D. Connor	Owner	8
FC-AFC Butte Blue Moon, L.M. Mr. and Mrs. B. Grunwald	B. Grunwald	8
FC & '66 NAFC Captain of Lomac, L.M. R. R. Deering	Owner	7
AFC Shamrock Acres Simmer Down, L.F. Mr. and Mrs. J. Marth	J. Marth	7
Waccamaw's Tinker, L.M. W. A. Chandler	Owner	6
AFC Smoke Tail's Cricket, L.M. Geo. D. Alt	Owner	6
FC-AFC Jetstone Muscles of Claymar, L.M. C. and M. D. Johnson	Margie Johnson	6
FC-AFC Sir Knight Falcon, L.M. P. E. and A. R. Pound	Perry Pound	6
FC-AFC Sand Gold Kim, L.F. J. D. Bernstein	Owner	6
AFC Black "R" of Birch, L.M. Dr. R. G. Gardner	Owner	6
Alamo Black Jack, L.M. N. M. Romano, Jr.	Owner	6
Polaris Luke, L.M. Dr. F. W. Partridge	Owner	5
AFC Copper City Buck, L.M. R. Sparks	Owner	5
FC-AFC Carbon Marker, L.M. Mr. and Mrs. T. E. Fajen, Jr.	T. E. Fajen, Jr.	5

FC-AFC Lucifer's Lady, L.F.
  Dr. R. L. Ellis   Owner   5
Black Rocky, L.M.
  Dr. R. M. Hutchinson   Owner   4
FC-AFC Samson's George of Glenspey, L.M.
  Mrs. W. L. Atkins   Owner   4
AFC Duke of Teddy Bear, L.M.
  C. J. Bierscheid   Owner   4
FC-AFC Flood Bay's Boomerang, L.M.
  L. S. Greenleaf, Jr.   Owner   4
AFC Jilly Girl, L.F.
  F. W. Miller   Owner   3
FC-AFC Frances Fishtail, L.F.
  R. H. Hecker   Owner   3
Rowdy's Sean of the Corkies, L.M.
  S. C. Shea   Owner   3
Gerry's Kaiwa of Rosamond, G.F.
  L. J. and Geraldine Miller   L. J. Miller   3
FC-AFC Torque of Daingerfield, L.M.
  Mrs. Joan H. Watkins   Owner   3
Moll-Leo Cayenne, G.M.
  J. D. Browning   Owner   3
FC-AFC Fisherman Bill of Delaware, L.M.
  Mr. and Mrs. M. B. Wallace, Jr.   Mrs. Wallace   3
FC-AFC Rill Shannon's Dark Del, L.F.
  M. R. Flannery   Owner   3
FC-AFC Stonegate's Arrow, L.M.
  Mr. and Mrs. B. Grunwald   B. Grunwald   3
FC-AFC Grady's Shadee Ladee, L.F.
  W. K. Chilcott, Jr.   Owner   3
AFC Gimp of Lakin, L.M.
  R. Sandahl   Owner   3
AFC Jingo Jo's Duckmaster, L.M.
  Hugh Adams   Owner   2
FC-AFC Mount Joy's Louistoo, C.M.
  E. C. Fleischmann   Mrs. Fleischmann   2
Jet's Target of Claymar, L.M.
  Mr. and Mrs. B. Grunwald   B. Grunwald   2
FC-AFC Tarblood of Absaraka, L.M.
  J. A. Love, Jr.   Owner   2
AFC Golden Rocket's Missile, G.M.
  B. F. Shearer, Jr.   Owner   2
Marelvan Mike of Twin Oaks, L.M.
  J. F. Nash   Owner   2
AFC Rosehill's Little Dutch Boots, L.F.
  M. R. Flannery   Owner   2
Black Michael O'Shea, L.M.
  Dr. F. L. Fletcher   Owner   2
FC-AFC Dairy Hill's Night Watch, L.M.
  A. A. Jones   Owner   2
FC-AFC Black Jet XVI, L.M.
  R. S. Humphrey   Owner   2
AFC Bean Ball, L.F.
  R. H. Hecker   Owner   2
AFC Columbine Loran, L.M.
  Jack Hogue   Owner   2
AFC Irwin's Toby, L.M.
  W. J. Hutchinson   Owner   1
FC-AFC Stilrovin Savannah Gay, G.F.
  Mrs. D. L. Walters   Owner   1

FC-AFC Chesanoma's Kodiak, C.M.		
Dr. W. E. Peltzer	Owner	1
FC-'65 NAFC Rebel Chief of Heber, L.M.		
Gus. F. Rathert	Owner	1
AFC Smoke Tail's Chico, L.M.		
H. A. Jacobs	Owner	1

Dogs Which Qualified But Did Not Run

Owner

FC-AFC Balsom's Mandy, L.F.	Dr. Ben B. Baker
AFC Billy Pawlesta, L.M.	Dr. Jesse W. Henderson
FC-AFC Bingo's Ringo, L.M.	Mr. and Mrs. Cliff Mortensen
AFC Buffalo Charlie, L.M.	Lee Gehrke
AFC Chap, L.M.	Douglas Wright, Jr.
FC-AFC Dessa Rae, L.F.	A. John Scharwat
FC-AFC Dobe's Desdemona, L.F.	Rupert A. Dobesh
'64 NAFC Dutchmoor's Black Mood, L.M.	A. Nelson Sills
FC-AFC Goodrich's Smoky Bear, L.M.	R. H. and D. D. Goodrich
AFC King High Siam, L.M.	S. G. B. Tennant
Oscar's Petite Lightning, L.F.	Mrs. R. M. Lewis
'64 NFC-AFC Ripco's V. C. Morgan, L.F.	J. D. Ott
Shawnee Ace of Spades, L.M.	P. and C. Lewis

Statistics

Starters	Dogs	Bitches	Total
Labradors	43	9	52
Goldens	3	2	5
Chesapeakes	3	—	3
Total	49	11	60

Starters Handled By	Men	Women	Total
	52	8	60

The 1967 Stake was held at the Krusen Ranch, McCall, Idaho. This is a truly picturesque area and the weather was ideal.

The Field Trial Committee consisted of: A. Belmont, S. H. Eliason, Jr., Dr. F. L. Flashman, Dr. F. L. Fletcher, Dr. J. C. Lundy, J. W. McAssey (chairman), K. M. Reiman, J. Romadka (Field Trial secretary), and S. Alan Williams.

Judges
(L to R): M. D. Orowitz, Hugh I. Klaren, E. H. Brown.

Field Trial Committee
(Standing L to R): S. Alan Williams, Dr. F. L. Flashman, J. Romadka (F.T. secretary), K. M. Reiman, Dr. F. Fletcher. (Kneeling L to R): S. H. Eliason, Jr., Dr. J. C. Lundy, A. Belmont, J. W. McAssey (chairman).

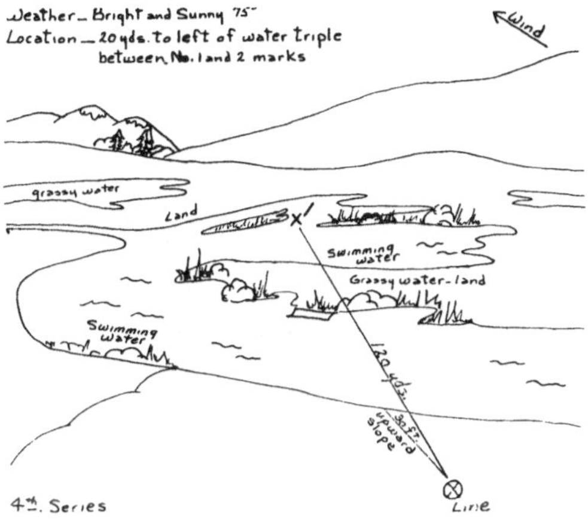

Weather – Bright and Sunny 75°
Location – 20 yds. to left of water triple
between No. 1 and 2 marks

Wind

grassy water

Land

3 X !

Swimming
water

Grassy water-land

Swimming
water

120 yds.

upward
slope

4th. Series

Line

4th Series — Water Blind

Traffic Committee
(Standing L to R): H. Seidell, C. O'Rourke, Dr. A. L. Ryan, R. Cadwalader, L. Larson.
(Kneeling L to R): Dr. R. C. Greenleaf, W. Horn, R. Sparks, Dr. F. W. Partridge.

67

Official Guns

(L to R): Front Row: Stephen Morrisey, Robert Reed, Donald L. Burnett (captain), Al Koppenhauer, William Becker. Back Row: C. A. Ostenberg, Frank Bates, Richard King, Robert Stubblefield, Paul Lalley, John Romadka, Loren Weston, Carrol Rice.

Hostess Committee

(L to R): Miss Maggie Lundy (chairman), Mrs. F. L. Flashman, Mrs. R. G. Gardner, Mrs. Peabody, Mrs. A. Belmont, Mrs. H. Shidler, Mrs. J. Romadka. (Not Shown): Mrs. S. A. Williams, Mrs. D. Adlin, Mrs. S. H. Eliason, Jr., Mrs. F. L. Fletcher, Mrs. L. C King, Mrs. N. Olson, Mrs. K. M. Rieman.

1968

NATIONAL AMATEUR CHAMPIONSHIP

STAKE

Auburn, Maine—Winner—Field Champion and 1967 National Amateur Champion Super Chief. (L to R): J. W. McAssey, Dr. R. C. Greenleaf (judges), August Belmont (owner and handler), W. W. Carity (judge).

NATIONAL AMATEUR CHAMPIONSHIP STAKE

Auburn, Maine — June 18-21, 1968

Judges: Warren W. Carity, Dr. Richard C. Greenleaf, John W. McAssey

Starting Dog — Owner	Handler	Series
FC & '67 NAFC Super Chief, L.M.		
August Belmont	Owner	WINNER
FC-AFC Jetstone Muscles of Claymar, L.M.		
Mr. and Mrs. C. P. Johnson	Mrs. Johnson	10
FC-AFC Glengarven's Mik, L.M.		
R. Vasselais	Owner	10
FC-AFC Fisherman Bill of Delaware, L.M.		
Mr. and Mrs. M. B. Wallace, Jr.	Mrs. Wallace	10
Targhee Sam, L.M.		
Blaine Murray	Owner	10
Dual & AFC Baron's Tule Tiger, C.M.		
Mrs. W. S. Heller	Owner	10
AFC Rosehill's Little Dutch Boots, L.F.		
M. R. Flannery	Owner	10
FC-AFC Rill Shannon's Dark Del, L.F.		
M. R. Flannery	Owner	10
AFC Bean Ball, L.F.		
R. H. Hecker	Owner	10
FC-AFC Lord Bomar, L.M.		
J. A. Love, Jr.	Owner	10
FC-AFC Dairy Hill's Mike, L.M.		
Harold Mack, Jr.	Owner	10
FC-AFC Shamrock Acres Simmer Down, L.F.		
Mr. and Mrs. J. Marth	J. Marth	10
Chipsal John Henry, L.M.		
M. Simonds	Owner	9
Misty's Sungold Lad, G.M.		
K. P. and V. D. Fisher	Valerie Fisher	9
AFC Billy Pawlesta, L.M.		
Dr. Jesse W. Henderson	Lee C. Broussard	9
'67 NFC & AFC Butte Blue Moon, L.M.		
Mr. and Mrs. B. Grunwald	B. Grunwald	8
AFC Jingo Jo's Duckmaster, L.M.		
Hugh Adams	Owner	8
AFC Cork of Evergreen, L.M.		
R. Vasselais	Owner	8
River Oaks Corky, L.M.		
John Trzepacz	Owner	8
FC-AFC Sir Knight Falcon, L.M.		
P. E. and Zola Pound	P. E. Pound	7
FC-AFC Hoss of Palm Grove, L.M.		
Geo. J. Gray	Owner	7
FC-AFC Floodbay's Baron O'Glengarven, L.M.		
A. B. Mason, Jr.	Owner	7
FC-AFC Torque of Daingerfield, L.M.		
Mrs. Joan H. Watkins	Owner	7
FC-AFC Creole Sister, L.F.		
Donald P. Weiss	Owner	6
AFC Stilrovin Tuppee Tee, G.F.		
Mrs. G. H. Flinn, Jr.	Owner	6
FC-AFC Cimaroc Tang, L.M.		
W. K. Laughlin	Owner	6

AFC Shamrock Acres Gun Away, L.M. Mrs. C. V. Brokaw, Jr.	Owner	6
FC-AFC Ripp'n Ready, G.M. W. D. Connor	Owner	5
AFC Cha Cha Dancer, L.M. R. N. Wolfe	Owner	5
FC-AFC Carbon Marker, L.M. Mr. and Mrs. T. E. Fajen, Jr.	T. E. Fajen, Jr.	5
FC-AFC Jet's Target of Claymar, L.M. Mr. and Mrs. B. Grunwald	B. Grunwald	5
AFC Hawk Hill's Sam of Devon, L.M. Virginia T. Wylie	Owner	4
FC-AFC Nodrog Penny, L.F. G. B. Olinger	Owner	4
Rover of Ramsey Place, L.M. G. R. Pidgeon	Owner	4
FC-AFC Royal's Moose's Moe, L.M. W. D. Connor	Owner	4
AFC Waccamaw's Tinker, L.M. W. A. Chandler	Owner	4
AFC Marelvan Mike of Twin Oaks, L.M. John F. Nash	Owner	3
Black Chief of Nakomis, L.M. C. B. Adams	T. M. Bouchard	3
FC-AFC Stonegate's Arrow, L.M. Mr. and Mrs. B. Grunwald	B. Grunwald	2
FC-AFC Col-Tam of Craignook, L.M. Mr. and Mrs. R. O. Bateman	R. O. Bateman	2
Bigstone Black Longshot, L.F. A. B. Mason, Jr.	Owner	2
FC-AFC Tarblood of Absaraka, L.M. J. A. Love, Jr.	Owner	1

Dogs Which Qualified But Did Not Run

	Owner
Ardyn's Black Bart, L.M.	Jack C. Murphy
FC-AFC Balsom's Mandy, L.F.	Dr. Ben B. Baker
AFC Button Boots, L.M.	Cliff Tennant
FC-AFC Camliag Pramero, L.M.	George E. Thrane
FC-AFC Chap, L.M.	J. Douglas Wright, Jr.
FC-AFC Cougar's Rocket, L.M.	James L. Casey
FC-AFC Dessa Rae, L.F.	A. John Scharwat
FC-AFC Dobe's Desdemona, L.F.	Rupert A. Dobesh
FC-AFC Flood Bay Boomerang, L.M.	L. S. Greenleaf, Jr.
AFC Gerry's Kaiwa of Rosamond, G.F.	L. J. and Geraldine Miller
FC-AFC Golden Rocket's Missile, G.M.	B. F. Shearer, Jr.
FC-AFC Grady's Shadee Ladee, L.F.	Wm. K. Chilcott, Jr.
FC-AFC Guy's Bitterroot Lucky, L.M.	Guy P. Burnett
FC-AFC Hairspring Trigger, L.M.	Dale Prentice
AFC Jupiter's Hi-Laurel, L.M.	Cliff Tennant
FC-AFC Mackenzie's Ripco Mac, L.M.	Mrs. Dean Parker
AFC Mount Joy's Bit O'Ginger, C.F.	Mrs. E. C. Fleischmann
FC-AFC Mount Joy's Louistoo, C.M.	Mrs. E. C. Fleischmann
FC Nodrog Nike, L.M.	Lyle Knight
Paha Sapa Warpath II, L.M.	A. J. Robinson
AFC Polaris Luke, L.M.	Dr. Francis W. Partridge
Radar Rip, L.M.	L. P. Floberg and H. Koessler
FC-'65 NAFC Rebel Chief of Heber, L.M.	Gus F. and Virginia Rathert
Serrana Sootana of Genesee, L.F.	Ray E. and Joan Bly
FC-AFC Shawnee Ace of Spades, L.M.	Perle and Gladys Lewis
FC-AFC Sir Mike of Orchard View, L.M.	Roger Vasselais
Velvet's Jezebel, L.F.	Dr. Frank L. Fletcher

Statistics

Starters	Dogs	Bitches	Total
Labradors	31	7	38
Goldens	2	1	3
Chesapeakes	1	—	1
Total	34	8	42

Starters Handled By	Men	Women	Total
	34	8	42

The 1968 Stake was held on a number of privately owned properties over an area some fourteen miles long. The weather was cool and clear throughout. The large proportion of dogs qualified but not entered can be laid at least in part to the travel distance involved in going to Maine, as of the twenty-seven dogs which did not run, twenty were from Pacific and Rocky Mountain States. The winner became the first dog to have won two National Amateur Championships.

The Field Trial Committee consisted of: Dr. Malcolm M. Filson (chairman), August Belmont, Sid H. Eliason, Jr., Michael R. Flannery, Dr. Forrest L. Flashman, Lewis S. Greenleaf, Jr., William K. Laughlin, John Romadka (field trial secretary), and S. Alan Williams.

Official Guns
(Standing L to R): Ted Wylie, R. Kelly, Dr. R. Mertens, S. Morrisey, R. E. L. Andrew,
R. Sibley, R. Hayes, A. W. Wilbor, L. E. Van Ingen. (Kneeling L to R): P. Lalley,
Chas. Smith (captain), D. Kingston.

6th Series

Field Trial Committee
(Standing L to R): L. S. Greenleaf, Jr., Dr. M. M. Filson (chairman), W. K. Laughlin, Dr. F. L. Flashman, J. Romadka (F.T. secretary) (Kneeling L to R): M. R. Flannery, A. Belmont, S. A. Williams.

8th Series

Hospitality Committee
(Standing L to R): Mrs. S. Alan Williams, Mrs. C. V. Brokaw, Jr., Mrs. Chas. Cooney, Mrs. Paul Lalley, Mrs. John Nash, Mrs. Lewis S. Haskell. (Seated L to R): Mrs. August Belmont, Mrs. Edwin E. Gesner (chairman), Mrs. Dudley Milliken.

Grounds Committee
(L to R): Ira Miller, Mrs. Wm. Bernhard, Mrs. F. B. Ginnel, Mrs. M. D. Orowitz, Dale Lundstrom.

1969

NATIONAL AMATEUR CHAMPIONSHIP

STAKE

Burlington, Wisconsin — Winner —
Field Champion and Amateur Field Champion
Guy's Bitterroot Lucky
Guy P. Burnett, owner and handler

NATIONAL AMATEUR CHAMPIONSHIP

Burlington, Wisconsin — June 17-20, 1969

Judges: Andrieus A. Jones, John A. Love, Jr., Dr. Edison E. Pierce

Starting Dog — Owner	Handler	Series
FC-AFC Guy's Bitterroot Lucky, L.M.		
Guy P. Burnett	Owner	WINNER
FC-AFC Misty's Sungold Lad, G.M.		
K. P. and V. D. Fisher	Valerie Fisher	10
FC-AFC Glengarven's Mik, L.M.		
R. Vasselais	Owner	10
FC-AFC Rosehill's Little Dutch Boots, L.F.		
M. R. Flannery	Owner	10
FC-AFC Torque of Daingerfield, L.M.		
Mrs. Joan H. Watkins	Owner	10
AFC Orion's Sirius, L.M.		
John M. Martin	Owner	10
AFC Cha Cha Dancer, L.M.		
R. N. Wolfe	Owner	10
Huck's Pride of Riverside, L.M.		
R. E. Cutler	Owner	10
'68 NFC-'67, '68 NAFC Super Chief, L.M.		
August Belmont	Owner	10
FC-AFC River Oaks Corky, L.M.		
M. R. Flannery	Owner	10
AFC Chipsal John Henry, L.M.		
Marshall Simonds	Owner	9
FC-AFC Rill Shannon's Dark Del, L.F.		
M. R. Flannery	Owner	9
AFC Tigathoe's Mainliner Mariah, L.F.		
A. C. Brown III	Owner	9
FC-AFC Grady's Shadee Ladee, L.F.		
W. K. Chilcott, Jr.	Owner	8
AFC Black Chief of Nakomis, L.M.		
Chas. B. Adams	T. M. Bouchard	8
AFC Timberlake Flying Muffin, L.F.		
Dr. R. R. Pfister	Owner	8
FC-AFC Jetstone Muscles of Claymar, L.M.		
C. P. and M. D. Johnson	Margie Johnson	8
FC-AFC Hoss of Palm Grove, L.M.		
George J. Gray	Owner	8
AFC Cork of Evergreen, L.M.		
R. Vasselais	Ruth Vasselais	8
AFC Paha Sapa Warpath II, L.M.		
A. J. Robinson	Owner	8
AFC Hiwood Stormy of Alaska, L.M.		
R. and J. A. McFall	Roy McFall	8
FC-AFC Nodrog Penny, L.F.		
G. B. Olinger	Owner	8
AFC Portneuf Valley Duke, L.M.		
R. Vasselais	Owner	8
AFC Dawn of Aladon, L.F.		
Virginia T. Wylie	Owner	8
FC-AFC Jupiter's Hi-Laurel, L.M.		
Cliff Tennant	Owner	8
AFC The Ballad of Tealbrook, L.M.		
Mr. and Mrs. B. A. King	Marshall Simonds	8

Doctor Pepper of Le-Mar, L.M. M. and L. Broussard	Lee Broussard	8
AFC Carr-Lab Penrod, L.M. August Belmont	Louise Belmont	7
AFC Mitch of Bitterroot, L.M. Carl F. Allen	Owner	6
AFC Carnmoney Brigadier, L.M. R. H. and D. D. Goodrich	R. H. Goodrich	6
FC-AFC Royal's Moose's Moe, L.M. W. D. Connor	Owner	6
FC-AFC Black Rocky, L.M. Dr. R. M. Hutchinson	Owner	5
Smokey of Park Avenue, L.M. R. D. and D. C. Borden	R. D. Borden	5
Coldwater's Brendan, L.M. G. and N. Moore	Gene Moore	5
FC-AFC Warpath Tuff, L.M. Dr. R. R. Pfister	Owner	5
Taliaferro's Tracer, L.M. Howard T. Jones	Owner	5
Ch.-AFC Shamrock Acres Simmer Down, L.F. J. and J. Marth	James Marth	5
Timcin's Black Domino, L.M. H. and L. Hill	Joan Williams	4
Dixieland Joe, L.M. Dr. J. M. Tudor	Owner	4
FC-AFC Fisherman Bill of Delaware, L.M. Mr. and Mrs. M. B. Wallace, Jr.	Audrey Wallace	4
FC-AFC Sandy of Sourdough, L.M. C. E. Bunn, Jr.	Owner	4
'67 NFC-AFC Butte Blue Moon, L.M. Mr. and Mrs. B. Grunwald	B. Grunwald	3
AFC Targhee Sam, L.M. Blaine Murray	Owner	3
FC-AFC Samson's George of Glenspey, L.M. Mrs. W. L. Atkins	Owner	3
FC-AFC Serrana Sootana of Genesee, L.F. R. E. and J. M. Bly	R. E. Bly	3
Ch.-AFC Tiger's Cub, C.M. Mrs. W. S. Heller	Owner	3
FC Misty of Otter Creek, L.F. R. H. Rovelstad	Owner	3
FC-AFC Floodbay's Baron O'Glengarven, L.M. A. B. Mason, Jr.	Owner	3
Deerwood Shantoo, L.F. O. S. Brewer	Owner	3
Koolwaters Colt of Tricrown, C.M. M. Paterno	Owner	2
AFC Hawk Hill's Sam of Devon, L.M. Virginia T. Wylie	Owner	2
AFC Waccamaw's Tinker, L.M. Wm. A. Chandler	Owner	2
Black Bandit, L.M. R. L. Horn	Owner	2
Tioga Joe, G.M. Vern Weber	Owner	2
FC-AFC Creole Sister, L.F. Donald P. Weiss	Owner	2
AFC Gwen's Trouble, L.F. Gwen L. Carraway	Owner	2

Andy's Partner Pete, L.M.
Mrs. C. V. Brokaw   Owner   2
FC-AFC Col-Tam of Craignook, L.M.
Mr. and Mrs. R. O. Bateman   R. O. Bateman   2

Dogs Which Qualified But Did Not Run

Owner

AFC Billy Pawlesta, L.M.	Dr. Jesse W. Henderson
FC-AFC Cougar's Rocket, L.M.	James L. Casey
FC-AFC Dobe's Desdemona, L.F.	Rupert A. Dobesh
AFC King Tut V, L.M.	Glenn P. Scheihing
FC-AFC Lord Bomar, L.M.	John A. Love, Jr.
AFC Marelvan Mike of Twin Oaks, L.M.	John F. Nash
FC-AFC Moll-Leo Cayenne, G.M.	James D. Browning
FC-AFC Mount Joy's Bit O'Ginger, C.F.	Mrs. E. C. Fleischmann
AFC Oscar's Petite Lightning, L.F.	Mrs. R. M. Lewis
Pat of Orchard Glenn, L.M.	Charles A. Biewen
AFC Polaris Luke, L.M.	Dr. Francis W. Partridge
FC-'65 NAFC Rebel Chief of Heber, L.M.	Gus F. and Virginia Rathert
FC-AFC Sir Knight Falcon, L.M.	Perry E. and Zola Pound
AFC Velvet's Jezebel, L.F.	Dr. Frank L. Fletcher

Statistics

Starters	Dogs	Bitches	Total
Labradors	40	14	54
Goldens	2	—	2
Chesapeakes	2	—	2
Total	44	14	58

Starters Handled By	Men	Women	Total
	45	13	58

The 1969 Stake was held on the Bong Wildlife and Recreation Area, Burlington, Wisconsin. This highly suitable area was formerly the Bong Air Force Base. Although the entry was large, the favorable weather and admirable mechanics combined to allow the completion of the Stake well within four days. The extra day provided by the commencement of the Stake on Tuesday was not used.

The Field Trial Committee consisted of: Warren W. Carity (chairman), John Romadka (Field Trial secretary), S. Alan Williams, Dr. Richard C. Greenleaf, Sid H. Eliason, Jr., Michael R. Flannery, S. G. Borden Tennant, Bing Grunwald and Thomas J. Reames.

Judges
(L to R): Andrieus A. Jones, Dr. Edison E. Pierce, John A. Love, Jr.

Field Trial Committee
(Standing L to R): J. Romadka (F.T. secretary), S. G. B. Tennant, M. R. Flannery, T. J. Reames, S. H. Eliason, Jr., B. Grunwald. (Kneeling L to R): Dr. R. C. Greenleaf, S. A. Williams, W. W. Carity.

Judge's Rain Shelter

Marshals
(Standing L to R): R. D. Borden, T. E. Fajen, Jr., F. Miller, W. Hallberg, R. Springer, N. M. Romano, Jr., L. Burrill, H. McInnis, R. Lambert. (Kneeling L to R): S. C. Shea, Mrs. A. W. Wilbor, R. N. Wolfe.

Game Stewards
(L to R) J. Dudley Ottley, Gil Johnson, Cliff Savell, Vern Weber, Co-Chairman; Chick Krause, Jerry Faris and Lee Broussard Co-Chairman.

Bird Throwers
(Standing L to R): W. Berth, T. Oungst, W. Voigt, C. J. Schomer, E. Carey, K. Wright. (Kneeling L to R): J. Weitzel, T. L. Sorenson, D. Huffstutter, J. Swan.

1970

NATIONAL AMATEUR CHAMPIONSHIP

STAKE

Cheney, Washington — Winner —
Field Champion and Amateur Field Champion
Andy's Partner Pete
Mrs. C. V. Brokaw, Jr., owner and handler.
(In background): C. Kostrewski, trainer.

NATIONAL AMATEUR CHAMPIONSHIP STAKE

Cheney, Washington — June 23-26, 1970

Judges: Dr. Richard G. Gardner, S. C. Shea, A. Wells Wilbor

Starting Dog — Owner	Handler	Series
FC-AFC Andy's Partner Pete, L.M.		
Mrs. C. V. Brokaw, Jr .	Owner	WINNER
Paha's Pow Wow, L.M.		
Dr. W. E. Peltzer	Owner	10
FC-AFC Clickety Click, G.M.		
M. G. Smith and L. P. Floberg	L. P. Floberg	10
Ray's Rascal, L.M.		
R. H. and D. D. Goodrich	R. H. Goodrich	10
FC-AFC Rosehill's Little Dutch Boots, L.F.		
M. R. Flannery	Owner	10
AFC Tigathoe's Mainliner Mariah, L.F.		
A. C. Brown III	Owner	10
FC-'69 NAFC Guy's Bitterroot Lucky, L.M.		
Guy P. Burnett	Owner	10
FC-AFC Royal's Moose's Moe, L.M.		
W. D. Connor	Owner	10
FC-AFC Creole Sister, L.F.		
Donald P. Weiss	Owner	10
FC-AFC River Oaks Corky, L.M.		
M. R. Flannery	Owner	10
FC Molybru Butch of Barmond, L.M.		
R. R. Deering	Owner	9
FC Smokey of Jetcin, L.M.		
D. E. Mann	Owner	9
FC-AFC Orion's Sirius, L.M.		
John W. Martin	Owner	9
Willow's Boe Longshot, L.M.		
Mr. and Mrs. D. H. Gearheart	D. H. Gearheart	8
AFC Ronaker's Novato Cain, G.M.		
D. S. MacTavish, Jr.	Owner	8
FC-AFC Floodbay's Baron O'Glengarven, L.M.		
A. B. Mason, Jr.	Owner	8
AFC Andy Black of Chestnut Hill, L.M.		
A. C. Frank, Jr.	Owner	8
FC Bigstone Flint, L.M.		
Mr. and Mrs. W. B. Carey	Sue Carey	8
AFC Deerwood Shantoo, L.F.		
O. S. Brewer	Owner	7
FC-AFC Moll-Leo Cayenne, G.M.		
J. D. Browning	Owner	7
'68 NFC-'67, '68 NAFC Super Chief, L.M.		
August Belmont	Owner	5
Pirate's Gold, L.M.		
W. and M. Murff	W. Murff	5
FC-AFC Misty's Sungold Lad, G.M.		
K. P. and V. D. Fisher	Valerie Fisher	5
FC-AFC Mitch of Bitterroot, L.M.		
Carl F. Allen	Owner	5
AFC Ralston Valley Dandy Jake, L.M.		
A. C. Donelly	Owner	5
FC-AFC Carnmoney Brigadier, L.M.		
R. H. and D. D. Goodrich	R. H. Goodrich	5

AFC Alamo Black Jack, L.M.		
N. M. Romano, Jr.	Owner	5
Dessa's Black Angel, L.M.		
Dr. and Mrs. M. W. Stroud	M. W. Stroud	5
Dual & AFC Tiger's Cub, C.M.		
Mrs. W. S. Heller	Owner	4
FC-AFC Serrana Sootana of Genesee, L.F.		
R. E. and J. Bly	R. E. Bly	4
FC-AFC Smokey of Park Avenue, L.F.		
R. D. and D. C. Borden	R. D. Borden	4
FC-AFC Jetstone Muscles of Claymar, L.M.		
C. P. and M. D. Johnson	Margie Johnson	4
FC Beau of Blair House, L.M.		
R. H. Grace	Owner	4
'67 NFC-AFC Butte Blue Moon, L.M.		
Mr. and Mrs. B. Grunwald	B. Grunwald	4
AFC Bayou Beau, L.M.		
W. J. Johnson	Owner	3
FC-AFC Randy Mayhall of Tina, L.M.		
G. Glenn Miller	Owner	3
Rolida's Stubby Bandit, L.M.		
T. F. Walsh	Owner	3
AFC Harang's Grumpy Express, L.M.		
J. W. Harang	Owner	3
Ern-Bar's Twinkle Boots, L.F.		
J. T. Walker II	Owner	3
Squire of Reo Raj, L.M.		
J. R. Cross	Owner	3
AFC Doctor Pepper of Le-Mar, L.M.		
M. and L. Broussard	Lee Broussard	3
AFC Beavercrest Sassy Sioux, L.F.		
W. E. Mahan	Owner	3
Copper Cities Colliery Cal, L.M.		
Josephine T. Reeve	Owner	3
FC-AFC Nodrog Penny, L.F.		
G. B. Olinger	Owner	3
Bob's Black Rebel, L.M.		
R. and M. L. Chance	Bob Chance	3
FC Shadow of Rocky Lane, L.M.		
John F. White	Owner	3
Bomar's Chris, L.M.		
J. N. Graham	Owner	2
AFC Rocky Road of Zenith, L.M.		
A. D. Pruitt	Owner	2
FC-AFC Rover of Ramsey Place, L.M.		
G. R. Pidgeon	Owner	2
FC-AFC Carr-Lab Penrod, L.M.		
August Belmont	Louise Belmont	2
Whitaker's Firefly, L.F.		
Robert Ladwig	Owner	2
FC-AFC Lord Bomar, L.M.		
John A. Love, Jr.	Owner	2
FC-AFC Grady's Shadee Ladee, L.F.		
W. K. Chilcott, Jr.	Owner	2
Wayside Black Buster, L.M.		
J. W. Morar	Owner	2
FC-AFC Samson's George of Glenspey, L.M.		
Mrs. W. L. Atkins	Owner	2
FC-AFC Jupiter's Hi-Laurel, L.M.		
Cliff Tennant	Owner	2

AFC Cherokee Chief V, L.M.		
J. H. Pettijohn	Owner	1
Midge of Greenwood, L.F.		
J. Boatright	Owner	1
AFC Little Miss Samantha, L.F.		
W. G. Wilson	Owner	1
AFC Gwen's Ringtail Velvet, L.F.		
W. C. Carraway	Owner	1
AFC Penny of Evergreen, L.F.		
Mrs. W. L. Atkins	Owner	1
AFC Dent's Midnight Rick, L.M.		
Jack Madsen	Owner	1

Dogs Which Qualified But Did Not Run

	Owner
AFC Chipsal John Henry, L.M.	Marshall Simonds
AFC Hawk Hill's Sam of Devon, L.M.	Virginia T. Wylie
FC-AFC Hoss of Palm Grove, L.M.	George J. Gray
Koolwaters Colt of Tricrown, C.M.	Michael Paterno
FC-AFC Marelvan Mike of Twin Oaks, L.M.	John F. Nash
FC-AFC Mount Joy's Bit O'Ginger, C.F.	Mrs. E. C. Fleischmann
FC My Rebel, L.M.	A. Wells Wilbor
FC-AFC Pelican Lake Peggy, L.F.	Mr. and Mrs. W. H. Gillespie
FC-AFC Velvet's Jezebel, L.F.	Dr. Frank L. Fletcher

Statistics

Starters	Dogs	Bitches	Total
Labradors	43	14	57
Goldens	4	—	4
Chesapeakes	1	—	1
Total	48	14	62

Starters Handled By	Men	Women	Total
	54	8	62

The 1970 Stake was held on the Turnbull National Wildlife Refuge at Cheney, Washington. The weather proved that if you go north in June, the weather is not always cool. The trial was plagued with a hot spell which produced 90 to 100° throughout.

The Field Trial Committee consisted of: J. J. Heneghan (chairman), John F. Nash (Field Trial secretary), S. H. Eliason, Jr., M. R. Flannery, Dr. R. C. Greenleaf, R. H. Hecker, Mrs. W. S. Heller, Dr. Dean Parker, and S. G. B. Tennant.

Judges
(L to R): A. Wells Wilbor, S. C. Shea, Dr. Richard G. Gardner.

Field Trial Committee
(L to R): M. R. Flannery, John F. Nash (F.T. secretary), Mrs. W. S. Heller, R. H. Hecker, J. J. Heneghan, S. H. Eliason, Jr., Dr. R. C. Greenleaf, Dr. Dean Parker.

Official Guns
(Front Row L to R): T. Werner, S. H. Eliason, Jr., D. Buttles, H. Snell, S. R. Johnson, W. J. Dahl. (Back Row L to R): J. Harkcom, S. Christopherson, S. J. Morrissey (capt.), Dr. E. B. Starkloff, D. Jones, A. W. Agnew, H. Pratt.

Game Stewards
(L to R): R. Tucker, J. Vanderzanden, D. Andrews, D. Thornton, J. Thompson, R. Goff (chief).

Hospitality Committee

(Standing L to R): Clara Allen, Sharon   Michael, Joan Greenleaf, Mebbie Heneghan, Betsy Eliason, Barbara Nash, Corky Olson. (Kneeling L to R): Evie Olson, Dorothy Brown, Pete Parker, Bonnie Flannery, Brownie Grunwald.

Bird Throwers

(Standing L to R): B. Hayden, V. C. Morgan, F. A. Dashnaw, J. Adix. (Kneeling L to R): G. Madsen, D. Michael, E. DeWitt, E. Minoggie, H. Loop.

1971

NATIONAL AMATEUR CHAMPIONSHIP

STAKE

Jackson Hole, Wyoming — Winner —
Field Champion and Amateur Field Champion
Dee's Dandy Dude
Michael Paterno, owner and handler.

NATIONAL AMATEUR CHAMPIONSHIP STAKE

Jackson Hole, Wyoming — June 22-25, 1971

Judges: Hugh Adams, Dr. Paul C. Kiernan, Paul Provenzano

Starting Dog — Owner	Handler	Series
FC-AFC Dee's Dandy Dude, LM. Michael Paterno	Owner	WINNER
FC-AFC Harang's Grumpy Express, L.M. J. W. Harang	Owner	10
AFC Hundred Proof Tad, L.M. J. S. Palmore	Owner	10
AFC Ralston Valley Dandy Jake, L.M. A. C. Donnelly	Owner	10
FC-AFC Warpath Rip, L.M. O. S. Brewer	Owner	10
FC-AFC Sandy of Sourdough, L.M. C. E. Bunn, Jr.	Owner	10
FC-AFC Jetstone Muscles of Claymar, L.M. Margie D. Johnson	Owner	10
FC-AFC Carr-Lab Penrod, L.M. A. Belmont	Louise Belmont	10
F-AFC Molybru Butch of Barmond, L.M. R. R. Deering	Owner	10
FC-AFC Tigathoe's Mainliner Mariah, L.F. A. C. Brown III	Owner	10
FC-AFC River Oaks Corky, L.M. M. R. Flannery	Owner	10
FC-AFC Smokey of Park Avenue, L.F. R. D. and D. C. Borden	R. D. Borden	10
FC-AFC Ray's Rascal, L.M. R. H. and D. D. Goodrich	R. H. Goodrich	8
AFC Paha Sapa Hardcase, L.M. L. L. Burrill	Owner	8
AFC Sauk Trail Deepwell "Doc", L.M. J. N. Boettcher	Owner	8
'67 NFC-NAFC Butte Blue Moon, L.M. Mr. and Mrs. B. Grunwald	B. Grunwald	7
Magic Marker of Timber Town, L.M. Marshall Simonds	Owner	7
Muktar of Offershire, L.M. R. Offerdahl	Owner	7
FC-AFC Carnmoney Brigadier, L.M. R. H. and D. D. Goodrich	R. H. Goodrich	7
'68 NFC-'67, '68 NAFC Super Chief, L.M. August Belmont	Owner	7
FC-AFC White's Mar-Ke-Tam Nerro, L.M. B. W. White	Owner	7
FC-AFC Rocky Road of Zenith, L.M. A. D. Pruitt	Owner	7
AFC Little Miss Samantha, L.F. W. G. Wilson	Owner	6
FC-AFC Royal's Moose's Moe, L.M. W. D. Connor	Owner	6
AFC Ready of Sacramento, G.M. R. and C. Leineke	Ron Leineke	6
AFC Ronaker's Novato Cain, G.M. D. S. MacTavish, Jr.	Owner	6

AFC Chuk Chukar Chuk, L.M.		
S. Gelardi	Owner	6
FC-AFC Mitch of Bitterroot, L.M.		
Carl Allen	Owner	6
FC-AFC Misty's Sungold Lad, G.M.		
K. P. and V. D. Fisher	Valerie Fisher	6
FC Tweet's Bebe, L.M.		
O. S. Brewer	Owner	6
FC-AFC Franklin's Tall Timber, L.M.		
R. and P. Magnusson	R. Magnusson	5
AFC King Tut V, L.M.		
G. P. Scheihing	Owner	5
Sam of Marlboro Country, L.M.		
D. J. Jones	Owner	5
FC-'70 NAFC Andy's Partner Pete, L.M.		
Mrs. C. V. Brokaw, Jr.	Owner	5
FC-AFC Dusty's Doctari, L.M.		
R. M. and B. E. Smith	R. M. Smith	5
FC-AFC Shadow of Rocky Lane, L.M.		
John F. White	Owner	5
AFC Bob's Black Rebel, L.M.		
R. and M. L. Chance	Bob Chance	5
AFC Brandy of Cortez, L.M.		
S. Thompson	Owner	5
FC-AFC Alamo Black Jack, L.M.		
N. M. Romano, Jr.	D. P. Weiss	5
Wingover Cherokee Chief, L.M.		
Elizabeth P. Milliken	D. L. Milliken	5
AFC Tioga Joe, G.M.		
Vern Weber	Owner	5
Pat's Penny Jo, L.F.		
Dr. L. D. and P. Ferucci	L. D. Ferucci	5
AFC Geechee, L.M.		
C. B. Harvey	Owner	5
'70 NFC-AFC Creole Sister, L.F.		
D. P. Weiss	Owner	5
AFC Gwen's Trouble, L.F.		
Gwen L. Carraway	Owner	4
Kinike Coquette, G.F.		
J. T. and S. S. Venerable	Sally Venerable	4
AFC Ern-Bar's Twinkle Boots, L.F.		
J. T. Walker II	Owner	4
AFC Dessa's Black Angel, L.M.		
Dr. and Mrs. M. W. Stroud	M. W. Stroud	4
AFC Sungold Sprite, G.F.		
V. D. Fisher	Owner	4
AFC Bellota Cacahuete, L.M.		
Josephine T. Reeve	R. Reeve	4
FC-AFC Hiwood Stormy of Alaska, L.M.		
R. and J. McFall	R. McFall	4
Round Valley's Lucky Tigger, L.M.		
S. Ammarell	Chip Ammarell	3
Bonnie Brooks Elmer, G.M.		
Mrs. G. H. Flinn, Jr.	Owner	3
FC-AFC Deerwood Shantoo, L.F.		
O. S. Brewer	Owner	3
Ottley's Jazzbo, L.M.		
J. D. Ottley	Owner	3
AFC River Oaks Rascal, L.M.		
J. M. Pilar	Owner	3

FC-AFC Billy Pawlesta, L.M.		
Dr. J. W. Henderson	Owner	3
AFC Shamrock Acres Drake, L.M.		
K. Anderson and J. Hogue	J. Hogue	3
Stilrovin Clipper Delane II, G.M.		
Mrs. G. H. Flinn, Jr.	Owner	3
FC-AFC Orion's Sirius, L.M.		
J. W. Martin	Owner	3
AFC Candlewood's Little Lou, L.M.		
Mary C. Howley	Owner	3
FC-AFC Serrana Sootana of Genesee, L.F.		
R. E. and J. Bly	R. E. Bly	3
AFC Squire of Reo Raj, L.M.		
J. R. Cross	R. D. Borden	2
AFC Midge of Greenwood, L.F.		
Joe Boatright	Owner	2
Dual-AFC Tiger's Cub, C.M.		
Mrs. W. S. Heller	Owner	2
FC-AFC J & L's Spooky, L.M.		
Josephine T. Reeve	Owner	2
FC Rodney's Mister M. L. Coon, L.M.		
G. Cassell and J. Bogrett	J. Bogrett	2
Mount Joy's Jez O'Meg, C.F.		
J. J. Mitchell & R. R. M. Carpenter, Jr.	J. J. Mitchell	1

Dogs Which Qualified But Did Not Run

	Owner
FC-AFC Clickety Click, G.M.	M. Smith and L. P. Floberg
FC-AFC Duke of Crookston, L.M.	Hugh I. Klaren
FC-'68 NAFC Guy's Bitterroot Lucky, L.M.	Guy P. Burnett
AFC Hawk Hill's Sam of Devon, L.M.	Virginia T. Wylie
FC-AFC Martens' Castaway, L.M.	Philip R. Fitzgerald
FC-AFC Monster Mike, L.M.	William B. Stone
FC-AFC Nodrog Penny, L.F.	Gordon B. Olinger
FC-AFC Paha's Pow Wow, L.M.	Dr. Wesley E. Peltzer
Dual-AFC Torque of Daingerfield, L.M.	Joan Shoemaker

Statistics

Starters	Dogs	Bitches	Total
Labradors	48	10	58
Goldens	6	2	8
Chesapeakes	1	1	2
Total	55	13	68

Starters Handled By	Men	Women	Total
	55	13	68

The 1971 Stake was held at the National Elk Refuge and nearby areas near Jackson, Jackson Hole, Wyoming. This area proved in the opinion of most to have as fine weather as could be asked for, truly beautiful scenery and fine trial grounds.

The Field Trial Committee consisted of: Donald L. Burnett (chairman), John F. Nash (Field Trial secretary), Sid H. Eliason, Jr., Michael R. Flannery, S. G. B. Tennant, Mrs. Walter S. Heller, Guy P. Burnett, Ernest J. Goppert, Jr., and Andrieus A. Jones.

Field Trial Committee

(Front Row, L to R) Mrs. Walter S. Heller, Third Vice-President; Sid Eliason, Jr., President; Don Burnett, Field Trial Chairman. (Back Row, L to R) Ernie Goppert, Jr., Field Trial Committee; Borden Tennant, Second Vice-President; John Nash, Secretary-Treasurer; Mike Flannery, First Vice-President; Guy Burnett, Fourth Vice-President and A. A. "Pete Jones, Field Trial Committee.

Judges

(L to R): Dr. Paul C. Kiernan, Paul Provenzano, Hugh Adams.

Marshals
(L to R): C. A. Rice, J. Hogue, J. Howard, S. Smith, O. J. Matthews, Mrs. A. W. Wilbor, J. Richards, G. Heicher, A. Donnelly, R. Stauffer, Gil Johnson.

Traffic Committee
(Back Row L to R): Dr. A. L. Ryan, W. Maeck, R. Meservey, A. Rieth, J. Nicholson. (Front Row L to R): H. Boeny, T. Evans, Dr. M. B. Samsel.

Grounds Committee
(Front Row, L to R) Bill Horn, Wilbur Saunders, Glenn Scheihing. (Back Row, L to R) Bob Shaver, Alex Zbitnoff, Richard Bartlett and Bob Honey.

Bird Throwers
(Standing L to R): D. Harmon, J. Correll, H. Shue, R. Crapo. (Kneeling L to R): C. Polityka, D. Millward, J. Fotheringham, H. Wolfe.

1972

NATIONAL AMATEUR CHAMPIONSHIP

STAKE

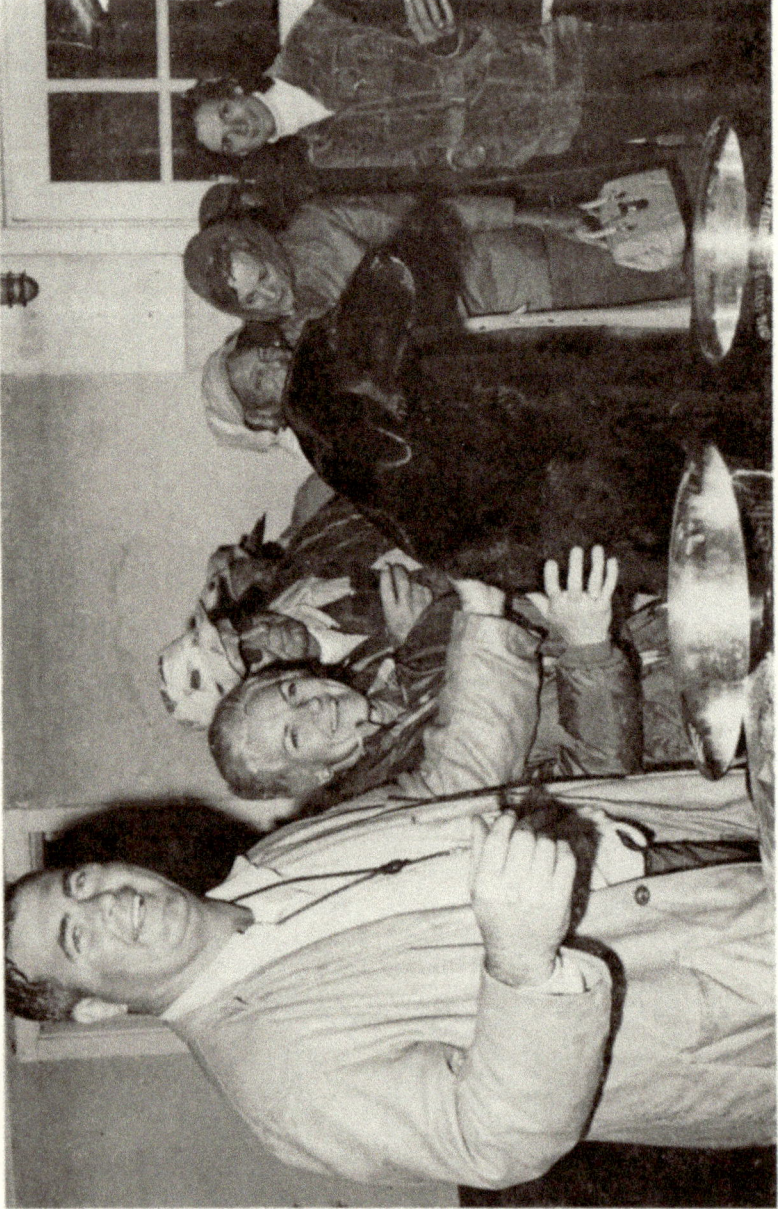

Meadeville, Pennsylvania — Winner — Field Champion and Amateur Field Champion River Oaks Corky Michael R. Flannery, owner and handler, and Bonnie Flannery

NATIONAL AMATEUR CHAMPIONSHIP STAKE

Meadeville, Pennsylvania — June 20-23, 1972

Judges: A. W. Agnew, L. L. Burrill, C. A. Rice

Starting Dog — Owner	Handler	Series
FC-AFC River Oaks Corky, L.M.		
M. R. Flannery	Owner	WINNER
FC-AFC Tweet's Bebe, L.M.		
O. S. Brewer	Owner	10
FC-'71 NAFC Dee's Dandy Dude, L.M.		
M. Paterno	Owner	10
FC-AFC Ray's Rascal, L.M.		
R. H. and D. D. Goodrich	R. H. Goodrich	10
FC-AFC Tigathoe's Mainliner Mariah, L.F.		
A. C. Brown III	Owner	10
Hunt's Cloud of Smoke, L.F.		
T. S. Flugstad	Owner	10
FC-AFC Royal's Moose's Moe, L.M.		
W. D. Connor	Owner	10
FC-AFC Midge of Greenwood, L.F.		
J. Boatright	Owner	10
AFC Magic Marker of Timber Town, L.M.		
M. Simonds	Owner	10
FC-AFC River Oaks Rascal, L.M.		
J. M. Pilar	Owner	10
AFC Pat's Penny Jo, L.F.		
Dr. L. D. Ferucci	Owner	9
Lucky's Lady in Red, L.F.		
Dr. C. W. Irwin	Owner	9
AFC Chief Sands, G.M.		
R. Sampson	Owner	9
FC-AFC Rocky Road of Zenith, L.M.		
A. D. Pruitt	Owner	9
FC-AFC Paha Sapa Warpaint, L.M.		
Mrs. A. C. Brown III	Owner	8
Evergreen Binx, L.M.		
B. Beier	Owner	8
Cody of Wanapum, L.M.		
Mrs. W. K. Laughlin	W. K. Laughlin	8
Royal Oaks Jill of Burgundy, L.F.		
A. C. Brown III	Owner	8
FC-AFC Shamrock Acres Drake, L.M.		
K. Anderson and J. Hogue	J. Hogue	8
'68 NFC-'67, '68 NAFC Super Chief, L.M.		
A. Belmont	Owner	7
'70 NFC-AFC Creole Sister, L.F.		
D. P. Weiss	Owner	7
FC-AFC Franklin's Tall Timber, L.M.		
R. and P. Magnusson	R. Magnusson	7
FC-AFC Ern-Bar's Twinkle Boots, L.F.		
J. T. Walker II	Owner	7
AFC Andy Black of Chestnut Hill, L.M.		
A. C. Frank, Jr.	Owner	7
AFC Lady's Brazos Pete, L.M.		
R. Cook	Owner	7
FC-AFC Ottley's Jazzbo, L.M.		
J. D. Ottley	Owner	7

FC-AFC Rodney's Mister M. L. Coon, L.M.		
G. Cassel and J. Bogrett	J. Bogrett	6
FC-AFC Shadow of Rocky Lane, L.M.		
J. F. White	Owner	6
Reimrock's Duke of Orleans, L.M.		
P. Roussos	Owner	6
FC-'70 NAFC Andy's Partner Pete, L.M.		
Mrs. C. V. Brokaw, Jr.	Owner	6
AFC Togom's Tiger of Abilena, L.M.		
S. Gacek	Owner	6
AFC Bob's Black Rebel, L.M.		
R. and M. L. Chance	R. Chance	6
AFC Twinkle's Mandy, L.F.		
J. T. Walker II	Owner	5
FC Baird's Centerville Sam, L.M.		
Mr. and Mrs. M. B. Wallace, Jr.	Audrey Wallace	5
AFC Hundred Proof Tad, L.M.		
J. S. Palmore	Owner	5
FC-AFC Orion's Sirius, L.M.		
J. W. Martin	Owner	5
Ol' Yeller, L.M.		
C. Prior	Owner	4
FC-AFC Misty's Sungold Lad, G.M.		
K. P. Fisher and V. F. Walker	Valerie Walker	4
AFC Tioga Joe, G.M.		
V. Weber	Owner	4
FC-AFC Pirate's Gold, L.M.		
W. and M. Murff	W. Murff	4
FC-AFC Warpath Rip, L.M.		
O. S. Brewer	Owner	4
FC-AFC Warpath Tuff, L.M.		
O. J. Matthews, Jr.	Owner	4
FC-AFC Martens' Castaway, L.M.		
P. R. Fitzgerald	Owner	4
Sir Caleb of Audlon, L.M.		
J. A. Stary, Jr.	Owner	4
FC Nodrog Punkie, L.M.		
W. R. Buxton	Owner	4
AFC Harrowby Dandy, L.M.		
C. L. Ruffalo	Owner	4
FC-AFC Carr-Lab Penrod, L.M.		
August Belmont	Louise Belmont	4
Aerco's Bit O'Honey, L.F.		
S. Vilagi	Owner	4
White River Duke, L.M.		
D. J. Wirth	Owner	4
Sun Dance's Babe, G.F.		
G. C. and C. B. Branch	Valerie Walker	3
FC-AFC Bigstone Flint, L.M.		
Mr. and Mrs. D. Crow	D. Crow	3
FC-AFC Carnmoney Brigadier, L.M.		
R. H. and D. D. Goodrich	R. H. Goodrich	3
FC-AFC Harang's Grumpy Express, L.M.		
J. W. Harang	Owner	3
'67 NFC-AFC Butte Blue Moon, L.M.		
Mr. and Mrs. B. Grunwald	B. Grunwald	3
AFC Kinike Coquette, G.F.		
J. and S. Venerable	Sally Venerable	3
FC-AFC Randy Mayhall of Tina, L.M.		
G. G. Miller	Owner	3

Ahab's Emancipator, L.M.		
Dr. and Mrs. G. B. Starkloff	G. B. Starkloff	3
Nilo Brandy Cork, L.M.		
Dr. A. G. Schultz	Owner	3
AFC Sauk Trail Deepwell "Doc", L.M.		
J. N. Boettcher	Owner	3
FC-AFC Shadow of Provincetown, L.M.		
Josephine T. Reeve	Owner	3
Wanapum Lucky Yo Yo, L.M.		
E. DeWitt	Gretchen Crow	3
Dual-AFC Tiger's Cub, C.M.		
Mrs. W. S. Heller	Owner	2
AFC Air Express, L.M.		
August Belmont	Louise Belmont	2
AFC Dairy Hill's Michikiniquia, L.F.		
A. A. Jones	Owner	2
AFC Copper Cities Colliery Cal, L.M.		
Josephine T. Reeve	Owner	2
Little Billie Joe, L.F.		
T. Voigt	Owner	1

Dogs Which Qualified But Did Not Run

	Owner
FC-AFC Alamo Black Jack, L.M.	Noxie M. Romano, Jr.
AFC Balsom's Snooper Honker, L.M.	Dr. Ben B. Baker
AFC Bellota Cacahuete, L.M.	Josephine T. Reeve
Bigstone Hard's Happy, L.M.	Alfred B. Hard
Black Irish Kelly, L.F.	Robert and Delores Mesch
Bow-Mar Black Brandy, L.M.	Carroll A. Rice
AFC Candlewood's Little Lou, L.M.	Mary C. Howley
Coll-A-Dene's Perky, L.M.	Thomas Helwig
FC-AFC Dusty's Doctari, L.M.	Ralph M. and Barbara E. Smith
AFC King Tut V. L.M.	Glenn P. Scheihing
AFC Nemo's Spyder of Round Valley, L.M.	Sib and Chip Ammarell
FC-AFC Ronaker's Novato Cain, G.M.	Desmond S. MacTavish, Jr.
FC-AFC Sandy of Sourdough, L.M.	Charles E. Bunn, Jr.
FC Swing Tarzan Swing, L.M.	James J. Heneghan
AFC Winrocks' Ripper, L.M.	Dr. John Anderson

Statistics

Starters	Dogs	Bitches	Total
Labradors	48	12	60
Goldens	3	2	5
Chesapeakes	1	—	1
Total	52	14	66

Starters Handled By	Men	Women	Total
	54	12	66

The 1972 Stake was held at the State of Pennsylvania's Pymatuning Waterfowl Area, near Meadeville. The area offers a variety of land and water ideal for retriever work. Unseasonable hurricane Agnes turned what had been billed as the "hot" National, into the wettest and windiest on record. Traditionally, the East draws the smallest number of entries when the Stake is held there. That the entry here was only two less than the record year in 1971, and qualifications soared to a new high of 81, all point to still bigger entries in the near future.

The Field Trial Committee consisted of: S. C. Shea (chairman), John F. Nash (Field Trial secretary), M. R. Flannery, S. G. B. Tennant, Mrs. W. S. Heller, G. P. Burnett, R. H. Johnson, C. E. Cooney and R. Magnusson.

Judges
(L to R): Lawrence L. Burrill, A. W. Agnew, Carroll A. Rice

Field Trial Committee
(Standing L to R): S. G. B. Tennant, Chas. E. Cooney, M R. Flannery, J. F. Nash (F.T. secretary), R. Magnusson. (Seated L to R): Guy P. Burnett, Mrs. W. S. Heller, S. C. Shea, R. H. Johnson.

Guns

(Standing L to R): M. M. Baker, C. S. Ostenberg, D. Doring, D. L. Mountcastle, A. Koppenhauer, H. Breton, D. C. Kingston, E. A. Wylie, R. Sadler, R. Sibley. (Seated L to R): J. W. McAssey, J. Columbo, C. Smith (captain), P. Lalley, M. Thompson.

Scene of 1st and 2nd Series

Handlers Watching Test Dog — 8th Series

Hospitality Committee

(Standing L to R): Gene Tennant, Rose Scott, Sue Gott, Nancy Tyler, Pat Magnusson, Rosemary Shea, Judy Martin. (Seated L to R): Brownie Grunwald, Bonnie Flannery, and Barbara Nash (co-chairmen), Marion Weiss, Marion Stroud.

PART III
OPEN ALL-AGE STAKES and
AMATEUR ALL-AGE STAKES

ALL TIME HIGH SCORING

(*National Championships Scored as 5 Point Wins)

(A) OPEN ALL-AGE STAKES

River Oaks Corky	L	Michael R. Flannery	199
*Spirit Lake Duke	L	Mrs. George Murnane	181
Black Panther	L	Carl W. Carlson	172½
Tarblood of Absaraka	L	John A. Love, Jr.	165
Michelle	L	Cyril R. Tobin	152½
Dairy Hill's Night Cap	L	Andreius A. Jones	148
*Massie's Sassy Boots	L	William T. Cline	147
*Major VI	L	Mrs. Fraser M. Horn	145½
*Whygin Cork's Coot	L	Mrs. George Murnane	137
Duxbak Scooter	L	Mrs. Grace Lambert	132
*Butte Blue Moon	L	Mr. & Mrs. Bing Grunwald	131
Techacko's Ranger	L	Cyril R. Tobin	127½
Black Boy XI	L	Lewis S. Greenleaf, Jr.	125½
Glengarven's Mik	L	Roger Vasselais	120
Pepper's Jiggs	L	Robert J. Pepper	119
Flood Bay Boomerang	L	Lewis S. Greenleaf, Sr.	115½
*Super Chief	L	August Belmont	112½
*Bracken's Sweep	L	Daniel E. Pomeroy	111½
*Del-Tone Colvin	L	Louis J. Snoeyenbos	111½
*Dolobran's Smoke Tail	L	Richard H. Hecker	110½
*Brignall's Gringo	L	Clifford N. Brignall	110
Canuck-Crest Cutty Sark	L	Mrs. A. P. Loening	109
Rip of Holly Hill	L	Mrs. William P. Roth	107
Shoremeadow Tidewater	L	Cyril R. Tobin	105½
Tar Baby's Little Sweet Stuff	L	Kensyle R. Carpenter	102½
Ace Hi Scamp of Windsweep	L	Mrs. Grace Lambert	101
Lord Bomar	L	John A. Love, Jr.	98½
*Royal's Moose's Moe	L	William D. Connor	98½
Baron's Tule Tiger	C	Mrs. Walter S. Heller	96
Happy Playboy	L	Mrs. Grace Lambert	95½
*King Buck	L	John M. Olin	93½
Dusty's Doctari	L	Mr. and Mrs. Ralph M. Smith	92
Ardyn's Ace of Merwalfin	L	Edwin Salvino	90
Rick of Charlemagne	L	Mrs. Reginald M. Lewis	89½
Cindy's Pride of Garfield	L	Mrs. Clifford V. Brokaw, Jr.	88½
Paha Sapa War Cloud	L	John A. Love, Jr.	88½
*Creole Sister	L	Donald P. Weiss	88
Rebel Chief of Heber	L	Mr. & Mrs. Gus F. Rathert	88
Macopin Maximum	G	Mrs. George Murnane	86
Tar Dessa Venture	L	John M. Preston	85
Van's Pride Ebony Shadow	L	W. E. Van Sickle	84½
Guy's Bitterroot Lucky	L	Guy P. Burnett	82
Carr-Lab Hilltop	L	Glenn B. Bump	81
Cougar's Rocket	L	James L. Casey	80
Sam Frizel of Glenspey	L	Mrs. Warner L. Atkins	80
Butch's Bitterroot Smokey	L	Joseph Albertson	79½
Little Pierre of Deer Creek	L	Mr. & Mrs. Paul Bakewell, Jr.	79½
*Mi-Cris Sailor	L	Mrs. George Murnane	79½
Oakcreek's Van Cleve	G	Alfred H. Schmidt	78½
Mr. Mac's Billy Boy	L	Mrs. George Murnane	78
Black Jet XVI	L	Mrs. R. S. Humphrey	77

Ace's Sheba of Ardyn	L	Mrs. William K. Laughlin	75½
Black Monk of Roeland	L	Mrs. D. L. Mesker	75½
*Cork of Oakwood Lane	L	Dr. A. Harold Mork	75
Ace of Southwood	L	John M. Olin	74½
Bigstone Flint	L	Mr. and Mrs. David Crow	74
Oakcreek's Fremont	G	Cyril R. Tobin	73½
Fisherman Bill of Delaware	L	Mr. & Mrs. Mahlon B. Wallace, Jr.	73
Truly Yours of Garfield	L	John M. Olin	72½
Howie's Happy Hunter	L	Mrs. Don H. Gearheart	72½
Bitterroot Chink-ee	L	Mrs. Martha B. Burnett	71½
*Bigstone Hope	L	Byron B. Grunwald	71
Keith's Black Magic	L	Daniel E. Pomeroy	71
Dee's Dandy Dude	L	Michael Paterno	70½
Sprig of Swinomish	L	Cyril R. Tobin	70½
Nethercroft Nemo of Nascopie	L	Mrs. Grace Lambert	69½
*Martens' Little Smoky	L	John M. Olin	69
Invail's Cavalier Carom	L	Mrs. C. V. Brokaw, Jr.	68½
Jetstone Muscles of Claymar	L	Mrs. Margie Johnson	68½
Carnation Butter Boy	L	Carnation Farm Kennels	67½
Samson's George of Glenspey	L	Mrs. Warner L. Atkins	67½
Zipper Dee Do	L	Timber Town Kennels	65½
Cimaroc Tang	L	William K. Laughlin	64½
Stonegate's Arrow	L	J. W. Kelsey	64½
Firelei's Hornet	L	Joseph Versay	64
Frances Fishtail	L	Richard H. Hecker	64
Jiggaboo of Mountaindale	L	Mr. & Mrs. Edward H. Brown	64
Ray's Rascal	L	R. H. and D. D. Goodrich	64
Staindrop Murton Marksman	L	John M. Olin	63½
The Golden Kid	G	Mrs. Gerald M. Livingston	63½
Glenairlee Rocket	L	F. F. Garlock	63
*Marvadel Black Gum	L	Mr. & Mrs. Paul Bakewell III	63
My Rebel	L	A. Wells Wilbor	63
Rip	G	Paul Bakewell III	63
Ace of Garfield	L	John M. Olin	62½
Black Corsair of Whitmore	L	Sandy F. Mackay	62½
Boley's Cascade	L	Ernest J. Goppert, Jr.	62
The Spider of Kingswere	L	Leonard S. Florsheim	62
Lord Beaver of Cork	L	Mrs. Grace Lambert	60½
Salt Valley Ottie	L	Sid H. Eliason, Jr.	60½
Freehaven Jay	L	James L. Free	60
Grady's Shadee Ladee	L	William K. Chilcott	60
Serrana Sootana of Genesee	L	R. E. and J. Bly	60
Beau of the Lark	L	Mr. & Mrs. Mahlon B. Wallace, Jr.	59½
Brazil's Black Jaguar	L	Mrs. Richard S. Humphrey	59½
Cream City Coed	L	Charles H. Morgan	59
Dessa Rae	L	A. J. Scharwat	59
*Shed of Arden	L	Paul Bakewell III	59
Black Prince of Sag Harbor	L	Mrs. Gerald M. Livingston	58½
Brandy Spirit of Netley	L	Mr. & Mrs. Theodore E. Fajen, Jr.	58½
Slo-Poke Smokey of Dairy Hill	L	Andreius A. Jones	58½
Warpath Rip	L	Oscar S. Brewer	58½

Most Wins (24) Black Panther, L. Carl W. Carlson

Most Placements (62) River Oaks Corky, L. Michael R. Flannery

River Oaks Corky
All-Time Winner of the Highest Number of
Open All-Age Points

Super Chief
All-Time Winner of Highest Number of Amateur All-Age Points and of
Combined Open and Amateur All-Age Points

(B) AMATEUR ALL-AGE STAKES

*Super Chief	L	August Belmont	242
Glengarven's Mik	L	Roger Vasselais	233
Dolobran's Smoke Tail	L	Richard H. Hecker	158½
Creole Sister	L	Donald P. Weiss	130
Sir Mike of Orchard View	L	Roger Vasselais	129½
*River Oaks Corky	L	Michael R. Flannery	126½
Tigathoe's Mainliner Mariah	L	Alanson C. Brown III	126½
Nickolas of Logan's End	G	Hugh Adams	123½
Rill-Shannon's Dark Del	L	Michael R. Flannery	118½
Baron's Tule Tiger	C	Mrs. Walter S. Heller	111
Jetstone Muscles of Claymar	L	Mrs. Margie Johnson	106½
Misty's Sungold Lad	G	K. P. Fisher and Mrs. Valerie F. Walker	104
*Dee's Dandy Dude	L	Michael Paterno	102
Dairy Hill's Mike	L	Harold Mack, Jr.	97½
Royal's Moose's Moe	L	William D. Connor	97½
Dairy Hill's Night Cap	L	Andreius A. Jones	96½
*Carr-Lab Hilltop	L	Glenn B. Bump	93½
Butte Blue Moon	L	Mr. and Mrs. Bing Grunwald	93
Shauna Buck	L	Mrs. August Belmont	90½
Carr-Lab Penrod	L	Mrs. August Belmont	89
*Rebel Chief of Heber	L	Mr. & Mrs. Gus F. Rathert	85
*Bracken's High Flyer	L	George L. Dukek	84½
Brandy Spirit of Netley	L	Mrs. Theodore E. Fajen, Jr.	84½
Frances Fishtail	L	Richard H. Hecker	82½
Cindy's Pride of Garfield	L	Mrs. Clifford V. Brokaw, Jr.	80½
*Guy's Bitterroot Lucky	L	Guy P. Burnett	80½
Rocky Road of Zenith	L	Andrew D. Pruitt	79½
Cougar's Rocket	L	James L. Casey	76½
Lord Bomar	L	John A. Love, Jr.	74½
Black Boy XI	L	Lewis S. Greenleaf, Jr.	72½
Nodrog Penny	L	Gordon B. Olinger	72½
Stilrovin Tuppee Tee	G	Mrs. George H. Flinn, Jr.	72
*Andy's Partner Pete	L	Mrs. C. V. Brokaw, Jr.	71½
Torque of Daingerfield	L	Mrs. Joan Watkins	71
Happy Thanksgiving	G	Miss Ann A. Fowler	70½
Rosehill's Little Dutch Boots	L	Michael R. Flannery	70½
Marelvan Mike of Twin Oaks	L	John F. Nash	70
Tiger's Cub	C	Mrs. Walter S. Heller	68
Bigstone Hope	L	Bing Grunwald	67½
Tarblood of Absaraka	L	John A. Love, Jr.	67½
*Ace's Sheba of Ardyn	L	William K. Laughlin	66
Black Brook's Lady Bimba	L	Mrs. Milton D. Orowitz	66
Del-Tone Colvin	L	Louis J. Snoeyenbos	66
Invail's Pennell	L	Clifford V. Brokaw, Jr.	64½
Ray's Rascal	L	Mr. & Mrs. Raymond H. Goodrich	64½
Salt Valley Ottie	L	Sid H. Eliason, Jr.	64
Col-Tam of Craignook	L	Mr. & Mrs. R. O. Bateman	63½
Carnmoney Brigadier	L	Mr. & Mrs. Raymond H. Goodrich	62½
*Dutchmoor's Black Mood	L	A. Nelson Sills	62½
Jibodad Velvet	L	Dr. Charles N. Versteeg	61½
Mainliner Mike II	L	J. W. McAssey-Mrs. G. H. Flinn, Jr.	61
Sam Frizel of Glenspey	L	Mrs. Warner L. Atkins	61
Della-Winn's Tar of Craignook	L	Dr. Donald S. Thatcher	60½

Mount Joy's Louistoo	C	Edward C. Fleischmann	60
Sand Gold Kim	L	Jerome Bernstein	60
Orion's Sirius	L	John W. Martin	59½
Paha Sapa Chief II	L	Wilbur T. Goode	59½
Black Jake of Devon	L	Peter Gill Wylie	58½
Princess Patricia Stieg	L	Richard H. Hecker	58½
Dairy Hill's Night Watch	L	Andreius A. Jones	58
Hawk Hill's Sam of Devon	L	Mrs. E. A. G. Wylie	58
*Captain of Lomac	L	Rudy R. Deering	57
Tar Baby's Little Sweet Stuff	L	Kensyle L. Carpenter	57
Lucinda of Crater Lake	L	Rolland G. Watt	56
Fisherman Bill of Delaware	L	Mrs. Mahlon B. Wallace, Jr.	55½

Most Wins (36) Super Chief, L. August Belmont
Most Placements (81) Glengarven's Mik, L. Roger Vasselais

(C) OPEN AND AMATEUR ALL-AGE STAKES

Dogs with an aggregate of 100 or more Open and Amateur Points, with at least 25% of the total in each major division.

*Super Chief	354½	*Bracken's High Flyer	138
Glengarven's Mik	353	Dusty's Doctari	129
River Oaks Corky	325½	Fisherman Bill of Delaware	128½
*Dolobran's Smoke Tail	269	Ray's Rascal	128½
Dairy Hill's Night Cap	244½	Torque of Daingerfield	128½
Tarblood of Absaraka	232½	Rick of Charlemagne	127½
*Butte Blue Moon	224	Nodrog Penny	125
*Creole Sister	218	Oakcreek's Van Cleve	125
Baron's Tule Tiger	207	Salt Valley Ottie	124½
Black Boy XI	198	Ardyn's Ace of Merwalfin	123½
*Royal's Moose's Moe	196	Rocky Road of Zenith	119
Sir Mike of Orchard View	178½	Sand Gold Kim	116½
*Del-Tone Colvin	177½	Black Jet XVI	115½
Nickolas of Logan's End	175½	Stonegate's Arrow	115
Jetstone Muscles of Claymar	175	Jibodad Velvet	112½
*Carr-Lab Hilltop	174½	Paha Sapa Chief II	112½
Lord Bomar	173	Bitterroot Chink-ee	111½
*Rebel Chief of Heber	173	Mount Joy's Louistoo	111
*Dee's Dandy Due	172½	La Sage's Neb	108½
Cindy's Pride of Garfield	169	Carmoney Brigadier	107½
Tigathoe's Mainliner Mariah	169	Grady's Shadee Ladee	107½
Rill Shannon's Dark Del	168	Petite Rouge	107½
Flood Bay Boomerang	163	Boley's Cascade	107
*Guy's Bitterroot Lucky	162½	Meg's Pattie O'Rourke	107
Misty's Sungold Lad	160½	Bigstone Flint	106½
Tar Baby's Little Sweet Stuff	159½	Truly Yours of Garfield	106½
Cougar's Rocket	156½	Dairy Hill's Night Watch	105½
Frances Fishtail	146½		
Brandy Spirit of Netley	143	*Marvadel Black Gum	104
Ace's Sheba of Ardyn	141½	*Captain of Lomac	103
Sam Frizel of Glenspey	141	Floodbay's Baron O'Glengarven	103
Carr-Lab Penrod	140½	*Andy's Partner Pete	102½
Dairy Hill's Mike	140	Black Monk of Roeland	102
*Bigstone Hope	138½		

OUTSTANDING CAMPAIGNS
(20 or More Points in a Year)
1967 - 1972

(*National Championships Scored as 5 Point Wins)

(A) OPEN ALL-AGE STAKES

1967

Super Chief	32½
Michelle	27
*Butte Blue Moon	25
Whygin Cork's Coot	25
Fisherman Bill of Delaware	23
Cimaroc Tang	22½
Flood Bay Boomerang	22
Lord Bomar	22
Rebel Chief of Heber	21½

1968

Whygin Cork's Coot	34½
Butte Blue Moon	31
Mr. Mac's Billy Boy	27
Glengarven's Mik	26½
Flood Bay Boomerang	26
*Super Chief	25½
Guy's Bitterroot Lucky	25
Michelle	25
Anzac of Zenith	24
Lord Bomar	23½
Tar Dessa Venture	22½
Canuck-Crest Cutty Sark	20

1969

River Oaks Corky	60½
Tar Dessa Venture	40½
Creole Sister	31
Dusty's Doctari	28

Cimaroc Tang	25
Mi-Cris Sailor	23
Cascade Charade	21½

1970

River Oaks Corky	42½
*Creole Sister	27
Invail's Cavalier Carom	25½
Bigstone Flint	25
Butte Blue Moon	22½
Whygin Cork's Coot	22

1971

River Oaks Corky	57½
Zipper Dee Do	29½
Shamrock Acres Super Value	26
Dusty's Doctari	25
Ray's Rascal	22½
*Mi-Cris Sailor	21
Rocky Road of Zenith	21
Dee's Dandy Dude	20½
Butte Blue Moon	20

1972

River Oaks Corky	37
Dee's Dandy Dude	33
Ray's Rascal	26½
Shamrock Acres Super Value	24½
Ace of Southwood	22
Zipper Dee Do	22
Baird's Centerville Sam	21
Willowmount El Diablo	20½

Most Wins (10) River Oaks Corky, L, Michael R. Flannery (1969)
Most Places (16) River Oaks Corky, L, Michael R. Flannery (1971)

(B) AMATEUR ALL-AGE STAKES

1967

*Super Chief	53
Glengarven's Mik	33½
Rill Shannon's Dark Del	31½
Rebel Chief of Heber	25
Butte Blue Moon	22½
Flood Bay Boomerang	22
Baron's Tule Tiger	21
Sir Mike of Orchard View	20

1968

*Super Chief	47½
Glengarven's Mik	41½

Torque of Daingerfield	37½
Guy's Bitterroot Lucky	33½
Marelvan Mike of Twin Oaks	31
Rill Shannon's Dark Del	28
Rosehill's Little Dutch Boots	24½
Cork of Evergreen	24
Jupiter's Hi-Laurel	23
Hawk Hills' Sam of Devon	21½
Royal's Moose's Moe	20

1969

River Oaks Corky	41
Super Chief	38
Tigathoe's Mainliner Mariah	34

Creole Sister 28½
Lord Bomar 26
Misty's Sungold Lad 26
Smokey of Park Avenue 24
Jetstone Muscles of Claymar 23
Glengarven's Mik 20½

1970

Creole Sister 42
Rocky Road of Zenith 34½
River Oaks Corky 28
Shamrock Acres Drake 25
Mitch of Bitterroot 24
*Andy's Partner Pete 23½
Duke of Crookston 20½
Super Chief 20

1971

*Dee's Dandy Dude 37
Ray's Rascal 29
Andy's Partner Pete 27
Bellota Cacahuete 27
Bigstone Flint 26
Misty's Sungold Lad 26
Super Chief 24½
River Oaks Corky 23½
River Oaks Rascal 21
Paha Sapa Warpaint 20½
Randy Mayhall of Tina 20½

1972

Dee's Dandy Dude 51
Tigathoe's Mainliner Mariah 30½
Misty's Sungold Lad 27
Carr-Lab Penrod 26½
Super Chief 25½
River Oaks Rascal 23½
Bob's Black Rebel 23
Martens' Castaway 21
Ottley's Jazzbo 21
Warpath Rip 20

Most Wins (9) Super Chief, L, August Belmont (1968)
Most Places (15) Glengarven's Mik, L, Roger Vasselais (1968)
(15) Tigathoe's Mainliner Mariah, L, Alanson C. Brown III (1969)

NUMBER AND SIZE
OPEN AND AMATEUR ALL-AGE STAKES
1951 - 1972

The below comparison covers the period starting with the first year in which an Amateur All-Age Stake was run. During the twenty year period, 1931 through 1950, Open All-Age stakes increased from one in the first year to fifty-two in 1950. For a year by year comparison of such stakes during that period, see the Labrador Retriever Club's 1966 Supplement.

	OPEN ALL AGE			AMATEUR ALL AGE		
	Trials	Starters	Avg.	Trials	Starters	Avg.
1972	139	6557	47.2	137	4818	35.2
1971	138	6010	43.6	135	4362	32.3
1970	134	5703	42.6	132	4134	31.3
1969	130	5430	41.8	128	3731	29.1
1968	127	4817	37.9	126	3798	30.1
1967	125	4332	34.7	120	3041	25.3
1966	123	4317	35.0	119	2958	24.8
1965	126	4281	33.4	118	3029	25.6
1964	119	4038	34.7	114	2889	25.3
1963	115	4006	34.8	109	2853	26.2
1962	111	3683	33.1	105	2685	25.5
1961	108	3562	32.9	99	2497	25.2
1960	106	3583	33.8	85	2277	24.0
1959	102	3301	32.4	95	2134	22.9
1958	100	3133	31.3	92	2079	22.6
1957	92	2939	32.0	83	1968	23.7
1956	84	2871	34.2	60	1502	25.0
1955	71	2369	33.5	39	967	24.0
1954	65	2114	32.5	37	976	26.3
1953	60	2324	38.8	35	891	25.5
1952	58	2071	35.7	39	855	22.0
1951	53	1950	36.0	32	727	22.0

ALPHABETICAL LIST OF FIELD TRIAL CLUBS

Showing the date each Club held its first trial, and indicating the abbreviation used hereafter in this book to designate each Club. Clubs marked (*) have not been active since the dates shown in parentheses after their respective names.

Alamo Retriever Field Trial Club	2- 8-57	ALM
Alaska Retriever Club	9- 4-70	ALK
Albuquerque Retriever Club	5- 6-67	ALB
American Amateur Retriever Club (formerly Illinois River FTA)	11-30-46	AAR
American Chesapeake Club	11-27-32	ACC
Atlanta Retriever Club	5- 8-70	ATL
Big Horn Basin Retriever Club	6-16-56	BHB
Brook Haven G.P.A. (1937)*	12-28-34	BRO
Buckeye Retriever Club	9-23-50	BUK
Calcasieu Retriever Club	10-16-70	CAS
California South Coast Retriever Club	3- 6-53	CSC
Carlisle Field Trial Club (1941)*	4- 5-40	CRL
Central Minnesota Retriever Club	6-18-49	CMI
Central Nebraska Retriever Club (formerly Hall Co. D&H Club)	5- 8-54	CNB
Central New York Retriever Club	5-30-58	CNY
Central Wyoming Retriever Club	8-28-70	CWY
Cheyenne Retriever Club	8-16-58	CHY
Colonial Retriever Field Trial Club	10- 8-49	COL
Del Bay Field Trial Club	10-20-45	DEL
Duluth Retriever Club	4-15-47	DUL
Eastern Idaho Retriever Club	7-28-68	EID
Eugene Retriever Club (1957)*	5- 1-54	EUG
Flat River Retriever Club	8-21-64	FRR
Fort Peck Retriever Club (1967)*	8- 3-63	FPK
Fort Pitt Retriever Club	6- 4-66	FTP
Golden Retriever Club of America	5-18-40	GOL
Great Salt Lake Retriever Club	5-22-59	GSL
Helena Retriever Club	10- 9-48	HEL
Idaho State Trial Association (1938)*	10-10-38	IST
Idaho Retriever Club	5-19-50	IDA
Irish Water Spaniel Club (1947)*	12- 4-37	IWS
Jacksonville Retriever Club	1-31-69	JAX
James River Retriever Club	3-26-71	JAM
Jayhawk Retriever Club	3-26-66	JAY
Kansas City Retriever Club	4- 2-55	KAN
Labrador Retriever Club	12-21-31	LAB
Lassen Retriever Club	3-29-57	LAS
Lincoln Trail Amateur Retriever Club	4- 2-71	LIT
Lone Star Retriever Club	2-24-56	LST
Long Island Retriever Field Trial Club	12-21-35	LIR
Madison Retriever Club	5- 5-56	MAD
Maine Retriever Trial Club	5-26-56	MAI
Manitowoc County Kennel Club	8-26-50	MAN
Maryland Retriever Club	11-19-49	MAR
Memphis Amateur Retriever Club	10-31-58	MEM
Michiana Retriever Club	8-23-68	MIC
Middle Tennessee Amateur Retriever Club	10-22-65	MTA
Mid-Illinois Ret. Club (formerly Wee-Ma-Tuk R.C. "WMT")	6- 5-64	MIL
Mid-Iowa Retriever C ub	5-14-65	MII
Midwest Field Trial Club	10-26-35	MIW
Minnesota Field Trial Association	5-21-38	MNS
Minot Retriever Club	8-13-60	MIT
Mississippi Valley Ret. Club (formerly Miss. Valley Kennel Club)	4-30-38	MIV
Missouri Valley Hunt Club	10-10-36	MOV
Mobile Amateur Retriever Club	2-24-61	MOB
Montana Retriever Club	10-11-47	MON
Mount Rushmore Retriever Club	9-15-62	MTR

National Amateur Retriever Club	6-20-57	NAM
National Retriever Club (formerly Nat'l Ret. Field Trial Club)	12- 5-41	NAT
Nebraska Dog and Hunt Club	9-25-42	NEB
North Dakota Retriever Club	10-21-44	NDK
Northern Retriever Field Trial Club (1947)*	6- 1-40	NRC
North East Wisconsin Kennel Club (1955)*	5-19-45	NEW
North Florida Amateur Retriever Club	2-14-64	NFL
North Louisiana Retriever Club	10-20-61	NLA
North State Field Trial Association (1936)*	10-16-36	NST
North Texas Retriever Club	5- 1-59	NTX
Northern California Retriever Trial Club	10- 1-48	NCA
Northwest Iowa Retriever Club (formerly N.W. Iowa Dog Club)	10- 1-49	NOI
Northwest Retriever Club	6- 2-45	NWR
Nutmeg Retriever Club (1967)* (merged with Shoreline Ret. Club)	5- 2-53	NUT
Ohio Valley Retriever Club	3-26-55	OHV
Oregon Retriever Trial Club	4-13-46	ORE
Phoenix Retriever Club	10- 9-70	PHO
Pikes Peak Retriever Club	8- 2-58	P'K
Port Arthur Retriever Club	2-24-56	PTA
Puget Sound Retriever Club	4-12-52	PUG
Redwood Empire Retriever Club	7-28-56	RED
Rocky Mountain Retriever Club	8-25-56	RKM
Rogue Valley Retriever Club	3-21-52	ROV
Rolling Rock Club (1941)*	10-30-36	RRC
Sagehens' Retriever Club	3-16-56	SAG
Samish Retriever Field Trial Club	3-16-57	SAM
San Diego Retriever Club	9- 1-72	SAD
Shasta Cascade Retriever Club	4-10-48	SHA
Sheridan Retriever Club	10- 2-54	SHE
Shoreline Retriever Club (see Nutmeg Retriever Club)	5- 2-68	SHO
Shrewsbury River Retriever Club	9-22-56	SHR
Sierra Nevada Retriever Club	5-30-58	SRN
Sioux Valley Retriever Club	8-30-58	SXV
Snake River Retriever Club	5-10-57	SNA
Sooner Retriever Club	4-28-72	SOO
Southern Arizona Retriever Club	2-14-58	SRZ
Southern California Retriever Club	3- 6-48	SCA
South Louisiana Retriever Club	5- 7-65	SLA
Spokane Retriever Club	5- 7-49	SPO
Superior Retriever Club (1966)*	6-16-56	SUP
Swamp Dog Club for Training and Trials	3-26-48	SWA
Tacoma Retriever Club	8- 6-55	TAC
Talbot Retriever Club	10-16-52	TAL
Tri-State Hunting Dog Association	6-11-49	TRI
Westchester Retriever Club	5-30-69	WCH
Western Montana Retriever Club	5-14-49	WMO
Western New York Retriever Club (formerly Rochester Ret. Club)	9-19-53	WNY
Willamette Valley Retriever Club	8-21-54	WIL
Wisconsin Amateur Field Trial Club	5- 7-38	WIS
Wolverine Retriever Club	9-25-54	WOL
Women's Field Trial Club	11-15-40	WOM

ALPHABETICAL LIST OF RETRIEVERS
PLACING IN AKC LICENSED
OPEN AND AMATEUR ALL-AGE STAKES
1967 - 1972

The total lifetime record of placements is included for all dogs which have placed in subject stakes during the period, January 1, 1967 through December 31, 1972. Progenitors marked (*) have also placed in subject stakes during the period under review. Information and pedigree data with respect to these will be found by referring to their places in the alphabetical list. Only field trial titles of alphabetically listed dogs are included. Titles of progenitors have been omitted throughout. Information with respect to prior records of certain of these progenitors may be found by reference to previous editions of the Labrador Book, and in the Books previously published by National Amateur Retriever Club.

LABRADOR RETRIEVERS - DOGS

ABENAKI'S SAGAMORE SA-267457 2/26/64 Dr. and Mrs. M. M. Filson
—By Sprucelane's Chippewa Chief (Paha Sapa Chief II - Lady of Sandy Hill) ex Canuck-Crest Sally* (Jet of Zenith-Canuck-Crest Tami O'Churchlee)
 AMATEUR—MAI 9/69-3; MAI 9/71-4.   (1½)

FC ACE HIGH SCAMP OF WINDSWEEP SA-412701 6/25/57 Mrs. Grace Lambert—By Cork of Oakwood Lane (Coastal Charger of Deer Creek - Akona Liza Jane of Kingdale) ex Queen's Ace (Blyth's Ace of Spades - African of Avandale)
 OPEN—NTX 3/61-1; MNS 5/61-2; CMI 6/61-1; MAD 8/61-1; WIS 4/62-1; NUT 5/62-1; WOM 10/62-3; NCA 3/63-3; SAG 3/63-1; MAN 8/63-1; MAR 10/63-3; NOI 9/63-2; SWA 11/63-2; LAB 4/64-1; SHR 5/64-1; NUT 5/64-2; MNS 5/64-2; MAR 10/64-1; WOM 10/64-4; LAB 4/65-2; MNS 5/64-2; CMI 5/65-2; TRI 6/65-3; DUL 8/65-2; MNS 9/65-1; MAD 5/66-1; MIL 6/66-2; TRI 6/67-2; SXV 9/67-4; MNS 9/67-3; LIR 10/67-4; SWA 11/67-4.   (101)

ACE HI INDIAN MAGIC SA-126374 8/28/60 Mrs. E. E. Pierce — By Paha Sapa Chief II (Freehaven Muscles - Treasure State Be Wise) ex Ace Hi Tammi (Cork of Oakwood Lane - Queen's Ace)
 OPEN—KAN 4/66-3; MEM 3/67-4.   (1½)
 AMATEUR—CNY 3/66-4; CNY 5/69-2.   (3½)

FC ACE OF GARFIELD SA-8433 7/22/59 John M. Olin—By Crowder (Cork of Oakwood Lane - Beautywood's Creole Jane) ex Pierre's Kit of Garfield (Shed's Prince of Garfield - Joy of Garfield)
 OPEN—MEM 2/64-3; MNS 5/64-1; TRI 5/64-3; WMT 6/64-4; MAD 8/64-4; AAR 5/65-1; TRI 6/65-1;OHV 10/65-1; MIV 10/65-1; MTA 10/65-3; NFL 2/66-1; MEM 3/66-2; MIW 10/66-2; MEM 10/66-1; NFL 2/67-4; MOB 2/67-3; KAN 3/67-1; MIW 4/67-3; MIV 10/67-2; MAD 5/67-3; WOL 5/68-3; MAN 8/68-1.   (62½)
 AMATEUR—4/66-3.   (1)

FC ACE OF SOUTHWOOD SA-398841 5/26/66 John M. Olin—By Ace of Garfield* (Crowder - Pierre's Kit of Garfield) ex Random Molly (Pepper's Jiggs - Random Shot)
 OPEN—SCA 2/69-4; WOM 4/69-3; LAB 4/69-4; SHO 5/69-1; MNS 9/69-4; WIS 9/69-1; KAN 10/69-3; LAB 11/69-4; JAX 2/70-2; NFL 2/70-1; NEB 4/70-3; MIW 4/70-3; WIS 5/70-4; MNS 5/70-2; AAR 5/70-1; NEB 4/71-3; MIW 4/71-4; WIS 4/71-3; MAD 5/71-4; GOL 5/71-4; AAR 5/71-4; TRI 5/71-1; MNS 9/71-2; WIS 9/71-1; KAN 3/72-3; MIV 4/72-2; NEB 4/72-1; MIC 8-72-2; AAR 9/72-1; MIW 10/72-2; MIV 10/72-1.   (74½)
 AMATEUR—WIS 9/69-4.   (½)

AHAB'S EMANCIPATOR SA-524728 10/1/67 Dr. and Mrs. Gene Starkloff—By Carnmoney Spud* (Bandit of Carnmoney - Carnmoney Boots) ex Mawod's Funf (Dairy Hill's Night Cap - Mawod's Drie)
OPEN—KAN 10/71-4. (½)
AMATEUR—MOB 3/72-2; LIT 4/72-1; AAR 5/72-2. (11)

FC-AFC AIR EXPRESS SA-566263 4/20/68 August Belmont—By Super Chief* (Paha Sapa Chief II - Ironwood Cherokee Chica) ex Dart of Netley Creek (Netley Creek's Sugar - Stonegate's Susie Q)
OPEN—SNA 8/71-1; WCH 5/72-4; MAI 9/72-1. (10½)
AMATEUR—WOM 4/71-1; MAR 10/71-2; CSC 2/72-2; IDA 8/72-2. (14)

FC-AFC ALAMO BLACK JACK SA-185895 3/12/62 Noxie M. Romano, Jr.—By Tony's Black Cork (Cork of Oakwood Lane - Del-Tone Cindy) ex Our Lady Midnight (Vogue Micky - Mirl's Graham Cracker)
OPEN—ALM 11/65-3; LST 3/66-4; GSL 5/67-3; NTX 3/68-4; PTA 10/69-3; LST 3/70-1; CAS 10/70-4; LST 10/70-1. (14½)
AMATEUR—SLA 9/66-1; NLA 10/66-2; SLA 10/67-3; PTA 10/68-4; ALM 11/68-4; NTX 10/69-4; PIK 5/70-2; RKM 5/70-1; NLA 10/70-4; ALM 11/70-2; LST 10/7-1; ALM 11/71-1. (32)

ALPAUGH'S WHISTLIN JIM SA-73258 8/10/60 Geo. L. Alpaugh—By Nic-O-Bet's Treveilyr Thunder (Treveilyr Swift - Manzanal Rain) ex Cork's Tar Baby (Cork of Oakwood Lane - Min-A-Jet of Reo Raj)
AMATEUR—SCA 9/67-4; CSC 9/68-2. (3½)

AMBER'S DANDY BEAU SA-312737 3/14/65 Orus J. Matthews, Jr.—By Ralston's Valley Floyd (Shamrock Acres Jim Dandy - Lady Ginger of Shady Lane) ex Amber of White Grass (Hap's Golden Boy - Aurora of Avandale)
OPEN—CNB 5/71-2. (3)
AMATEUR—ALB 5/68-3; PIK 8/68-4; PIK 5/69-4; PIK 9/69-4; CNB 5/70-4; CWY 8/70-4; MOV 9/70-2. (6½)

AFC ANDY BLACK OF CHESTNUT HILL SA-377663 1/24/65 Armin C. Frank, Jr.—By Dutchmoor's Black Mood* (Calypso Clipper - Jet's Tammy) ex Dory II (Roy's Rowdy - Paha Sapa Kate)
OPEN—MAR 10/72-4. (½)
AMATEUR—FTP 5/68-3; LIR 10/68-4; SWA 11/68-3; BUK 4/69-2; LAB 11/69-1; DEL 3/70-1; SAG 3/71-3; LIR 10/71-2; JAX 3/72-1; MAR 5/72-4. (25)

FC-NARFC '70 ANDY'S PARTNER PETE SA-400162 12/17/64 Mrs. Clifford V. Brokaw, Jr.—By Alpine Cherokee Rocket (Cherokee Buck - Nelgard's Madam Queen) ex Ja Dar's Miss Kim (Black Banner - Queen Deborah)
OPEN—NFL 2/69-1; TAL 3/69-4; WOM 4/69-4; MAN 8/69-1; COL 9/69-4; LAB 11/69-3; TAL 4/70-4; MAR 5/70-1; OHV 10/71-4; LIR 10/71-4; LAB 4/72-3; FRR 8/72-2; OHV 9/72-2; LAB 11/72-1. (31)
AMATEUR—MIC 8/68-3; DEL 10/68-1; WOM 10/68-4; MOB 2/69-4; MTA 3/69-4; WOL 5/69-4; CNY 5/69-3; FRR 8/69-4; SWA 10/69-1; MOB 2/70-2; MEM 3/70-3; LAB 3/70-4; MAR 5/70-3; CNY 5/70-3; NAM 6/70-1; MAN 8/70-2; FRR 8/70-3; LIR 10/70-1; WOM 10/70-2; JAX 3/71-1; NFL 3/71-1; BUK 9/71-1; WOL 10/71-2; LIR 10/71-3; WOM 10/71-2; SWA 11-71-1; TAL 4/72-4; LAB 4/72-1; WOM 10/72-3. (71½)

FC ANZAC OF ZENITH SA-197088 3/24/63 Carnation Farm Kennels —By Black Mike of Lakewood (Vicky's Duffy Boy - Thornwood Bracken Scout) ex Jezebel of Normandy (Yankee Clipper of Reo Raj - Belle of Zenith)

Ace High Scamp of Windsweep

Ace of Garfield

Ace of Southwood

Andy's Partner Pete

OPEN—NWR 4/66-1; IDA 5/67-3; SNA 5/67-1; SPO 5/67-2;
LAS 2/68-1; NCA 3/68-2; ROV 3/68-1; PUG 4/68-4; SPO
5/68-1; WMO 5/68-4; WIL 8/68-1.   (38)
AMATEUR—SHA 4/66-4; SNA 5/66-1.   (5½)

APRIL FOOLS YELLOW JACKET SA-40128 4/1/60 Don L. and Patsy
Rice—By Flashes Black Drake (Black Flash of Hellgate - Bannerman
Lady Anne) ex Sparkle Plenty of Whitmore (Black Rogue of Whit-
more - Okanagon Queen of Flathead)
AMATEUR—WMO 5/67-2; HEL 9/67-3.   (4)

ARCHIE THE COCKROACH SA-453832 4/19/66 Robert A. and
Barbara S. Stubblefield—By David's Idaho Pete (Night Fighter - Paha
Sapa Wacincala) ex Mountain Crest's Black Velvet (Tarblood of
Absaraka* - Duxbak Lady III)
AMATEUR—GSL 8/70-4.   (½)

ARDYN'S BLACK BART SA-146530 3/17/62 Jack C. Murphy — By
Breckonhill's Shannon O'Moore (Breckonhill Ben - Erin O'Moore) ex
Ardyn's Mercy Bound (Holly's Ace of Ardyn - Ace's Topsy of Winniway)
AMATEUR—SPO 10/66-1; PUG 4/67-4; TAC 8/67-1; PUG
8/67-2; SPO 9/67-4.   (14)

ARROYO SECO ROCKET SA-370193 8/3/63 H. C. Shearer—By Crook's
El Toro (Crook's Tahoe Pat - Black Rapids of Baranof) ex Arroyo Seco
Cindy (Curnshaw Bat-Jac Boy - Panther's Flyaway Cinders)
OPEN—ALK 8/71-4.   (½)
AMATEUR—ROV 3/68-2.   (3)

FC ATTAWAN PUCKA SAHIB SA-128617 12/25/60 Mr. and Mrs. A. B.
Mason Jr. — By Paha Sapa Chief II (Freehaven Muscles - Treasure
State Be Wise) ex Penny Girl (Cork of Oakwood Lane - Min-A-Jet
of Reo Raj)
OPEN—COL 10/64-1; SWA 3/65-3; SXV 9/65-1; MAI 9/65-1;
SWA 3/66-1; LIR 4/66-2; CNY 5/66-3; SWA 11/66-3; LIR
4/67-3; LIR 4/68-3.   (28)

FC-AFC BAIRD'S CENTERVILLE SAM SA-383706 1/24/66 Mr. and Mrs.
M. B. Wallace, Jr.—By Crozier's Sparkle (Innistona Pheasant - Castle-
more Sylver of Wallasey) ex Henry's Charm (Flashes Black Drake -
Macushla of Rockmont)
OPEN—SLA 2/70-1; ATL 5/70-4; MIV 10/70-1; MTA 10/70-4;
MEM 10/70-4; MII 6/71-1; MIV 10/71-2; MOB 11/71-4; NFL
3/72-2; MOB 3/72-2; MTA 4/72-4; MEM 4/72-1; LIT 4/72-3;
MIL 5/72-1; SXV 9/72-3; WIS 9/72-4.   (41)
AMATEUR—MIL 6/70-2; MIV 4/71-3; MIV 10/71-3; MTA
10/71-4; MTA 4/72-2; MEM 4/72-1; MIV 10/72-1.   (18½)

FC-AFC BAIR'S SAMBO II SA-578995 7/9/67 Howard W. and Beverly
Bair—By Hap (Hamer's Tar Baby - Hamer's Lady Buff) ex Swinomish
Shady Teena (Swinomish Big Chance - Shady Bingo II)
OPEN—SCA 3/72-1.   (5)
AMATEUR—NCA 3/71-1; SHA 5/71-4.   (5½)

FC-AFC BALSOM'S SNOOPER HONKER SA-544131 10/5/67 Dr. B. B.
Baker—By Singing Woods War Cloud (Paha Sapa Chief II - Fallwood's
Hi Top Boots) ex Redd (Crowder - Bigstone Ricky)
OPEN—SHA 9/70-3; GSL 8/71-3; SHA 9/71-3; NCA 9/71-3;
NCA 3/72-3; SHA 4/72-1.   (10)
AMATEUR—GSL 8/71-1; SHA 9/71-2; NCA 9/71-2; SCA 3/72-2;
ROV 3/72-4.   (14½)

BAR ME NONE SA-374778 5/19/65 Robert Dobbs—By Rip Van Winkle III (Sun Valley Tuck - Jet of Hawthorne II) ex Ruby's Jet (Salt Valley Ottie - Sid's Rusty)
    AMATEUR—GSL 5/69-4. (½)

AFC BAYOU BEAU SA-229469 1/28/63 Wayne J. Johnson—By Medlin's Texas Jack Tar (Boley's Tar Baby - Medlin's Cricket) ex Jethaven Black Lucky (Paha Sapa Chief II - Bayou Black Belle)
    OPEN—PTA 3/68-3; LST 10/68-4; PTA 10/69-1. (6½)
    AMATEUR—SLA 2/67-3; SLA 9/67-1;LST 10/68-2; NLA 10/69-4; ALM 10/69-4; LST 3/70-1; NLA 3/70-3; PTA 10/70-4. (16½)

BAYOU PIRATE SA-225453 7/22/60 Daniel W. Martin—By Del-Tone Colvin (Cork of Oakwood Lane - Del-Tone Bridget) ex Black Belle of Mylla (Snikeb's Owl Car - Greenway Shadow)
    AMATEUR—SLA 2/66-3; PTA 3/66-2; NTX 10/67-1; LST 10/67-4; PTA 3/68-4. (10)

BEAU GENTRY SA-600817 6/12/68 Thomas F. Hubbard—By Ridgewood All Is Jake (Ridgewood Playboy - Mueller's Scout) ex Timcin's Queen of Spades (Timcin's Black Domino* - Black Satin Doll)
    AMATEUR—MIL 6/72-4. (½)

FC-AFC BEAU OF BLAIR HOUSE SA-363311 2/21/65 Mr. and Mrs. Don H. Gearheart—By Cache Valley Drifter (Sunday Shoes - Belle of Bear River) ex Springer's Cleo (Black Cougar - Bay City Katie Jane)
    OPEN—GSL 8/69-4; LAS 2/70-2; GSL 5/70-1; SRN 5/70-1; GSL 8/70-2; ALK 9/70-4; ATL 4/71-1; LAB 4/71-2; LAB 11/71-3; SNA 5/72-3; MON 6/72-1; IDA 8/72-3; NCA 9/72-4. (33½)
    AMATEUR—SHA 4/69-2; SAG 7/69-1; SAG 3/70-1; SHA 9/70-2; MAR 10/71-3. (17)

BEAVERCREST BLACK TARTAR II SA-395670 1/11/66 Wm. J. Maeck —By Beavercrest's Bolo (Black Marauder of Whitmore - Corsair's Jet of Whitmore) ex Queen of Valentine (Massie's Sassy Boots - Judy of Valentine)
    AMATEUR—SNA 5/69-4; WMO 5/71-3. (1½)

BEAVERCREST GOIN' GUS SA-485418 3/3/67 Dr. A. L. Ryan—By Beavercrest Kannonball Kidd (Paha Sapa Chief II - Shady Haven Farm Topper) ex Belle High (Butch's Bitterroot Smoky - Massie's Sassy Littlecloud)
    AMATEUR—IDA 5/71-4. (½)

BEAVER STATE HOPE SA-718914 1/6/69 Dr. R. C. Greenleaf — By Tyker Baby* (Tar Baby's Little Sweet Stuff - Dessa Rae*) ex Acute Accent* (Ripco's Peter Pan - Shoe's Del-Tone Femme)
    OPEN—TAC 8/72-2. (3)

FC BEL-AIRE LUCKY BOY SA-604506 11/23/67 Mrs. Grace Lambert— By Guy's Bitterroot Lucky* (Beavercrest Toreador - Pickrel's Ebony Babe) ex Jilly's Tiger Lil (Duxbak Scooter* - Jilly Girl*)
    OPEN—TRI 6/71-2; MIL 6/71-2; MIT 8/71-3; NDK 8/71-1; LIR 10/71-3. (13)
    AMATEUR—KAN 4/69-4; NOI 10/70-4. (1)

BELLE SHAIN'S STEAMBOAT MAN SA 421154 11/11/65 Mr. and Mrs. E. Rob Leatherbury—By Ebony Mood's Bingo* (Dutchmoor's Black Mood* - Bigstone Lady B) ex Delta's Queen Bee (Martens' Hi Style Buck - Bigstone Ricky)
    OPEN—ATL 4/72-4. (½)
    AMATEUR—NFL 11/70-4; NFL 11/71-4. (1)

AFC BELLOTA CACAHUETE SA-416532 11/14/65 Josephine T. Reeve
—By Carr-Lab Penrod* (Paha Sapa Chief II - Ironwood Cherokee
Chica) ex Midnight Chuckar (Gun Thunder Oly* - Midnight Sue
of Calumet)
OPEN—GSL 5/71-3; ACC 8/71-3. (2)
AMATEUR—SNA 8/70-3; ACC 8/70-4; SRZ 2/71-1; CSC 2/71-1;
GSL 5/71-1; ACC 9/71-4; MON 9/71-4; HEL 9/71-1; WMO
9/71-1; PHO 10/71-3. (28½)

BIGSTONE COUNT BLACK RIP SA-247878 1/13/64 John A. Cassidy—
By Count Yurmarbles Again (Bingo Again - Bigstone Bracken) ex Lady
Blackduck (Blake's Black Timber Crusader - Kellogg's Black Lady)
AMATEUR—LAB 11/67-2; SHR 3/68-3; DEL 3/69-4; WOM
4/69-2; DEL 10/69-2. (10½)

FC-AFC BIGSTONE FLINT SA-329701 10/21/64 Mr. and Mrs. David
Crow—By Martens' Mister Nifty* (Royal of Garfield - Martens' Black
Badger) ex Dick's Black Scamp (Yankee Bob - Glen-Water Fan Fare)
OPEN—JAY 3/69-4; WIS 4/69-4; PIK 5/69-1; MAD 8/69-1;
MNS 9/69-3; MOV 9/69-3; NLA 10/69-1; NEB 4/70-1; CNB
5/70-1; PIK 8/70-1; CHY 8/70-1;ALM 11/70-1; MEM 4/71-2;
ALB 7/71-1; NLA 10/71-1; PTA 10/71-3; LST 10/71-2; LST
3/72-1; NLA 3/72-1; SLA 3/72-4; ALB 5/72-4; PIK 5/72-2. (74)
AMATEUR—FRR 8/69-2; NTX 3/70-3; NLA 3/70-4; PIK
5/70-4; LST 3/71-3; PTA 3/71-2; SLA 4/71-2; ALB 7/71-1;
RKM 8/71-1; SLA 10/71-2; NTX 10/71-2; PTA 10/71-2; ALM
2/72-3; RKM 8/72-4. (32½)

BIGSTONE HARD'S HAPPY SA-456121 3/26/66 Alfred B. Hard—By
Martens' Mister Nifty* (Royal of Garfield - Martens' Black Badger) ex
Don's Ginny Soo (Don-El's Doo Lee - Beautywood's Creole Jane)
OPEN—NWR 4/72-3. (1)
AMATEUR—TAC 4/70-4; HEL 9/70-4; WMO 9/71-4; ORE
3/72-1; IDA 5/72-3; HEL 9/72-2. (10½)

FC BIGSTONE SCOUT SA-281717 9/24/63 Mr. and Mrs. T. E. Fajen
—By Bigstone Butch (Bigstone Editor - Bigstone Dinah Girl) ex
Martens' Black Dot (Cork of Oakwood Lane - Beautywood's Creole
Jane)
OPEN—MIW 10/69-2; KAN 10/69-2; MAN 8/71-1; BUK 9/71-
2; WNY 10/71-2. (17)
AMATEUR—MNS 9/70-3; MIW 4/71-4; MNS 5/71-1; MNS
5/72-4; WIS 9/72-3. (8)

FC-AFC BILLY PAWLESTA SA-156685 3/12/62 Dr. J. W. Henderson—
By Robbet's Black Hope (Staindrop Murton Marksman - Ebony Duchess)
ex Toto of Audlon (Bracken's Sweep - Little Trouble of Audlon)
OPEN—SLA 9/66-2; NLA 10/66-3; LST 10/66-4; LST 10/68-3;
ALM 11/69-3; CAS 10/70-1; PTA 10/70-3. (12½)
AMATEUR—NLA 10/64-4; ALM 2/66-1; LST 3/66-2; NTX
3/66-1; PTA 10/66-1; PTA 10/67-3; LST 3/68-1; PTA 3/68-1;
LST 10/68-3; PTA 10/68-1; ALM 10/69-3; PTA 10/70-2. (39½)

BITTERROOT'S TAURUS SA-786114 4/6/70 Arnold Boudreaux — By
Guy's Bitterroot Lucky* (Beaver Crest Toreador - Pickrel's Ebony
Babe) ex Royal Oaks September Song (Super Chief - Shamrock Acres
Whygin Tardy)
AMATEUR—PTA 10/72-4. (½)

AFC BLACK BANDIT SA-240168 12/17/62 Richard Horn—By Ace Bingo
(Bingo Again - Bigstone Dinah Girl) ex Green Ridge Sally (Del-Tone
Colvin - Shady Haven Farm Jet)

OPEN—MTR 5/67-4; DUL 8/67-4; KAN 3/68-2; CMI 5/68-3; MII 5/69-3; MIT 8/69-4. (6½)

AMATEUR—MOV 9/65-3; CNB 5/67-4; MII 5/67-2; MNS 5/67-4; MIT 8/67-3; MOV 9/67-4; KAN 3/68-4; NEB 4/68-2; CNB 5/68-3; TRI 5/68-2; MIT 8/68-1 SXV 8/68-3; MOV 9/68-3; NOI 9/68-2; CNB 5/69-3; MIT 8/69-3; MTR 5/70-1; SXV 8/70-4; SXV 5/71-4; MOV 9/71-2; NDK 8/72-2. (38)

BLACKBERRY BRANDY V SA-544810 6/24/66 William F. Weh—By St. Louie's Trouble of Audlon (Beautvwood Rare Trouble - Trouble's Double of Audlon) ex Stardust's Sheba (Jeffsboy of Candlewood - Shamrock Acres Stardust)

AMATEUR—MNS 5/71-4; MAD 8/71-4; DUL 8/71-3; MAD 8/72-2; MAN 8/72-4. (5½)

AFC BLACK CHIEF OF NAKOMIS SA-158423 1/25/62 Charles Adams —By Rod Iron of Chalet (Saber of Chalet - Candylick of Chalet) ex Princess of New Hope (Onyx Chief of Rice - Cinderella of Aitken)

OPEN—MNS 9/67-4. (½)

AMATEUR—MNS 5/66-1; MNS 5/67-1; MAD 8/67-4; MNS 9/67-4; MNS 5/68-4; CMI 5/68-1; MAD 8/68-1; MNS 5/69-3; CMI 5/69-2; MNS 5/70-3. (26½)

FC BLACK DUKE OF SHERWOOD SA-292324 6/23/64 L. Marvin Roberts, M.D.—By Prince of Rapids Hollow (Little Dipper of Maryglo-Queen of Rapids Hollow) ex Queen of High Tide (Jelley's Sir Michael - Cyrier's Princess)

OPEN—JAY 3/70-3; HEL 9/70-3; ALM 2/71-3; KAN 4/71-4; MON 6/71-3; BHB 6/71-1; HEL 9/71-4. (10)

AMATEUR—NTX 3/71-4; KAN 10/71-4. (1)

BLACKFOOT LOBO SA-478015 12/7/66 Mr. and Mrs. Don H. Gearheart—By Raglando Rodarbal (Flashes Black Drake - Macushla of Rockmont) ex Queen's Folly (Breits Black Wind - Potter's Blackfoot Princess)

OPEN—MIT 8/70-2; NDK 8/70-2; WOM 10/71-3; NTX 10/72-2. (10)

AMATEUR—NTX 10/72-1. (5)

AFC BLACK JAKE OF DEVON SA-960258 10/18/58 Peter Gill Wylie By Black Nipper of Devon (Marvadel Black Thorn - Wardwyn Windbound) ex Gina (Chukker of Bonniehurst - Sandy of Indianola)

OPEN—SWA 3/64-3; NUT 5/64-1; LST 3/65-4; PTA 3/65-3; SHR 5/65-4; SRZ 2/66-4; BUK 9/66-4. (9)

AMATEUR—LAB 11/62-4; MAR 10/63-4; SWA 3/64-1; WOM 4/64-2; MAI 5/64-2; LIR 10/64-2; DEL 10/64-4; MOB 2/65-2; PTA 3/65-4; WOM 4/65-1; SHR 5/65-4; MAI 5/65-1; CNY 5/65-3; WNY 9/65-1; MAR 10/65-2; LIR 10/65-2; SRZ 2/66-2; SHR 4/66-2; MAI 5/66-2; CNY 5/66-2; MAR 10/66-3; DEL 10/66-4; LAB 11/66-4; CSC 2/67-2. (58½)

FC-AFC BLACK JET XVI SA-968754 3/29/58 R. S. Humphrey—By Cork's Rocket of Swinomish (Mike of Swinomish - Cork's Jill) ex La Dee of River Lake (Little Blackie of Holly Hill - Ebony Lady VI)

OPEN—LAB 4/61-2; LIR 5/61-1; SWA 11/61-1; CNY 5/62-1; DEL 10/62-4; SWA 11/62-1; CSC 2/63-4; SCA 3/63-1; TAL 3/63-4; SHR 5/63-2; MAI 5/63-2; WNY 9/63-4; COL 9/63-2; SWA 11/63-3; TAL 3/64-1; TAC 8/64-2; MAI 9/64-1; DEL 10/64-3; LAB (S) 11/64-1; WNY 9/65-1; LAB (S) 11/65-2; SAG 3/66-2; WOM 4/66-1; LIR 10/66-4; SAG 3/67-3; WNY 9/67-4. (77)

AMATEUR—LAB 4/61-3; LIR 5/61-4; MAI 9/63-4; SHR 5/64-3; NUT 5/64-1; TAC 8/64-1; COL 10/64-4; COL 10/65-1; WOM 6/65-1; COL 10/66-1; WOM 10/66-1; WOM 4/67-1. (38½)

Baird's Centerville Sam

Bigstone Flint

Black Jake of Devon

Black Jet XVI

FC-AFC BLACK MICHAEL O'SHEA SA-137174 7/7/61 Frank L.
Fletcher, M.D.—By Problem Boy Duke of Wake (Ponto's Ponto of
Wake - Kavanagh's Ripple) ex Smoky's Gal Tammy (Butch's Bitterroot
Smoky - Fenbroke's Meath)

OPEN—WMO 9/66-1: IDA 5/67-2; EID 7/68-2; SNA 8/68-4;
SPO 5/69-3; HEL 9/69-2.   (15½)

AMATEUR—SNA 8/65-2; ACC 8/66-3; HEL 9/66-1: ACC
8/67-4; WMO 9/67-2; IDA 5/68-4; IDA 8/68-4; IDA 5/69-2;
SNA 8/69-2.   (19½)

BLACK NIG PRINCE SA-508402 4/26/67 Les Jante — By Martens'
Scrubby Giant* (Crowder - Martens' Little Bullet) ex Eee Gee's Nell
(Eee Gee's Starr - Celene's Pal Amber)

OPEN—CNB 5/71-1.   (5)

FC-AFC BLACK ROCKY SA-199719 8/13/62 Roy M. Hutchinson M.D.
—By One-Dollar Bill (Paha Sapa Chief II - Snow Queen) ex Iowa
Black Nipper (Kewanee's Swamp Buster - Dakota Black Shirley)

OPEN—PTA 3/67-1; JAY 3/69-1; MIT 8/69-2.   (13)

AMATEUR—MOV 9/65-2; PTA 3/67-3; MII 5/67-3; MII
5/68-2; CMI 5/68-2; MNS 5/69-2.   (14)

AFC BLACK "R" OF BIRCH SA-96669 8/1/59 Richard C. Gardner M.D.
—By Snake River George (Snake River Steen - Jane Lou) ex Black
Lou of Strahenweis (Dan McGraw of Wake - Ten Mile Annie)

OPEN—IDA 8/62-4; HEL 9/62-3; WMO 9/62-4; GSL 8/63-3:
SNA 5/64-4; GSL 5/65-4; SNA 8/65-4 ACC 8/66-3; PUG
4/67-3.   (6½)

AMATEUR—WMO 9/62-4; SNA 5/63-4: GSL 5/63-2; GSL
8/63-4; GSL 5/64-3: IDA 8/64-1; SNA 8/64-4: GSL 8/64-3;
SNA 5/65-1; GSL 5/66-1; ORE 3/67-1; SNA 5/67-3; IDA 8/67-4;
GSL 8/68-2.   (31½)

BLACK SORCERER OF SUNSET SA-114360 9/20/61 Jack F. Mitchell
—By Danny's Black Mac (Rip's Kimo of Filoli - Lucinda of Crater
Lake) ex Belle of Sunset (Jibodad Dandy - Peggy of Long Lake II)

AMATEUR—PUG 8/68-3.   (1)

FC BLITZ VON MOBILE SA-238281 6/8/63 Carroll A. Rice—By Ricky's
Buck (Martens' Hi Style Buck - Bigstone Ricky) ex Viewpoint Black
Jodi (Buster Boy - Black Sheba of Random Lake)

OPEN—MOB 11/66-1; LST 3/68-3; MON 9/68-2; CNB 3/69-2;
MOV 9/69-2.   (15)

AMATEUR—MOB 7/66-4; RKM 5/68-3; MON 5/68-3; CWY
8/70-2.   (5½)

BOATSWAIN'S STORMY SPIRIT SA-484076 12/25/66 Allen & Jeanette
Sharpe—By Stormy of Spirit Lake Gal (Ace Bingo - Spirit Lake Gal)
ex Cork Harbour's Princess (Del-Tone Buck* - O' Torq's Kimberly)

OPEN—LST 10/70-4; SLA 4/71-4.   (1)

AMATEUR— NFL 2/70-4; MIC 8/70-4.   (1)

FC-AFC BOB'S BLACK REBEL SA-374921 3/27/65 Bob and Mary Lou
Chance—By Smoky Le Blanc (Robbet's Black Hope - Cuzz's Corky)
ex Beaumark's Lady Tamee (Gladrock Duke - Beaumark's Yeoward
Lass)

OPEN—LST 2/69-4; LST 3/70-4; SLA 10/70-1; PTA 10/70-2;
CAS 9/72-4; LST 10/72-4.   (10)

AMATEUR—LST 10/69-1; NTX 10/69-2; SLA 2/70-4; PTA
3/70-3; CAS 10/70-1; PTA 10/70-1; ALM 11/70-4; ALM 2/71-1;
NTX 3/72-1; NLA 3/72-1; CAS 9/72-1; PTA 10/72-2; LST
10/72-1.   (48)

BODORO'S COALEY SA-253992 2/16/63 Robert Oberg—By Del-Tone Buck* (Martens' Hi Style Buck - Glen-Water Fan Fare) ex Valgaard Lady of Shady Lane (Yankee Clipper of Reo Raj - Rock Haven's Black Angel)
    OPEN—RKM 5/67-3. (1)

BOISE'S BLACK BART SA-438950 4/18/66 Charles O'Rorke—By Skyline Black Panther (Skyline Donner - Smith's Cindy Lou) ex Jet of Clear Lake (Black Mike of Lakewood - Rhea of Lakewood)
    AMATEUR—WMO 9/69-3. (1)

AFC BOMAR'S BLACKFOOT WOG SA-604672 12/1/67 Wayne E. Mahan and Horace H. Koessler—By Lord Bomar* (Blackfoot's Happy New Year - Peg's Blackfoot Queen) ex Lady Jane XI (Duke of Ashton - Black Diamond Liz)
    OPEN—SHE 9/71-3; BHB 6/72-4; EID 7/72-3. (2½)
    AMATEUR—WMO 9/70-2; RKM 8/71-3; CWY 8/71-4; SHE 9/71-3; SPO 5/72-3; WMO 5/72-4; MON 6/72-4; BHB 6/72-4; CHY 8/72-3; CWY 8/72-2; HEL 9/72-1; WMO 9/72-4. (19½)

BOMAR'S CHRIS SA-347450 2/21/65 James W. Graham — By Lord Bomar* (Blackfoot's Happy New Year - Peg's Blackfoot Queen) ex Cristy (Galleywood Bigshot of Rice - Minnie of Base Line)
    AMATEUR—SPO 9/69-2; NWR 4/70-3; GOL 5/70-1. (9)

BOMBER II SA-422670 6/11/66 Otto D. McCaughan—By Meatball of District Ten (Trockmorton of Gosnel - Kim Von Guard) ex Wandarin Heights Shannon (Black Monk of Roeland - Manzanal Lilac)
    AMATEUR—SPO 5/70-4. (½)

BOW-MAR BLACK BRANDY SA-481907 4/5/67 Carroll A. Rice—By Sir Knight Falcon* (Patch of Bonniehurst - Faindi Kalp Asswad) ex Nodrog Penny* (Mainliner Mike - Beautywood's Rebel Queen)
    OPEN—NTX 3/70-2; PTA 3/71-3; RKM 8/72-3; HEL 9/72-3. (6)
    AMATEUR—MTA 5/71-4; MON 6/71-3; PIK 8/71-1; CWY 8-71-3; PIK 8/72-4; MOV 9/72-4. (8½)

AFC BRANDY OF CORTEZ SA-467905 7/27/66 Steve Thompson—By Camliag Pramero* (Mainliner Mike - Beautywood's Rebel Queen) ex Tempa Jigg of Moore Hill (Pepper's Jiggs - Starfire of Timberlake)
    OPEN—SRN 5/69-4; CSC 9/69-2; SRN 5/70-3. (4½)
    AMATEUR—GSL 5/69-2; SRN 5/70-3; PHO 10/70-1; ALB 5/71-1; SRN 5/71-2; PHO 10/71-2; SCA 9/72-2. (23)

FC-AFC BRANDY SPIRIT OF NETLEY SA-83525 7/11/57 Mr. and Mrs. T. E. Fajen—By Crozier's Silver Lance (Staindrop Saighdeer - Staindrop Murton Modesty) ex Bonnie Star of Netley (Tanda of Treesholme - De Forest Golden Windrush)
    OPEN—TRI 6/61-4; WIS 4/62-3; MNS 5/62-1; MAD 8/62-1; GOL 5/63-1; MAD 8/63-4; MAN 8/63-3; SXV 8/63-3; MNS 9/63-1; WIS 9/63-4; MIW 10/63-4; WIS 4/64-4; WOL 5/64-2; AAR 5/64-1; FRR 8/64-4; AAR 9/64-4; WIS 4/65-1; MAD 5/65-2; MAN 8/65-4; FRR 8/65-1; AAR 9/65-3; WIS 9/65-2; MIW 10/65-3; MAD 5/66-2; TRI 6/66-4; MAD 8/66-3; DUL 8/66-3. (58½)
    AMATEUR—MNS 5/62-1; OHV 9/62-1; MOV 10/62-2; LST 3/63-2; GOL 5/63-1; MNS 5/63-1; AAR 5/63-4; TRI 5/63-4; SHE 6/63-3; MAD 8/63-1; MNS 9/63-1; MIW 10/63-4; MOV 10/63-1; WIS 5/64-2; TRI 5/64-2; AAR 9/64-2; MNS 9/64-2; WIS 9/64-2; MIW 10/64-1; WIS 4/65-4; GOL 5/65-4; AAR 5/65-1; MIW 10/65-1; MIW 4/66-4; WOL 5/66-2; SHE 6/66-4; MAD 8/66-2; MAN 8/66-3; WIS 9/66-4; MII 5/67-4; AAR 5/67-3. (84½)

BRANT OF BLENHEIM SA-747327 5/15/65 Robin Heather—By Star of South Shaughnessy (Kimbow General Monty - Jibodad Topsy) ex Cowman's Ramah of Mishikamav (Rhett of Coldwater II - Crevamoy's Princess Kelly)
OPEN—LAS 2/70-3. (1)

FC BRAZIL'S BLACK JAGUAR SA-197211 9/19/61 Mrs. R. S. Humphrey—By Legs of Wake (Ponto's Ponto of Wake - Jody of Wake) ex Labcroft Darling Zahm's Peggy (Nodak's Timothy - Labcroft Kittiwake)
OPEN—WIL 8/64-1; LAB(S) 11/64-3; LIR 4/65-2; NUT 5/65-2; MAI 9/65-2; SRZ 2/66-2; LIR 4/66-4; WOM 4/66-2; LAB 4/66-4; WOM 10/66-3; SCA 3/67-4; NUT 5/67-1; MAI 9/67-1; COL 9/67-4; SRZ 2/68-1; CSC 2/68-1; SCA 3/68-3; CSC 2/69-1; SCA 2/69-3; JAY 3/69-2; BUK 9/69-1; CSC 2/70-4. (59½)
AMATEUR—CSC 2/64-4; LAS 10/64-4; SPO 10/64-3; MAI 9/67-1. (7)

FC-AFC BRECKONHILLS SEAN O'MOORE SA-97685 5/11/60 Gene R. Moore—By Breckonhill's Ben (Glenhead Jimmy - Quail of Auburn) ex Erin O'Moore (Ripco's Peter Pan - Lady Coleraine's Velvet)
OPEN—ORE 9/65-1; ROV 3/66-2; NWR 9/66-2; PUG 4/68-3. (12)
AMATEUR—TAC 8/63-4; SPO 10/64-2; WIL 8/64-4; PUG 8/65-2; SPO 10/65-4; PUG 8/66-2; PUG 4/67-2; GSL 5/67-2; WIL 8/68-1; SPO 9/68-3; TAC 4/69-4. (23½)

BROADMOOR REX SA-182696 10/16/61 Robert A. Adams—By Peter-Dee of Hawkhome (Smith's Dusky - Black Rebecca) ex La-Dee of River Lake (Little Blackie of Holly Hill - Ebony Lady VI)
AMATEUR—SNA 5/67-4. (½)

BROTHER LEM OF UPLAND FARM SA-204811 1/25/63 Charles Elmes —By Skeeter of Upland Farm (Flip of Timber Town - Ardgowan's Scotch Mist) ex Belle of Upland Farm (Yankee Clipper of Reo Raj - Belle of Zenith)
AMATEUR—MOB 2/66-3; TRI 6/67-4; MAR 10/67-4; LAB (S) 11/67-4; ATL 5/70-3. (4½)

BRUCE'S HAPPY WARRIOR SA-543771 12/28/67 Bruce and Upton Henderson—By Guy's Bitterroot Lucky* (Beavercrest Toreador - Pickrel's Ebony Babe) ex Soot's Shadow of Genesee (Paha Sapa Chief II - Princess Sootana of Buffalo)
AMATEUR—RKM 8/70-3. (1)

BUCK OF WHITTINGTON SA-440657 12/13/66 Henry R. Miller, III —By Alvaleigh's Hussar (Peter of Gaymark* - Alvaleigh's Hussy) ex Bonython Copper (Bonython Simba - Amber Storm)
AMATEUR—DEL 3/70-3; SWA 11/70-3; JAM 3/71-4; MAR 5/71-1; TAL 4/72-3; WCH 5/72-4; LIR 5/72-4. (9½)

BUCK OF WOODLAWN SA-189549 1/25/63 John Van Bloom — By Del-Tone Buck* (Martens' Hi Style Buck - Glen-Water Fan Fare) ex The Contesse (Trevrchamp Minyok - Beck'aven Peggy)
OPEN—NEB 4/67-3; PIK 8/67-2. (4)

FC BUCK'S HOBO SA-270807 5/6/64 Henry A. Bronner—By Del-Tone Buck* (Martens' Hi Style Buck - Glen-Water Fan Fare) ex Jet Noir La Petite (Del-Tone Colvin - Black Belle of Mylla)
OPEN—PIK 5/69-4; MTR 5/69-4; MON 5/69-3; BHB 6/69-3; MOB 2/70-1; NLA 3/70-3; PIK 5/70-1; BHB 6/70-4; RKM 8-71-2; SHE 9/71-4; CAS 9/71-2; ALM 11/71-2; ATL 4/72-1; CAS 9/72-3; NLA 10/72-2. (33)
AMATEUR—SLA 10/70-2; NLA 3/71-2; NLA 3/72-3; CAS 9/72-3. (8)

BUCKSKIN BULLET SA-538575 5/14/66 Don and Margie Smith—By Nilo Smoky's Black Powder (Martens' Little Smoky* - Nilo Pete's Ida) ex Margie's Sugar Lady (Kelley's Clem - Berda's Cindy)
AMATEUR—SCA 9/71-2. (3)

BUCKSKIN TORQUIN SA-564672 3/27/68 G. T. Hall, Jr.—By Copper City Buck* (Diamond Jig - Big Mountain Yip) ex Moon Shine Bobdee (Torque of Daingerfield* - Gotch Outa Beauregard)
AMATEUR—PUG 4/72-2; SPO 5/72-2. (6)

BUMBLE BUZZ OF BEE STING SA-451766 6/14/66 Ken Anderson—By Bigstone's Crowder Cap (Crowder - Bigstone Goldie) ex Cimaroc Lady Jean (Nodak Boots - Hull's Oma)
OPEN—AAR 5/69-3; MOV 4/70-2; CMI 5/70-4; ATL 4/71-3; MNS 9/71-3. (6½)

NRFC '67-AFC BUTTE BLUE MOON SA-251930 6/2/63 Mr. and Mrs. Byron B. Grunwald—By Beavercrest Storm Cloud (Del-Tone Colvin - Beavercrest Shore Leave) ex Macushla of Rockmont (Beavercrest Toreador - Apache Teardrop)
OPEN—CNB 5/66-2; MON 6/66-1; RKM 8/66-3; MON 9/66-4 MOV 9/66-4; ALM 2/67-2; LST 3/67-1; MOV 9/67-3; NOI 9/67-1; MOV 10/67-1; KAN 10/67-3; NAT 11/67-1; NFL 2/68-2; PTA 3/68-1; NTX 3/68-1; KAN 3/68-1; SHE 8/68-1; MOV 9/68-2; MIW 10/68-1; MII 5/69-1; TRI 5/69-1; CHY 8/69-4; SHE 8/69-4; MON 9/69-3; JAY 3/70-1; KAN 4/70-4; MIW 4/70-2; RKM 5/70-3; MON 6/70-2; CHY 8/70-3; SHE 9/70-2; HEL 9/70-2; MON 9/70-2; KAN 4/71-1; MOV 4/71-4; NEB 4/71-2; RKM 5/71-1; MTR 5/71-4; MOV 9/71-3; KAN 10/71-1; NEB 4/72-4; ALB 5/72-1; KAN 10/72-1. (131)
AMATEUR—CNB 5/66-4; MAD 8/66-4; MAN 8/66-2; NOI 10/66-4; MIW 10/66-3; MOV 10/66-2; KAN 10/66-1; LST 3/67-2; JAY 3/67-2; MAD 8/67-3; SXV 9/67-1; NOI 9/67-1; MIW 10/67-4; KAN 10/67-1; ALM 3/67-3; MOV 10/68-2; MOV 10/68-3; KAN 10/68-1; ALM 2/69-1; KAN 3/69-2; MOV 10/69-1; KAN 10/69-2; MII 5/70-2; SHE 9/70-2; NOI 10/70-3; MOV 10/70-4; ALM 2/71-3; MIW 4/71-1; WIS 4/71-4; BHB 6-71-1; MOV 9/71-3; NOI 10/71-3; LST 3/72-3; KAN 3/72-2; MIT 8/72-3; CHY 8/72-1. (93)

BUTTE KING OF THE ROAD SA-416535 11/4/65 Wilbur Saunders—By Tar of Rock Montana (Flashes Black Drake - Sparkle Plenty of Whitmore) ex Greenlief's Black Imp* (Beavercrest Storm Cloud - Macushla of Rockmont)
AMATEUR—BHB 6/69-4. (½)

AFC BUTTON BOOTS SA-150925 4/27/62 Cliff Tennant—By Boot's & Belle's Tag-a-Long (Massie's Sassy Boots - Belle of Zenith) ex Shay's Black Beauty (Nookachamps' Duke - Lady of Winwood)
OPEN—ORE 9/65-3; NWR 9/67-2. (4)
AMATEUR—SAM 3/64-1; WIL 8/65-4; SPO 10/65-1; TAC 4/66-3; SPO 5/66-3; WIL 8/66-4; NWR 4/67-4; SPO 5/67-3; ORE 3/68-4; NWR 4/68-2; IDA 5/68-1. (23)

AFC CAESAR OF SWINOMISH SA-68998 12/5/58 Gene H. Hill—By Mike of Swinomish (Nigger of Swinomish - Stitches of Holly Hill) ex Shady Bingo II (Nodak Ar-Dee - Shady Bingo)
AMATEUR—WIL 8/64-3; WIL 8/65-1; ORE 4/66-2; TAC 8/66-2; TAC 4/67-1; WIL 8/67-3; SHA 4/68-3. (19)

FC CALIPH OBSIDIAN HOBII SA-225197 2/1/63 Ed. Carey—By King Cole of Menomin* (Black Gum Gus - Rushmore's Black Shaw) ex Jinjo Black's Jet Jewel (West Island Pons' Pride - Rodney's Pitch Black)

Brandy Spirit of Netley

Butte Blue Moon

Captain of Lomac

OPEN—GOL 5/67-1;MIW 10/67-1; SLA 2/68-3; BUK 4/68-4;
TRI 5/68-1; FRR 8/68-1; SLA 2/69-3; WOL 5/69-4; TRI 5/69-4;
MAD 8/69-4; FRR 8/70-1; OHV 10/70-2; MIW 10/70-4; MNS
9/71-4; NOI 10/71-1; MTA 10/71-2.   (41)
AMATEUR—MIW 10/68-4.   (½)

FC-AFC CAMLIAG PRAMERO SA-147565 /3-26/60 Geo. Thrane—By
Mainliner Mike (Skipper of Rodall II - Wendy of Candlewood) ex
Beautywood's Rebel Queen (Roy's Rowdy - Beautywood's Repeat)
OPEN—CNB 5/64-3; CHY 5/64-1; BHB 5/64-4; IDA 8/64-2;
CHY 8/64-4; COL 10/64-4; MEM 3/65-4; CNB 5/65-2; RKM
5/65-1.   (19)
AMATEUR—COL 10/64-1; CHY 5/64-1; DEL 10/64-2; SWA
11/64-3; MEM 3/65-3; CNB 5/65-1; CHY 8/65-3; KAN 10/65-4;
MTR 5/67-4; PIK 8/67-3; RKM 8/67-1; SHE 9/67-1; GSL
8/68-2.   (36)

FC-AFC CANDLEWOOD'S BEAU OF BEAUMONT SA-578632 4/11/68
Dr. Joe L. Koch—By Martens' Little Smoky* (Crowder - Martens'
Little Bullet) ex Naughty Mary of Audlon (Del-Tone Buck* - Sweet
Georgia Brown of Audlon)
OPEN—RKM 5/72-1; MTR 5/72-4; MNS 9/72-2; SLA 9/72-1.   (13½)
AMATEUR—SLA 9/72-3.   (1)

FC-AFC CANDLEWOOD'S LITTLE LOU SA-509496 4/14/67 Mary C.
Howley — By St. Louie's Trouble of Audlon (Beautywood's Rare
Trouble - Trouble's Double of Audlon) ex Shamrock Acres Belle Aire
(Beautywood's Rare Trouble - Shamrock Acres Domino Queen)
OPEN—AAR 5/71-2; MAD 8/71-1; SLA 10/71-4; TRI 6/72-1.   (13½)
AMATEUR—TRI 6/70-1; OHV 10/70-2; MIW 10/71-2; MEM
10/70-3; MOV 10/71-2; DUL 8/72-1.   (20)

CANUCK-CREST GALLANT SA-350377 4/23/64 Harold S. Schutt, Jr.
and C. Porter Schutt—By Riskin* (Black Boy of Whitmore - Paha Sapa
Rapid Water) ex Canuck-Crest Tami O'Churchlee (Beautywood's
Carbon Copy - Twink of Belle Isle)
OPEN—MTA 3/69-3.   (1)

FC-NARFC '66 CAPTAIN OF LOMAC SA-176506 4/18/59 Rudy R.
Deering—By Spook of Manhattan (Spook of Granon - Cymro Queen)
ex Country Club's Little Deb (Crevamoy's Black Devil - Porthwidgen
Jo)
OPEN—PUG 8/63-3; ORE 3/64-4; PUG 8/64-3; CSC 2/65-2;
NWR 4/65-2; TAC 8/65-2; WIL 8/65-2; PUG 8/65-1; NWR
9/65-1; PUG 4/66-1; PUG 8/66-3; SAM 3/67-1; PUG 4/67-1;
NWR 4/68-4; SAM 8/68-1.   (46)
AMATEUR—TAC 8/63-3; WIL 8/63-3; SAM 3/64-1; TAC
4/64-2; TAC 8/64-3; PUG 8/64-3; SPO 5/65-3; TAC 8/65-3;
PUG 8/65-1; NWR 9/65-3; SAM 3/66-1; PUG 4/66-1; NAT
4/66-1; PUG 8/66-1; SAM 3/67-1; NWR 4/67-2; SPO 4/68-2;
SRN 5/68-1; NWR 9/68-3.   (57)

FC CARBO COMPUTER SA-398899 3/6/66 Mrs. Clifford V. Brokaw,
Jr.—By Shamrock Acres Gun Away* (Beautywood Rare Trouble -
Marlab's Gypsy) ex Personality Plus (Greatford Glenfarg Bragg - West
Island Cleopatra)
OPEN—BUK 4/69-2; WOL 5/69-1; NFL 2/70-2; SHO 9/70-4;
LIR 5/71-2; MAR 5/71-4; WOM 10/72-4; LAB(S) 11/72-3.   (16½)
AMATEUR—WOL 9/70-2; LIR 10/70-3; JAM 3/71-2; LAB
4/71-2.   (10)

FC-AFC CARBON MARKER SA-62914 8/27/60 Thomas J. Reames—
By Ace Bingo (Bingo Again - Bigstone Dinah Girl) ex Green Ridge
Sally (Del-Tone Colvin - Shady Haven Farm Jet)

OPEN—WIS 4/65-2; WIS 9/65-1; SHE 6/66-4; AAR 9/66-2; AAR 9/67-4; MOV 9/67-1; WIS 9/68-2; FRR 8/69-3; MIC 8/69-2; NTX 10/69-4. (24½)

AMATEUR—WMT 6/64-4; MIW 4/65-1; MAD 5/65-4; GOL 5/65-3; AAR 5/65-2; AAR 9/65-1; MIW 4/66-3; MAD 8/66-1; MIW 4/67-4; MNS 9/67-3; WIS 9/67-3; MOV 9/67-3; MIW 10/68-2; WIS 4/69-4; MIC 8/69-4; NOI 9/69-3; MIW 10/69-3; KAN 10/69-4; MOV 4/70-4; MAD 5/70-3; MII 5/70-3; WOL 5/70-4. (36)

FC CARNATION BUTTERBOY SA-306298 6/16/64 Carnation Farm Kennels—By Galleywood Gunner (Galleywood Shot - Galleywood Gina) ex Carnation Raven (Noah of Swinomish - Imp of Holly Hill)

OPEN—NWR 9/67-3; SHA 4/68-4; MON 5/68-3; TAC 8/68-1; SHA 8/68-4; ORE 3/69-2; PUG 4/69-3; RED 7/69-2; WIL 8/69-4; PUG 8/69-1; SHA 9/69-3; SCA 3/70-1; NCA 3/70-1; PUG 4/70-4; GOL 5/70-4; TAC 8/70-1; SRZ 2/71-3; CSC 2/71-4; ROV 3/71-1; TAC 4/71-4; NWR 4/71-1; IDA 5/71-2; PUG 4/72-1; NWR 4/72-1; TAC 8/72-1. (67½)

FC CARNATION RAINSTAR SA-615367 10/7/67 Carnation Farm Kennels—By Anzac of Zenith* (Black Mike of Lakewood - Jezebel of Normandy) ex Happy's Twinkle* (Night Cap Again - Miss Behavior)

OPEN—PUG 8/70-3; SPO 5/71-2; WMO 5/71-3; RED 7/71-2; PUG 8/71-3; NWR 9/71-1; CSC 2/72-1. (19)

FC CARNMONEY BILLY JO SA-151982 1/2/59 Chas J. Bjork — By Carnmoney Rockette (Cork of Oakwood Lane - Little Peggy Black Gum) ex Glen-Water Fever Pitch (Craigend Rock - Peggy of Carnmoney)

OPEN—FTP 8/63-3; FTP 8/64-1; MON 9/64-2; FTP 8/67-2. (12)

AMATEUR—MON 9/64-2; CSC 2/66-4; MIT 8/66-1. (8½)

FC-AFC CARNMONEY BRIGADIER SA-537477 6/29/66 Ray H. and Dorothea Goodrich—By Bandit of Carnmoney (Chuck of Bracken - Stonegate's Black Cindy) ex Castlemore Sheila of Cordova (Castlemore Shamus - Miss Kate of Cordova)

OPEN—SRV 5/69-1; SAM 8/69-2; NCA 3/70-2; SAG 3/70-1; IDA 8/70-3; ACC 8/70-3; SHA 9/70-1; SCA 3/71-3; SHA 4/71-3; SRN 5/71-1; NCA 9/71-2; CSC 2/72-2; SCA 3/72-3; SAG 3/72-3; IDA 5/72-4; ACC 7/72-1; SAG 7/72-3; SAD 9/72-4. (45)

AMATEUR—ORE 3/69-1; IDA 4/69-1; SRN 5/69-4; SAG 7/69-3; TAC 8/69-2; SNA 8/69-3; ACC 8/69-2; SHA 9/69-4; CSC 2/70-1; EID 7/70-3; ACC 8/70-1; CSC 10/70-3; SAG 3/71-1; SAG 7/71-2; SCA 9/71-1; LAS 2/72-3; IDA 5/72-1; SAG 7/72-4; SAD 9/72-2; NCA 9/72-1; SCA 9/72-3; CSC 9/72-2. (62½)

CARNMONEY MAGNUM SA-648328 5/10/64 V. P. Lakusta—By Bandit of Carnmoney (Chuck of Bracken - Stonegate's Black Cindy) ex Carnmoney Penny Dhu (Carnmoney Carbon Copy - Stonegate's Next O'Kin)

OPEN—GSL 8/69-2; WMO 9/69-3. (4)

AMATEUR—WMO 9/70-4. (½)

CARNMONEY SPUD SA-429749 7/14/64 Harold Mack, Jr.—By Bandit of Carnmoney (Chuck of Bracken - Stonegate's Black Cindy) ex Carnmoney Boots (Nodak Boots - The Duchess of Rose Hill)

OPEN—SCA 9/70-4; PHO 10/70-4; SAG 3/71-1; GSL 5/71-4; SAG 7/71-4. (7)

AMATEUR—NCA 3/72-1. (5)

FC-AFC CARR-LAB PENROD SA-270506 4/28/64 Mrs. August Belmont —By Paha Sapa Chief II (Freehaven Muscles - Treasure State Be Wise) ex Ironwood Cherokee Chica (Cherokee Buck - Glen-Water Fantom)

OPEN—WOL 5/68-4; PIK 8/68-2; MAI 9/68-1; NCA 9/69-2; MAI 9/69-1; SAG 3/70-4; TAL 4/70-1; WNY 9/70-2; WOM 4/71-2; WCH 5/71-2; MAR 5/71-3; SHO 9/71-4; WOM 9/71-1; SWA 11/71-2; WCH 5/72-1; IDA 8/72-2; SWA 11/72-2. (51½)
AMATEUR—SAG 3/67-3; SWA 11/67-1; SHA 9/68-1; MAR 10/68-4; SAG 3/69-4; SHR 4/69-3; MAR 5/69-2; LIR 5/69-3; PIK 8/69-3; MAR 10/69-1; DEL 10/69-1; WOM 10/69-2; TAL 4/70-4; MAR 5/70-4; SHO 9/70-1; WNY 9/70-3; WOM 4/70-4; MAI 9/70-4; COL 10/70-2; MAR 10/70-3; SWA 11/70-1; SHR 4/71-2; WCH 5/71-3; MAR 5/71-2; TAC 8/71-3; IDA 8/71-3; MAI 9/71-2; COL 10/71-2; LIR 10/71-4; SRZ 2/72-1; SCA 3/72-4; JAM 3/72-2; LAB 4/72-3; WCH 5/72-2; SNA 8/72-1; SHO 9/72-3; WOM 10/72-1; SWA 11/72-2. (90)

CASCADE'S RODNEY ST. CLAIR SA-189534 12/9/62 Jere W. Bogrett —By Boley's Cascade (King Chukker of Robbinsdale - Mem of Greeymar) ex Queen Eby of Lakenham (Paha Sapa Chief II - Eby of Beaver Creek)
AMATEUR—MON 9/65-3; PIK 4/66-2; RKM 5/66-4; CHY 5/66-4; HEL 9/67-2. (8)

CEDARHAVEN J. B., SA-608746 12/17/67 John A. Love, Jr.—By Mitch of Bitterroot* (Beavercrest Toreador - Pickrel's Ebony Babe) ex Sills Little Smoky Lewbonnie (Martens' Little Smoky* - Hunt's Charming Annebelle)
OPEN—CWY 8/71-4. (½)
AMATEUR—SHE 9/71-2; RKM 8/72-1; MON 9/72-4. (8½)

FC CEDAR HAVEN MATADOR SA-288339 10/20/63 Mrs. Wm. P. Roth—By Odessa's King (Ardvn Ace - Lady Cinder Mattausch) ex Pride's Black Duchess (Noah of Swinomish - Carnation Pride)
OPEN—TAC 8/67-3; ORE 9/67-1; SAM 9/67-4; LST 10/67-1; SAG 3/68-1; SNA 5/68-3; WMO 9/68-1; WMO 5/69-3. (23½)

CENTENNIAL CHUKALUK SA-490194 1/4/67 Marvin and Sandra K. Sundstrom—By Centennial Cric* (Avalanche Burnt Sage - Queen Eby of Lakenham) ex Dyke's Potlach (Ripco's Peter Pan - Dyke's Decoy of Pantherlake)
OPEN—PUG 8/69-4; ORE 9/69-2; NWR 4/71-3; SPO 10/71-4; PUG 4/72-3; NWR 9/72-2. (9)

CENTENNIAL CRIC SA-305926 3/14/64 Marvin Sundstrom — By Avalanche Burnt Sage (Satan III - Constant Winner of Avalanche) ex Queen Eby of Lakenham (Paha Sapa Chief II - Eby of Beaver Creek)
AMATEUR—SPO 5/67-4; TAC 8/67-4. (1)

AFC CHA CHA DANCER SA-315713 5/10/64 Robert N. Wolfe — By Duke of Ashton (Birchwood Yodel - Lightning Bolt Peggy of Arcola) ex Black Diamond Liz (Paha Sapa Chief II - Penny Girl)
OPEN—MNS 5/69-4. (½)
AMATEUR—DUL 8/67-1; SXV 9/67-4; MNS 9/67-1; CMI 5/68-4; TRI 5/68-1; MNS 9/68-3; NOI 9/68-1; MAD 5/69-3. (23)

CHAMPAGNE EL TORO SA-660314 4/23/68 Florence Saunders—By Bomar's Chris* (Lord Bomar* - Cristy) ex Champagne Cassie (Pokey of Sourdough - Gee Gee)
AMATEUR—HEL 9/71-3; MON 6/72-2; HEL 9/72-4. (4½)

AFC CHAP SA-78967 4/23/60 J. Douglas Wright, Jr.—By Baird's Shed of Nashville (Deer Creek's Hit Parade - Louisiana Checo) ex Dixie Bingo (Bingo Again - Bigstone Peggy)
OPEN—NLA 3/68-3. (1)
AMATEUR—MEM 3/65-1; MOV 4/65-2; MOV 10/65-3; MTA 10/65-2; MEM 10/65-4; MEM 10/66-1; MEM 3/67-3; MTA 3/67-2; MTA 10/67-2; MEM 10/67-1; MEM 3/68-3; MTA 10/68-3; MEM 10/68-3. (32½)

CHAUNCEY OF ELLENWOOD SA-280068 8/27/64 John E. Taylor—By
Galleywind Swift (Hiwood John - Merry-Go-Round Tradewinds) ex
Marv's Sussie (Hello Joe of Rocheltree - Ty's Lace)
AMATEUR—KAN 3/69-3.   (1)

AFC CHEROKEE CHIEF V SA-180894 12/28/62 J. H. Pettijohn, Jr.—
By Otter O'Vyrnwy (Grouse-A-Dee - Creedy Park Stella) ex Renegade
Sioux (Paha Sapa Chief II - Semloh's Deb of Walden Pond)
OPEN—NEB 4/66-4; KAN 5/67-4; KAN 10/70-3 ALB 5/71-3.   (3)
AMATEUR—KAN 10/65-1; KAN 10/67-2; JAY 3/68-3; KAN
3/68-3; MII 5/68-4; KAN 10/68-3; KAN 10/69-3; JAY 3/70-1;
KAN 4/70-3; ALB 5/70-4.   (19)

CHEROKEE PEACE PIPE SA-425618 10/11/68 Eugene M. Batman—By
Cherokee Chief V* (Otter O'Vyrnwy - Renegade Sioux) ex Sugar
Plum's Tar Baby (Marshwise Snapshooter - B-B Swift)
OPEN—CAS 9/71-3.   (1)
AMATEUR—KAN 10/72-4.   (½)

FC CHIEF BLACK FEATHER SA-4/28/64 J. Kent Sweezey—By Paha
Sapa Chief II (Freehaven Muscles - Treasure State Be Wise) ex
Ironwood Cherokee Chica (Cherokee Buck - Glen-Water Fantom)
OPEN—SHO 5/68-2; FTP 5/68-3; SLA 2/69-2; SHO 5/69-3;
SLA 2/70-2; FTP 6/70-3; BUK 9/70-2; LAB 4/71-1; JAM 3/72-3.   (21)

CHIEF CODY OF LE-MAR SA-568093 4/7/68 Lee & Marjorie Broussard
—By Super Chief* (Paha Sapa Chief II - Ironwood Cherokee Chica)
ex Duxbak's Patsy Del Norte (Duxbak Scooter* - Jilly Girl*)
OPEN—PTA 10/72-4.   (½)
AMATEUR—LST 10/72-3.   (1)

CHIEF CONSULTATION SOUTH BAY SA-576436 4/14/68 Dr. E. C.
McRee—By Super Chief* (Paha Sapa Chief II - Ironwood Cherokee
Chica) ex Kara (Royal Beaver of Romany - Big Oaks Black Belle)
OPEN—ALB 7/72-2.   (3)

CHIEF STORM CLOUD SA-550000 10/5/67 Hugh Adams—By Singing
Woods War Cloud (Pata Sapa Chief II - Fallwoods Hi Top Boots) ex
Redd (Crowder - Bigstone Ricky)
OPEN—EID 7/71-1.   (5)

AFC CHIPSAL JOHN HENRY SA-249618 2/26/64 Marshall Simonds—
By Sprucelane's Chippewa Chief (Paha Sapa Chief II - Lady of Sandy
Hill) ex Canuck-Crest Sally* (Jet of Zenith - Canuck-Crest Tami
O'Churchlee)
OPEN—DEL 3/69-4.   (½)
AMATEUR—LAB 4/67-1; WNY 9/67-2; LAB (S) 11/67-1; LAB
4/68-3; SHO 5/68-4; CNY 5/68-3; MAI 9/68-4; WOM 4/69-1;
LAB 4/69-4; MAR 5/69-1; LIR 5/69-4; MTA 3/70-3; DEL
3/70-2; SHR 4/70-1; LIR 5/70-4; MAI 9/70-3;.   (37½)

CHIPS OF BIRCHWOOD SA-199109 10/6/62 Mrs. G. Hronis — By
Citation of Franklin (Kingswere Black Ebony - Dark Flight From
Franklin) ex Lokate of High Point (Tar of Rockingell - Nelgard's
Gracious Lady)
AMATEUR—AAR 9/67-4; WIS 9/68-4; AAR 5/69-4; WIS 9/70-1.   (6½)

FC CHOC OF SAN JUAN SA-191050 1/3/63 David Butler—By Lee Labs
Jimi (Clear Weather - Ace's Bonnie of Winniway) ex La Belle (Sir La
Ferro - Ward's Golden Sugarfoot)
OPEN—WMO 5/66-3; TAC 8/66-4; WMO 8/66-3; SPO 10/66-4;
TAC 8/67-2; SHE 9/67-1; MON 9/67-1; HEL 9/67-2; WMO
9/67-4.   (19½)
AMATEUR—SHE 9/67-4; TAC 8/68-4.   (1)

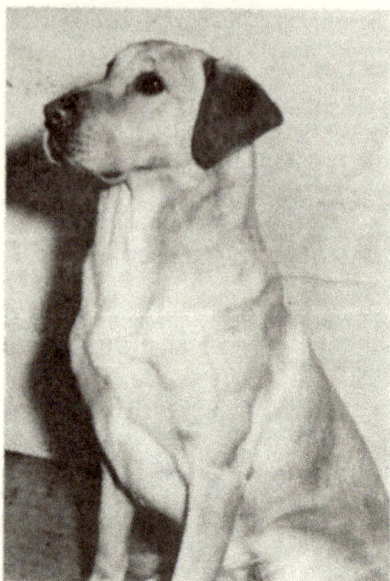

Carnation Butter Boy

Carnmoney Brigadier

Carr-Lab Penrod

Cimaroc Tang

CHUCK OF CRAIGEND ROCK SA-553677 7/17/66 R. A. White—By
Green Timbers' Shamus (Castlemore Shamus - Green Timbers' Little
Gem) ex Faro's Princess Christine (Faro's Prince of Cottonwood - Faro's
Little Willow)
AMATEUR—PUG 4/71-2; NWR 4/71-3.   (4)

AFC CHUK CHUKAR CHUK SA-450864 4/2/66 Salvatore C. Gelardi
—By Black Sorcerer of Sunset* (Danny's Black Mac - Belle of Sunset)
ex Black Witch of Sunset (Pepper's Jiggs - Happy Valley Patzy)
OPEN—RED 7/70-1.   (5)
AMATEUR—LAS 2/70-1; SAG 7/70-1; WIL 8/70-1; SHA 9/70-4;
LAS 2/71-2; RED 7/72-3.   (19½)

CIMAROC COON WILLIE SA-432833 10/7/66 M. H. Kurkjian, Jr.—
By Nassau* (Bigstone's Crowder's Cap - Cimaroc Lady Jean) ex
Cimaroc Blond Bomber (Martens' Scrubby Giant - Martens' Black Tagg)
OPEN—CMI 5/72-4.   (½)

CIRRUS SEA SERPENT SA-764762 5/28/68 Earl F. Robinson — By
Cirrus Eclipse (Beaver Crest Storm Cloud - Raven Cirrus) ex Chipaking
Chick (Copper City Buck* - Chipaking Smoke Signal)
AMATEUR—WMO 9/72-3.   (1)

FC-AFC CIMAROC TANG SA-215192 6/13/63 William K. Laughlin—By
Cimaroc Tar Baby (Crowder - Bigstone Bang) ex Cimaroc Lady (Royal
of Garfield - Martens' Lady Jane)
OPEN—SRZ 2/67-4; CSC 2/67-2; SAG 3/67-1; SHR 4/67-1; CNY
5/67-2; COL 9/67-3; LAB (S) 11/67-1; NCA 3/68-1; SAG
3/68-3; TAL 4/68-1; WOM 4/68-3; FTP 5/68-1; SCA 2/69-1;
NCA 3/69-1; KAN 3/69-4; MAR 5/69-4; COL 9/69-2; MAR
10/69-2; SWA 10/69-2; LAB 11/69-1.   (64½)
AMATEUR—MIT 8/65-3; WOM 4/67-2; MAI 9/67-3; LIR
10/67-4; DEL 10/67-3; NCA 3/68-2; SAG 3/68-1; WOM 4/68-2;
SHO 5/68-2; WOM 10/68-2; NCA 3/69-4; DEL 10/69-3; WOM
10/69-1.   (30)

FC CINDER FELLA OF STONESTHROW SA-169898 2/28/62 John
M. Olin — By Beau's Buzzsaw of Stonesthrow (Beau Brummel of
Wyndale - Lady of Lancaster) ex Bart's Jeri of Stonesthrow (Smudge's
Bingo - Sparkle Plenty II)
OPEN— PIK 5/65-2; SXV 10/65-3; KAN 10/65-2; PIK 4/66-2;
NTX 10/66-1; MOB 2/67-4; MEM 3/67-3; WIS 4/67-1; AAR
5/67-1; OHV 9/67-3; TRI 5/68-3; MIC 8/68-4; MNS 9/68-2;
OHV 9/68-3; MIW 10/68-2.   (36)
AMATEUR—NOI 10/66-3; MIW 10/66-4; NTX 10/66-4; NEB
4/67-2; WIS 4/67-2.   (8)

CLAYMAR'S ACADEMY AWARD SA-305386 11/2/64 Oscar S. Brewer
—By Stonecastle Jack (Staindrop Ringleader - Bigstone Sugar) ex Jet
Firefly of Dacity (Marshwise Snapshooter - Jigger of Dacity)
OPEN—MAN 8/68-4.   (½)
AMATEUR—NTX 3/68-3.   (1)

CLAYMAR'S CRASH DIVER SA-426774 1/4/66 James W. Aston, Jr.
M.D.—By Jetstone Muscles of Claymar* (Stonecastle Jack - Jet Firefly
of Dacity) ex Buck's Dolly (Del-Tone Buck* - Woodland's Ebony Major)
AMATEUR—PIK 5/70-3.   (1)

CLOUD BURST SA-586886 5/14/68 F. E. Rose, Jr.—By Camliag Pramero*
(Mainliner Mike - Beautywoods Rebel Queen) ex Tina of Gray
Summit (Black Watch of Horseshoe - Purina's Black Magic)
AMATEUR—SLA 3/72-2.   (3)

FC CODY OF WANAPUM SA-690038 5/9/69 Wm. K. Laughlin — By
Spring Farms Lucky* (Paha Sapa Chief II - Ironwood Cherokee Chica)
ex Toni of Wanapum (Pepper's Jiggs - Ar-Dee's Sassy Holly)
OPEN—ORE 9/71-3; SPO 10/71-1; WNY 9/72-1; MAI 9/72-2.　　　(14)
AMATEUR—SPO 10/71-3; LAB 4/72-2.　　　(4)

FC-AFC COLDWATER'S BRENDAN SA-478526 7/10/65 Gene & Nancy
Moore—By Rhett of Coldwater II (Ink of Coldwater - Judy of Coldwater) ex Masai's Star (Gung-Ho of Granton* - Masai Phantom Sprig
of Olrega)
OPEN—IDA 8/68-1; TAC 4/70-2; SOO 4/72-2; BHB 6/72-3.　　　(12)
AMATEUR—TAC 8/68-3; SPO 9/68-4; TAC 4/69-3; TAC
8/69-3; SHE 9/70-3; MTR 5/72-1.　　　(9½)

COLEY'S GRAND CLIPPER SA-285859 8/30/64 Roy McFall—By Hiwood
Stormy of Alaska* (Del-Tone Colvin - Lady Roxanne of Muldoon)
ex Sally Jacona of Indian Spring (Marian's Timothy - Lockerbie
Araminta)
AMATEUR—TAC 4/68-4; SRZ 2/69-2; ROV 3/69-4.　　　(4)

COLL-A-DENE'S PERKY SA-620587 6/26/68 Thomas R. Hellwig—By
Rupert White Bear (Loughderg Strokestown Blackguard Boy - Rupert
Marleigh Bingham) ex Coll-A-Dene's Rockette Dee (Jetstone Muscles
of Claymar* - Melissa of Oakridge)
OPEN—PIK 5/71-3; ALB 7/71-2; PTA 3/72-3; NLA 3/72-3.　　　(6)
AMATEUR—NLA 10/71-1; LST 10/71-2; NLA 3/72-4.　　　(8½)

COLL-A-DENE'S SQUIRE SA-496517 7/20/67 Gregory D. and Judith
Belding—By Coll-A-Dene's Royal Salute (Petite Rouge* - Shamrock
Acres Gret) ex Shamrock Acres Kerry Dancer (Shamrock Acres Sonic
Boom - Whygin Campaign Promise)
OPEN—SLA 9/72-4.　　　(½)

COLONEL SMOKEY SQUIRREL SA-205108 1/1/63 William Daley—By
Dyke (King of Nanticoke Acres - Spooks II) ex Nilo Smoky's Cassan-
dra (Stonegate's Ace of Spades - Nilo Cinderella)
AMATEUR—SCA 9/70-2.　　　(3)

FC-AFC COL-TAM OF CRAIGNOOK SA-114812 1/18/61 Mr. and Mrs.
R. O. Bateman—By Del-Tone Colvin (Cork of Oakwood Lane - Del-
Tone Bridget) ex Tam-O-Shanter of Craignook (Black Mamba of
Kingswere - Tar of Random Lake)
OPEN—MIW 10/65-2; MEM 3/66-1; WIS 4/67-4; MAN 8/67-3;
AAR 9/67-1; MIW 10/67-3; MII 6/68-2; MAN 8/69-4.　　　(19)
AMATEUR—GOL 5/63-4; WIS 9/63-2; WEC 6/64-3; MAN
8/64-2; FRR 8/64-3; WIS 9/64-3; MIW 10/64-2; WOL 4/65-3;
FRR 8/65-1; MIW 10/65-3 SHE 6/66-2; AAR 9/66-2; MIW
10/66-1; WIS 4/67-4; AAR 9/67-1; WIS 9/67-1; MIW 10/67-2;
MAD 8/68-2; MIW 4/69-1; MAN 8/69-3; WIS 9/69-3; MIW
10/69-2; MTA 10/69-4; MIW 4/70-2; MAD 5/70-2.　　　(63½)

COL-TAM'S STORMY SA-400717 5/8/66 Jack L. Woodland—By Col-
Tam of Craignook* (Del-Tone Colvin - Tam-O'-Shanter of Craignook)
ex Polly of Arroyo (Bouser Von Nimelo - Cedar Creek's Heide)
OPEN—ALK 8/71-3.　　　(1)

AFC COLUMBINE LORAN SA-134008 7/30/61 Jack E. Hogue — By
Columbine Copper (Rusty of Bonny - Pensive Penni Dardanella) ex
Miss Rusty Jig a Boo (Rusty of Bonny - Miss Jig a Boo)
OPEN—ALB 5/69-4.　　　(½)
AMATEUR—CNB 5/64-1; PIK 5/65-4; CNB 5/65-4; RKM
5/65-3; CHY 5/65-1; PIK 8/66-3; CHY 8/66-4; ALB 5/67-1;
PIK 5/67-4; SHE 9/67-3; MTR 5/68-1.　　　(25)

CONNORS' HUNTER SA-647218 9/20/68 Ron and Sally Connors—By
Warpath Tuff* (Del-Tone Colvin - Paha Sapa Wacincala) ex Storm-
along A' Go Go (Sarchek - Bayduck's Ginny)
OPEN—PIK 8/72-3. (1)
AMATEUR—JAY 3/72-2; BHB 6/72-3; ALB 7/72-1; CYW
8/72-1. (14)

CONQUISTADOR OF FORTUNE SA-625868 10/17/67 Henry M. Tullis
—By Kranwood's Charlie f Falcona (Paha Sapa Chief II - Algo-Ken's
Char-Sue) ex Homestead's Dolly (Kranwood's Charlie of Falcona -
Homestead Jody)
AMATEUR—ALB 5/71-2. (3)

CONTY'S BLACK CHIP SA-672706 11/13/68 Frank A. Conty—By Rip's
Smokey Duke (Poe's Smo of Rocklane - Rip's Gal) ex Princess Patsy
La Coquetta (Rio Bravo Quate - La Coquetta de La Totah)
AMATEUR—PIK 5/71-1; PIK 8/71-3. (6)

AFC COPPER CITIES COLLIERY CAL SA-411342 5/6/66 Josephine T.
Reeve—By Bellota Punch (Paha Sapa Chief II - Bay City Zany Jane)
ex Samantha of San Rafael (Bigstone Buck II - Bigstone Sugar's Pam)
OPEN—HEL 9/69-4. (½)
AMATEUR—PUG 8/69-1; MON 9/69-2; SNA 5/70-3; ACC
8/70-3; SRN 5/71-4; SNA 8/71-1; MON 9/71-3; SRZ 2/72-4;
SNA 5/72-1; GSL 5/72-4. (22½)

FC-AFC COPPER CITY BUCK SA-111000 8/5/60 Robert Sparks—By
Diamond Jig (Kellogg's Nick - Kellogg's Dusky) ex Big Mountain Yip
(Whitmore's Valiant Knight - Lindy Lou IV)
OPEN—HEL 9/64-2;SHE 6/66-1; HEL 9/66-4; WMO 5/67-1;
SAM 3/68-3; HEL 9/68-4. (15)
AMATEUR—HEL 9/64-1; WMO 9/65-2; WMO 5/66-4; WMO
9/66-2; WMO 5/68-4. (12)

FC-AFC CORK OF EVERGREEN SA-255583 3/6/64 Roger Vasselais—
By Del-Tone Buck* (Martens' Hi Style Buck - Glen-Water Fan Fare)
ex Jac-Lor Miss Cindy (Manzanal Duffer - Savage Sue)
OPEN—LAB (S) 11/67-2; TAL 3/68-4; SWA 11/68-4; SHR
4/69-4; LIR 5/70-1; LAB (S) 11/70-3. (10½)
AMATEUR—MAI 5/67-2; TRI 6/67-2; FRR 8/67-4; SWA 11/67-
4; MEM 3/68-1; MTA 3/68-3; TAL 3/68-1; LIR 4/68-2; MAR
5/68-3; WNY 9/68-3; COL 9/68-2; SWA 11/68-1; BUK 4/69-4;
LAB 4/69-3; SHO 5/69-4; TRI 5/69-2; TAL 3/70-2; WNY
9/71-4; LAB (S) 11/71-4; NFL 3/72-2. (43)

CORKY'S RAMBLIN RILEY SA-773614 5/17/69 Michael R. Flannery—
By River Oaks Corky* (Martens' Mister Nifty* - Don's Ginny Soo)
ex Moody's Dell (Del-Tone Buck* - Rill-Shannon's Dark Del)
OPEN—ALK 8/72-4. (½)

FC-AFC COUGAR'S ROCKET SA-145039 2/7/61 James L. Casey—By
Black Cougar (Cork of Oakwood Lane - Bigstone Breeze) ex Bay City
Katie Jane (Gypsy Duke - Countess of Terravilla)
OPEN—WIL 8/63-1; SAG 8/63-2; SHA 9/63-2; NCA 9/63-1;
SCA 9/63-4; CSC 9/63-4; LAS 10/63-1; CSC 2/64-3; NWR
4/64-4; ACC 8/64-4; PUG 8/64-4; SHA 9/64-2; NCA 9/64-2;
SCA 9/64-1; CSC 10/64-1; LAS 10/64-2; LAS 2/65-4; SCA
3/65-3; ROV 3/65-3; ORE 4/65-4; SNA 5/65-1; RED 7/65-2;
SNA 8/65-3; SRN 5/66-4; NCA 9/66-3; SRN 5/67-1; RED 7/66-
1; NCA 9/67-4; GSL 8/68-1; IDA 8/68-4; SAG 8/68-4; CSC
9/68-3; ALM 11/68-4; SRN 5/69-2; SAG 7/69-3; ACC 8/69-3. (80)

AMATEUR—SAG 3/63-1; ROV 3/63-3; SNA 5/63-1; GSL 5/63-1; RED 7/63-2; SAG 8/63-4; CSC 2/64-1; NCA 3/64-3; ORE 3/64-2; ACC 7/64-1; SAG 9/64-3; SHA 9/64-4; SCA 9/64-1; CSC 10/64-1; LAS 10/64-1; SCA 3/65-4: NWR 4/65-1; SNA 5/65-3; SHA 5/65-2; RED 7/65-1; SHA 4/66-3; SAG 9/67-4; SCA 9/67-2; CSC 9/67-2; NCA 3/68-3; SRN 5/69-2; ACC 8/69-4. (76½)

FC COUNTER SMOKE SA-52831 4/16/60 Mrs. Geo. R. Pidgeon—By LaSage's Smoky (Oak Creek Monarch - Princess Pat of Tanca Moor) ex Nelgard's Counter Point (Freehaven Muscles - Ladies' Day at Deer Creek)
OPEN—GOL 5/64-1; MEM 3/65-3; WOL 5/65-4; MOB 2/66-1; MOV 4/66-4; GOL 5/66-3; WOL 5/66-2; NLA 3/67-2; MII 6/67-4; MAN 8/67-4; WIS 9/67-4; MOB 11/67-3. (21½)
AMATEUR—SLA 9/66-3. (1)

FC COUNTRY CLUB'S EL-CID SA-253501 11/16/62 John M. Olin—By Nascopie Dark Destroyer (Cork of Oakwood Lane - Blyth's Queen of Spades) ex Cowman's Stylish Girl (Craigend Rock - Crevamoy's Princess Kelly)
OPEN—NFL 2/68-4; AAR 5/68-2; MNS 9/68-3; WIS 9/68-4; KAN 3/69-1. (10)

COUNTRY'S DELIGHT CAESAR SA-530474 12/1/67 Anthony Stary—By Lord Bomar* (Blackfoot's Happy New Year - Peg's Blackfoot Queen) ex Lady Jane XI (Duke of Ashton - Black Diamond Liz)
OPEN—WOL 9/71-4; BUK 4/72-2; WIS 4/72-1; CNY 5/72-4. (9)

COUSIN JACK OF UPLAND FARM SA-286763 10/31/64 Roger Vasselais—By Skeeter of Upland Farms (Flip of Timber Town - Ardgowan's Scotch Mist) ex Belle of Upland Farm (Yankee Clipper of Reo Raj - Belle of Zenith)
OPEN—BUK 4/69-4. (½)
AMATEUR—WOM 10/67-3; NTX 3/68-2; DEL 10/68-3; JAX 1/69-2; NFL 2/69-4; TAL 3/69-3; SHR 4/69-4; MAR 5/69-4; WNY 9/69-2; LIR 10/69-3; SWA 10/69-3. (15½)

AFC CREOLE CARPETBAGGER SA-471518 1/27/67 Donald P. Weiss—By Ridgewood Playboy (La Sage's Smoky - Nelgard's Counter Point) ex Jac-Lor Miss Cindy (Manzanal Duffer - Savage Sue)
OPEN—NTX 3/72-3; NTX 10/72-1. (6)
AMATEUR—SLA 10/70-4; LST 10/70-4: NTX 3/71-2; NTX 10/71-3; LST 10/71-3; SOO 4/72-3; CAS 9/72-2; NLA 10/72-1; NTX 10/72-2; MEM 10/72-1. (23)

CROOK'S JOLLY ROGER SA-265756 8/3/63 Wayne and Charles Crook —By Crook's El Toro (Crook's Tahoe Pat - Black Rapids of Baranof) ex Arroyo Seco Cindy (Cumshaw Bat-Jac Boy - Panther's Flyaway Cinders)
OPEN—CSC 9/66-3; NCA 9/68-2. (4)
AMATEUR—10/65-3. (1)

CROZIER'S FIREBRAND SA-751403 7/31/68 J. McNeely DuBose, M.D. —By Innycot Sailor (Innycott Solitaire - Redgame Blair) ex Willou's Red River Belle (Glengarven's Rookie - Willou's Useless Rory)
OPEN—SWA 11/71-4. (½)

DAIRY HILL'S MAD HATTER SA-477287 4/29/67 A. A. Jones—By Crook's El Toro (Crook's Tahoe Pat - Black Rapids of Baranof) ex Dairy Hill's Toddy Tot* (Dairy Hill's Night Cap - Carr-Lab Babe)
AMATEUR—PHO 10/70-4; ALB 5/71-3; GSL 5/71-3; EID 7/71-2; GSL 8/71-2; SCA 9/71-3; SNA 5/72-3; SAG 7/72-2; EID 7/72-3; PHO 10/72-3. (15½)

FC-AFC DAIRY HILL'S MIKE SA-914668 9/27/57 Harold Mack, Jr.—
By Slo-Poke Smokey of Dairy Hill (Red's Black Jack - Bonnie of
Tahknecht) ex Dairy Hill's Flame's Fury (Black Demon of Granton -
Manzanal Kindle)

    OPEN—SHA 4/61-3; WIL 8/61-1; SAG 9/61-4; CSC 9/62-3;
LAS 2/63-2; CSC 2/64-1; SHA 5/64-2; HEL 9/64-1; SHE 9/64-4;
LAS 10/64-4; SHA 5/65-3; ACC (S) 8/65-4; SCA 9/65-2; SAG
3/66-4; TAC 4/66-2; GSL 5/67-2; GSL 8/67-4; SAG 9/67-4;
NWR 4/68-1; ACC 8/68-3. (42½)

    AMATEUR—TAC 4/61-4; SWA 11/61-1; SRZ 2/62-2; MCA
3/62-1; ROV 3/62-2; SAG 5/62-4; GSL 5/62-4; SAG 8/62-3; GSL
8/62-4; SCA 9/62-1; LAS 2/63-3; SCA 3/63-2; SAG 8/63-1; NCA
9/63-1; CSC 2/64-2; SAG 3/64-1; ROV 3/64-4; RED 7/64-4; SRZ
2/65-4; ORE 4/65-3; SHA 5/65-1; SRN 5/65-1; SHE 8/65-2;
SCA 3/66-1; SAG 3/66-3; RED 7/66-3; IDA 8/66-3; SCA 9/66-3;
CSC 9/66-1; LAS 2/67-2; CSC 2/67-4; SHA 4/67-4; GSL 5/67-1;
IDA 8/67-1; SHA 9/67-2; ROV 3/68-4; GOL 7/68-3; ACC
8/68-4; SAG 8/68-4. (97½)

FC-AFC DAIRY HILL'S NIGHT WATCH S-954552 2/20/58 A. A. Jones
—By Dairy Hill's Night Cap (Slo Poke Smokey of Dairy Hill - Dairy
Hill's Flame's Fury) ex Carr-Lab Jill (Carr-Lab Ditto Gainer - Carr-
Lab Pride's Angel)

    OPEN—NCA 9/60-3; SRZ 2/61-4; ROV 3/61-3; RKM 8/61-4;
NCA 9/61-3; SCA 3/62-2; NCA 3/62-3; SAG 8/62-4; GSL 8/62-3;
NCA 3/63-1; ROV 3/63-3; SHA 4/63-3; IDA 5/63-1; BHB
6/63-3; SNA 8/63-1; ROV 3/64-3; ACC 8/64-3; IDA 5/64-4;
SAG 3/65-2; NCA 9/66-1; SCA 9/66-2; CSC 9/66-2; LAS 2/67-4;
SRZ 2/67-3; ROV 5/67-3; NCA 9/67-3. (47½)

    AMATEUR—ROV 3/61-2; IDA 5/61-2;RKM 8/61-3; TAL
3/62-4; SWA 3/62-4: WOM 4/62-3; SRN 5/62-4; TAC 8/62-4;
NCA 9/62-1; CSC 2/63-4; ROV 3/63-2; SRN 2/63-2; IDA 8/63-1;
RED 7/64-1; LAS 2/65-4; RED 7/65-4; GSL 8/65-3; ACC 8/65-1;
NCA 9/65-2; SCA 9/65-4; CSC 2/66-2; GSL 8/66-2; ACC 8/66-1;
CSC 9/66-2; NCA 3/67-4; SAG 3/67-4; ACC 8/67-3. (58)

DAIRY HILL'S PLANTERS PUNCH SA-248674 1/12/64 Rupert A.
Dobesh—By Dairy Hill's Night Cap (Slo Poke of Smokey of Dairy
Hill - Dairy Hill's Flame's Fury) ex Techacko's Cinder (Massie's Sassy
Boots - Nodak Tar Pride)

    AMATEUR—GSL 5/68-4; SCA 9/68-1; SNA 5/69-3; ACC 8/69-3;
GSL 5/70-1; GSL 8/71-4; SNA 8/71-3. (14)

DAIRY HILL'S TOP BANANA SA-396890 11/12/65 A. A. Jones—By
Mawod's Shorty (Dairy Hill's Night Cap - Mawod's Drie) ex Grace-
Arts's Winalot (Nascopie Dark Destroyer - Grace-Art's Classy Boots)

    AMATEUR—ROV 3/69-1. (5)

DAJO'S BLACK VELVET SA-65774 8/25/59 David E. Zinschlag—By
Royal of Garfield (Roy's Rowdy - Pierre's Kit of Garfield) ex Martens'
Lady Jane (Jet Black Sin - Beautywood's Creole Jane)

    AMATEUR—MNS 5/65-1; CMI 5/65-2; DUL 8/66-4; CMI
5/67-2. (11½)

DAKOTA JAKE SA-277625 7/8/64 Perry and Zola Pound—By Del-Tone
Colvin (Cork of Oakwood Lane - Del-Tone Bridget) ex Paha Sapa
Wacincala (Freehaven Muscles - Treasure State Be Wise)

    AMATEUR—CHY 8/68-4; SHE 8/68-4. (1)

FC DANNY'S COLE BLACK SLATE SA-249836 12/30/68 Mrs. Grace
Lambert—By Blake's Cole Black Banner (Black Banner - Lone Lake's
Corkette) ex Wondawhere You Are (King High Siam - Tar of Cheyenne)

    OPEN—MNS 5/70-3; TRI 6/70-3; MOV 4/71-1; SXV 9/71-4;
NOI 10/71-2; NOI 7/72-1; MAN 8/72-3; MNS 9/72-3. (17½)

    AMATEUR—DUL 8/68-3. (1)

Col-Tam of Craignook

Cougar's Rocket

Dairy Hill's Mike

Dairy Hill's Night Watch

FC DAVE'S DEMETRIUS SA-126073 9/29/61 Dave and Sharon Magana
—By Rip Van Winkle III (Sun Valley Tuck - Jet of Hawthorne II)
ex Ruby's Jet (Salt Valley Ottie - Sid's Rusty)
OPEN—SNA 5/65-3; GSL 8/65-4; ACC 9/67-1; GSL 5/68-4;
HEL 9/68-3; SNA 5/69-2. (11)
AMATEUR—SLC 5/65-1. (5)

DEADLY DUDLEY'S DEKE SA-312039 1/30/65 D. B. Whitson—By Jet
Skipper (Black Tar of Avandale - Wendyadee) ex Gypsy's Gun Ho
(Sandy's Sunny - Bentley's Lady Jan)
AMATEUR—NDK 8/69-3. (1)

DEADLY DUDLEY'S DUXBAK COOT SA-355145 9/30/65 D. B. Whit-
son — By Duxbak Scooter* (Baker's Jerry - Carnmoney Moira) ex
Random Shot (Alpine Cherokee Rocket - Freeze Out Flats' Black Jewel)
AMATEUR—MIT 8/71-2. (3)

DEELITE'S MR. BONES SA-172854 10/6/61 Rebecca and Charles R.
Sherman—By Sage of Sanfray (La Sage's Smokey - Cream City Clip-
per) ex Sheer Dee Lite (Labcroft Brandy - Whileaway Crathie)
OPEN—MOB 11/67-4; NFL 11/67-4. (1)

FC-NARFC '71 DEE'S DANDY DUDE SA-459172 2/16/67 Michael
Paterno—By Ridgewood Playboy (La Sage's Smokey - Nelgard's Counter
Point) ex Grady's Shadee Ladee* (Black Mike of Lakewood - Jezebel
of Normandy)
OPEN—SHE 7/69-3; SCA 9/69-2; ALM 2/70-4; JAY 3/70-2;
WCH 5/70-3; EID 7/70-3; GSL 8/70-3; MAI 9/70-1; WOM
10/70-3; SWA 7/70-4; ALM 2/71-2; LST 3/71-2; JAY 3/71-3;
WCH 5/71-3; LIR 5/71-1; MAI 9/71-1; COL 10/71-3; MAR
10/71-4; DEL 10/71-3; ALM 2/72-1; PTA 3/72-1; TAL 4/72-2;
LAB 4/72-1; WCH 5/72-3; LIR 5/72-1; EID 7/72-4; GSL 8/72-2;
WNY 9/72-4; SHO 9/72-4; COL 9/72-4; LIR 10/72-2; DEL
10/72-3. (70½)
AMATEUR—ALM 2/70-2; PTA 3/70-4; WOM 4/70-3; CNY
5/70-4; IDA 8/70-1; MAI 9/70-2; COL 10/70-3; PTA 3/71-1;
WOM 4/71-4; WCH 5/71-4; LIR 5/71-4; MAR 5/71-4; CNY
5/71-1; NAM 6/71-1; SHO 9/71-1; MAI 9/71-3; COL 10/71-1;
MAR 10/71-1; DEL 10/71-2; WOM 10/71-3; ALM 2/72-4; LST
3/72-1; PTA 3/72-2; NFL 3/72-1; TAL 4/72-1; MAR 5/72-2;
EID 7/72-2; GSL 8/72-1; WNY 9/72-1; SHO 9/72-1; COL
9/72-2; MAR 10/72-4; LIR 10/72-1; DEL 10/72-2. (102)

FC DEL-TONE BUCK, SA-139689 7/30/61 Albert M. Stoll—By Martens'
Hi Style Buck (Cork of Oakwood Lane - Beautywood's Creole Jane)
ex Glen-Water Fan Fare (Cork of Oakwood Lane - Little Peggy Black
Gum)
OPEN—MIT 8/63-2; SXV 8/63-4; MEM 10/63-4; PTA 3/64-3;
TRI 5/64-2; MIT 8/64-3; SXV 9/64-1; MNS 9/64-4; NFL
2/65-3; MOV 4/65-2; SUP 6/65-4; FTP 8/65-2; MEM 10/65-3;
SXV 10/66-3; ALM 2/67-1; NEB 4/67-4; FTP 8/67-3; MIT
8/67-4; MEM 10/67-1; MOB 2/69-3; DUL 8/69-4; WIS 10/69-2. (40½)
AMATEUR—SLA 2/70-3. (1)

DEL-TONE REX SA-218179 9/4/62 Richard Heins — By Beautywoods
Rare Trouble (Roy's Rowdy - Beautywood's Repeat) ex Glen-Water
Fury (Cork of Oakwood Lane - Little Peggy Black Gum)
OPEN—DUL 8/67-2; CMI 5/69-4. (3½)

AFC DENT'S MIDNIGHT RICK SA-307745 12/12/64 Jack Madsen—
By Stillwater's Royal Rick (Carr-Lab Hilltop - Stillwater's Lady Jeep)
ex MacGene's Tinker Bell (Ripco's Peter Pan - MacGene's Charcoal
Cinders)

OPEN—PUG 4/70-2; SPO 5/70-1; TAC 8/70-4; PUG 4/71-4. (9)
AMATEUR—SPO 5/68-3; TAC 8/68-2; PUG 4/69-2; NWR
4/70-2; PUG 8/71-1. (15)

FC-AFC DESSA'S BLACK ANGEL SA-227060 10/28/63 Dr. and Mrs.
M. W. Stroud—By Tar Baby's Little Sweet Stuff (Tar Baby of Holly
Hill - Debbie of Holly Hill) ex Dessa Rae* (Odessa's King - Jerry)
OPEN—WNY 9/70-4; MAD 5/71-2; MIW 10/71-3; OHV 4/72-3;
AAR 5/72-1; BUK 9/72-2; OHV 9/72-4; ATL 10/72-1. (19)
AMATEUR—WOL 9/69-1; MTA 3/70-4; SHR 4/70-4; BUK
4/70-4; WOL 5/70-1; FTP 6/70-4; MIC 8/70-1; NFL 3/71-2;
BUK 4/71-1; FTP 6/71-2; MIC 8/71-2; BUK 9/71-4; NFC
3/72-4; MOB 3/72-3; SLA 3/72-3; GOL 5/72-3; FTP 6/72-2;
ALK 8/72-4; BUK 9/72-4; WOL 9/72-4; SWA 11/72-4. (40)

FC DESSA'S LITTLE TAR BABY SA-227059 10/28/63 Douglas David
—By Tar Baby's Little Sweet Stuff (Tar Baby of Holly Hill - Debbie
of Holly Hill) ex Dessa Rae* (Odessa's King - Jerry)
OPEN—SAM 3/66-2; TAC 4/66-4; NWR 4/66-4; WMO 5/66-4;
PUG 8/68-3; CSC 2/69-2; ROV 3/69-3; NWR 4/69-1; SPO
5/69-2; RED 7/69-1; NWR 9/69-4; ORE 9/69-4; ROV 3/70-3;
TAC 4/70-1; PUG 4/70-1; RED 7/70-4; SPO 10/70-2; ORE
4/71-1; TAC 4/71-1; SNA 5/71-4; SPO 5/71-1; AAR 9/71-4;
SHA 9/71-2. (57)
AMATEUR—SAM 3/66-4; IDA 5/66-3; SPO 5/67-2; ORE 9/68-4;
ORE 4/70-2; TAC 4/70-3; SHA 5/70-4; PUG 4/71-3. (10½)

DICK'S BLACK DUKE SA-396834 12/20/64 H. V. P. Lewis—By Black
Mike XVIII (Creswoods Little Imp - Penny IX) ex Penny Girl II
(Duke of Robin's Roost - Lone Lake's Duchess)
AMATEUR—CNB 5/68-4. (½)

DIXIELAND COOT'S TIGER BABY SA-560607 5/18/67 Phil Mac-
Millan—By Whygin Cork's Coot* (Cork of Oakwood Lane - Whygin
Dark Ace) ex Star Fire of Audlon (Paha Sapa Chief II - Star of Fate)
AMATEUR—NDK 8/71-4; MIT 8/72-4. (1)

DIXIELAND JOE SA-229455 3/10/63 Dr. John Tudor—By Kewanee's
Yogi (Boley's Tar Baby - Bigstone Smoky) ex Duxbak Cindy (Baker's
Jerry - Carnmoney Moira)
OPEN—NLA 10/66-2; MTI 10/66-3; NFL 11/63-4; SLA 10/67-2;
NLA 3/68-4; MTI 10/68-4. (8½)
AMATEUR—NLA 3/69-1; MIW 4/69-2; MEM 4/71-3. (9)

FC-AFC DOCTOR PEPPER OF LE-MAR SA-373818 12/21/65 Marjorie
and Lee Broussard—By Cher Te Beau of Repmen (Cher Te Neg -
Calcasieu Queen) ex Cathy-Chris' Yellow Sue (Colonel's Mr. Chips -
Barnes Sugar Bee)
OPEN—PTA 10/68-1; LST 10/69-2; PTA 3/70-3; NLA 10/70-2. (12)
AMATEUR—NTX 10/68-2; ALM 11/68-3; SLA 9/69-4; LST
10/69-3; ALM 2/70-1; LST 3/70-4; NLA 10/70-3; NLA 3/71-4;
CAS 9/71-3; CAS 9/72-4; PTA 10/72-3; ALM 11/72-1. (20)

DONALD GRUNTS RAY SA-488874 5/20/67 Howard W. and E. Ida
Ray—By Katy's Boy (Bib N. Tucker - Sommers Beau Kay) ex Pareenca
Apache Tear (Rip of Fairchild - Ebony Vixen)
AMATEUR—NCA 9/69-1; NCA 9/70-4; NCA 3/71-4; NCA 3/72-3. (7)

FC DOUBLE PLAY OF AUDLON SA-110623 6/23/61 Charles Elmes—
By Nodak Boots (Massie's Sassy Boots - Spider Wise) ex Pawlesta
Fleetfoot of Audlon (Beautywoods' Carbon Copy - Toto of Audlon)
OPEN—MAN 8/66-4; WOL 5/67-1; MII 6/67-2; DUL 8/67-3;
WIS 9/67-3; MOB 10/69-2; NFL 11/69-2. (16½)
AMATEUR—SLA 3/67-1; MOV 10/67-2. (8)

FC-AFC DUKE OF CROOKSTON SA-136694 5/1/64 Hugh I. Klaren
—By Michael of Pepin View (Cork of Oakwood Lane - Del-Tone Lass)
ex Breezeway's Tiny Lady (Count of Zenith - Blondie of Zenith)
    OPEN—WMT 6/65-3; MTA 3/66-4; WIS 4/67-3; MAD 8/67-1;
    MOB 2/68-4; MAD 5/68-1; MAN 8/68-3; AAR 8/68-1; MEM
    2/69-4; MIW 4/69-2; MAD 5/69-2; MIC 8/69-3; AAR 9/69-4;
    MOV 10/69-4; JAX 2/70-4.   (28)
    AMATEUR—MAD 5/70-4; AAR 5/70-3; TRI 6/70-3; MAD
    8/70-3; MII 6/70-1; AAR 9/70-1; WIS 9/70-3; MIW 10/70-1;
    MOV 4/71-1; AAR 5/71-3; MIW 10/71-2.   (29½)

FC-AFC DUKE OF TEDDY BEAR SA-147529 5/31/61 Charles J. Bierschied—By Teddy Bear (Bud - Cheta) ex Dulcie (Nicky of Hager's
Acres - Kelvin Groves Mamie)
    OPEN—SHE 6/64-2; RKM 8/65-1; CHY 8/66-4; PIK 5/67-1;
    RKM 5/68-2.   (16½)
    AMATEUR—PIK 8/63-1; RKM 5/64-2; RKM 8/64-2; RKM
    5/65-2; RKM 8/65-1; RKM 8/66-1; CHY 8/66-1; RKM 5/69-2.   (32)

FC-AFC DUSTY'S DOCTARI SA-440071 3/5/66 Ralph and Barbara E.
Smith—By Joy's Coal Dust* (Ace of Balboa - Smokey Flame) ex Miss
Tehama Tar (Silver Duke - Miss Conception)
    OPEN—MON 5/68-1; BHB 6/68-4; TAC 8/68-3; SNA 8/68-2;
    SAG 8/68-3; NCA 9/68-1; SCA 9/68-3; TAC 4/69-4; PUG
    4/69-1; SHA 4/69-1; GSL 5/69-2; SHE 7/69-1; SAG 7/69-4;
    EID 7/69-2; SNA 8/69-3; ACC 8/69-1; LAS 2/70-1; SRZ 2/70-3;
    NCA 3/70-4; NWR 4/70-2; SNA 5/70-2; GSL 5/70-3; WMO
    5/70-4; BHB 6/70-3; SNA 8/70-3; NCA 9/70-4; CSC 2/71-2;
    SCO 3/71-2; SAG 3/71-3; PUG 4/71-1; SHA 4/71-2; IDA
    5/71-3; GSL 5/71-1; EID 7/71-4; IDA 8/71-4; PHO 10/71-2;
    SRZ 2/72-2; SNA 5/72-2.   (92)
    AMATEUR—CSC 9/68-3; WMO 5/69-2; MON 5/69-3; SAG
    7/69-2; SCA 9/69-4; SRZ 2/70-3; SCA 2/70-2; ACC 8/70-2;
    SRZ 2/71-2; SCA 3/71-1; ACC 8/71-1; SRZ 2/72-2; SAD 9/72-1;
    CSC 9/72-4.   (37)

NARFC '64 DUTCHMOOR'S BLACK MOOD SA-35121 2/17/60 A.
Nelson Sills—By Calypso Clipper (Yankee Clipper of Reo Raj - Bigstone
Bobber) ex Jet's Tammy (Boley's Tar Baby - Spirit Lake Jet)
    OPEN—MAR 10/65-3..   (1)
    AMATEUR—MAR 10/62-4; WOM 10/62-2; SWA 3/63-1; DEL
    10/63-2; TAL 3/64-1; MAR 10/64-1; WOM 10/64-1; NAM
    6/64-1; TAL 3/65-1; LIR 4/65-2; SHR 5/65-2; SWA 3/66-1;
    LAB 4/66-1; MAI 9/66-4; LIR 10/66-4; DEL 10/66-3; LAB (S)
    11/66-1; TAL 3/67-2.   (62½)

DUTCH'S BLACK LUCIFER SA-722593 5/30/67 Gary and Barbara Cole
—By Mac's Black Beau (Kellogg's Cork of Lost River - Mac's Black
Dawn) ex Gypsy Rose Satan (Hyatt's Kynowocky - Lady Troubles)
    AMATEUR—LAS 2/71-4.   (½)

DUXBAK BLACK OAK SA-449524 11/2/61 John M. Olin—By Duxbak
Scooter* (Baker's Jerry - Carnmoney Moira) ex Duxbak Queen (Black
Squeek of Netley Creek - Duxbak Trixie)
    OPEN—MAD 8/67-3; MEM 3/68-3.   (2)

FC DUXBAK SCOOTER SA-137325 4/11/58 Mrs. Grace Lambert—By
Baker's Jerry (Prince of Lowestoft - Kendahar Kitt) ex Carnmoney
Moira (Brant of Bardonda - Sandylands Jilly)
    OPEN—MAI 5/62-1; TRI 6/62-1; MNS 10/62-1; WOM 10/62-2;
    SCA 3/63-2; NUT 5/63-2; DUL 5/63-3; SUP 6/63-3; NDK
    8/63-2; SXV 8/63-1; MAR 10/63-4; DEL 10/63-2; WOM 10/63-1;

Dee's Dandy Dude

Dusty's Doctari

Dutchmoor's Black Mood

Duxbak Scooter

WOM 4/64-1; LAB 4/64-3; DUL 5/64-3; ALM 11/64-1; CMI
6/64-2; DEL 10/64-1; LST 3/65-1; NTX 3/65-3; WOM 4/65-1;
LAB 4/65-1; SHR 5/65-1; GOL 5/65-1; MNS 5/65-3; CMI
5/65-4; TRI 6/65-4; DUL 6/65-1; DEL 10/65-2; WOM 10/65-4;
CMI 5/66-2; MII 6/66-3; FTP 8/66-3; MIT 8/66-3; DUL 8/66-2;
MTR 9/66-1; MAR 10/66-1; LIR 10/66-2; DEL 10/66-2; LIR
4/67-2; CMI 5/67-1.   (132)
AMATEUR—MNS 5/64-1; DUL 5/64-4; MNS 9/65-3.   (8½)

EASY DOES IT OF VALHALLA SA-594072 5/31/68 Dr. and Mrs. Roy J.
    Brinkman — By Geechee* (Ridgewood Playboy - Grace-Art's Smart
    Lady) ex Valhalla Trooper's Persimmon (Medlin's Texas Trooper -
    Betsy's Copy Kat)
    AMATEUR—ATL 10/72-3; MIT 10/72-1; ALM 11/72-3.   (7)

FC-AFC EBBANEE'S RICOCHET SA-140772 3/2/59 Mrs. C. V. Brokaw,
    Jr.—By Blair's Black Victory (Greatford Fizz - Killarney Jet Lady)
    ex Ebbanee's War Dancer (Cal-Vada's Li'le Black Falcon - Crevamoy's
    Flirt)
    OPEN—TAL 3/63-3; BUK 9/63-1; LAB(S) 11/63-4; LIR 4/64-2;
    WOL 9/64-3; TAL 3/65-2; TRI 6/65-2; FRR 8/65-3; OHV
    10/65-4; WOM 4/66-4.   (18½)
    AMATEUR—DUL 8/63-4; LIR 10/63-4; OHV 10/64-3; NUT
    5/64-2; WOL 5/64-2; AAR 5/64-1; DEL 10/64-1; LAB (S)
    11/64-4; WOM 4/65-4; LAB 4/65-4; MAI 5/65-4; MAN 8/65-3;
    OHV 10/65-1; DEL 10/65-1; SWA 11/65-4; LAB (S) 11/65-2;
    TAL 3/66-3; MOB 2/67-1; LAB 4/67-4.   (41)

EBONY MOOD'S BINGO SA-157681 6/1/62 E. E. Jackson III—By
    Dutchmoor's Black Mood* (Calypso Clipper - Jet's Tammy) ex Bigstone
    Lady B (Bigstone King II - Bigstone Bounce)
    OPEN—SLA 9/67-4; MEM 10/68-3; JAX 1/69-4; SLA 9/69-1;
    MOB 10/69-4; MOB 11/70-3.   (8½)

EGGERS ROYAL BLUE SA-246744 4/2/63 H. A. and Betty Jo Eggers
    —By Washek's Diamond Duke (Gulf Coast Casper - Petersen's Black
    Gal) ex Evelyn's Diana (Lonnie's Pride - Comanche's Cissy of Texas)
    AMATEUR—LST 10/66-3; SLA 9/67-2.   (4)

ELECTRICITY OF AUDLON SA-43337 4/11/60 Mrs. Fred Benners—By
    Hiwood John (Galleywood Swift - Hiwood Peggy) ex Merry-Go-Round
    Tradewinds (Cork of Oakwood Lane - Grangemead Watfor)
    OPEN—MOV 4/63-3; GOL 5/63-2; SLA 5/65-4; WMT 6/65-2;
    NTX 10/65-4; ALM 2/67-4; NTX 10/67-2; NTX 10/68-3.   (12½)
    AMATEUR—MTA 3/66-4; NTX 3/66-3; PTA 10/66-3; MTA
    3/67-4; NLA 3/67-2; PIK 8/67-4; RKM 8/67-2; NTX 10/67-2;
    ALM 2/68-4; NTX 3/70-4.   (13½)

EL NEGRO SAM SA-217000 8/12/63 Paul William Rabeler—By Black
    Flash of Hellgate (Samson of Avandale - Claire of Avandale) ex Aldice
    of Avandale (Cutbank Bobolink - Savina of Avandale)
    OPEN—BHB 6/67-4.   (½)
    AMATEUR—BHB 6/69-2; EID 7/69-2.   (6)

ERN-BAR'S ANDY OF ANZAC SA-530617 10/7/67 Carnation Farm
    Kennels—By Anzac of Zenith* (Black Mike of Lakewood - Jezebel of
    Normandy) ex Happy's Twinkle* (Nightcap Again - Miss Behavior)
    OPEN—TAC 4/72-3; WMO 5/72-3.   (2)

EVERGREEN BINX SA-667591 12/10/68 Mr. and Mrs. David Crow—By
    Samson's George of Glenspey* (Sam Frizel of Glenspey* - Thunder
    Chief's Shiri) ex Penny of Evergreen* (Martens' Mister Nifty* - Pre-
    Don Jacky)

OPEN—ALM 2/72-3; SHE 9/72-4; ALM 11/72-1. (6½)
AMATEUR—MOV 9/71-1; MII 5/72-1; NOI 7/72-4; CWY
8/72-3; ALM 11/72-4. (12)

FARO'S MATHEW SA-549677 11/16/63 Willie Taylor—By Faro's Trey
of Spades (Cowman's Black Atom - Tammy of Cinder's Targ) ex
Faro's Molly (Country Club's Joey - Gem of Avandale)
AMATEUR—NWR 4/68-4. (½)

FIELDMARSHALL HEINZ GUDERIAN SA-352815 9/7/65 Donald E.
deZurik—By Duxbak Scooter* (Baker's Jerry - Carnmoney Moira) ex
Jilly Girl* (Paha Sapa Chief II - Penny Girl)
OPEN—MNS 5/72-3. (1)
AMATEUR—MNS 5/72-1. (5)

FC-AFC FISHERMAN BILL OF DELAWARE SA-57901 6/13/60 Mr.
and Mrs. M. B. Wallace, Jr.—By Prince William of Erie (Labcroft
Brandy - Margaret of Erie) ex Gambler's Lady (Buckeye Sambo -
Skipper Sue)
OPEN—MIW 4/63-4; NFL 2/64-3; MOB 2/64-2; WIS 4/64-3;
WMT 6/64-3; MOV 10/65-2; MOB 11/65-2; SLA 2/66-4; KAN
4/66-1; GOL 5/66-4; MII 6/66-4; MAN 8/66-2; MOV 10/66-1;
MTA 10-66-2; MOB 2/67-2; SLA 2/67-2; MEM 3/67-2; MTA
3/67-3; NLA 3/67-3; MOV 4/67-3; MIW 4/67-1; MTA 10/67-1;
MEM 10/67-3; MOV 4/68-4; AAR 5/68-4; MII 6/68-1; MIT
8/68-3; NLA 10/68-1; JAX 1/69-3; NFL 2/69-3; MOB 2/69-2;
AAR 8/69-2. (73)
AMATEUR—MOV 4/63-4; WIS 4/63-3; AAR 5/63-1; MOV
4/64-3; WMT 6/64-1; MOB 2/65-4; SLA 5/65-3; MTA 10/65-3;
MEM 10/65-3; NFL 2/66-2; MOB 2/66-4; WIS 4/66-4; AAR
5/66-4; MII 6/66-1; SLA 9/66-4; MOV 10/66-3; MTA 10/66-3;
MOV 4/67-1; MAD 5/67-4; MII 6/67-2; MOV 10/67-3; MTA
10/67-3; MEM 10/67-3; MOB 2/68-1; MII 6/68-4; MOV 10/68-1;
MIW 4/69-4; AAR 5/69-1. (55½)

FC FLINT'S NIFTY ARROW SA-562599 6/16/67 Mrs. Grace Lambert
—By Bigstone Blaze (Martens' Mister Nifty* - Dick's Black Scamp)
ex Spade O'Cedar (Lolu's Sweet Billy - Queen of Spades XIII)
OPEN—CMI 5/70-2; WIS 9/70-3; MNS 5/71-3; CMI 5/71-1;
MAD 8/71-3; WOM 4/72-1; CMI 5/72-2; MAR 10/72-2. (22)

FC-AFC FLOOD BAY BOOMERANG SA-191300 3/12/62 Lewis S.
Greenleaf, Jr.—By Beautywood Rare Trouble (Roy's Rowdy - Beauty-
wood's Repeat) ex Glengarven's Black Shadow (Par of Carnmoney -
Glengarven's Babe)
OPEN—MIV 4/64-3; COL 10/64-2; MAR 10/64-3; LIR 4/65-4;
WOM 4/65-2; LAB 4/65-3; CNY 5/65-2; COL 10/65-1; MAR
10/65-4; LIR 10/65-4; DEL 10/65-3; WOM 10/65-1; SRZ 2/66-3;
NCA 3/66-1; SAG 3/66-3; LAB 4/66-3; MAI 5/66-1; AAR 9/66-1;
BUK 9/66-1; MAI 9/66-3; MAR 10/66-3; LIR 10/66-1; WOM
10/66-1; LAB (S) 11/66-2; SRZ 2/67-2; CSC 2/67-1; NCA
3/67-4; TAL 3/67-4; SHR 4/67-3; MAI 5/67-2; FTP 6/67-2;
COL 10/67-1; DEL 10/67-3; NCA 3/68-4; SAG 3/68-4; JAY
3/68-1; LIR 4/68-1; WOM 4/68-1; LAB 4/68-2; WNY 9/68-3;
SWA 11/68-2; LAB 11/62-2; CNY 5/69-1. (115½)
AMATEUR—NCA 3/66-1; LIR 4/66-1; WOM 4/66-2; LIR
10/66-1; WOM 10/66-2; CSC 2/67-1; LIR 4/67-2; LAB 4/67-2;
SHE 6/67-1;MAI 9/67-4; LR 10/67-2; WOM 10/67-2; CSC
2/68-2; LIR 4/68-3. (47½)

FC-AFC FLOODBAY'S BARON O' GLENGARVEN SA-253076 3/15/62
Austin B. Mason, Jr.—By Beautywood Rare Trouble (Roy's Rowdy -
Beautywood's Repeat) ex Glengarven's Black Shadow (Par of Carn-
money - Glengarven's Babe)

OPEN—LAB 4/66-2; SXV 9/66-4; SLA 2/67-3; MAI 5/67-1; COL 9/67-2; MAR 10/67-4; LIR 10/67-3; WOM 10/67-1; MEM 3/68-1; MTA 3/68-1; SHR 3/68-3; WOM 4/68-4; CNY 5/68-3; BUK 9/68-1; MAR 10/68-3; TAL 3/69-1; SHR 4/69-2; LAB 4/69-2; LIR 10/69-4; DEL 3/70-1; CNY 5/70-3; WOM 4/70-3; WOM 10/70-4; LIR 5/71-4; COL 10/71-4. (57½)

AMATEUR—CMI 5/64-3; COL 9/66-4; SLA 2/67-4; MEM 3/67-1; LIR 4/67-1; SHR 4/67-2; COL 9/67-4; SLA 2/68-1; DEL 3/68-3; LIR 10/68-2; SWA 11/68-2; SHR 4/69-2; WOM 4/69-3; LAB 4/69-1; MTA 3/70-2; DEL 3/70-4; TAL 4/70-1; COL 10/70-4. (45½)

FRANKIE OF RIVERNOOK SA-179414 7/5/62 Mr. and Mrs. Don H. Gearheart—By Nodak Boots (Massie's Sassy Boots - Spider Wise) ex Glen-Water Fal-Lal (Cork of Oakwood Lane - Little Peggie Black Gum)
OPEN—SHR 3/68-4; DEL 3/68-4; DEL 10/68-4; MEM 2/69-1. (6½)

FC-AFC FRANKLIN'S TALL TIMBER SA-358903 9/27/65 Roger and Pat Magnusson—By Del-Tone Buck* (Martens' Hi Style Buck - Glen-Water Fan Fare) ex Franklin's Gold Charm (Kinley Comet of Harham - Sunset Road of Franklin)
OPEN—AAR 9/70-1; WNY 9/70-1; BUK 4/71-3; GOL 5/71-3; MIC 8/71-4. (12½)

AMATEUR—FRR 8/69-3; OHV 9/69-4; WOL 5/70-4; WNY 9/70-2; OHV 10/70-3; JAX 3/71-2; MIV 4/71-4; WIS 4/71-1; FRR 8/71-1; OHV 10/71-3; OHV 4/72-4; BUK 4/72-3; AAR 5/72-3; MIC 8/72-1; BUK 9/72-2; OHV 9/72-4; FRR 8/72-3. (32½)

FROSTY FORTUNE OF FLOSUM SA-236466 12/25/62 Mike Musolf —By Great Lakes Duke (Buff of Bur-Mur Farm - Goldie of Wright) ex Duchess of Jolor (Brooklyn's King - Cinderella Sue)
AMATEUR—CMI 5/67-4; DUL 8/69-2. (3½)

GAHONK'S TRAVELLER SB-12002 10/6/69 Dr. and Mrs. William N. Bernhard—By My Rebel* (Yankee Clipper of Reo-Raj - Duchess of Millers Haven) ex Canvasback Dee (Ace-Hi Royal Flush - Duxbak Dandy)
OPEN—TAL 4/72-4. (½)

GAYFEATHERS DOMINO SA-447841 10/1/66 Irwin S. and Dagmar Brown—By Cherokee Chief V* (Otter O'Vyrnwy - Renegade Sioux) ex Sugarplum's Tar Baby (Marshwise Snapshooter - B-B Swift)
OPEN—CNB 5/70-4; MII 5/72-4; CHY 8/72-4. (1½)

GAYLAB'S GABRIEL SA-600628 11/14/67 C. E. Leech—By Castlemore Shamus (Strokestown Duke of Blaircourt - Hilldown Sylver) ex Birdie's Misty (Crozier's Cinco' Cork - Rockwall's Birdie)
OPEN—NEB 4/71-4. (½)
AMATEUR—MIT 8/71-4; MIT 8/72-2. (3½)

GAYLAB'S SHAMUS SA-573601 11/14/67 Dr. John M. Tudor — By Castlemore Shamus (Strokestown Duke of Blaircourt - Hilldown Sylver) ex Birdie's Misty (Crozier's Cinco' Cork - Rockwall's Birdy)
OPEN—LIT 4/72-2. (3)

GEE BABY SA-147761 5/29/62 Dr. and Mrs. Clifford M. Boone—By Riefler's Dutch (Medlin's Cork of Grapevine - Medlin's Cricket) ex Pretty Nifty (Robbets Coaldust - Cinders of Richland)
AMATEUR—ALM 2/67-4; NTX 3/68-4. (2)

AFC GEECHEE SA-307699 5/18/64 Dr. Charles B. Harvey—By Ridgewood Playboy (La Sage's Smoky - Nelgard's Counter Point) ex Grace-Art's Smart Lady (Nascopie Dark Destroyer - Grace-Art's Classy Boots)

OPEN—NFL 11/69-4; MTA 3/70-4; MTA 10/70-2; JAX 3/71-2;
SLA 10/71-2.   (10)

AMATEUR—NFL 2/68-1; NFL 2/69-2; NFL 11/69-1; JAX
2/70-4; SLA 10/70-1; MTA 10/70-2; MOB 11/70-3; NFL 3/71-3;
ATL 10/71-2; MEM 10/71-4; MOB 11/71-4; NFL 3/72-3; MAD
5/72-2; FTP 6/72-4.   (32)

GEECHEE'S BUCK SA-429311 5/1/66 Howard T. Jones—By Geechee*
   (Ridgewood Playboy - Grace-Art's Smart Lady) ex Jumper of Spring
   Valley (Nodak Boots - Glen-Water Fan Fare)
   AMATEUR—ATL 10/71-1.   (5)

GEECHEE'S DANIEL DEXTER SA-460352 12/29/66 Dr. J. R. Winburn
   —By Geechee* (Ridgewood Playboy - Grace-Art's Smart Lady) ex
   Bigstone Molly Dee (Royal of Garfield - Bigstone Duchess II)
   OPEN—PIK 5/72-3.   (1)
   AMATEUR—NFL 11/72-4.   (½)

GENTLEMAN JIGGS SA-678855 1/25/68 Hugh I. Klaren—By Koskinen's
   Colonel (Love's Black Rock - Rubelle of Avandale) ex Cheyenne's Lady
   (Kangas of Mount-View-Farm - Rangewise Little Jody)
   OPEN—MAN 8/70-2.   (3)
   AMATEUR—ATL 10/72-2.   (3)

AFC GIMP OF LAKIN SA-182303 6/14/61 Robert Sandahl—By Bingol
   Bengul Bouncer (Chip of Maple Knoll - Masons Mingamongo) ex
   Lady Carbon Daglo (Trevr-Champ Minyok - Shady Haven Farm Jet)
   OPEN—CNB 5/67-2; NEB 4/68-4.   (3½)
   AMATEUR—SXV 9/65-2; MIV 10/65-4; MII 5/66-2; KAN
   10/66-2; KAN 3/67-2; CNB 5/67-1; JAY 3/68-2; KAN 3/68-2.   (23½)

FC-AFC GLENGARVEN'S MIK SA-151980 8/23/59 Roger Vasselais—
   By Glengarven's Kim (Yankee Clipper of Reo Raj - Burndale's Cedar
   Lass) ex Gordon's Black Babe (Gordon's Smokey - Bitterroot Assa)
   OPEN—MIT 8/62-1; NDK 8/62-3; WOL 5/63-3; CMI 6/63-4;
   COL 9/63-3; SWA 3/64-1; LIR 4/64-3; CNY 5/64-1; MAN
   8/64-4; FRR 8/64-2; WNY 9/64-4; BUK 9/64-1; ALM 2/65-3;
   SWA 3/65-1; BUK 9/65-1; WOL 9/65-1; MTA 3/66-1; TAL
   3/66-2; LIR 4/66-3; SHR 4/66-3; MNS 5/66-3; CMI 5/66-1;
   BHB 6/66-2; OHV 9/66-1; SWA 11/66-4; NTX 3/67-2; WOM
   4/67-3; TRI 6/67-4; FRR 8/67-1; MAR 10/67-2; SWA 11/67-2;
   MOB 2/68-1; NTX 3/68-2; NLA 3/68-1; WAL 5/68-1; COL
   9/68-2; MAR 10/68-1; WOM 10/68-4; CMI 5/69-2; TRI 5/69-3;
   LIR 10/69-1.   (120)

   AMATEUR—PTA 3/63-1; TAL 3/63-1; WOM 4/63-4; WOL
   5/63-1; CNY 5/63-4; MAN 8/63-1; WOL 9/63-2; COL 9/63-2;
   MAR 10/63-1; LIR 10/63-1; SWA 11/63-2; MEM 2/64-4; LAB
   4/64-2; WOL 5/64-3; AAR 5/64-2; FRR 8/64-1; WNY 9/64-3;
   BUK 9/64-4; MAR 10/64-2; LIR 10/64-3; SWA 11/64-1; NFL
   2/65-2; ALM 2/65-1; LST 3/65-4; SWA 3/65-4; TAL 3/65-2;
   WOL 5/65-1; BUK 9/65-3; WOL 9/65-1; DEL 10/65-4; NFL
   2/66-1; MOB 2/66-1; MEM 3/66-3; MTA 3/66-2; SWA 3/66-4;
   SHR 4/66-1; WOM 4/66-3; LAB 4/66-2; MAD 5/66-1; MII
   5/66-1; CMI 5/66-3; BHB 6/66-2; OHV 9/66-2; MAR 10/66-2;
   LIR 10/66-3; DEL 10/66-2; NFL 2/67-3; NTX 3/67-1; LIR
   4/67-4; WOM 4/67-4; CMI 5/67-1; MII 6/67-1; SHE 6/67-3;
   FRR 8/67-3; BUK 9/67-4; MAI 9/67-2; COL 9/67-1; MAR
   10/67-1; SWA 11/67-3; MOB 2/68-3; SLA 2/68-3; MTA 3/68-1;
   NLA 3/68-4; WOM 4/68-1; LAB 4/68-1; MAR 5/68-2; WOL
   5/68-3; CNY 5/68-4; WNY 9/68-1; BUK 9/68-4; COL 9/68-1;
   MAR 10/68-3; LIR 10/68-1; DEL 10/68-2; JAX 1/69-1; NFL
   2/69-1; MOB 2/69-1; SLA 2/69-1; MEM 2/69-4; LIR 5/70-2;
   LIR 10/70-4.   (233)

150

Fisherman Bill of Delaware

Flood Bay Boomerang

Glengarven's Mik

GLEN'S LADY'S CASPER SA-387316 9/3/64 Frank Roehl — By Nilo Captain's Courageous (King Buck - Truly Yours of Garfield) ex Glen's Lady of the Mountains (Bali Machree Smokey - Lloyd's Park Avenue Lady)
OPEN—RKM 5/69-2. (3)

GOOSE SPOOKER SA-293428 2/14/63 Dr. Frank C. Henry—By Lignite's Old Yeller (Lignite of Keogh - Owyhee Ebony Belle) ex Mistress of Sterling (Ripco's Peter Pan - Rieben's Taffy)
OPEN—SHA 9/67-4. (½)

GRAND ADMIRAL RAEDER SA-242603 3/15/62 Geo. M. Hansen III —By Kingdale's Decoy (Kiska Pete Junior - Tri-Stada Gun Moll) ex Duckwind Dark Dawn (Slo-Poke Smokey of Dairy Hill - Kingdale's Ink Spot)
AMATEUR—DUL 6/65-4; TRI 6/67-3; DUL 8/68-2; NWR 9/68-3. (5½)

GREAT SMOKE CLOUD SA-528026 3/8/67 Dr. J. W. Aston, Jr.—By Raven Mike of Stonegate (Stonegate's Brazen Beau - Midge of Stonegate) ex Skookum Scooter (Castlemore Shamus - Birdie's Misty)
OPEN—PIK 5/72-4. (½)
AMATEUR—ALM 2/72-1; SOO 4/72-4. (5½)

GUEYDAN OF BEAUMARK SA-298348 2/7/64 S. G. B. Tennant — By Black Jack Yappee (Nodak's Timothy - How Hi Ginger) ex Denna (Gladrock Duke - Tronic Clover)
AMATEUR—NLA 10/68-4; PTA 3/69-2. (3½)

AFC GUNG-HO OF GRANTON SA-168850 6/23/58 Wilbur Saunders— By Cal-Vada's Li'l Black Falcon (Murray of Avandale - Cal-Vada's Snowball) ex Jibodad Topsy (Chuck of Bracken - Jibodad Gypsy)
OPEN—WMO 9/63-3; SNA 8/64-4; WMO 5/65-3; WMO 9/65-3; IDA 5/66-4; HEL 9/66-2; WMO 9/66-4; SNA 5/67-4; MON 9/67-3. (9)
AMATEUR—HEL 9/63-1; SNA 8/64-1; HEL 9/64-4; WMO 9/64-4; IDA 5/65-3; MON 6/65-3; MON 9/65-1; SRZ 2/66-4; MON 6/66-2; SNA 8/66-3; HEL 9/66-4; WMO 9/66-3; IDA 5/67-4; SNA 8/67-3; MON 9/67-2; WMO 9/67-3. (29½)

GUNNER OF GUNTHUNDER SA-368042 2/21/65 C. Alan Fischer—By Cache Valley Drifter (Sunday Shoes - Belle of Bear River) ex Springer's Cleo (Black Cougar - Bay City Katie Jane)
AMATEUR—NCA 9/68-3; MIV 4/69-4. (1½)

FC GUN THUNDER OLY SA-133017 12/17/61 Mrs. William P. Roth— By Tar Baby's Little Sweet Stuff (Tar Baby of Holly Hill - Debbie of Holly Hill) ex Tad's Cork of Laketree (Shoremeadow Tidewater - Cork's Bobber of Swinomish)
OPEN—ORE 4/66-1; SHA 4/66-2; LAS 2/67-1; SRZ 2/67-1; SCA 3/67-1; CSC 2/68-2; SRN 5/68-1; RED 7/68-1; WIL 8/68-3; SAM 8/68-3; NWR 9/68-2. (41)

FC-NARFC '69 GUY'S BITTERROOT LUCKY SA-308959 8/12/64 Guy P. Burnett—By Beavercrest Toreador (Sentinel of Whitmore - Semloh's Peggy) ex Pickrel's Ebony Babe (Teddy Carbon Copy - Invail's Salty's Thyme)
OPEN—SNA 5/67-2; SPO 5/67-1; WMO 5/67-3; SNA 8/67-1; HEL 9/67-3; SPO 9/67-3; SNA 5/68-4; SPO 5/68-3; WMO 5/68-1; BHB 6/68-1; EID 7/68-4; SNA 8/68-1; MON 9/68-1; HEL 9/68-2; IDA 5/69-2; SNA 5/69-1; WMO 5/69-2; MII 6/69-3; HEL 9/69-3; WMO 9/69-1; SCA 3/70-4; SPO 5/70-2; WMO 5/70-1; EID 7/70-1; SNA 8/70-2; NCA 9/70-2; SNA 8/71-2; WMO 9/71-4. (82)

AMATEUR—SPO 5/67-1; WMO 5/67-1; BHB 6/67-2; WMO 9/67-4; SPO 9/67-2; SRZ 2/68-2; SNA 5/68-1; SPO 5/68-1; WMO 5/68-2; MON 5/68-2; BHB 6/68-4; EID 7/68-2; SNA 8/68-1; MON 9/68-1; HEL 9/68-3; SRZ 2/69-1; CSC 2/69-1; MII 6/69-2; NAM 6/69-1; HEL 9/69-3; SRZ 2/70-1; CSC 2/70-2; SCA 3/70-4; SNA 8/70-2. (80½)

FC-AFC HAIRSPRING TRIGGER SA-150997 3/26/60 H. Dale Prentice —By Mainliner Mike (Skipper of Rodall II - Wendy of Candlewood) ex Beautywood's Rebel Queen (Roy's Rowdy - Beautywood's Repeat)
OPEN—CHY 5/63-4; RKM 5/64-4; PIK 8/65-3; RKM 8/66-4; CHY 8/66-3; PIK 5/67-4; PIK 8/67-1; RKM 5/68-3. (10)
AMATEUR—PIK 4/64-2; RKM 8/64-4; PIK 8/65-2; RKM 5/66-1; CHY 5/66-2; RKM 5/67-4; RKM 5/68-1. (20)

FC HANK'S SPOOK SA-535525 9/3/67 James L. Doherty—By Big Black Rippis (Hyatt's Big Bill Bronsey - Lady of Churn Creek) ex Bianca (Hap - Coll-A-Dene's Snow Flake)
OPEN—SCA 9/70-2; PHO 10/70-2; NCA 3/71-4; KAN 4/71-2; SRN 5/71-4; EID 7/71-2; GSL 8/71-4; SNA 8/71-3; SCA 9/71-1; CSC 10/71-3; LAS 2/72-1; NEB 4/72-2; GSL 8/72-1; IDA 8/72-1; NCA 9/72-2. (41½)
AMATEUR—CSC 9/72-1. (5)

HAPPY HOLLOW'S EL CHAMPO SA-808251 4/6/70 Ross Eggestein —By Guy's Bitterroot Lucky* (Beavercrest's Toreador - Pickrel's Ebony Babe) ex Royal Oaks September Song (Super Chief* - Shamrock Acres Whygin Tardy)
AMATEUR—MNS 9/72-3. (1)

FC HAPPY PLAY BOY SA-234174 2/26/63 Mrs. Grace Lambert — By Castlemore Shamus (Strokestown Duke of Blaircourt - Hilldown Sylver) ex Suzie (Flee Island's King Fish - Glengarven's Gay Lady)
OPEN—MIT 8/65-2; CMI 5/66-4; MIT 8/66-4; DUL 8/66-4; NDK 8/66-1; MNS 9/66-3; WOM 10/66-4; SHR 4/67-4; LAB 4/67-4; MNS 5/67-4; CMI 5/67-3; TRI 6/67-1; NDK 8/67-2; DEL 10/67-2; MNS 5/68-1; CMI 5/68-2; TRI 5/68-2; MNS 9/68-1; LIR 10/68-4; MNS 5/69-2; WIS 9/69-3; NOI 9/69-1; LIR 10/69-2; DEL 10/69-1; PTA 3/70-1; SHR 4/70-1; WCH 5/70-2; MNS 5/70-4; LIR 10/70-3; SHR 4/71-2; WOM 4/71-3; WCH 5/71-1; WOM 4/72-2; TAL 4/72-1; MAR 5/72-3; LIR 10/72-1. (95½)

FC-AFC HARANG'S GRUMPY EXPRESS SA-439268 2/18/66 Jack W. Harang—By Martens' Busy Digger (Rowdy Dow of Minyok - Ivanhoe Sally) ex Shining Jackie (Mr. Bing II - Ebony of Abbeville)
OPEN—PTA 10/69-4; NLA 10/70-3; MEM 10/70-2; MEM 4/71-1; MII 6/71-3; DUL 8/71-1. (15½)
AMATEUR—SLA 9/69-3; NLA 10/69-2; LST 10/69-2; PTA 10/69-3; ALM 10/69-1; NFL 2/70-2; ALM 2/70-4; LST 3/70-3; NLA 10/70-1; MIV 10/70-3; MTA 10/70-4; SLA 4/71-4; MEM 4/71-2; MIV 10/71-1; ATL 4/72-2; MEM 4/72-3. (36½)

HARROWBY DANDY SA-305633 9/7/64 Carl L. Ruffalo — By Lord Beaver of Cork (Cork of Oakwood Lane - Martens' Lady Jane) ex Bar-Jon Bell (Ron-Els Lickety Split - Beebee of Audlon)
OPEN—TRI 6/70-2. (3)
AMATEUR—MNS 5/69-4; MNS 9/70-4; MII 5/71-4; MNS 9/71-1; WIS 4/72-3; GOL 5/72-1; MNS 5/72-3; TRI 6/72-4; SRN 9/72-2; WIS 9/72-1. (22)

FC HARROWBY WHEELER DEALER SA-229269 7/15/63 C. S. Weyerhauser—By Duxbak Scooter* (Baker's Jerry - Carnmoney Moira) ex Bit O' Ginger (Del-Tone Colvin - Cloe of Endo Trail)
OPEN—NLA 10/67-3; MIV 10/68-2; MEM 10/68-1; MOB 11/68-3 (10)
AMATEUR—MTA 10/68-1. (5)

153

AFC HAWK HILL'S SAM OF DEVON SA-121879 9/5/61 Virginia T. Wylie—By Black Jake of Devon* (Black Nipper of Devon - Gina) ex Winds Way Bab of Houqua (Woodcroft Dusker - Winds Way Dinah)
   OPEN—BUK 9/65-2; LIR 10/66-4; WOM 4/67-4; CSC 2/68-3; LIR 4/68-4; SAM 3/70-3; DEL 10/70-2. (9½)
   AMATEUR—SHR 5/65-3; MAR 10/65-4; MAI 5/66-1; LAB (S) 11/66-3; LIR 10/67-3; LAB (S) 11/67-3; SRZ 2/68-1; CSC 2/68-4; WOL 9/68-1; MAR 10/68-2; MEM 10/68-1; LAB 11/68-2; SRZ 2/69-4; JAY 3/69-2; SHO 5/69-2; MAR 5/69-3; CNY 6/69-1; SRZ 2/70-4; NCA 3/70-2; WCH 5/70-1; COL 10/70-1; SWA 11/70-4; LAB (S) 11/70-4. (58)

FC HERMITAGE HILL DRAKE SA-317320 9/3/64 A. P. Clark — By Labcroft Timmy of Blackbrook (Nodak's Timothy - How-Hi Ginger) ex Miss Chief Cinder (Kasey Cole - Charkey)
   OPEN—WOL 5/69-3; FRR 8/69-2; WNY 9/69-3; BUK 9/69-3; MTA 3/70-2; MIC 8/70-3; AAR 8/70-4; WOL 5/71-2; FTP 5/71-3; MAD 5/72-3; GOL 5/72-4; MIC 8/72-1. (21)
   AMATEUR—BUK 4/68-2; WOL 9/68-4. (3½)

HERMITAGE HILL TIMBERDOODLE SA-494751 10/25/66 Barbara Davis—By Ace-Hi's Royal Flush (Cork of Oakwood Lane - Queen Ace) ex Wellwatt Pitch Patty's Julie (Smudge's Pitch - Canuck-Crest Bonnie)
   OPEN—BUK 9/71-4. (½)

HEY YOU OF LAKE VIEW SA-208142 5/20/63 Jack E. Hogue — By Mike of Lake View (Cork of Lucky Lake - Lassie of Lakeview II) ex Fisher's Babe (Crowder - Bigstone Ricky)
   AMATEUR—ALB 5/67-3. (1)

HIELAN HAVOC SA-234748 10/5/62 Daniel S. Barnes—By Nascopie of Highland Park (Cork of Oakwood Lane - Blyth's Queen of Spades) ex Jacona the Lark (Marian's Timothy - Lockerbie Araminta)
   AMATEUR—LAS 2/68-2; NWR 4/69-2; TAC 8/69-4; SAM 3/70-3; PUG 4/70-4. (8)

HIGH LOW JICK SA-417011 6/18/66 John A. Love, Jr.—By Tar Baby's Little Sweet Stuff (Tar Baby of Holly Hill - Debbie of Holly Hill) ex Sugar Sweet (Paha Sapa Chief II - Snow Queen)
   OPEN—CWY 8/71-3; SHE 9/72-3; PIK 8/72-4. (2½)
   AMATEUR—CWY 8/71-1; RKM 5/72-3; RKM 8/72-3; CHY 8/72-2; HEL 9/72-3. (11)

HI GO NIKI SA-200153 2/16/63 D. B. Whitson—By Del-Tone Buck* (Martens' Hi Style Buck - Glen-Water Fan Fare) ex Valgaard Lady of Shady Lane (Yankee Clipper of Reo Raj - Rock Haven's Black Angel)
   AMATEUR—MIT 8/70-1. (5)

HI-LINE KING PEPPER SA-302101 8/30/64 Harold Shidler—By Bewise Little Jeff (Paha Sapa Chief II - Shady Haven Farm Topper) ex Queen of The Valley (Glenkarnock's Busy Boy - Beavercrest's Grand Duchess)
   AMATEUR—WMO 5/29-3. (1)

HI-M's JAKE THE GIANT KILLER SA-839689 10/16/69 Michael Paterno—By Guy's Bitterroot Lucky* (Beavercrest's Toreador - Pickrel's Ebony Babe) ex Carr-Lab Spirit (Del-Tone Buck* - Miss Chief Cherokee)
   AMATEUR—MAI 9/72-1; MAR 10/72-2; DEL 10/72-3. (9)

FC HIWINDS OF SOUTH BAY SA-40398 4/11/60 August Belmont—By Hiwood John (Galleywood Swift - Hiwood Peggy) ex Merry-Go-Round Trade Winds (Cork of Oakwood Lane - Grangemead Watfor)

OPEN—NCA 3/64-1; WOM 4/64-3; 10/64-3; GSL 5/65-2; WNY 10/65-4; COL 10/65-2; LIR 10/65-3; SWA 10/65-3; LAB (S) 11/65-4; LIR 4/66-1; WOL 5/66-1; SRN 5/66-3; WNY 9/66-3; MAR 10/66-2; SCA 3/67-3; LAB 4/67-3. (33)

AMATEUR—SWA 11/63-4; TAL 3/64-3; WOM 4/64-3; WNY 9/64-4; LIR 10/64-1; SCA 3/65-1; LIR 4/65-3; NUT 5/65-3; SRN 5/65-4; WNY 9/65-2; LIR 10/65-1; SWA 11/65-2; LAB (S) 11/65-3; TAL 3/66-2; SHR 4/66-4; WNY 9/66-2; MAI 9/66-3; MAR 10/66-4; SHR 4/67-3; NUT 5/67-2; CNY 5/67-3. (40½)

FC-AFC HIWOOD STORMY OF ALASKA SA-176464 10/25/62 Roy and Josephine McFall — By Del-Tone Colvin (Cork of Oakwood Lane - Del-Tone Bridget) ex Lady of Roxanne of Muldoon (Staxigoe Stinger - Queen's Flip of Avandale)
OPEN—SAM 3/69-3; CSC 2/71-3; NCA 3/71-1; PUG 4/71-2; LAS 2/72-4. (10½)

AMATEUR—TAC 4/68-1; PUG 4/68-4; LAS 2/69-3; SCA 2/69-3; NCA 3/69-1; SAM 3/69-2; ROV 3/69-2; SRZ 2/71-3; SAM 3/71-4; ROV 4/71-1; TAC 4/71-3; ALK 8/71-4; SAM 3/72-4; ALK 8/72-3. (28)

FC-AFC HOSS OF PALM GROVE SA-237031 12/20/63 George J. Gray —By Koskinen's Dirk (Dirk of Avandale - Kromm's Penny of Skoal) ex Gal (Dee Dot's Greatford Duke - Bigstone Rebel Babe)
OPEN—GOL 5/67-2; MNS 5/67-3; MOB 11/67-2; NFL 11/67-1; NFL 2/68-1; NLA 10/68-2. (20)

AMATEUR—MNS 9/66-4; MTR 9/66-3; MOV 9/66-1; NLA 10/66-4; MTA 10/66-2; PTA 3/67-1; WIS 9/67-4; MOV 9/67-1; NFL 2/68-3; MOB 2/68-4; MNS 9/68-2; WIS 9/68-1; SLA 9/68-1; NLA 10/69-1; NFL 11/69-2; JAX 2/70-2. (46)

AFC HUCK'S PRIDE OF RIVERSIDE SA-248640 11/21/63 Robert E. Cutler—By Yankee Joe (Yankee Clipper of Reo Raj - The Contesse) ex Blue Lady (Star Chief - Miquel's Moppet)
OPEN—MII 5/69-4; MII 5/70-3; MII 5/72-3. (2½)

AMATEUR—MII 5/69-1; CMI 5/69-1; SXV 8/69-2; NOI 9/69-4; NOI 10/70-1; SXV 9/71-3; MII 5/72-2. (22½)

FC-AFC HUNDRED PROOF TAD SA-533212 7/23/67 John S. Palmore— By Dunvegan Jock (Otter O'Vyrnwy - Renegade Sioux) ex Queen of Dotken (Nilo Brackenbank Buck - Cork's Rough Shadow)
OPEN—MTA 4/71-3; FTP 6/71-4; BUK 9/713; NFL 11/71-3; FTP 6/72-1. (10½)

AMATEUR—MTA 10/70-2; NFL 11/70-2; MTA 4/71-1; BUK 4/71-2; FTP 6/71-4; OHV 10/71-4; MTA 10/71-2; MIV 4/72-1; LIT 4/72-3; FTP 6/72-3; MIV 10/72-2; MIT 10/72-3. (27)

HUNT'S NIPPER OF LITTLE SMOKY SA-478902 3/3/67 Merritt Pizitz —By Martens' Little Smoky* (Crowder - Martens' Little Bullet) ex Hunt's Charming Annabelle (Del-Tone Buck* - Jac-Lor Miss Cindy)
OPEN—MIV 10/71-3. (1)

I GO LICORICE SPLIT TO SA-406596 3/7/66 W. F. Somerhiser — By Martens' Scrubby Giant* (Crowder - Martens' Little Bullet) ex Martens' Black Tagg (Royal of Garfield - Martens' Lady Jane)
OPEN—MOV 9/69-4; CNB 9/70-3. (1½)

AMATEUR—MII 5/69-4; MOV 9/72-3. (1½)

INASHOTTE DEE CHUGGY SA-467907 7/18/66 Harold Mack Jr.— By Portneuf Valley Duke* (Spirit of Bear River - Twin Lakes Lady) ex Belle High (Butch's Bitterroot Smoky - Massie's Sassy Little Cloud)
AMATEUR—NCA 3/71-3; SRZ 2/72-3. (2)

155

Guy's Bitterroot Lucky

Happy Playboy

Hawk Hill's Sam of Devon

Invail's Cavalier Carom

FC INVAIL'S CAVALIER CAROM SA-223571 7/8/63 Mrs. C. V. Brokaw Jr.—By Ebbanee's Ricochet* (Blair's Black Victory - Ebbanee's War Dancer) ex Martens' Jumper (Cork of Oakwood Lane - Beautywood's Creole Jane)

    OPEN—GOL 5/66-1; OHV 10/66-4; NUT 5/67-3; MEM 3/68-4; TAL 3/68-2; MAN 8/68-2; FRR 8/68-3; MIC 8/68-2; NFL 2/69-4; MOB 2/69-4; LAB 4/69-3; SHO 5/69-4; CNY 5/69-2; MTA 3/70-1; WCH 5/70-1; LIR 5/70-2; CNY 5/70-2; MAN 8/70-3; SHO 9/70-2; LIR 10/70-4; SWA 11/70-1; CNY 5/71-1; LAB (S) 11/71-2; SHR 4/72-1; WOL 5/72-3; FRR 8/72-3; DEL 10/72-4; WOM 10/72-1. (68½)

INVAIL'S GUNNER SA-777023 12/22/69 Dr. H. S. Liebert, Jr. — By Shamrock Acres Gun Away* (Beautywood Rare Trouble - Marlab Gypsy) ex Tioga's Tabatha (Caliph Obsidian Hobii - Sandy's Black Mahria)

    AMATEUR—LAB (S) 11/72-4. (½)

INVAIL'S MEDICINE MAN SA-101099 5/5/62 Dr. and Mrs. D. S. Reive—By Salty of Sugar Valley (Treveilyr Swift - Zipper of Sugar Valley) ex Martens' Jumper (Cork of Oakwood Lane - Beautywood's Creole Jane)

    OPEN—WOL 9/68-1. (5)

    AMATEUR—WOL 9/65-2; WOL 5/66-4. (3½)

AFC IRWIN'S TOBY SA-167724 1/15/58 Wm. J. Hutchinson — By VanWagner's Kernel (Blyth's Ace of Spades - Saskatoon Judy) ex Kim of Brimherst (Prince Roderick of the Court - Tar'N Feather Clan)

    AMATEUR—WNY 9/63-4; NFL 2/64-3; MEM 2/64-3; BUK 4/65-3; CNY 5/65-2; WNY 9/66-1; NFL 2/67-1; MOB 2/67-2; BUK 4/67-2. (22½)

FC-AFC IVY PAT SA-205581 12/18/61 R. C. Greenleaf, M.D. — By Pepper's Jiggs (Ardyn's Ace of Merwalfin - Black Magic of Van Nola View) ex Jibodad Velvet (Rip of Holly Hill - Jibodad Gypsy)

    OPEN—PUG 8/65-4; SAM 3/66-1; PUG 8/67-3; ORE 9/67-4; SPO 9/67-1; NWR 9/68-3; SPO 9/68-2. (16)

    AMATEUR—ORE 4/65-2; PUG 8/65-4; SPO 5/66-4; WMO 5/66-2; NWR 9/66-4; ROV 3/67-2; ORE 9/68-3; SAM 3/69-4; SHA 4/69-4; SPO 5/69-2; ORE 9/69-4; PUG 8/70-4. (16½)

FC-AFC J. & L.'s SPOOKY SA-206561 6/17/63 Josephine T. Reeve—By Killand's King Cole (Fairchild's Knobby - Nodak Night Light) ex Nodak Miss Que (Nodak Black Target - Nodak Candy)

    OPEN—NEB 4/66-2; WMO 9/68-4; MON 9/69-2; PHO 10/70-1. (11½)

    AMATEUR—WMO 9/65-1; NEB 4/66-2; CNB 5/66-2; GSL 5/67-3; PTA 10/67-4; PUG 8/68-4; WMO 5/69-1; HEL 9/69-2; WMO 8/69-4; SRZ 2/70-2; GSL 5/70-2; SNA 8/70-4; SHA 9/70-3; PHO 10/70-2. (32)

JACKSON'S RIPSNORTER SA-172209 8/27/62 Dora E. Mayfield — By Spirit Lake Smokey (West Maple Joker - Dee Ann) ex Lady Charkey of Evergreen (Kasey Cole - Charkey)

    OPEN—CHY 8/64-4; MAN 8/67-2; ALB 5/69-3. (4½)

    AMATEUR—RKM 8/67-3; OHV 9/68-4; CHY 8/70-3. (2½)

JAC-LOR BLARNEY STONE SA-488174 1/27/67 Pete Roussos — By Ridgewood Playboy (La Sage's Smoky - Nelgard's Counter Point) ex Jac-Lor Miss Cindy (Manzanal Duffer - Savage Sue)

    OPEN—JAX 3/71-4; MEM 4/72-3. (1½)

    AMATEUR—MTA 4/72-3; MOB 11/72-1. (6)

JAC-LOR REBELLION SA-523788 1/27/67 Dr. John O. Ramsey — By
Ridgewood Playboy (La Sage's Smoky - Nelgard's Counter Point) ex
Jac-Lor Miss Cindy (Manzanal Duffer - Savage Sue)
    AMATEUR—PTA 3/72-4. (½)

FC JAMIE'S LITTLE TIGGER SA-374518 12/18/65 Marion H. Dailey—
By Dutchmoor's Pooh Bear (Clypso Clipper - Jet's Tammy) ex Howmor's Dark Gypsy (Marshwise Snapshooter - Topsy's Peg)
    OPEN—MNS 5/71-1; JAY 3/72-1; KAN 3/72-2; MOV 9/72-3;
    KAN 10/72-3. (15)
    AMATEUR—CNB 5/71-4. (½)

FC-AFC JET'S TARGET OF CLAYMAR SA-138869 1/14/62 Mr. and
Mrs. Byron B. Grunwald—By Stonecastle Jack (Staindrop Ringleader -
Bigstone Sugar) ex Jet Firefly of Dacity (Marshwise Snapshooter -
Jigger of Dacity)
    OPEN—KAN 10/65-1;NTX 3/66-1; MIV 4/66-3; BHB 6/66-1;
    NOI 10/66-4; MIW 10/66-4; MII 5/67-1; BHB 6/67-2; SHE
    6/67-3; PTA 3/68-4; MII 5/68-2. (29½)
    AMATEUR—PIK 5/65-2; PIK 8/65-4; NTX 10/65-2; PTA
    3/66-4; SHE 9/66-3; NOI 10/66-1; MIV 10/66-4; MAD 8/67-1;
    MIV 10/67-4; NFL 2/68-2; MTR 5/68-4. (22½)

FC-AFC JETSTONE MUSCLES OF CLAYMAR SA-133987 1/14/62
Margie D. Johnson—By Stonecastle Jack (Staindrop Ringleader - Bigstone Sugar) ex Jet Firefly of Dacity (Marshwise Snapshooter - Jigger
of Dacity)
    OPEN—RKM 8/64-4; NTX 10/64-2; NEB 4/65-2; CNB 5/65-4;
    RKM 8/65-3; MTA 9/65-3; MIW 10/65-1; JAY 3/66-4; CNB
    5/66-3; MII 5/66-1; BHB 6/66-3; JAY 3/67-4; CNB 5/67-1; RKM
    8/67-1; CHY 8/67-2; JAY 3/68-4; NEB 5/68-1; PIK 5/68-1;
    KAN 10/68-2 MIV 4/69-4; NEB 4/69-4; RKM 8/69-3; CHY
    8/69-3; MOV 9/70-2; NEB 4/71-1; BHB 6/71-4; MON 9/71-4;
    HEL 9/71-1; RKM 5/72-2. (68½)
    AMATEUR—CNB 5/64-2; CHY 8/64-3; MTR 9/64-4; NOI
    10/64-2; LST 10/64-3; NEB 4/65-3; SXV 9/65-1; RKM 9/65-2;
    CHY 8/65-4; MOV 9/65-1; NOI 10/65-2; KAN 10/65-3; JAY
    3/66-1; MIW 4/66-1; CNB 5/66-3; CHY 5/66-1; BHB 6/66-3;
    SXV 9/66-1; JAY 3/67-1; PIK 8/67-2; SXV 9/67-3; JAY 3/68-1;
    NEB 4/68-4; RKM 8/68-2; SXV 8/68-2; KAN 10/68-4; PTA
    3/69-3; NTX 3/69-1; JAY 3/69-3; KAN 3/69-4; NEB 4/69-3; RKM
    5/69-3; RKM 8/69-1; CHY 8/69-2; MOV 9/69-1; MIW 9/69-4;
    NEB 4/70-4; ALB 5/70-2; RKM 8/70-4; CHY 8/70-4; JAY 3/71-3;
    CNB 5/71-3; CHY 8/71-2. (106½)

AFC JINGO JO'S DUCKMASTER SA-234276 2/20/62 Hugh Adams—
By Duke of Erin-Go-Bra Carnmoney (Chuck of Bracken - Stonegate's
Black Cindy) ex Duckmaster Teal (Ebbanee's Ricochet* - Nodak's
Delight)
    OPEN—NCA 9/66-2; SHA 4/67-3; SNA 8/67-3; ACC 8/67-3;
    SCA 3/68-2. (9)
    AMATEUR—ROV 3/66-1; SHA 4/66-2; IDA 5/66-4; GSL
    8/66-3; IDA 8/66-1; ACC 8/66-4; CSC 9/66-4; SRZ 2/67-1; SRN
    5/67-3; RED 7/67-1; SNA 8/67-1. (31½)

JO-ANNE'S BLACK BLADE SA-417076 2/27/66 Mrs. Stephen V. Gardner
—By Castlemore Shamus (Strokestown Duke of Blaircourt - Hilldown
Sylver) ex Pelican Lake Peggy* (Castlemore Shamus - Birdie's Misty)
    OPEN—SWA 10/69-1. (5)

FC JO-DO'S JET FIRE SA-237896 2/28/63 Dr. F. O. Wright — By
Macopin Huron (Spirit Lake Duke - Beautywood's Peggydidit) ex
Sharmain's Black Ghost (Spirit Lake Duke - Dee Ann)

OPEN—PTA 3/67-4; MII 8/67-3; CNB 5/68-1; CMI 5/68-1; NDK 8/68-4; RKM 8/68-3; MII 6/69-2; MNS 9/69-2; LST 10/69-4; ALM 2/70-2; MIV 4/70-3; PIK 5/70-4; MTR 5/70-1; RKM 8/70-4; CAS 10/70-3; LST 10/70-2; ALM 11/70-3; PIK 5/71-4; RKM 5/71-2; NLA 10/71-4. (38½)

JOHN HENRY OF OAKRIDGE SA-226720 9/5/63 Mr. and Mrs. Alan Williams—By Namahbin of Oakridge (Nilo Possibility - Jet of Oakridge) ex Grace-Art's Bouncing Baby (Nascopie Dark Destroyer - Grace-Art's Classy Boots)
AMATEUR—MEM 10/67-4; AAR 5/68-4. (1)

JOHN'S SPIKE SA-397129 1/28/65 Glen Stewart—By Paha Sapa Chief II (Freehaven Muscles - Treasure State Be Wise) ex Regina Di Campi* (Marshwise Snapshooter - Stormy Cindy)
OPEN—BHB 6/69-4; EID 7/69-3; PTA 3/71-2. (4½)

FC JOLOR'S COMPOBASSO SA-179840 3/3/62 Mrs. Geo. Murname— By Mark Chidley Swift (Solo of Poverty Gulch - Inky's Harbor Lassie) ex Mark's Mate of Jolor (Chidley Bounder - Tracy's Chidley Dot)
OPEN—LIR 4/65-1; WOM 4/65-3; MEM 3/66-1; MAI 9/66-4; DEL 10/67-1. (16½)

JONES' DADDY WAGS SA-284331 3/12/64 C. W. Tyler—By Sad Sam Jones* (Mister Jones of Niskayuna - Flicker of Timber Town) ex Honor of Clitheroe (Chipsdale Early Win - Black Stomper)
AMATEUR—BUK 4/69-3. (1)

FC-AFC JOY'S COAL DUST S-904776 7/6/57 Jack Gardner—By Ace of Balboa (Pan of Podington - Queen of Balboa) ex Smokey Flame (Slo Poke Smokey of Dairy Hill - Dairy Hill's Flame's Fury)
OPEN—NCA 9/60-4; CSC 9/60-3; SLC 5/61-4; NCA 9/61-2; RED 7/62-4; ACC 8/62-2; NCA 9/62-3; SCA 9/62-3; CSC 9/62-4; SAG 3/63-2; ROV 3/63-1; SHE 6/63-2; IDA 8/64-1; SAG 9/64-2; NCA 3/65-2; SAG 9/65-4. (33½)
AMATEUR—LAS 2/60-4; RED 7/60-4; SAG 9/60-1; RED 7/61-3; SAG 9/61-3; CSC 2/62-4; ROV 3/62-1; SHA 9/62-3; CSC 9/62-2; NCA 3/63-3; ACC 8/63-1; SCA 2/64-4; SRN 5/64-1; LAS 10/64-2; NCA 3/65-2; SAG 3/65-4; ROV 3/65-2; SAG 7/65-1; NCA 3/66-2; ALB 5/67-4. (49)

J'S BIG WATER BUCK SA-145521 12/15/61 John L. Fredrickson—By Royal of Garfield (Roy's Rowdy - Pierre's Kit of Garfield) ex Martens' Lady Jane (Jet Black Sin - Beautywood's Creole Jane)
AMATEUR—DUL 8/67-4; DUL 8/68-4; MNS 9/69-2. (4)
FC-AFC JUPITER'S HI-LAUREL SA-166518 8/14/62 Cliff Tennant — By Jupiter of Stony Knoll (Marian's Timothy - Beautywood's Lady Fair) ex Smith's Cindy Lou (Black Prince XIII - Lake Desire Queen)
OPEN—ORE 9/66-4; ORE 3/67-2; WIL 8/67-3; PUG 8/67-2; SPO 9/67-4; ROV 3/68-3; TAC 4/68-2; WIL 8/68-2; ORE 9/68-3; SPO 9/68-1; LAS 2/69-1; ROV 3/69-4; TAC 8/69-1; IDA 8/69-2; TAC 8/70-3; SAM 9/70-3. (36½)
AMATEUR—TAC 4/66-2; TAC 8/66-4; ORE 9/66-4; SAM 3/67-3; PUG 4/67-3; WIL 8/67-1; NWR 9/67-1; ORE 3/68-1; TAC 4/68-3; IDA 5/68-2; WIL 8/68-3; NWR 9/68-1; ORE 9/68-1; SPO 9/68-2; LAS 2/69-2; ROV 3/69-3; IDA 8/69-2; NWR 9/69-2; NWR 4/70-4; GOL 5/70-2; TAC 4/71-4. (53)

JUST SAMSON SA-459726 3/6/66 Mrs. Albert P. Loening—By Shamrock Acres Gun Away* (Beautywood Rare Trouble - Marlab Gypsy) ex Personality Plus (Greatford Glenfarg Bragg - West Island Cleopatra)
OPEN—WOL 5/68-2. (3)

FC-AFC KEG OF BLACK POWDER SA-121307 3/29/61 James Culbertson—By Wasatch Renegade (Paha Sapa Chief II - Shady Shawnee) ex Uneva Drake's Lucky Lady (Uneva Drake - Lisnamallard Clodogh)
OPEN—PIK 5/65-1; CHY 5/65-2; ALB 5/67-2. (11)
AMATEUR—NTX 3/65-1; CHY 5/65-4; DUL 6/65-2; PIK 8/65-3; NTX 3/66-2; KAN 4/66-2; JAY 3/67-3. (16½)

KENNON'S JOCKEAUX SA-362721 (11/30/65) Bob Kennon, Jr.—By Jetstone Muscles of Claymar* (Stonecastle Jack - Jet Firefly of Dacity) ex Lady's Pie Doe (Dutchmoor's Etaoin Shrdlu - Lady B. Good II)
AMATEUR—PTA 10/69-4. (½)

KENTUCKIAN SA-303114 7/6/64 R. C. Greenleaf, M.D.—By Kellog's Cork of Lost River (Kellogg's Nick - Bigstone Belle Boji) ex Mac's Black Dawn (Techako's Ranger - B. I.'s Ginger Girl)
OPEN—WMO 5/69-4. (½)
AMATEUR—TAC 4/69-1; NWR 4/69-4. (5½)

AFC KIM O'SAGE SA-75689 10/24/60 M. R. Flannery — By Avalanche Burnt Sage (Satan III - Constant Winner of Avalanche) ex Hull's Oma (Bingo Again - Bigstone Dinah Girl)
OPEN—MNS 9/66-4; GOL 5/67-4; MNS 5/68-2. (4)
AMATEUR—LIR 4/64-3; CNY 5/64-1; MEM 10/64-1; SLA 5/65-1; MAD 8/65-3; AAR 9/65-3; OHV 9/66-3; MOB 11/66-2; MTA 3/67-3; MAD 5/67-3; AAR 5/67-2; MAN 8/67-2; BUK 9/67-3; MOB 11/67-4. (31½)

FC KING COLE OF MENOMIN S-1963619 5/20/58 Daniel C. Searle—By Black Gum Gus (Stonegate's Captain - Little Peggy Black Gum) ex Rushmore's Black Shaw (Jet Black Sin - Beautywood's Creole Jane)
OPEN—MIW 4/62-1: AAR 5/62-4; MAN 8/62-1; AAR 8/63-2; MNS 9/63-4; MIV 10/63-1; MTA 3/68-4. (19½)

KING KONG II SA-317329 11/27/64 Lyle Knight — By Nodrog Nike* (Mainliner Mike - Beautywood Rebel Queen) ex Walt's Honey Bee (Willie M - Crowder's Black Sal)
AMATEUR—CMI 5/72-4. (½)

AFC KING TUT V SA-292522 9/17/64 Glenn P. Scheihing — By Pepper's Jiggs (Ardyn's Ace of Merwalfin - Black Magic of Van Nola View) ex Random Shot (Alpine Cherokee Rocket - Freeze Out Flat's Black Jewel)
OPEN—MON 5/68-4; MON 9/68-3; WMO 9/68-2; SNA 5/69-4. (5)
AMATEUR—SHE 8/68-2; MON 9/68-3; WMO 9/68-1; CNB 5/69-1; BHB 6/69-3; MON 8/69-3; MON 6/70-1; HEL 9/70-3; WMO 9/70-3; CNB 5/71-1; SHE 9/71-1; MON 9/71-1; BHB 6/72-2. (41)

KNIGHT TRAIN SA-330216 8/28/64 S. F. Frye—By Bo Jet II (Pepper's Jiggs - Pepper's Maggie) ex LaChatelaine De La Meute (Styx du Lac Pons - Lady Tork of Medo)
OPEN—TAC 8/69-3; NWR 4/70-4. (1½)
AMATEUR—SAM 3/68-3. (1)

KNOTS SA-600372 2/2/68 Amelia L. and C. B. Pierson, Jr.—By Black Point of Avandale (Black Point Black Decoy - Black Brenda of Avandale) ex Camelot (Dutchmoor's Black Mood - Sassafras of Rodinary Point)
AMATEUR—LAB (S) 11/72-2. (3)

KOOTENAI BUCK SA-642789 10/26/68 L. J. Carrier — By Winter's Shadow (Irene's Blackie - Irene's Lady) ex Garnet of Coeur D'Alene (Gold Kebo - Marg O'Coeur D'Alene)
AMATEUR—WMO 5/72-3. (1)

KOSKINEN'S PYEWACKET SA-885830 1/6/70 Ray Koskinen — By Koskinen's Geronimo (Koskinen's Colonel - Rangewise Li'l Tuff) ex Gun Thunder's Shadee Ladee (Gun Thunder Oly* - Grady's Shadee Ladee*)
OPEN—WMO 9/72-1. (5)

KRACKEN OF TIMBER TOWN SA-375816 10/22/65 Kenneth Krueger —By Duxbak Scooter* (Baker's Jerry - Carnmoney Moira) ex Dinah of the Reward (Attawan Pucka Sahib - Jet of the Reward)
OPEN—CWY 8/70-3. (1)
AMATEUR—LAB (S) 11/71-2. (3)

LAD CROWDER'S RANGER SA-367617 5/8/65 Mrs. B. A. Richardson —By Bigstone Crowder's Cap (Crowder - Bigstone Goldie) ex Cimaroc Lady Jean (Nodak Boots - Hull's Oma)
OPEN—MON 9/68-4; NTX 10/68-2; NFL 11/68-1. (8½)

AFC LADY'S BRAZOS PETE SA-370441 1/19/66 Richard A. Cook—By Nicholas of the Navasot (Robbet's Black Hope - Cuzz's Corky) ex Mark's Koko Lady (Huckster's Little Black Sambo - Andy's Black Cinderella)
OPEN—NTX 3/70-3. (1)
AMATEUR—NTX 10/69-3; KAN 4/70-2; KAN 10/70-3; SOO 4/72-1; CNB 5/72-1. (15)

AFC LAKELAND TIGER OF BRUCE SA-393093 8/14/65 E. M. Cohn —By Peppi of Lakewood (Del-Tone Buck* - Lakewood's Resolution) ex Shady Dutchess of Duluth (Bingo of Glendale - Queenie of Rose Lake)
OPEN—NDK 8/68-1. (5)
AMATEUR—MNS 5/68-1; MNS 9/68-4; MNS 9/69-4; MNS 5/70-4; MNS 9/70-1. (11½)

FC LAKENHAM PAHA SUN DANCE SA-18444 10/14/61 Walter Candy III—By Paha Sapa Chief II (Freehaven Muscles - Treasure State Be Wise) ex Eby of Beaver Creek (Cork of Oakwood Lane - Martens' Little Bullet)
OPEN—CSC 10/65-1; CSC 9/67-4; ROV 3/68-2; BHB 6/68-3; GOL 7/68-4. (10)
AMATEUR—SRN 5/66-2. (3)

LAKESHORE COWIE SA-542211 8/21/66 Max Holman—By Del-Tone Buck* (Martens' Hi Style Buck - Glen-Water Fan Fare) ex Lakeshore Jody (Nodak Boots - Bill's Black Beauty)
OPEN—RKM 5/70-2. (3)

LAKESIDE DEAN'S SHADOW SA-202783 6/15/63 Dr. Alfred Schultz —By Pomme De Terre Pete (Cork of Oakwood Lane - Del-Tone Lass) ex Glen's Lady of the Mountains (Balla Machree Smokey - Lloyd's Park Avenue Lady)
AMATEUR—SLA 3/68-4; LIT 4/71-4. (1)

LAND-O-LAKES SUNBURST SA-342451 2/1/62 Hugh McInnis—By Sir Buck of Belle Isle (Rex of the Ridge II - Honey of Belle Isle) ex Millham Mist (Dusty of Hamdere - Sheila of Carlisle)
OPEN—NLA 3/69-3. (1)
AMATEUR—MEM 2/69-3; MIV 4/69-2; MEM 10/69-4; MOB 10/69-3; NFL 11/69-3; SLA 2/70-2; MIV 5/70-2; ATL 5/70-2; NTX 11/70-3. (16½)

FC LARRY'S LASSER SA-345068 4/20/65 Gale M. and Noreen Roberts —By Ripco's Western Blend (Ripco's Peter Pan - Peppy of Lopez) ex Morgan's Anne (Pepper's Jiggs - Carr-Lab Pride)

OPEN—ORE 3/69-3;ROV 3/70-2; NWR 4/70-3; GOL 5/70-1; SAG 7/70-2; NWR 9/70-2; ORE 4/71-2; SHA 4/71-1; WIL 8/71-1; WMO 9/71-1; TAC 4/72-1; NWR 4/72-1; WMO 5/72-1.   (44½)

FC LASSER'S CAPTAIN HOOK SA-582404 3/16/68 Dr. Wm. D. Swancutt—By Larry's Lasser* (Ripco's Western Blend - Morgan's Anne) ex Ripco's Lady Jo (Ripco's Peter Pan - Agraselda of Creek Road)
OPEN—WMO 5/70-3; TAC 8/70-2; MON 5/71-4; RED 7/71-3; IDA 8/71-3; BHB 6/72-3; SAG 7/72-1; TAC 8/72-3.   (15½)
AMATEUR—WIL 8/71-2; SAG 3/72-3.   (4)

LEROY III SA-797218 8/30/69 C. R. Tobin — By Techako's Ranger (Massie's Sassy Boots - Nodak Tar Pride) ex Michelle* (Black Mike of Lakewood - Kemper's Sassy Sue)
OPEN—WIL 8/72-3; KAN 10/72-2.   (9)

LINCOLN OF BEL AIR SA-559157 5/20/67 Richard Reeve—By Jetstone Muscles of Claymar* (Stone Castle Jack - Jet Firefly of Dacity) ex Iowa Black Nipper (Kewanee's Swamp Buster - Dakota Black Shirley)
AMATEUR—SNA 5/72-4; SNA 8/72-4.   (1)

FC-AFC LORD BOMAR SA-73516 1/6/61 John A. Love, Jr. — By Blackfoot's Happy New Year (Navajo Tar of Sunnymede - Navajo Corky of Bigstone) ex Peg's Blackfoot Queen (Sambo of Somonauk II - Benson's Black Patu)
OPEN—WMO 5/65-4; NTX 10/65-2; LST 10/65-2; ALM 11/65-1; MIW 4/66-3; GSL 5/66-1; CHY 5/66-4; WMO 5/66-1; SHE 9/66-1; HEL 9/66-3; MTR 9/66-2; MOV 9/66-1; KAN 10/66-2; KAN 3/67-3; PIK 5/67-3; WMO 5/67-4; MAD 8/67-2; MAN 8/67-1; RKM 8/67-3; CHY 8/67-3; MON 9/67-2; HEL 9/67-4; WMO 9/67-1; MIV 10/67-3; GSL 5/68-2; WMO 5/68-2; BHB 6/68-2; SHE 6/68-3; EID 7/68-1; GSL 8/68-4; SHE 8/68-2; HEL 9/68-1; MON 5/69-2; GSL 8/68-1; SHE 8/69-1.   (98½)
AMATEUR—WMO 5/64-1; WMO 5/65-1; MON 9/65-4; SHE 6/66-3; PIK 8/66-1; MTR 9/66-2; ALB 5/67-2; MTR 5/67-2; MON 6/67-1; SHE 9/67-2; MON 9/67-3; MON 5/68-1; BHB 6/68-1; SHE 6/68-3; RKM 8/68-4; CHY 8/68-3; MON 9/68-4; MON 5/69-1; BHB 6/69-1; CHY 8/69-1; SHE 8/69-3; MON 9/69-1; HEL 9/69-1; MON 6/70-4; BHB 6/70-4.   (74½)

LUCKY'S BITTERROOT SHASTA SA-638135 7/26/68 L. J. Miller and Dr. Wm. Weirich—By Guy's Bitterroot Lucky* (Beavercrest Toreador - Pickrel's Ebony Babe) ex Miss Tehama Tar (Silver Duke - Miss Conception)
OPEN—WMO 5/71-2; PUG 8/72-3; PHO 10/72-4.   (4½)
AMATEUR—ORE 9/72-4.   (½)

LUCKY'S SHAST BEAU SA-858483 11/23/69 Peter F. Lane—By Guy's Bitterroot Lucky* (Beavercrest's Toreador - Pickrel's Ebony Babe) ex Miss Tehama Tar (Silver Duke - Miss Conception)
AMATEUR—GSL 8/72-4.   (½)

LUKE OF PATTY JIMSUE SA-546968 8/16/67 Glen Madsen — By Bair's Black Sambo (Hap - Swinomish Lady Teena) ex Patty JimSue (Ripco's Peter Pan - Mollie Muldoon)
OPEN—TAC 8/71-2.   (3)

LULAKE'S RICKIE SA-439800 5/1/66 James E. Rentz — By Geechee* (Ridgewood Playboy - Grace-Art's Smart Lady) ex Jumper of Spring Valley (Nodak Boots - Glen-Water Fan Fare)
OPEN—MOB 2/70-2; NFL 11/72-4.   (3½)
AMATEUR—NFL 11/70-3; NFL 11/71-3.   (2)

FC-AFC MACKENZIE'S RIPCO MAC SA-77461 4/24/60 Mrs. Dean
Parker—By Ripco's Peter Pan (Rip of Holly Hill - Whitmores Rowdy
Lady) ex Black Queen IX (Breckonhill Ben - Jeepers of Woldgate)
OPEN—TAC 4/63-3; SAM 9/63-2; TAC 4/64-4; PUG 8/64-1;
SAM 9/64-3; WMO 9/64-2; SPO 5/65-4; SAM 3/66-4; PUG
4/67-4; NWR 4/67-4; NWR 9/67-1. (20½)
AMATEUR—SPO 9/62-3; ORE 3/63-4; PUG 4/63-1; TAC
4/63-2; NWR 4/63-3; NWR 9/63-4; SAM 3/64-4; IDA 8/64-4;
WIL 8/64-2; NWR 4/66-1; TAC 8/67-3; NWR 9/67-3. (22)

AFC-FC MACKENZIE'S RIPCO TAR SA-133119 4/6/61 Joan H.
Shoemaker—By Ripco's Peter Pan (Rip of Holly Hill - Whitmore's
Rowdy Lady) ex Misty Gem (Hiwood Peat - Cosmic Gem)
OPEN—SAM 3/64-1; SPO 5/64-4; WMO 9/64-1; NWR 9/65-3;
PUG 4/66-3; NWR 9/66-4; ORE 9/66-3; TAC 4/67-4; SAM
9/67-3. (15½)
AMATEUR—NCA 3/64-1; SAM 3/64-3; NWR 4/64-2; NWR
9/64-2; SAM 3/65-3; TAC 4/65-1; ORE 9/65-4; IDA 8/66-4. (19)

FC-AFC MAGIC MARKER OF TIMBER TOWN SA-523713 10/26/67
Marshall Simonds—By Chief Black Feather* (Paha Sapa Chief II -
Ironwood Cherokee Chica) ex Canuck-Crest Tami O'Churchlee
(Beautywood's Carbon Copy - Twink of Belle Isle)
OPEN—JAM 3/71-2; LAB 4/71-4; LAB (S) 11/71-1; JAM
3/72-4; WOM 4/72-3; COL 9/72-1; LIR 10/72-4; WOM 10/72-3. (16½)
AMATEUR—WOM 10/70-1; JAM 3/71-3; LIR 5/71-3; CNY
5/71-4; SHO 9/71-4; WOM 10/71-4; LAB (S) 11/71-1; JAM
3/72-1; SHR 4/72-2; LIR 5/72-3; MAI 9/72-3. (23½)

AFC MALLARD OF DEVIL'S GARDEN S-964100 11/4/58 Richard H.
Johnson—By Bingo Again (Rip's Bingo - Shady Lady IV) ex Ottertail
Penny (Sparky of Minnesota - Cindy of Ottertail)
OPEN—NFL 2/64-4; NFL 2/67-1; NFL 11/67-2. (8½)
AMATEUR—COL 9/61-1; MEM 10/61-2; MOB 2/62-1; COL
9/62-4; MEM 10/62-1; NTX 3/63-3; NFL 2/62-2; MOB 2/64-1;
TAL 3/64-4; NFL 2/65-3; MOB 11/67-2; NFL 11/68-3. (33)

FC-AFC MARELVAN MIKE OF TWIN OAKS SA-209663 4/2/63 John
F. Nash—By Blyth's Black Joe of Marel Van (Blyth's Ace of Spades -
Blyth's Imp) ex Neb's Deb (La Sage's Neb - Belle Isle's Wendy)
OPEN—FRR 8/67-2; MIV 4/68-2; WNY 9/68-2; OHV 9/68-4;
MTA 10/68-2; OHV 9/69-1; MTA 10/69-4; MEM 10/69-3;
WIS 5/70-1; WOL 9/70-2. (28)
AMATEUR—WOL 5/67-2; CNY 5/67-1; FRR 8/67-2; MUK
9/67-1; MIV 4/68-1; WOL 5/68-1; CNY 5/68-1; FTP 5/68-1;
WNY 9/68-2; BUK 9/68-2; OHV 9/68-1; BUK 9/69-2; OHV
9/69-3; MIW 10/69-1; BUK 4/70-2; CNY 5/70-1; BUK 9/70-4;
WOL 9/70-1; BUK 4/71-4. (70)

MARK V SA-222028 7/14/63 J. D. Ott—By Man of Night (Butchboy -
Ruth of Avandale) ex Dixie Bell (Tug-O'Mike - Mother Fletcher's
Black Lady)
OPEN—SPO 5/65-2; SAM 3/67-3; ORE 9/67-3. (5)

MARK DUCK'S DAGO SA-138019 4/1/61 Carl L. Ruffalo—By Mark
Duck's My Spud (Jet Black Sin - Peggy of Gervais) ex Shirley's Bea
(Black Bruin of the Corkies - Cleo's Petrovich)
AMATEUR—MAD 5/66-4; DUL 8/67-2; NOI 9/67-3. (4½)

MARK OF GLOSTER SA-149449 6/7/62 John Ramsey—By Medlin's
Cork of Grapevine (Cork of Oakwood Lane - Martens' Little Bullet)
ex Pat's Error Mitzie (Staindrop Ringleader - Nilo Jewel)
AMATEUR—NTX 10/67-4; ALM 11/67-3; ALM 2/69-2. (4½)

163

Jetstone Muscles of Claymar

Lord Bomar

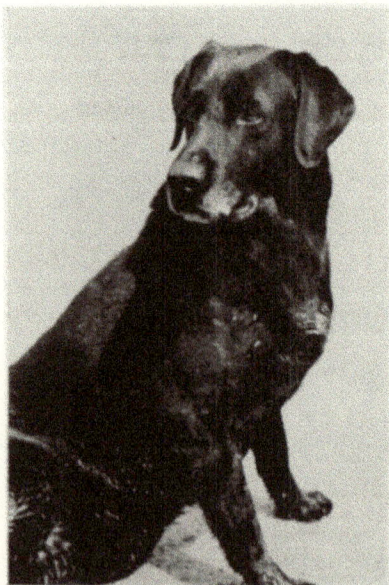

Marelvan Mike of Twin Oaks

Martens' Little Smoky

FC-AFC MARTENS' CASTAWAY SA-529236 9/20/67 Philip R. Fitzgerald
—By My Rebel* (Yankee Clipper of Reo Raj - Duchess of Miller's
Haven) ex Martens' Little Susie (Martens' Mister Nifty* - Martens'
Black Doll)
    OPEN—JAY 3/71-1; MII 5/71-2; MNS 5/71-2; SXV 9/71-2;
    CNB 5/72-3; DUL 8/72-1.   (20)
    AMATEUR—MOV 9/70-1; CMN 5/71-4; MIT 8/71-1; DUL
    8/71-1; NDK 8/71-2; SXV 9/71-1; NEB 4/72-3; MII 5/72-3;
    MNS 5/72-2; CMI 5/72-1; MIT 8/72-1; DUL 8/72-3; MNS
    9/72-1.   (44½)

NRFC '65 MARTENS' LITTLE SMOKY S-986861 3/4/59 John M. Olin
—By Crowder (Cork of Oakwood Lane - Beautywood's Creole Jane)
ex Martens' Little Bullet (Jet Black Sin - Radde's Neenah of Crow
Wing)
    OPEN—MEM 10/63-3; MNS 5/64-4; WMT 6/64-1; DUL 8/64-2;
    WIS 9/64-2; MIW 10/64-1; MEM 10/64-1; NFL 2/65-2; MOB
    2/65-2; MAD 5/65-3; AAR 5/65-4; AAR 9/65-1; MOV 9/65-4;
    OHV 10/65-3; MTA 10/65-2; MEM 10/65-1; NST 11/65-1; KAN
    10/66-4; MEM 10/66-3; NFL 2/67-3; MIV 4/67-1; WIS 4/67-2;
    WOL 9/67-2; KAN 10/67-4; MEM 10/67-2 MIV 4/68-3; WIS
    4/68-3; MAD 5/68-4; AAR 8/68-3; WOL 9/68-3.   (69)

MARTENS' MISTER LUCKY SA-228764 8/20/63 H. C. Eby — By
Martens' Mister Nifty* (Royal of Garfield - Martens' Black Badger) ex
Martens' Black Doll (Crowder - Martens' Little Bullet)
    OPEN—CSC 10/70-2.   (3)
    AMATEUR—GSL 5/68-3.   (1)

FC MARTENS' MISTER NIFTY SA-51087 8/1/59 Lawrence Martens—
By Royal of Garfield (Roy's Rowdy - Pierre's Kit of Garfield) ex
Martens' Black Badger (Cork of Oakwood Lane - Martens' Little Bullet)

    OPEN—MIT 8/62-4; MIT 8/63-1; DUL 8/63-3; MOV 9/63-2;
    MIT 8/64-4; DUL 8/64-3; MII 5/65-1; MNS 5/65-4; NDK
    8/65-2; MOV 9/65-1; MIT 8/66-1; NOI 10/66-3; MAD 5/67-2;
    MII 5/67-4; CMI 5/67-4; MIT 8/67-2; NDK 8/67-4.   (38)

MARTENS' MISTER STUBBS SA-608577 2/8/68 Gary Ahlgren—By
Martens' Scrubby Giant* (Crowder - Martens' Little Bullet) ex Pelican
Lake Biddy (Castlemore Shamus - Birdie's Misty)
    AMATEUR—CMI 5/71-3.   (1)

MAR-TEN'S MONEYMAKER SA-476449 9/30/66 Charles Hays — By
Dajo's Black Velvet (Royal of Garfield - Martens' Lady Jane) ex
Duchess of Rock (Yankee Clipper of Reo Raj - Queen Liz of Reo Raj)
    AMATEUR—SXV 9/70-3.   (1)

FC MARTENS' SCRUBBY GIANT SA-119789 5/19/60 Lawrence Martens
—By Crowder (Cork of Oakwood Lane - Beautywood's Creole Jane)
ex Martens' Little Bullet (Jet Black Sin - Radde's Neenah of Crow Wing)
    OPEN—SUP 6/65-2; NDK 8/65-1; MIT 8/67-1; MNS 9/67-1;
    MNS 5/68-4.   (18½)

FC MARTENS' STORMY SA-109039 9/1/59 John M. Olin—By Royal
of Garfield (Roy's Rowdy- Pierre's Kit of Garfield) ex Martens' Black
Badger (Cork of Oakood Lane - Martens' Little Bullet)
    OPEN—MAD 5/64-3; MEM 3/65-2; KAN 4/65-3; MAD 5/65-4;
    WOL 5/65-2; AAR 5/65-3; WIS 9/65-3; MTA 10/65-1; MEM
    10/65-1; MIV 4/66-2; AAR 5/66-1; WIS 9/66-2; MEM 10/66-4;
    MOB 2/67-1; MTA 3/67-4; NEB 4/67-1; OHV 9/67-4.   (43)

MARTIN'S SCOKIM SA-301700 12/28/63 Charles Martin—By Stan's
Licorice Ladd (Beavercrest Dirk - Cindy of Valentine) ex Tarb of
Argyll (Tarblood of Absaraka* - Cricket of Prophy-Cup)
    OPEN—SHE 6/68-2; SHE 8/68-3.   (4)

MASAI OF ABERDEEN SA-418810 2/17/66 Cliff Tennant—By Pepper's Jiggs (Ardyn's Ace of Merwalfin - Black Magic of Van Nola View) ex Sheena V (Ebbanee's Ricochet* - Exploiter Lady)
AMATEUR—TAC 4/72-4; NWR 4/72-4; SHA 4/72-2. (4)

FC MEDLIN'S OTTO OF TOOTHACRES SA-185383 10/7/62 C. Thurman Clem, D.D.S.—By Medlin's Cork of Grapevine (Cork of Oakwood Lane - Martens' Little Bullet) ex Medlin's Cricket (King Buck - Duchess Suzana)
OPEN—NLA 10/66-1; ALB 5/67-3; GSL 5/67-1; SHE 9/67-4; PTA 10/67-3. (12½)
AMATEUR—NLA 10/67-4. (½)

FC MEDLIN'S TEXAS RUFF SA-71978 9/25/60 K. Rufus Deskins—By Medlin's Cork of Grapevine (Cork of Oakwood Lane- Martens' Little Bullet) ex Medlin's Cricket (King Buck - Duchess Suzana)
OPEN—MON 9/64-3; NLA 10/64-4; LST 10/64-2; ALM 11/64-1; ALM 11/66-4. (10)
AMATEUR—NLA 10/63-3; NTX 10/63-3; NTX 10/64-1; NTX 3/69-3. (8)

MEDLIN'S TEXAS TROOPER SA-118531 10/1/61 Dr. and Mrs. Roy Brinkman—By Medlin's Cork of Grapevine (Cork of Oakwood Lane - Martens' Little Bullet) ex Medlin's Cricket (King Buck - Duchess Suzana)
OPEN—PTA 3/67-3. (1)

FC MEDLIN'S TINY BOOM SA-151315 10/1/61 Fred Buxton and Radford Byerly—By Medlin's Cork of Grapevine (Cork of Oakwood Lane - Martens' Little Bullet) ex Medlin's Cricket (King Buck - Duchess Suzana)
OPEN—ALM 11/64-4; NLA 3/66-1; PIK 4/66-1; GSL 8/66-3; ALM 2/67-3; NFL 11/68-2. (15½)
AMATEUR—LST 10/65-3; NTX 3/67-3; NLA 3/67-4. (2½)

METO OF DEVIL'S GARDEN SA-118444 11/8/61 R. H. Johnson—By Mallard of Devil's Garden* (Bingo Again - Ottertail Penny) ex Bay City Katie Jane (Cork of Oakwood Lane - Bigstone Breeze)
OPEN—NFL 11/68-4. (½)
AMATEUR—TAL 3/67-3; MOB 11/67-3; NFL 11/68-1. (7)

MI-CRIS DRAMBUIE CKC 592688 12/12/63 Barry Clute—By Highlander's Bojangles (Salty of Sugar Valley - Highlander's Diana) ex Twink of Belle Isle (Yankee Clipper of Reo Raj - Fallwood's Lucky Lady)
AMATEUR—FRR 8/69-1; WIS 4/71-2; MAD 5/71-3. (9)

NRFC '71 MI-CRIS SAILOR SA-470951 8/8/66 Mrs. George Murnane —By Highlander's Bojangles (Salty of Sugar Valley - Highlander's Diana) ex Mi-Cris Black Lady (Ace-Hi Crusader - Skeet of Crevamoy)
OPEN—MAI 9/68-2; WOM 10/68-1; SCA 2/69-2; NCA 3/69-2; SHR 4/69-1; WOM 4/69-2; SHO 5/69-2; MAR 5/69-1; LIR 5/69-4; CNY 5/69-4; MAD 8/70-3; NDK 8/70-3; WOL 9/70-4; MOB 11/70-1; JAX 3/71-1; CHY 8/71-2; MAI 9/71-2; LIR 10/71-1; NAT 11/71-1; JAM 3/72-1; MAR 5/72-1; MIT 8/72-1; NDK 8/72-1. (79½)

MIKE OF BURRVIEW ACRES SA-786465 3/31/69 John M. Olin—By Burnham's Ex (Happy Playboy* - Splash of Frontier) ex Suzie Q (Nibs III - Maggie L.)
OPEN—MIV 10/72-4. (½)

MIDNIGHT IN THE BIGHORNS SA-29757 2/15/60 Jack S. Gourley— By Black Flash of Hellgate (Samson of Avandale - Claire of Avandale) ex Princess Pat X (Quinlan's Black King - Queen V)
AMATEUR—BHB 6/67-1; HEL 9/67-4. (5½)

FC MINOT'S MAGIC MARKER SA-356251 9/30/65 Mr. L. J. Campbell
—By Duxbak Scooter* (Baker's Jerry - Carnmoney Moira) ex Random
Shot (Alpine Cherokee Rocket - Freeze Out Flats' Black Jewel)
OPEN—DEL 3/70-3; DEL 10/70-4; LAB (S) 11/70-4; MAR
10/71-1; WOM 10/71-4; ATL 4/72-2. (10½)

MISS JAN'S DOBIE SA-188381 2/27/62 John W. Mecom, Jr.—By Bob
of Random Lake II (The Black Mambo of Kingswere - Cream City
Clipper) ex Montana Sue (George Lowball Poker - Miss Flukum)
OPEN—NLA 10/64-2; NTX 3/66-3; SHE 9/67-3; PTA 10/67-4;
ALB 5/68-3. (6½)

FC-AFC MITCH OF BITTERROOT SA-310647 8/12/64 Carl F. Allen—
By Beavercrest Toreador (Sentinel of Whitmore - Semloh's Peggy) ex
Pickrel's Ebony Babe (Teddy Carbon Copy - Invail's Salty's Thyme)
OPEN—WMO 9/68-3; TAC 4/69-3; IDA 5/69-4; WMO 5/69-1;
MIL 6/69-4; WMO 9/69-2; WMO 9/70-3; ORE 3/72-2; SPO
9/72-3. (16)
AMATEUR—TAC 8/68-1; WMO 9/68-2; IDA 5/69-3; SPO
5/69-1; WMO 5/69-4; TAC 8/69-1; NWR 8/69-4; WMO 9/69-2;
SPO 9/69-3; IDA 5/70-2; SPO 5/70-1; WMO 5/70-2; TAC
8/70-2; WMO 9/70-1; SPO 10/70-1; WMO 5/72-2. (51)

MITCH'S DANDY BOUNCER SA-541526 12/7/67 Dr. Samuel F. Mazella
—By Mitch of Bitterroot* (Beavercrest's Toreador - Pickrel's Ebony
Babe) ex Sills' Little Smokey Lewbonnie (Martens' Little Smoky -
Hunt's Charming Annabelle)
OPEN—NFL 3/72-3; SHR 4/72-4; CNY 5/72-3. (2½)

FC MOBY DICK SA-471823 4/19/66 Carnation Farm Kennels — By
Stillwaters Royal Rick (Carr-Lab Hilltop - Stillwaters Lady Jeep)
ex Navajo Toni of Sunnymede (Navajo Tar of Sunnymede Navajo
Corkey of Bigstone)
OPEN—GSL 5/69-3; ORE 9/70-1; ORE 4/71-3; TAC 4/71-2;
IDA 5/71-4; WMO 5/71-1; ROV 3/72-4. (16)

FC-AFC MOLYBRU BUTCH OF BARMOND SA-515776 2/26/65 Rudy
R. Deering — By Pee Cee Dee Rowdy of Bardonda (Topper of
Granton - Green Timber's Jo) ex Syldonnell's Dixie (Craigend Rock -
Country Club's Little Bullet)
OPEN—SAM 3/70-1; SAM 9/70-1; SAM 3/71-2; TAC 4/71-3;
NWR 9/71-2; TAC 4/72-4. (17½)
AMATEUR—NWR 9/67-2; PUG 4/70-1; NWR 4/72-3. (9)

MOON ROCKET OF ZENITH SA-710568 5/6/69 W. E. and Joy Bowen
—By Rocky Road of Zenith* (Black Mike of Lakewood - Jezebel of
Normandy) ex Black Bunny of Lakewood (Ridgewood Playboy-Grady's
Shadee Ladee*)
OPEN—MTA 10/72-1. (5)

MONDOR'S JET SA-119840 7/13/61 Ernest B. Mondor—By Lile Nick of
Brignall (Brignall's Nick - Brignall's Waaf) ex Black Duchess of Palm
Desert (Big Oaks' Black Rip - Big Oak's Black Trouble)
AMATEUR—SCA 9/64-4; SRZ 2/67-2; SCA 3/68-3. (4½)

FC-AFC MONSTER MIKE SA-304816 12/7/64 Ben Mitchel, M.D.—By
Ironwood Latigo (Alpine Cherokee Rocket - Ironwood Black Panda)
ex Hasley's Midnight Star (Shades of Robin - Laika of Murray Hill)
OPEN—KAN 10/69-4; NLA 3/70-1; PIK 8/70-2; MOV 9/70-3;
MIW 10/70-2; PTA 10/70-4; CAS 9/72-2; ALM 11/72-3. (17)
AMATEUR—MOV 9/68-4; MIV 10/68-4; MAN 8/69-4; SXV
8/69-4; NLA 3/70-2; MTR 5/70-2; SXV 9/70-1; ALB 7/72-4;
RKM 8/72-2. (16½)

MORTY'S EBONY MAGIC SB-93609 2/2/68 Dr. R. D. Sandilands—By
Mixed Up Morty of Hi-Noon (Turner's Smokey Boy - Flashy Girl) ex
Duckworth's Black Mandy (Black Boy of Whitmore - Paha Sapa
Rapid Water)
OPEN—WMO 4/72-3. (1)

MOUNTAIN VIEW'S BUFF SA-26847 11/14/59 Frank and Rita Aylstock
—By Satan of Yellowstone (Tarblood Charkie - Gem of Jardine) ex
Her Majesty Pat (Sandy's Sunny - Madam Queen III)
OPEN—CSC 10/65-2. (3)
AMATEUR—SRZ 2/67-4. (½)

FC MR. LUCKY OF OAK HILL SA-373983 5/19/64 Pat and John
Van Bloom — By Dutchmoor's Pooh Bear (Calypso Clipper - Jet's
Tammy) ex Howmoor's Dark Gypsy (Marshwise Snapshooter - Topsy's
Peg)
OPEN—MON 5/68-2; SHE 6/68-1; SXV 8/68-3; CNB 5/69-4;
ALM 2/70-1; IDA 8/70-4; KAN 10/70-4. (15½)
AMATEUR—SHE 6/69-3; MOV 9/70-4; KAN 10/70-2. (4½)

FC MR. MAC'S BILLY BOY SA-239806 3/11/63 Mrs. Geo. Murnane—
By Carnmoney Billy Jo* (Glen-Water Fever Pitch - Carnmoney Rock-
ette) ex Rill Shannon Dark Dell* (Del-Tone Colvin - Glengarven's
Black Bess)
OPEN—FTP 6/67-3; BUK 9/67-3; WOL 9/67-3; OHV 9/67-1;
WOM 10/67-2; SLA 2/68-4; SHR 3/68-1; DEL 3/68-1; WNY
9/68-4; COL 9/68-1; DEL 10/68-1; DEL 10/68-1; WOM 10/68-3;
NLA 3/69-4; SHR 4/69-3; LAB 4/69-1; LIR 5/69-2; MTA
10/69-3; DEL 3/70-2; SHR 4/70-2; DUL 8/70-1; WOM 4/70-1;
MOB 11/70-4; JAX 3/71-3; MTA 4/71-1; MIT 8/71-1; SHO
9/71-3; MAI 9/71-3. (78)
AMATEUR—MIT 8/66-2. (3)

FC-AFC MUKTAR OF OFFERSHIRE SA-440989 10/24/66 Ray Offerdahl
—By My Rebel* (Yankee Clipper of Reo Raj - Duchess of Miller's
Haven) ex Pen-Pep Dolly (Pepper's Jiggs - Penny Girl)
OPEN—NOI 10/70-1; CNB 5/71-3; CMI 5/71-2; CNB 5/72-2;
NDK 8/72-2. (15)
AMATEUR—CMI 5/70-3; KAN 10/70-4; MII 5/71-3; CMI
5/71-1; NDK 8/71-3; CMI 5/72-3; NDK 8/72-1; MOV 9/72-2. (17½)

MUSCLES JET JOCK SA-472914 1/31/67 Col. and Mrs. W. B. Twichell
—By Jetstone Muscles of Claymar* (Stonecastle Jack - Jet Firefly of
Dacity) ex Lady's Pie Doe (Dutchmoor's Etaoin Shrdlu - Lady B.
Good II)
OPEN—MIC 8/70-4. (½)
AMATEUR—NFL 11/72-1. (5)

FC MY REBEL SA-223985 6/1/63 A. Wells Wilbor—By Yankee Clipper
of Reo Raj (Stonegate's Captain - Little Peggy Duchess - Jet's Gum) ex Duchess
of Miller's Haven (Duke of Ashton - Prana's Replica of Bingo)
OPEN—NEB 4/66-1; DUL 8/66-1; KAN 10/66-3; NEB 4/67-2;
CMI 5/67-2; TRI 6/67-3; SXV 8/68-2; WIS 9/68-3; NTX
10/68-1; NEB 4/69-2; MNS 5/69-1; MIV 4/70-1; NEB 4/70-4;
CMI 5/70-3; MNS 9/70-3; NOI 10/70-2; MII 5/71-1; MIT
8/71-4; DUL 8/71-3; WIS 9/71-2; MOV 9/71-1; NOI 7/72-2. (63)
AMATEUR—DUL 8/69-1; CMI 5/70-1; WOM 4/72-3. (11)

AFC MYSAKS MAJOR BUCK SA-291489 7/30/64 Robert D. Blue—
By Ebony Buck of Chandler (Sam of Blaircourt - Tamara) ex Golden
Miss Muffet (Thimothy Safari Ringo - Switzer's Black Dawn)
AMATEUR—MII 5/68-1; TRI 5/68-4; CNB 5/68-4; NEB 4/70-3;
CNB 5/70-3; MII 5/70-3; SXV 9/71-2; NOI 10/71-2; NOI 7/72-1. (20)

MYSTERY ICABOD SA-219828 11/22/62 Jay C. Thompson — By Paha Sapa Chief II (Freehaven Muscles - Treasure State Be Wise) ex Jet of Hart (Hartchamp of Greybull - Poco's Black Judy)
AMATEUR—SNA 8/68-3. (1)

FC NASSAU SA-243717 5/17/63 M. H. Muse and Jack Peterson—By Bigstone Crowder's Cap (Crowder - Bigstone Goldie) ex Cimaroc Lady Jean (Nodak Boots - Hull's Oma)
OPEN—MII 5/68-4; DUL 8/68-4; MNS 9/68-4; ALM 11/68-1; NDK 8/69-2; SXV 8/69-4; NOI 9/69-4; SXV 9/71-3. (11½)
AMATEUR—ALM 11/68-2. (3)

FC NASSAU'S NAR OF MINNEWASKA SA-358399 10/18/65 Mrs. Grace Lambert—By Nassau* (Bigstone Crowder's Cap - Cimaroc Lady Jean) ex Nodak Miss Que (Red River Jet - Nodak Candy)
OPEN—SXV 8/69-3; WOL 9/69-3; WOM 10/69-2; LST 3/70-2; TRI 6/70-4; DUL 8/70-3; MIL 6/70-2; MNS 9/70-4; DEL 10/70-1; SHR 4/71-1; CMI 5/71-4; MIT 8/71-2; LAB 4/72-2; MAN 8/72-1; WIS 9/72-3. (35½)

NEB'S MIDNIGHT REBEL SA-157594 3/26/62 Mrs. Robert E. Eckis— By La Sage's Neb (La Sage's Smoky - Cream City Clipper) ex Raven-camp Black Heel (Black Boy XI - Lady Twing of Oak Orchard)
OPEN—WNY 9/65-2; CNY 5/67-4. (3½)
AMATEUR—WNY 9/65-3; WNY 9/66-4; BUK 9/66-3; CNY 5/67-4. (3)

FC-AFC NEMO'S SPYDER OF ROUND VALLEY SA-537146 11/24/67 Chip Ammarell — By Nethercroft Nemo of Nascopie* (Timbershed Totem of Nascopie II - Nimrod's Wendy of Windy Mains) ex Blitz of Round Valley (Alpine Cherokee Rocket - Yankee's Ebony Girl)
OPEN—AAR 9/71-3; MIW 10/71-2; NTX 3/72-1; SHE 9/72-1. (14)
AMATEUR—MIC 8/70-3; LIT 4/71-3; GOL 5/71-2; WOL 5/71-4; FRR 8/71-3; OHV 10/71-2; MIW 10/71-1; MIW 10/72-2. (17½)

FC NETHERCROFT NEMO OF NASCOPIE SA-281100 3/10/62 Mrs. Grace Lambert—By Timbershed Totem of Nascopie II (Chuck of Bracken - Crevamoy Lou) ex Nimrod's Wendy of Windy Mains (Nimrod's Rip Van Winkle - Sally)
OPEN—CMI 5/65-3; MNS 9/65-2; MNS 5/66-1; FTP 8/66-4; NDK 8/66-2; TAL 3/67-3; WOM 4/67-1 LAB 4/67-2; MAD 5/67-1; NDK 8/67-1; DEL 10/67-4; MEM 3/68-2; MAD 8/68-2; WIS 9/68-1; MNS 5/69-3; DUL 8/69-2; SXV 8/69-1; LAB 5/70-2; MAD 8/70-4; MNS 9/70-2; WIS 9/70-1; MIV 4/71-2; CMI 5/71-3; TRI 6/71-4; WIS 10/71-4; NOI 10/71-3. (69½)

NETLEY CREEK'S BLACK BRUTE (SA-974304 10/26/68 Don H. and Caro Gearheart—By Ravenhill's Bass (Pepper's Jiggs - Dart of Netley Creek) ex Penny of Delta (Smokey of Delta Plaza - Black Lady of Valentine)
OPEN—SCA 9/72-4. (½)
AMATEUR—PHO 10/72-4. (½)

NICOLL'S COMEBACK SA-508528 2/9/66 Keith Nicolls—By Collinwood Duke (Bushwacker's Jake - Irish Ridge Hap) ex Nicoll's Blackie (Keystone Laddie II - Foxleigh Rebel Girl)
OPEN—FTP 6/72-4. (½)

AFC NILO BRANDY CORK SA-554527 1/30/68 A. G. Schultz, M.D.—By Martens' Little Smoky* (Crowder - Martens' Little Bullet) ex Keith's Brandy (Castlemore Shamus - Techako's Dart)
AMATEUR—MIL 6/71-1; MIW 4/72-2; LIT 4/72-4; MII 6/72-1; AAR 9/72-1. (18½)

Mi-Cris Sailor

Mister Mac's Billy Boy

My Rebel

Nethercroft Nemo of Nascopie

FC NILO BRIAN BORU SA-384483 1/15/66 A. G. Schultz, M.D.—By
Staindrop Talent (Scotney Dusty - Staindrop Cindy) ex Nilo Pete's Ida
(Pomme de Terre Pete - Staindrop Isla)
OPEN—MIV 10/69-2; MIL 6/70-1; AAR 9/70-2. (11)
AMATEUR—MIW 10/71-4; MIW 10/72-3. (1½)

FC NILO STAINDROP CHARGER SA-406766 5/30/66 John M. Olin—
By Staindrop Talent (Scotney Dusty - Staindrop Cindy) ex Nilo Ida's
Pretender (Pomme de Terre Pete - Staindrop Isla)
OPEN—MIW 10/69-1; KAN 4/70-2; MII 5/70-2; AAR 5/70-3;
TRI 6/70-1; WIS 9/70-2; LIT 4/71-1; MIV 4/71-3; MIW 4/71-2;
WIS 9/71-3; MIV 4/72-3; MIW 4/72-1; MAD 5/72-2; MNS
9/72-4; WIS 9/72-2. (42½)

FC NODROG NIKE SA-94361 3/26/60 Lyle Knight—By Mainliner Mike
(Skipper of Rodall II - Wendy of Candlewood) ex Beautywood's Rebel
Queen (Roy's Rowdy - Beautywood's Repeat)
OPEN—FTA 8/64-3; SUP 6/65-1; FTP 8/65-4; DUL 8/65-3;
SXV 9/65-2; MTR 9/65-2; FTP 8/66-1. (18½)
AMATEUR—MIT 8/66-4; MIT 8/67-1; NDK 8/68-2. (8½)

FC-AFC NODROG PUNKIE SA-504005 4/5/67 Wilford L. Buxton—By
Sir Knight Falcon* (Patch of Bonniehurst - Faindi Kalp Asswad) ex
Nodrog Penny* (Mainliner Mike - Beautywood's Rebel Queen)
OPEN—KAN 10/70-2; ALM 2/71-1; NTX 3/71-2; SOO 4/72-3;
CNB 5/72-1; MIT 8/72-4; CHY 8/72-3; MOV 9/72-1. (23½)
AMATEUR—CHY 8/71-4; CWY 8/71-2; NTX 3/72-3; RKM
5/72-4; MOV 9/72-1. (10)

OLD VAV SA-272594 6/24/64 E. Rob Leatherbury — By Cork's Bingo
(Crowder - Bigstone Bang) ex Longshot's Rebel Rouser (Yankee Clipper
of Reo Raj - Star of Fate)
OPEN—WIS 4/69-3; MTA 10/69-1; WOL 5/70-3; MIT 8/70-4;
MNS 5/72-4. (8)
AMATEUR—NFL 11/67-2; MEM 10/70-2. (6)

OL' YELLER SA-490179 5/9/67 Cactus Pryor — By Mark of Gloster*
(Medlin's Cork of Grapevine - Pat's Error Mitzie) ex Friday at
Waxahachie Creek (Circle T. Thatch - Boomerang's Rebound)
OPEN—CWY 8/70-4; ALB 7/71-4; PIK 8/71-1. (6)
AMATEUR—ALB 5/71-2; ALM 11/71-2; ALM 2/72-2. (9)

ONYX GREATFORD PRIDE SA-129969 1/13/62 Wm. B. Carey — By
Rice's Busy Gamekeeper (Greatford Scale - Snipe of Euston) ex
Ariadne of Greersliegh (Diant Swandyke Creamcracker - Whinbush
Greer)
OPEN—AAR 9/66-4; WIS 9/66-4; NTX 3/67-3. (2)
AMATEUR—WOL 9/67-4. (½)

ORION OF RIVER PARK SA-224863 10/5/63 Brian F. Hunter — By
King Donald D. (Sukey V Smoker - Charcoal Belle of Colusa) ex
Madame Hepzibah Hoo-Ha (Mizar of Glenarden - Starlite II)
AMATEUR—SAG 3/70-2; SRN 5/70-2. (6)

FC-AFC ORION'S SIRIUS SA-348610 7/10/65 John W. Martin — By
Rocket of Flint (Sam of Blaircourt - Tamara) ex Crystodigin Martin
(Royal of Garfield - Martens' Lady Jane)
OPEN—MIV 4/69-1; FRR 8/69-1; AAR 5/70-4; FRR 8/70-3;
WOL 9/70-3; SWA 11/70-3; BUK 4/71-4; GOL 5/71-1; WOL
5/71-1; OHV 10/71-1; OHV 4/72-1; BUK 9/72-4. (34½)
AMATEUR—FRR 8/68-4; AAR 8/68-4; WOL 9/68-2; KAN
10/68-2; WIS 4/69-3; GOL 5/69-2; WNY 9/69-3; WOL 9/69-2;
OHV 9/69-1; MTA 10/69-1; MIC 8/70-2; BUK 9/70-2; OHV
10/70-1; FRR 8/71-4; BUK 9/71-3; WOL 9/71-3; OHV 10/71-1;
WNY 9/71-2; OHV 4/72-2; BUK 4/72-1; OHV 9/72-1. (59½)

FC-AFC OTTLEY'S JAZZBO SA-485575 12/30/66 J. Dudley Ottley—By
Sam Sloan Creek (Dare Devil of Warwick - Smolnie) ex Tina Rose
(Copperhill Loughderg Brogeen - Goldfinch)
OPEN—MTA 10/70-3; ATL 4/71-2; ATL 10/71-4; MOB 11/71-2;
JAX 3/72-1; ATL 4/72-3; ATL 10/72-4; MEM 10/72-2.   (17)
AMATEUR—MEM 3/70-4; ATL 5/70-4; MOB 3/71-3; ATL
4/71-1; MTA 4/71-3; MOB 11/71-2; NFL 11/71-1; ATL 4/72-1;
MTA 4/72-1; FTP 6/72-1; ATL 10/72-1; MOB 11/72-3.   (37)

PADDLER OF WINTERGREEN SA-341035 5/14/65 Erwin R. Jones—
By Labcroft Timmy of Black Brook (Nodak's Timothy - How-Hi
Ginger) ex Miss Chiff Cinder (Kasey Cole - Charkey)
OPEN—MAR 5/70-3; MAN 8/70-4; MNS 10/71-4; MEM 10/71-4;
BUK 4/72-3.   (3½)

AFC PAHA SAPA HARDCASE SA-324662 4/4/65 Larry L. Burrill—By
Rebel Chief of Heber* (Paha Sapa Chief II - Penny Girl) ex Ripco's
Lady Pam (Ripco's Peter Pan - Coleraine's Lady Velvet)
OPEN—MAD 8/69-3; NDK 8/70-1; DUL 8/71-4.   (6½)
AMATEUR—CMI 5/69-4; MII 5/70-1; TRI 6/70-2; NDK 8/70-4;
TRI 6/72-1; NDK 8/72-3; SXV 9/72-3.   (16)

FC PAHA SAPA JACK SA-133542 12/6/61 Herbert Fleishhacker, Jr.—By
Paha Sapa Chief II (Freehaven Muscles - Treasure State Be Wise) ex
Mark's Mondak Penny (Nilo Possibility - Mueller's Cuddles)
OPEN—NWR 4/65-3; SAM 9/65-4; LAS 2/66-1; SNA 5/66-3;
SPO 5/66-4; SNA 8/66-1.   (13)
AMATEUR—SCA 9/67-3.   (1)

PAHA SAPA JAY SA-300599 12/9/64 Donald P. Weiss—By Paha Sapa
Chief II (Freehaven Muscles - Treasure State Be Wise) ex Princess
Sootana of Buffalo (Tarblood Buffalo Chief - Lady Gretchen of Buffalo)
OPEN—PTA 3/69-4.   (½)

PAHA SAPA MEDICINE MAN SA-75259 6/21/60 Mr. Oscar S. Brewer
—By Paha Sapa War Cloud (Burrhaven Bones - Paha Sapa Princess)
ex Miss Debit of Shady Valley (King Chukker of Robbinsdale - Mem
of Greeymar)
OPEN—CHY 8/64-3; MON 9/64-1; SHE 9/66-4.   (6½)
AMATEUR—MOV 9/64-3; ALM 2/65-3; JAY 3/66-4; AAR
5/66-3; MIL 6/66-4; SHE 9/66-2; KAN 10/66-4; ALM 2/67-3.   (8½)

PAHA SAPA PRIDE OF CASEY SA-599941 7/7/68 Cliff and Una Savell
—By Paha Sapa Hardcase* (Rebel Chief of Heber* - Ripco's Lady
Pam) ex Evangeline Tar Baby (Coco Sunset - Zip's Cajun Lady)
OPEN—PTA 10/71-4.   (½)
AMATEUR—NLA 10/71-4.   (½)

FC-AFC PAHA SAPA WARPAINT SA-484616 7/17/66 Mrs. Alanson C.
Brown III — By Paha Sapa Chief II (Freehaven Muscles - Treasure
State Be Wise) ex Ironwood Cherokee Chica (Cherokee Buck - Glen-
Water Fantom)
OPEN—MAI 9/70-2; LAS 2/71-2; SRZ 2/71-2; JAM 4/71-3;
FRR 8/71-2; SWA 11/71-1.   (18)
AMATEUR—WNY 9/70-4; WCH 5/71-2; CNY 5/71-3; SAG
7/71-3; MAN 8/71-3; FRR 8/71-2; COL 10/71-3; WNY 9-71-1;
DEL 10/71-4; WOM 10/71-1; LIR 5/72-2; SHO 9/72-4; LIR
10/72-3.   (25½)

FC-AFC PAHA SAPA WARPATH SA-88862 12/1/60 Dr. and Mrs. Rietz
—By Paha Sapa Chief II (Freehaven Muscles - Treasure State Be
Wise) ex Paha Sapa Belle (Burrhaven Bones - Paha Sapa Princess)

172

OPEN—NEB 4/65-3; BHB 6/65-1; SHE 9/65-2; KAN 10/65-4; MII 5/66-2; MIW 10/66-3; PTA 3/67-2; JAY 3/67-3; MTR 5/67-1; KAN 10/67-2. (25½)

AMATEUR—MTR 9/63-2; KAN 4/65-3; MIV 4/65-4; NEB 4/65-3; RKM 8/65-4; MTR 9/65-4; NOI 10/65-3; PTA 3/66-1; KAN 4/66-3; NEB 4/67-4; MIW 4/67-2: MTR 5/67-3; SHE 6/67-4; KAN 10/67-4; MIC 8/68-4; SXV 8/68-1. (24½)

FC-AFC PAHA SAPA WARPATH II SA-205730 6/11/63 Don F. Bader —By Paha Sapa Warpath* (Paha Sapa Chief II - Paha Sapa Belle) ex Shadow of Dakota (Dakota Duke - Shiela Shamrock)
OPEN—MNS 5/68-3; CMI 5/68-4: RKM 8/68-2; PIK 8/69-2; CHY 8/71-1; SXV 10/71-1; JAY 3/72-2; CNB 5/72-4; ALB 7/72-3. (22)

AMATEUR—NEB 5/66-4; JAY 3/67-4; KAN 3/68-1; MNS 5/68-2; CMI 5/68-3; PIK 8/68-1; RKM 8/68-3; JAY 3/69-1; TRI 5/69-4. (21½)

PAHA'S POW ON TAP SA-922931 12/22/70 Roger Vasselais—By Paha's Pow Wow* (Paha Sapa Chief II - Ironwood Cherokee Chica) ex Dolly of Audlon (Duxbak Scooter* - Little Dollface of Audlon)
OPEN—SHO 9/72-1. (5)

AMATEUR—SWA 11/72-3. (1)

FC-AFC PAHA'S POW WOW SA-455896 7/18/66 Dr. W. E. Peltzer—By Paha Sapa Chief II (Freehaven Muscles - Treasure State Be Wise) ex Ironwood Cherokee Chica (Cherokee Buck - Glen-Water Fantom)
OPEN—ACC 8/69-2; IDA 8/70-1; SNA 8/70-1; ACC 8/70-1. (18)

AMATEUR—IDA 5/70-1; GSL 5/70-3; GSL 8/70-1; IDA 8/70-3. (12)

PAM'S BLACK SPLASH SA-482099 5/17/67 J. R. Leonard — By My Rebel* (Yankee Clipper of Reo-Raj - Duchess of Millers Haven) ex Mike's Lizzie Odom* (Gee Baby - Dee Dee Baby)
AMATEUR—NLA 10/72-3; ALM 11/72-2. (4)

PANTHER BABY SA-222729 10/28/63 Mr. J. J. Heneghan — By Tar Baby's Little Sweet Stuff (Tar Baby of Holly Hill - Debbie of Holly Hill) ex Dessa Rae* (Odessa's King - Jerry)
OPEN—WIL 8/66-4; SAM 3/67-2; ORE 3/67-3; IDA 5/67-4; RED 7/67-4; TAC 8/67-4; IDA 8/67-3; SAM 9/67-2; SPO 9/67-2; LST 10/67-3; SHA 9/68-2. (17)

AMATEUR—SPO 5/69-4; PUG 8/69-3; SPO 10/70-4. (2)

PANTHER OF THE COEUR D'ALENE'S SA-183348 3/14/62 Horace H. Koessler—By Odessa's King (Ardyn Ace - Lady Cinder of Mattausch) ex Pride's Black Duchess (Noah of Swinowish - Carnation Pride)
OPEN—BHB 6/71-2. (3)

AMATEUR—MON 9/69-4; SHE 9/70-4; MON 9/70-4; WMO 6/71-2. (4½)

AFC PARKY SA-203028 12/18/61 Richard Reeve — By Pepper's Jiggs (Ardyn's Ace of Merwalfin - Black Magic of Van Nola View) ex Jibodad Velvet (Rip of Holly Hill - Jibodad Gypsy)
OPEN—ACC 8/70-4. (½)

AMATEUR—SRN 5/67-4; SRZ 2/68-3; CSC 2/68-3; SAG 3/68-2; WIL 8/69-1; WMO 5/70-3; SNA 8/70-1. (16½)

PAT OF ORCHARD GLEN SA-262776 3/29/64 Charles A. Biewen — By Bat-Jac's Tinny Tim (Cumshaw Bat-Jac's Boy - Ademala's Fay) ex Wandarin Heights Shannon (Black Monk of Roeland - Manzanal Lilac)
OPEN—SHA 4/69-2. (3)

AMATEUR—NCA 3/69-3; SAG 3/69-1. (6)

FC PATSY'S THUNDERCHIEF SA-563940 4/7/68 R. R. Johnson, Jr.—
By Super Chief* (Paha Sapa Chief II - Ironwood Cherokee Chica) ex
Duxbak's Patsy Del Norte (Duxbak Scooter* - Jilly Girl*)
OPEN—MTA 10/71-1; MOB 11/71-3; MTA 4/72-3; MIC 8/72-3;
AAR 9/72-4; WNY 9/72-3; CAS 9/72-1. (14½)
AMATEUR—SLA 9/72-4; MTA 10/72-4. (1)

PEIGAN'S BOLLE BLAKE SA-484399 4/2/66 Sheila and Wm. Sabbag,
M.D. — By Crook's El Toro (Crook's Tahoe Pat - Black Rapids of
Baranof) ex Luka of Casey's Rocket* (Cougar's Rocket* - Pacific
Mokee)
AMATEUR—SCA 9/70-3; SNA 8/71-4. (1½)

FC PELICAN LAKE BOO BOO SA-469218 2/27/66 Cal Barry — By
Castlemore Shamus (Strokestown Duke of Blaircourt - Hilldown Sylver)
ex Pelican Lake Peggy* (Castlemore Shamus - Birdie's Misty)
OPEN—WOL 9/68-4; DEL 10/68-2; SWA 10/69-4; SLA 2/70-3;
MAR 5/70-2; WOL 5/70-4; FTP 6/70-1; WOL 9/70-1; BUK
4/71-1; MAD 5/71-3; WOL 5/71-4; FTP 6/71-2. (28)

PEPPER'S OMEGA SA-124174 12/18/61 Bob Pepper — By Pepper's
Jiggs (Ardyn's Ace of Merwalfin - Black Magic of Van Nola View) ex
Jibodad Velvet (Rip of Holly Hill - Jibodad Gypsy)
OPEN—SAM 3/66-3; SPO 5/66-1; SPO 5/67-4. (6½)

PETER OF GAYMARK SA-126453 4/25/61 Mrs. Paul Kiernan — By
Beautywood's Carbon Copy (Webway's Crusader - Gilmore's Peggy) ex
Nilo Solo's Margie (Solo of Poverty Gulch - Nilo Buck's Pride)
OPEN—MIT 8/65-3; NDK 8/65-4. (1½)
AMATEUR—SWA 11/66-2; CNY 5/67-2; DEL 3/69-3. (7)

FC-AFC PETITE ROUGE SA-85985 4/4/60 Mrs. Warner L. Atkins—By
Robbet's Black Hope (Staindrop Murton Marksman - Ebony Duchess)
ex Cuzz's Corky (Dandy Dan of Repmen - Sprigella)
OPEN—LST 10/62-4; KAN 3/63-1; NEB 4/63-2; CNB 5/63-3;
BHB 6/63-4; KAN 3/64-2; MIW 4/64-2; CNB 5/64-1; MON
5/64-3; MAD 8/64-2; NTX 10/64-4; KAN 10/64-4; PTA 3/65-4;
NLA 3/65-1; MIV 4/65-1; MON 6/65-2; BUK 9/65-3; NOI
10/65-2; NEB 4/66-3; CNB 5/66-1; MII 5/66-3; CHY 5/66-2;
MON 6/66-3; MAD 8/66-4; LST 3/67-3. (56)
AMATEUR—NEB 4/63-1; MIW 4/63-2; MON 9/63-4; ALM
2/64-3; PTA 3/64-2; NTX 3/64-1; MON 5/64-2; BUK 9/64-2;
WOL 3/64-3; OHV 10/64-4; MIW 10/64-3; NTX 3/65-2; NLA
3/65-2; KAN 4/65-1; MON 6/65-4; BHB 6/65-1; BUK 9/65-2;
KAN 4/66-1; NTX 10/66-3. (51½)

PIN OAKS LITTLE OTTER SA-188687 12/28/62 Jim Culbertson—By
Otter O'Vrnwy (Grouse-A-Dee - Creedypark Stella) ex Renegade
Sioux (Paha Sapa Chief II - Semloh's Deb of Walden Pond)
OPEN—MON 6/67-2. (3)
AMATEUR—JAY 4/66-3; RKM 5/67-3. (2)

PIPERS HIGHLAND DRUMMER SA-497970 6/15/67 Mary Lindsay
Schwyn—By Riskin* (Black Boy of Whitmore - Paha Sapa Rapid
Water) ex Canuck-Crest Packwood Peggy (Spirit Lake Duke - Canuck-
Crest Tami O'Churchlee)
OPEN—NTX 10/71-2. (3)

FC-AFC PIRATE'S GOLD SA-438442 10/9/66 Bill and Millie Murff—By
Tabak (Mountain View's Buff - Mik-El's Tawny of Dewmar) ex Big
Oaks Dianne Gold of Ibaden (Big Oaks Black Rip - Sherry Gold of
Ibaden)

174

OPEN—CSC 9/69-3; CSC 2/70-2; SCA 9/70-3; CSC 10/70-3;
SCA 3/71-4; CSC 10/71-1; ALM 11/71-1; SCA 3/72-4; SCA
9/72-3. (18)

AMATEUR—SCA 9/69-1; CSC 2/70-4; SCA 3/70-3; NCA 9/70-2;
CSC 10/70-4; CSC 2/71-2; SCA 3/71-3; ALM 11/71-3; CSC
2/72-4; SCA 3/72-3; ALB 5/72-4; SAD 9/72-4; CSC 9/72-3. (18½)

POCATELLO CHIEF SA-793536 6/13/69 Pat and John Van Bloom—By
Spring Farms Lucky* (Paha Sapa Chief II - Ironwood Cherokee Chica)
ex Cedar Ridge Jodi (Beavercrest Kannonball Kid - Queen of Valentine)
OPEN—MON 9/72-3. (1)

AFC POLARIS LUKE SA-319489 4/14/64 Dr. Francis W. Partridge—
By Fenbroke's Beau (Fenbroke's Beaufort - Jetstream Jezebel) ex
Countess of Sheridain (Fenbroke's Heythorp - Duchess of Sheridain)
OPEN—WMO 9/67-2; IDA 8/68-3; SNA 8/68-3; ACC 8/68-2. (8)

AMATEUR—IDA 5/67-1; SNA 5/67-2; HEL 9/67-1; WMO
5/68-3; ACC 8/68-1; IDA 5/69-4; SNA 5/69-1; EID 7/69-4; SNA
8/69-4; ACC 8/69-1; WMO 5/71-4. (31)

POLARIS PETER SA-646602 10/10/68 Dr. Francis W. Partridge—By
Guy's Bitterroot Lucky* (Beavercrest's Toreador - Pickrel's Ebony
Babe) ex Velvet's Jezebel* (Pepper's Jiggs - Jebodad Velvet)
OPEN—SNA 8/72-4; WMO 9/72-4. (1)
AMATEUR—GSL 5/72-2. (3)

AFC PORTNEUF VALLEY DUKE SA-248523 6/24/63 Roger Vasselais
—By Spirit of Bear River (Spirit Lake Duke - Belle of Bear River) ex
Twin Lakes Lady (Bob's Bannock Jake - Midnight Lady II)
OPEN—LAB 4/68-4; MAI 9/69-4. (1)

AMATEUR—WNY 9/67-4; SWA 11/67-2; WOM 4/68-4; MAR
5/68-4; BUK 9/68-3; SWA 11/68-4; JAX 1/69-4; NFL 2/69-3;
MOB 2/69-2; SLA 2/69-3; BUK 4/69-1; BUK 9/69-3; COL
9/69-2; LIR 10/69-4; LIR 5/70-3. (22)

AFC POTOMAC BUDDY SA-361769 4/9/65 G. W. Faulhaber — By
Jet of Zenith (Massie's Sassy Boots - Thornwood Rhea) ex Stormy
Snowy (Alvaleigh's Rapscallion - Rocky's Pat)
OPEN—SRZ 2/68-3; ALB 4/70-4; SRZ 2/71-4; PHO 10/71-4;
SAD 9/72-3. (3½)

AMATEUR—ALB 5/68-2; SRZ 2/69-3; CSC 2/69-4; SCA 2/69-4;
CSC 9/69-3; GSL 5/70-4; PHO 10/70-3; NTX 11/70-2; PHO
10/71-1. (15½)

PROBLEM BOY'S DINNY SA-119874 7/7/61 L. C. King—By Problem
Boy Duke of Wake (Ponto's Ponto of Wake - Kavanagh's Ripple) ex
Smoky's Gal Tammy (Butch's Bitterroot Smokey - Fenbroke's Meath)
AMATEUR—IDA 5/67-2; ACC 8/67-2. (6)

QUIEN SABE'S BLACK ACE SA-107987 7/29/61 E. E. Jackson III
—By Quien Sabe (La Sage's Smoky - Cream City Clipper) ex Gale of
Cedar Creek (Cork of Oakwood Lane - Lady Gale)
OPEN—NTX 3/65-4; ALB 5/67-4. (1)

FC-AFC RADAR RIP SA-332586 4/23/65 Richard S. Humphrey — By
Lord Bomar* (Blackfoot's Happy New Year - Peg's Blackfoot Queen)
ex Cinder Gal of Seneca (Ravencamp Woodlark - Cape Vincent's Niger)
OPEN—NTX 10/67-1; KAN 3/68-3; PUG 8/71-2; MON 9/71-1;
ORE 9/72-2. (17)

AMATEUR—NLA 10/67-3; LST 10/67-3; ALM 11/67-2; JAY
3/68-4; GSL 8/67-2; IDA 8/67-4; TAC 8/70-1. (14)

AFC RALSTON VALLEY DANDY JAKE SA-314035 10/21-64 Alvah C. Donnelly—By Shamrock Acres Jim Dandy (Brodhead's Bar Booze - Whygin Gentle Julia of Avec) ex Sprite of Ralston Valley (Zelstone Sparkle - Spirit of Avandale)

    OPEN—PIK 5/69-2; SHE 6/69-2; RKM 5/70-4; MTR 5/71-3; JAY 3/72-3.   (8½)

    AMATEUR—ALB 5/69-3; SHE 6/69-2; CHY 8/69-3; CNB 5/70-1; CHY 9/71-1; NEB 4/71-4; RKM 5/71-1; ALB 7/71-3; RKM 8/71-2; CNB 5/72-2.   (27½)

FC RANDY DANDY OF HOLLY HILL SA-268426 5/4/63 Bill Swanland —By Castlemore Shamus (Strokestown Duke of Blaircourt - Hilldown Sylver) ex Glengarven's Dainty Dell (Glengarven's Kim - Lady Ginner of Malachi)

    OPEN—PUG 8/68-4; ORE 9/68-4; SPO 9/68-3; SAM 8/69-3; PUG 8/69-3; SAM 9/70-2; SAM 3/71-1; SPO 5/71-4; SPO 10/71-2; ORE 3/72-3;PUG 4/72-4; ORE 9/72-4.   (17½)

FC-AFC RANDY MAYHALL OF TINA SA-393816 3/30/66 G. Glenn Miller—By Ebony Mood's Bingo* (Dutchmoor's Black Mood* - Bigstone Lady B) ex Tina of Grey Summit (Black Watch of Horseshoe - Purina's Black Magic)

    OPEN—MTA 3/69-2; MIT 8/69-3; NDK 8/69-3; MOB 10/69-3; ATL 5/70-1; MIT 8/70-1; DUL 8/70-2; NFL 11/71-2; ALM 2/72-2; SAG 3/72-1.   (30)

    AMATEUR—NLA 3/69-2; MIW 4/69-3; AAR 5/69-2; AAR 8/69-2; SLA 9/69-1; DEL 10/70-2; MOB 11/70-2; ALM 2/71-2; ATL 4/71-4; MAN 8/71-2; SLA 10/71-1; NLA 10/71-2; NTX 10/71-1; PTA 10/71-3; SLA 9/72-1.   (46½)

FC-AFC RAY'S RASCAL SA-558031 10/2/67 Raymond H. and Dorothea Goodrich—By Carnmoney Spud* (Bandit of Carnmoney - Carnmoney Boots) ex Miss Fiddlesticks (Black Mike of Lakewood - Kemper's Sassy Sue)

    OPEN—ROV 3/70-4; IDA 5/70-4; RED 7/70-2; IDA 8/70-2; SHA 9/70-2; CSC 10/70-1; CSC 2/71-1; SAG 3/71-4; SAG 7/71-1; RED 7/71-1; IDA 8/71-2; SCA 9/71-4; NCA 9/71-4; CSC 10/71-2; NCA 3/72-1; IDA 5/72-1; SNA 5/72-1; ACC 7/72-4; SAG 7/72-2; SCA 9/72-2; CSC 9/72-1.   (64)

    AMATEUR—LAS 2/70-4; IDA 5/70-3; SNA 5/70-1; RED 7/70-1; EID 7/70-1; CSC 10/70-2; LAS 2/71-3; SAG 3/71-2; SHA 4/71-2; SAG 7/71-1; RED 7/71-2; IDA 8/71-1; ACC 8/71-2; NCA 9/71-3; CSC 10/71-1; SCA 3/72-1; IDA 5/72-1; SAG 7/72-1; NCA 9/72-2.   (64½)

REBCHA'S SUPER DUPER SA-612325 4/20/68 Z. Z. White—By Butte Blue Moon* (Beavercrest Storm Cloud - Macushla of Rockmont) ex Nodrog Penny* (Mainliner Mike - Beautywood Rebel Queen)

    OPEN—SXV 9/72-2.   (3)

FC-NARFC '65 REBEL CHIEF OF HEBER SA-82627 12/25/60 Gus F. and Virginia Rathert—By Paha Sapa Chief II (Freehaven Muscles - Treasure State Be Wise) ex Penny Girl (Cork of Oakwood Lane - Min-A-Jet of Reo Raj)

    OPEN—LAS 2/63-4; SCA 2/64-3; ROV 3/64-1; SRN 5/64-3; RED 7/64-3; SAG 9/64-1; NCA 9/64-1; LAS 2/65-1; SCA 3/65-2; NCA 3/65-3; SRN 5/65-1; LAS 2/66-2; NCA 3/66-2; ROV 3/66-1; SHA 4/66-3; SRN 5/66-2; SAG 9/66-2; SHA 9/66-1; SCA 9/66-3; CSC 2/67-3; NCA 3/67-1; ROV 3/67-1; SHA 4/67-2; SRN 5/67-4; ACC 9/67-2; SCA 9/67-2; CSC 9/67-3; SRZ 2/68-4; RED 7/68-4; SAG 8/68-2; NCA 9/68-3; CSC 9/68-1.   (88)

Orion's Sirius

Ray's Rascal

Rebel Chief of Heber

River Oaks Rascal

AMATEUR—SHA 9/63-3; SCA 2/64-3; ROV 3/64-4; SHA 5/64-2; SAG 9/64-4; LAS 10/64-3; NAM 6/65-1; LAS 2/65-1; SRZ 2/65-1; CSC 2/65-1; SCA 3/65-3; RED 7/65-3; SAG 9/65-2; SHA 9/65-3; NCA 9/65-1; ROV 3/66-3; NCA 9/66-1; SCA 9/66-1; LAS 2/67-1; SCA 3/67-4; NCA 3/67-1; SHA 4/67-2; SAG 9/67-3; SHA 9/67-1; SCA 9/67-1; CSC 9/67-4; SAG 3/68-3; GOL 7/68-4; RED 7/68-2; SAG 8/68-3; NCA 9/68-1; CSC 9/68-4.   (85)

FC-AFC REIMROC'S DUKE OF ORLEANS SA-359030 1/22/65 Pete Roussos—By Ridgewood Playboy (La Sage's Smoky - Nelgard's Counter Point) ex Topsy Turvy Tar Baby (Nigger of Dacity - Glen-Water Fal-Lal)
OPEN—NFL 11/67-3; NFL 11/70-3; MOB 3/71-2; MTA 4/71-4; ATL 10/71-3; MOB 11/72-1; NFL 11/72-1.   (16½)
AMATEUR—MEM 2/69-2; NLA 9/69-3; MIV 4/70-3; JAX 3/71-4; ATL 4/71-3; ATL 10/71-4; MOB 11/71-1; MOB 3/72-4; MEM 4/72-2; MOB 11/72-2.   (18½)

RE-MAR'S BLACK BUCK SA-228224 8/29/63 Mrs. Robert E. Eckis— By Del-Tone Buck* (Martens' Hi Style Buck - Glen-Water Fan Fare) ex Valgaard Lady of Shady Lane (Yankee Clipper of Reo Raj - Rock Haven's Black Angel)
OPEN—FRR 8/67-4.   (½)

REMOHCS EBONY ACE SA-408311 4/4/66 Dr. J. R. Winburn, Jr.— By Martens' Little Smoky* (Crowder - Martens' Little Bullet) ex Vanspride Ebony Shadow* (Stonecastle Jack - Jet Firefly of Dacity)
OPEN—NTX 3/69-1.   (5)
AMATEUR—ATL 10/72-4.   (½)

AFC RENEGADE PEPE SA 101589 3/29/61 Wm. O. Tarrant — By Wasatch Renegade (Paha Sapa Chief II - Shady Shaunee) ex Uneva Drake's Lucky Lady (Uneva Drake - Lisnamallard Clodogh)
OPEN—PIK 5/65-3; RKM 8/65-2; JAY 3/66-2; KAN 4/66-2; RKM 5/66-4; RKM 8/66-2; NTX 10/67-3; SXV 8/68-4; MOV 9/68-4; NOI 9/68-3.   (16½)
AMATEUR—PIK 5/65-1; NTX 3/66-4; JAY 3/66-2; PIK 4/66-1; RKM 5/67-1; RKM 5/68-2; JAY 3/69-4.   (22)

RILLE ANN'S BURR SA-612171 6/12/68 Mr. and Mrs. Byron B. Grunwald—By Butte Blue Moon* (Beavercrest Storm Cloud - Macushla of Rockmont) ex Mark's Jigger of Joy (Ace of Garfield* - Random Molly)
OPEN—MAI 9/72-3.   (1)
AMATEUR—MIT 8/70-2; SHO 9/71-2; LAB (S) 11/71-3; LAB (S) 11/72-1.   (12)

RILLE ANN'S COLE BUCK BLAZER SA-527167 7/22/67 L. P. Floberg —By Del-Tone Buck* (Martens' Hi Style Buck - Glen-Water Fan Fare) ex Rille Ann's Lady (Del-Tone Colvin - Oma's Sassy)
AMATEUR—CMI 5/69-3; JAY 3/70-3.   (5)

RILLE ANN'S MICKEY SA-515183 7/22/67 Roger Vasselais — By Del-Tone Buck* (Martens' Hi Style Buck - Glen-Water Fan Fare) ex Rille Ann's Lady (Del-Tone Colvin - Oma's Sassy)
OPEN—MAI 9/72-3.   (1)
AMATEUR—MIT 8/70-2; SHO 9/71-2; LAB (S) 11/71-3; LAB (S) 11/72-1.   (12)

RIMROCK ROSCOE SA-179515 12/29/62 Dr. and Mrs. G. B. Starkloff —By Rimrock Ringo (Rimrock Rufus - Rubel's Belle of Bear Tooth) ex Beavercrest Warpath (Beavercrest Kannonoall Kidd - Semloh's Peggy)
OPEN—SHE 9/66-2.   (3)
AMATEUR—MIW 10/65-4; CHY 8/66-3; KAN 3/67-3; MIV 4/67-2; MIW 4/67-1; GOL 5/67-4; AAR 5/67-4.   (11½)

RINCON VALLEY JET SA-127235 5/18/61 Harold Shidler—By Black
Monk of Roeland (King Chukker of Robbinsdale - Mem of Greeymar)
ex Runaway's Sacagewea (Wardwyn Jackpot - Runaway Rocket)
OPEN—RED 7/67-3; SPO 5/68-4.   (1½)
AMATEUR—SRN 5/66-3; SRZ 2/67-3.   (2)

RINGO FROM HAPPY HOLLOW SA-273235 7/3/64 Dutchmoor Ken-
nels—By Del-Tone Buck* (Martens' Hi Style Buck - Glen-Water Fan
Fare) ex Delia Dancer (Claude of Avandale - Cherokee's Lucky Lady)
OPEN—PIK 8/69-4.   (½)

RIPCO'S REPEATER SA-317676 1/10/65 Michael R. Flannery—By
Ripco's Peter Pan (Rip of Holly Hill - Whitmore's Rowdy Lady) ex
Shoe's Del-Tone Femme (Del-Tone Colvin - Bridget Sue of Mercer)
AMATEUR—SLA 2/69-2; FTP 5/69-4.   (3½)

RIPPLE RIVER SA-722186 9/17/69 Roy McFall—By River Oaks Corky*
(Martens' Mister Nifty* - Don's Ginny Soo) ex Tyker's Lucky Penny*
(Tyker Baby - Halroy's Christmas Carol)
AMATEUR—ALK 8/22-2.   (3)

RIPSHIN ROOSTER SA-510059 2/3/67 Dr. James J. Lange—By Mac-
Gene's Fall Guy (Rico's Peter Pan - MacGene's Highland Lass) ex
Washington's Tootie Kazootie (Katanga Pepper - Black Diamond Liz)
OPEN—DUL 8/72-4.   (½)

RIP VON BLACK WINKLE SA-215191 5/19/63 Hugh Adams — By
Cougar's Rocket* (Black Cougar - Bay City Katy Jane) ex Pacific
Mo Kee (Shasta Swede of Bracken - Mistletoe Meadow Lark)
OPEN—IDA 8/67-1.   (5)
AMATEUR—SCA 3/68-4.   (½)

FC RISKIN SA-291125 2/21/62 Lindsay and Rich Schwyn—By Black Boy
of Whitmore (Riverside Rebellion - Cindy Strathblane) ex Paha Sapa
Rapid Water (Del-Tone Colvin - Paha Sapa Wi)
OPEN—CSC 9/67-2; ACC 8/68-4; SCA 9/68-4; CSC 9/68-2;
ALM 11/68-3; RED 7/69-4; EID 7/69-4; SNA 8/69-2; SCA
9/69-1; CSC 9/69-1; ACC 8/70-2.   (25)

FC-NARFC '72 RIVER OAKS CORKY SA-399497 3/26/66 Michael R.
Flannery—By Martens' Mister Nifty* (Royal of Garfield - Martens'
Black Badger) ex Don's Ginny Soo (Don-El's Doo Lee - Beautywood's
Creole Jane)
OPEN—MIC 8/68-3; MIW 10/68-4; JAX 1/69-1; SLA 2/69-1;
MEM 3/69-2; NLA 3/69-2; BUK 4/69-1; GOL 5/69-2; AAR
5/69-1; FTP 5/69-4; MIL 6/69-1; DUL 8/69-1; MIC 8/69-1; AAR
8/69-1; WNY 9/69-1; WOL 9/69-1; DEL 9/69-3; JAX 2/70-3;
MOB 2/70-4; MEM 3/70-4; SHR 4/70-4; MAD 5/70-1; WOL
5/70-1; FTP 6/70-2; MIC 8/70-2; ALK 9/70-2; BUK 9/70-1;
FRR 8/70-2; MIW 10/70-1; MIV 10/70-2; NFL 11/70-1; NFL
3/71-2; MOB 3/71-1; LIT 4/71-4; MTA 4/71-3; BUK 4/71-2;
WIS 4/71-2; MAD 5/71-1; AAR 5/71-1; FTP 6/71-1; MAN
8/71-2; FRR 8/71-1; AAR 9/71-1; BUK 9/71-1; WNY 9/71-1;
OHV 10/71-3; DEL 10/71-2; JAX 3/72-2; MOB 3/72-4; BUK
4/72-4; MAD 5/72-1; WOL 5/72-2; AAR 5/72-4; FTP 6/72-2;
MAD 8/72-3; MAN 8/72-4; ALK 8/72-1; FRR 8/72-1; BUK
9/72-3; WOL 9/72-2; OHV 9/72-3; SWA 11/72-1.   (199)
AMATEUR—WIS 4/68-2; MAD 5/68-1; WOL 5/68-2; TRI
5/68-3; MAN 8/68-2; SLA 2/69-4; MEM 2/69-1; MTA 3/69-1;
FTP 5/69-1; MIL 6/69-1; MAD 8/69-2; MAN 8/69-1; DUL
8/69-3; MIC 8/69-1; AAR 8/69-1; WOL 9/69-4; WOM 10/69-3;
SLA 2/70-1; MTA 3/70-1; MIV 4/70-1; MAR 5/70-1; ALK
9/70-2; NFL 11/70-1; MOB 3/71-1; MTA 4/71-2; MAD 5/71-4;
WOL 5/71-1; FTP 5/71-1; WOL 9/71-1; OHV 4/72-1; BUK
4/72-2; NAM 6/72-1; ALK 8/72-1; BUK 9/72-3.   (126½)

179

FC-AFC RIVER OAKS RASCAL SA-603599 7/24/68 Joseph Pilar—By River Oaks Corky* (Martens' Mister Nifty* - Don's Ginny Soo) ex Random Rapscallion (Duxbak Scooter* - Random Shot)

    OPEN—MIW 4/71-3; MIC 8/71-1; SRZ 2/72-4; MOB 3/72-1; GOL 5/72-1; AAR 5/72-3. (17½)

    AMATEUR—FRR 8/70-1; WOL 9/70-4; MIW 10/70-4; JAX 3/71-3; NFL 3/71-4; MIW 4/71-2; MAD 5/71-2; WOL 5/71-2; MIL 6/71-4; MAD 8/71-1; AAR 9/71-1; JAX 3/72-4; MAD 8/72-1; MAN 8/72-1; WOL 9/72-1; MIW 10/72-1; OHV 9/72-2. (50½)

RIVER OAKS ROWDY BEAR SA-721676 5/17/69 Mr. and Mrs. Bing Grunwald—By River Oaks Corky* (Martens' Mister Nifty* - Don's Ginny Soo) ex Moody's Dell (Del-Tone Buck* - Rill-Shannon's Dark Del)

    OPEN—LST 3/72-2; RKM 8/72-2; SHE 9/72-2. (9)

RIVER ROAD BIPPY SA-773461 5/25/69 Dr. Armand Jaques—By Mi-Cris Drambuie* (Highlander's Bojangles - Twink of Belle Isle) ex Chere Te Negresse (Mr. Black of Bissonet - Flash's Lady Boots)

    OPEN—CHY 8/72-2. (3)

RIVER ROAD REHO SA-402099 5/1/65 John M. Bacon—By Charley of Avandale (Zelstone Sparkle - Zelstone Queen) ex Cricket Diana (Gustav of Obsidian - Stormy Twink)

    OPEN—SLA 9/68-4. (½)

ROBINHOOD'S GEECHEE JUNIOR SA-523961 5/22/67 Mr. and Mrs. Mahlon B. Wallace, Jr.—By Geechee* (Ridgewood Playboy - Grace-Art's Smart Lady) ex Hetero Pam of Southlands (Rock of Canterbury - Aqua Jill of Dover)

    OPEN—LIT 4/72-4; MIT 8/72-3; DUL 8/72-3; SXV 9/72-4. (3)

ROCKBEND'S KAMAKURA SA-503359 9/8/67 Mrs. Alanson C. Brown III—By Carr-Lab Penrod* (Paha Sapa Chief II - Ironwood Cherokee Chica) ex Rockbend's Redhead (Del-Tone Buck* - Rockbend's Fan Marker)

    OPEN—MAR 10/71-2. (3)

    AMATEUR—WNY 9/71-3. (1)

ROCKBEND'S MAGIC MARKER SA-440171 1/5/66 James R. Smith—By Sage Joker* (Sage of Sanfray - Sheer Dee Lite) ex Rockbend's Redhead (Del-Tone Buck* - Rockbend's Fan Marker)

    OPEN—MAD 8/70-2. (3)

    AMATEUR—AAR 5/72-4. (½)

ROCKET OF FRONTIER SA-818965 6/27/68 Mrs. Gaylord Donnelly—By Martens' Little Smoky* (Crowder - Martens' Little Bullet) ex Ike's Blue Lady (Nilo Mister President - Pippin of Picardy)

    OPEN—AAR 5/72-2. (3)

FC-AFC ROCKY ROAD OF ZENITH SA-384628 2/9/66 Andrew Pruitt —By Black Mike of Lakewood (Vicky's Duffy Boy - Thornwood Bracken Sweet) ex Jezebel of Normandy (Yankee Clipper of Reo Raj - Belle of Zenith)

    OPEN—GOL 5/70-2; ALK 9/70-3; SLA 10/70-4; NTX 11/70-3; LST 3/71-4; NTX 3/71-1; SLA 4/71-2; SHA 4/71-4; WIL 8/71-2; PUG 8/71-1; SAM 9/71-3; NLA 10/71-2; NLA 3/72-2; IDA 5/72-3; SPO 5/72-1; PUG 8/72-2; SAM 9/72-3; ALM 11/72-2. (42½)

    AMATEUR—WIL 8/69-4; WMO 9/69-1; SAM 3/70-2; ROV 3/70-2; TAC 4/70-2; NWR 4/70-1; IDA 5/70-4; WMO 5/70-4; TAC 8/70-4; PUG 8/70-2; ALK 9/70-1; NWR 9/70-1; MON 9/70-3; CAS 10/70-3; LST 10/70-2; ALM 11/70-3; TAC 4/71-2; NWR 4/71-4; MTR 6/71-2; TAC 8/71-1; PUG 8/71-2; ORE

9/71-1; PTA 3/72-1; ORE 3/72-2; PUG 4/72-1; SPO 5/72-4; WIL 8/72-4; PUG 8/72-3; NWR 9/72-3; SPO 9/72-3; LST 10/72-2. (79½)

ROCKY'S DARTEGA SA-317225 1/24/64 Mrs. Edward J. Keady—By Castlemore Shamus (Strokestown Duke of Blaircourt - Hilldown Sylver) ex Birdie's Misty (Crozier's Cinco' Cork - Rockwall's Birdie)
OPEN—TAL 3/68-3; FTP 5/69-2; WNY 9/69-2; LAB 5/70-4; MAI 9/70-4; COL 10/71-2. (11)
AMATEUR—TAL 3/69-1; SWA 10/69-2; MTA 10/72-2; NFL 11/72-3. (12)

FC-AFC RODNEY'S MR. M. L. COON SA-570862 2/9/68 George Cassel and Jere Bogrett—By Cascade's Rodney St. Clair* (Boley's Cascade - Queen Eby of Lakenham) ex Queen of Opal's Black Pepper (Black Flash of Hellgate - Queen of Opal)
OPEN—WMO 9/70-1; SNA 5/71-1; SNA 8/71-4; NTX 10/71-1; MON 6/72-4; BHB 6/72-1. (21)
AMATEUR—SNA 5/71-4; HEL 9/71-2; BHB 6/72-1; EID 7/72-4. (9)

ROLIDA'S STUBBY BANDIT SA-232512 1/14/63 T. F. Walsh—By Bondill's Black Bandit (Flying Ebony of Franklin - Bigstone Corky) ex Rolida's Ebony Angel (Tan Beau's Nordake Dach - Genell's Black Judy)
OPEN—PIK 8/67-3. (1)
AMATEUR—CHY 8/67-2; CNB 5/70-2; PIK 5/70-1; RKM 5/70-3; PIK 8/70-4. (12½)

FC ROUND VALLEY'S LUCKY TIGGER SA-650554 1/1/69 Dr. David J. Collon—By Spring Farm's Lucky* (Paha Sapa Chief II - Ironwood Cherokee Chica) ex Blitz of Round Valley (Alpine Cherokee Rocket - Yankee's Ebony Girl)
OPEN—PTA 3/71-1; WOL 9/72-4; OHV 9/72-1; MIW 10/72-4; MTA 10/72-2. (14)
AMATEUR—LST 3/71-1; WOL 9/71-4. (5½)

FC-AFC ROVER OF RAMSEY PLACE SA-192706 3/16/63 George R. Pidgeon—By Del-Tone Buck* (Martens' Hi Style Buck - Glen-Water Fan Fare) ex Valgaard Lady of Shady Lane (Yankee Clipper of Reo Raj - Rock Haven's Black Angel)
OPEN—MIV 10/66-4; MIV 4/68-1; MIV 10/68-3; MOB 11/68-2; MAD 5/69-3; AAR 5/69-4; SLA 9/69-3; NLA 10/69-2; MIV 10/69-1; MTA 10/69-2: MEM 10/69-4; MEM 3/70-3; BUK 4/70-2; WIS 5/70-3; MII 5/70-1; MIL 6/70-3; NFL 4/71-3; MOB 3/71-3; MEM 10/71-2. (39½)
AMATEUR—MEM 3/67-4; MEM 10/67-2; MOB 11/67-1; MTA 10/68-2; MEM 10/68-4; MOB 11/68-2; MOB 2/70-1; MEM 3/70-1; MEM 10/70-4. (25½)

ROWDY'S SEAN OF THE CORKIES SA-223988 6/29/63 S. C. Shea— By Roy's Rowdy (Cork of Oakwood Lane - Beautywood's Creole Jane) ex Princess Nickawampus (Pepper's Jiggs - Jibodad Velvet)
OPEN—MIL 6/68-3; FTP 5/69-1; BUK 8/69-2. (9)
AMATEUR—FRR 8/66-1; WIS 4/67-3; GOL 5/67-3; MTA 3/68-4; OHV 9/68-3; FTP 5/69-3; BUK 9/70-3. (10½)

NRFC '72-AFC ROYAL'S MOOSE'S MOE SA-246647 3/22/63 W. D. Connor—By Royal's Moose (Royal of Garfield - Martens' Lady Jane) ex Spirit Lake Gal (Trevrchamp Minyok - Joe's Eager Beaver)
OPEN—MNS 5/66-4; MNS 5/67-1; SXV 9/67-2; NOI 9/67-2; KAN 10/67-1; SLA 2/68-1; LST 3/68-1; NEB 4/68-2; MOV 9/68-3; KAN 3/69-2; NEB 4/69-1; WIS 4/69-1; RKM 8/69-1; AAR 8/69-3; MAD 5/70-4; SHO 9/70-1; MOV 9/70-1; KAN 10/70-1; JAY 3/71-4; KAN 4/71-3; PIK 5/71-1; RKM 8/71-1; ALB 5/72-2; MAD 8/72-2; RKM 8/72-4; CHY 8/72-1; MOV 9/72-4; MEM 10/72-1; NAT 11/72-1. (98½)

181

AMATEUR—CMI 5/66-1; TRI 6/66-4; MNS 9/66-3; MOV 9/66-2; KAN 10/66-3; NEB 4/67-3; PTA 3/68-2; CNB 5/68-1; PIK 8/68-2; SXV 8/68-4; COL 9/68-4; MIW 10/68-1; MIV 10/68-2; LST 2/69-3; NEB 4/69-5; WIS 4/69-1; MAD 8/69-1; WNY 9/69-4; MOV 9/69-2; KAN 5/70-1; NEB 4/70-1; WIS 5/70-4; MAD 8/70-1; WIS 9/70-4; JAY 3/71-1; KAN 4/71-4; MIV 4/71-2; RKM 6/71-2; JAY 3/72-1; ALB 5/72-1; PIK 5/72-2; MTR 5/72-3; MAD 8/72-3; KAN 10/72-3; MEM 10/72-2. (97½)

FC ROYL JAY SA-281614 5/19/64 Leroy A. Croshaw—By Dutchmoor's Pooh Bear (Calypso Clipper - Jet's Tammy) ex Howmor's Dark Gypsy (Marshwise Snapshooter - Topsy's Peg)
OPEN—SXV 9/67-1; MNS 5/69-1; KAN 3/72-4. (10½)

SAD SAM JONES S-97891 4/11/58 C. W. Tyler—By Mister Jones of Niskayuna (St. Jones Blackie - Wyandotte Pin-Up) ex Flicker of Timber Town (Sir Cabot of Timber Town - Candlelight of Timber Town)
AMATEUR—FRR 8/66-4; WOL 9/66-4; WOL 9/67-3. (2)

FC-AFC SAGE JOKER SA-81788 8/11/60 Ellen W. and John V. Eliot, Jr. —By Sage of Sanfray (La Sage's Smoky - Cream City Clipper) ex Sheer Deelight (Labcroft Brandy - Whileaway Crathie)
OPEN—WIS 4/64-1; MAN 8/64-1; AAR 9/64-1; MAD 8/65-2; WIS 4/66-4; AAR 5/66-4. (19)
AMATEUR—MIW 4/65-3; AAR 5/65-4; MNS 9/65-4; WIS 9/65-1; AAR 5/66-2; AAR 5/68-1; MAD 5/69-1; GOL 5/69-3. (21)

SAGE RAMBLER SA-82503 11/8/60 Edwin Ross — By Sage Rider (Queenie's Buck - Diadem) ex Rexana (Topsy's Rex - Pat V)
AMATEUR—MAD 5/67-1. (5)

FC SAGE'S SASKERAM PETE SA-129205 10/6/61 Dr. and Mrs. R. Kesky —By Sage of Sanfray (La Sage's Smoky - Cream City Clipper) ex Sheer Deelight (Labcroft Brandy - Whileaway Crathie)
OPEN—BHB 6/65-3; WIS 9/65-4; WIS 4/66-3; FRR 8/66-4; WIS 9/66-3; MIW 10/66-1; NFL 2/67-2; NTX 3/67-4; MIW 4/67-2; WIS 4/68-1; MAD 5/68-2. (23½)

FC SALT VALLEY EPAMINONDAS SA-127197 12/7/60 Frank C. Ash— By Salt Valley Ottie (Butch's Bitterroot Smokey - Fenbroke's Meath) ex Thats Mandy (Freehaven Muscles - Treasure State Be Wise)
OPEN—PIK 8/64-1; RKM 8/64-3; WNY 9/65-3; WNY 9/67-3; NOI 9/68-1. (13)
AMATEUR—IDA 5/64-2; SNA 5/65-2; GSL 5/65-2. (9)

SALT VALLEY ESPRESSO SA-734140 2/10/68 Carroll A. Rice — By Samson's George of Glenspey* (Sam Frizel of Glenspey - Thunder Chief's Shiri) ex Penny of Evergreen* (Martens' Mr. Nifty* - Pre-Don Jacky)
OPEN—RKM 5/72-4. (½)

FC-AFC SAM FRIZEL OF GLENSPEY S-829932 6/19/56 Mrs. Warner L. Atkins—By Liseter Timber (Comus of Timbertown - Liseter Echo) ex Flash of Glenspey (Ledgeland's Peter - Princess of Barrington)
OPEN—MOV 9/60-4; NTX 3/61-3; KAN 3/61-1; CNB 5/61-3; MNS 5/61-1; KAN 10/61-4; NTX 3/62-1; KAN 3/62-3; CNB 5/62-1; AAR 9/62-2; OHV 9/62-2; NTX 10/62-4; NTX 3/63-3; MIW 4/63-1; WIS 4/63-1; MAD 8/63-2; NEB 4/64-3; RKM 5/64-1; MAD 8/64-1; MAN 8/64-2; KAN 10/64-1; NLA 3/65-3; KAN 4/65-1; MIW 4/65-1; NOI 10/65-3; MIW 10/65-4; KAN 10/65-3; MAD 8/66-2. (80)
AMATEUR—CNB 5/61-2; MIV 4/62-3; KAN 3/62-2; CNB 5/62-4; LST 10/62-3; NLA 10/62-4; NTX 3/63-1; MON 5/63-2;

Rocky Road of Zenith

Royal's Moose's Moe

Sam Frizel of Glenspey

Samson's George of Glenspey

MIV 10/63-2; KAN 10/63-1; NTX 3/64-2; MON 5/64-1; MIW 10/64-4; LST 3/65-2; PTA 3/65-1; NTX 3/65-3; NOI 10/65-1; MEM 3/66-1; NFL 2/67-4; LST 3/67-1; PTA 3/67-2. (61)

SAM OF ARROWHEAD LAKE SA-464812 3/22/67 Dr. J. D. Ramsey— By Playboy's Black Cloud (Ridgewood Playboy - Topsy Turvy Tar Baby) ex Royal Lady in Black (Royal of Garfield - Kadet Fields Velvet) OPEN—SOO 4/72-4. (½)

FC SAM OF DIXIE RAPIDS SA-527728 10/5/67 Charles V. Allain—By Skipper of the Rapids (Timberlane Shadows - Satan of Rolling Hills) ex Shining Black Dixie (Martens' Busy Digger - Shining Jackie)
OPEN—ALB 5/71-1; CAS 9/71-4; SLA 3/72-1. (10½)
AMATEUR—CAS 10/70-4; ALB 5/71-4; MTA 4/72-4. (1½)

SAM OF MARLBORO COUNTRY SA-268155 6/29/63 Dan. J. Jones— By Tuxedo of Green Point (Hartfiel's Sunburst Lad - Hartfiel's Midnight Lady) ex Mike's Nancy (Clover Creek's Bo-Marc - Lancelot's Guinevere)
AMATEUR—PUG 8/70-3; NWR 9/70-3; PUG 4/71-1. (7)

FC-AFC SAMSON'S GEORGE OF GLENSPEY SA-223731 4/12/63 Mrs. Warner L. Atkins—By Sam Frizel of Glenspey* (Liseter Timber - Flash of Glenspey) ex Thunder Chief's Shiri (Paha Sapa Chief II - Zipper's Swift Anne)
OPEN—CHY 9/65-2; MTR 9/65-1; MOV 10/65-3; SLA 2/66-3; LST 3/66-1; NTX 3/66-2; MIW 4/66-4; MON 6/66-2; RKM 8/66-1; MON 9/66-1; JAY 3/67-2; MIW 4/67-4; MII 5/67-3; RKM 5/67-2; MOV 9/67-2; ALM 11/67-3; ALM 2/68-4; NEB 4/68-3; CNB 5/68-2; MII 5/68-1; KAN 10/68-4; ALM 2/69-4; MIV 4/69-2; MIW 4/69-1; NTX 3/70-1; NEB 4/70-2. (67½)
AMATEUR—MON 9/66-1; MIW 10/67-1; MOV 9/68-1; PTA 3/69-1; ALM 2/70-3; PTA 3/70-2; MIW 4/70-1; DEL 10/70-4; MTA 4/71-4; MEM 4/71-4. (30½)

SAM'S THUNDER CLOUD SA-225806 7/24/63 Robert L. and Alice M. Brown—By Sam of Hunter Mountain (Mike of Hunter Mountain - Lady Salle) ex Black Dixie Princess (Kashpureff Silver King - Kashpureff Kathreen)
OPEN—NCA 9/69-1. (5)
AMATEUR—NCA 9/67-1. (5)

FC-AFC SANDY OF SOURDOUGH SA-212126 6/15/63 Charles E. Bunn, Jr.—By Pokey of Sourdough (Timewaster's Shadow - Benson's Black Patu) ex Gee Gee (Clinker II - Melan)
OPEN—WOL 9/66-4; MTA 3/67-2; LIR 4/67-4; MAI 5/67-4; FTP 6/67-4; LAB (S) 11/67-3; SLA 9/68-2; MTA 3/69-1; NLA 10/69-3; MTA 3/70-3; NLA 10/70-1; MIV 10/70-4; MTA 10/70-1; NLA 3/71-1; MTA 10/71-3. (32½)
AMATEUR—BUK 4/66-2; PIK 8/66-2; WOL 9/66-2; NTX 3/69-4; MIS 4/69-1; AAR 8/69-3; NLA 10/69-3; MIT 8/70-4; NDK 8/70-2; MIV 10/70-2; MTA 10/70-1; NTX 11/70-1; MEM 4/71-1; NDK 8/71-1; MTA 10/71-1; MEM 10/71-2; MEM 4/72-4; LIT 4/72-2. (54½)

SAUK TRAIL BLACK MOUSE SA-338536 1/29/65 David Collon — By Dutchmoor's Etaoin Shrdlu (Calypso Clipper - Jet's Tammy) ex Sauk Trail Black Pine (Comanche of Thunderbolt - Sauk Trail Black Fox)
OPEN—OHV 10/69-4; AAR 5/70-2. (3½)

FC-AFC SAUK TRAIL DEEPWELL "DOC" SA-490968 2/26/67 Jack Boettcher—By Stormy of Spirit Lake Gal (Ace Bingo - Spirit Lake Gal) ex Sauk Trail Velvet Cougar (Cougar's Rocket* - Jibodad Velvet)

184

OPEN—IDA 8/69-4; SHA 9/69-2; LAS 2/70-4; ORE 4/70-2; SRN 5/70-2; ORE 9/70-2; ROV 3/71-2; WIL 8/71-4; ORE 9/71-2; PUG 4/72-2; WIL 8/72-1. (27½)

AMATEUR—RED 7/69-2; SHA 9/69-2; ORE 9/69-3; SPO 9/69-4; ROV 3/70-3; PUG 4/70-3; SHA 4/71-1; WIL 8/71-4; SHA 9/71-1; NWR 9/71-1; PUG 4/72-3; SHA 4/72-3; TAC 8/72-3; WIL 8/72-2; SHA 9/72-2; ORE 9/72-3. (35)

FC SAUK TRAIL SENATOR SA-641396 11/4/68 Oscar S. Brewer—By Lord Bomar* (Blackfoot's Happy New Year - Peg's Blackfoot Queen) ex Sauk Trail Velvet Cougar (Cougar's Rocket* - Jibodad Velvet)
OPEN—MOV 9/71-4; KAN 10/71-3; LST 3/72-3; KAN 3/72-1; MTR 5/72-1; PIK 5/72-1; CHY 8/72-3; HEL 9/72-2. (21½)
AMATEUR—SHE 9/71-4; ALB 5/72-2. (3½)

FC-AFC SAZERAC MAC S-965869 12/9/58 Dr. J. Fertitta—By Glenhead Zuider (Glenhead Jimmy - Ariston Jet) ex Carefree Lass (Feast of Fyvie - Camoran Crocus)
OPEN—PTA 9/62-2; NTX 10/62-1; NTX 10/63-1; ALM 11/63-4; PTA 3/64-2; NLA 3/64-3; NTX 10/64-3; PTA 10/64-1; ALM 11/64-2; NTX 10/65-3; SLA 9/66-3; NTX 10/66-3; PTA 10/66-3; LST 10/66-2; SLA 9/67-1; NLA 10/67-2; ALM 11/67-2. (44½)
AMATEUR—NLA 3/63-2; NLA 10/63-4; ALM 2/64-1; NLA 3/64-2; MAD 8/64-1; NTX 10/64-3: PTA 10/64-4; LST 10/64-2; ALM 2/65-4; NLA 10/65-4; PTA 10/65-1; MAD 8/66-3; PTA 10/66-2; ALM 11/66-2. (34)

SEAFIELD CHIEF SA-269826 4/24/64 Robert K. Plant, M.D. — By Syldonnel's Douk (Chuck of Bracken - Country Club's Little Bullet) ex Cindy of Bardonda (Phantom Prince of Richmond - Greentimber Boots of Bardonda)
AMATEUR—ORE 3/69-3. (1)

FC-AFC SHADOW OF PROVINCETOWN SA-564529 2/29/68 Josephine T. Reeve—By Charles of Burgundy (Blackie of Westview - Je Suis Pret) ex Tarbaby's Mistake (Black Jet XVI* - Boot's Tar Baby)
OPEN—CSC 10/70-4; SNA 5/71-2; GSL 8/71-2; ROV 3/72-1; IDA 5/72-2; GSL 5/72-3; WMO 5/72-4; SNA 8/72-1; SCA 9/72-1. (26)
AMATEUR—IDA 8/71-4; SNA 8/71-2; WMO 9/71-3: PHO 10/71-4; SNA 5/72-2; GSL 5/72-1; EID 7/72-1; NCA 9/72-3; PHO 10/72-1. (27)

FC-AFC SHADOW OF ROCKY LANE SA-372771 1/2/66 John F. White —By Glor-Loral Watch My Smoke (Annwyn's Shedrow - Glor-Loral Lightning Ebony) ex Topsy Turvy Tar Baby (Nigger of Dacity - Glenwater Fal-Lal)
OPEN—WIS 4/69-2; MEM 10/69-2; MOB 10/69-1; JAX 2/70-1; BUK 4/70-4; MII 5/70-4; MEM 4/71-4; MII 5/71-3; DUL 8/71-2; NDK 8/71-4; AAR 9/71-4; WOL 9/71-1; MOB 3/72-3; MIV 4/72-1; LIT 4/72-1; SLA 9/72-2. (41½)
AMATEUR—MEM 10/69-3; MOB 2/70-4; MEM 3/70-2; WIS 5/70-1; DUL 8/70-2; MIL 6/70-4; MOB 11/70-1; SLA 10/71-3; MIV 10/71-4; MOB 11/71-3; MOB 3/72-1; MII 6/72-2. (28½)

SHAG OF SHANTY BAY SA-387762 1/2/66 John P. Roughen — By Glor-Loral Watch My Smoke (Annwyn's Shedrow - Glor-Loral Lightning Ebony) ex Topsy Turvy Tar Baby (Nigger of Dacity - Glen-Water Fal-Lal)
AMATEUR—AAR 9/71-4; TRI 6/72-3. (1½)

FC-AFC SHAMROCK ACRES DRAKE SA-389721 3/23/66 Keith Anderson and Jack Hogue—By Ridgewood Playboy (La Sage's Smoky - Nelgard's Counter Point) ex Shamrock A of Ralston Valley (Zelstone Sparkle - Spirit of Avandale)

OPEN—MON 9/69-4; PIK 8/70-3; PIK 5/71-2; CWY 8/71-2; MON 9/71-2; SHE 9/71-1; JAY 3/72-4; NEB 4/72-3; ALB 7/72-4; MON 9/72-2. (20½)

AMATEUR—MTR 5/69-3; SHE 8/69-2; MOV 9/69-4; MON 6/70-2; BHB 6/70-1; EID 7/70-2; PIK 8/70-2; RKM 8/70-1; HEL 9/70-2; MON 9/70-2; NEB 4/71-1; PIK 5/71-2; MON 6/71-1; ALB 7/71-4; NEB 4/72-4; CNB 5/72-3; PIK 5/72-3; MTR 5/72-4; SHE 9/72-1; MON 9/72-2; PIK 8/72-3. (55)

AFC SHAMROCK ACRES GUN AWAY SA-150157 9/30/61 Mrs. Clifford V. Brokaw, Jr.—By Beautywood Rare Trouble (Roy's Rowdy - Beautywood's Repeat) ex Marlab Gypsy (Marlab Murky Mike - Marlab Top Tune)
OPEN—MOB 2/68-3; MTA 3/68-3; BUK 4/68-2; MAD 8/68-3. (6)

AMATEUR——MAI 5/65-2; MAN 8/65-2; NUT 5/67-4; MAI 5/67-3; MAN 8/67-1; WOL 9/67-1; MAN 8/68-3; BUK 8/68-2; OHV 9/68-2. (24½)

SHAMROCK ACRES MODOC PAINTER SA-646899 1/14/69 Virginia T. Wylie—By Super Chief* (Paha Sapa Chief II - Ironwood Cherokee Chica) ex Shamrock Acres Smoky Cinder (Martens' Little Smoky* - Shamrock Acres Miss Cinders)
AMATEUR—WNY 9/72-3. (1)

SHAMROCK ACRES NYLIC NED SA-519944 10/12/67 Chet McCrory —By Super Chief* (Paha Sapa Chief II - Ironwood Cherokee Chica) ex Could Be's Miss Erable (Mighty Manfred of Maryglo - Beer's Mug)
AMATEUR—NCA 9/72-4. (½)

SHAMROCK ACRES SUPER DRIVE SA-466881 3/7/67 Wm. K. Laughlin—By Super Chief* (Paha Sapa Chief II - Ironwood Cherokee Chica) ex Could Be's Miss Erable (Mighty Manfred of Maryglo - Beer's Mug)
OPEN—WOM 4/71-4; MAI 9/71-4; WNY 9/71-4; CNY 5/72-1; LAB (S) 11/72-2. (9½)

SHAMROCK ACRES SUPERSTITION SA-470518 3/7/67 Dr. John Morgan—By Super Chief* (Paha Sapa Chief II - Ironwood Cherokee Chica) ex Could Be's Miss Erable (Mighty Manfred of Maryglo - Beer's Mug)
OPEN—WOM 4/70-2; COL 10/70-3; SWA 11/71-3; JAX 3/72-3; JAM 3/72-2. (9)

AMATEUR—WOM 10/70-4; LAB (S) 11/70-3; CNY 5/71-2; SWA 11/71-2; JAM 3/72-3; CNY 5/72-3; LIR 10/72-4; WOM 10/72-2; LAB (S) 11/72-3. (14)

FC SHAMROCK ACRES SUPER VALUE SA-649586 1/31/68 J. J. Heneghan—By Super Chief* (Paha Sapa Chief II - Ironwood Cherokee Chica) ex Shamrock A of Ralston Valley (Zelstone Sparkle - Spirit of Avandale)
OPEN—PUG 8/70-4; IDA 5/71-1; SAG 7/71-2; TAC 8/71-1; IDA 8/71-1; SAM 9/71-2; SHA 9/71-1; CSC 2/72-3; NCA 3/72-2; SAM 3/72-3; ORE 3/72-1; NWR 4/72-2; SPO 5/72-4; RED 7/72-1; SHA 9/72-4; NWR 9/72-4; SPO 9/72-1. (51)

SHANTOO TAR BUCK SA-317643 2/25/65 Dan Mahoney—By Gadwall's Thunder (Paha Sapa Chief II - Gadwall's Golden Blarney) ex Stormy's Black Cinderella (Tiger of Cottonwood - Stormy Lady II)
OPEN—ALB 5/70-3; BHB 6/71-3. (2)

FC-AFC SHAWNEE ACE OF SPADES SA-108688 6/21/61 Perle and Gladys Lewis—By Nilo Smoky's Ace of Spades (Stonegate's Ace of Spades - Nilo Cinderella) ex Lady of Ahab (Nilo Black Tail Buck - Bess III)

OPEN—MEM 10/65-4; WOL 5/66-3; AAR 5/66-3; NDK 8/66-4; MTA 10/66-4; NFL 11/66-3; MAD 5/67-4; GOL 5/67-3; AAR 9/67-3; WIS 9/67-1; ALM 2/68-3. (13)

AMATEUR—MEM 10/63-4; WMT 6/65-4; MTA 10/65-4; GOL 5/67-1. (6½)

SHOREMEADOW CHALLENGE SA-117891 7/31/61 Douglas Proby— By Shoremeadow Barnacle Bill (Shed's Black Shadow - Nodak's Topps) ex Beautywood's Lady Fair (Webway's Crusader - Gilmore's Peggy)

OPEN—NWR 9/65-2. (3)

AMATEUR—TAC 4/67-3. (1)

SILLS' BLACK BANDIT SA-786889 12/23/69 Mr. and Mrs. David Crow —By Anzac of Zenith* (Black Mike of Lakewood - Jezebel of Normandy) ex Sills' Little Smokey Lewbonnie (Martens' Little Smoky*- Hunt's Charming Annabelle)

OPEN—MON 9/72-1; HEL 9/72-4; LST 10/72-2. (8½)

SILVER SQUIRE SA-381525 5/14/65 E. Peterson and G. B. Brunner— By Shane of Shannon Hills (Rice's Busy Gamekeeper - Galleywood Hotshot of Rice) ex Tammy of Shannon Hills (Noir Chien Arf - Jill of Bluffview)

OPEN—SXV 9/71-1. (5)

FC SINDBAD IV SA-349762 9/20/65 Robert M. Newbury—By Ridgewood Playboy (La Sage's Smoky - Nelgard's Counter Point) ex Odell's Nancy II (Harrel's Buster of Blackus - Rahat of Beaver Bay)

OPEN—MIW 10/69-4; NFL 2/70-3; GOL 5/71-2; MOV 9/71-4; MIW 10/71-1. (10)

AMATEUR—MAD 8/70-4; MEM 4/71-3. (1½)

AFC SIR CALEB OF AUDLON SA-601060 5/20/68 Joseph A. Stary, Jr.— By Del-Tone Buck* (Martens' Hi Style Buck - Glen-Water Fan Fare) ex Jet Star of Audlon (Paha Saa Chief II - Star of Fate)

OPEN—WOL 9/72-1. (5)

AMATEUR—WIS 9/71-1; MIW 10/71-3; MEM 10/71-1; MII 6/72-3; WOL 9/72-3. (13)

FC-AFC SIR KNIGHT FALCON S-979796 2/5/59 Perry E. and Zola R. Pound—By Patch of Bonniehurst (Bonniehurst King Tut - Bonniehurst Toi Jet) ex Faindi Kalp Asswad (Malish Kalp Asswad - Black Cloud Katchina)

OPEN—CNB 5/63-4; MON 9/63-4; ALM 2/64-1; KAN 3/64-4; PIK 8/64-4; MTR 9/64-4; MOV 9/64-4; NOI 10/64-1 MON 6/65-4; PIK 8/65-1; SHE 9/65-1; PIK 5/67-2; MTR 5/68-2; CHY 8/68-4. (30)

AMATEUR—MTR 9/62-3; CNB 5/63-2; RKM 8/63-4; MTR 9/63-1; SHE 9/64-1; MTR 9/64-1; SHE 9/65-1; RKM 8/66-3; PIK 5/67-1; CHY 8/67-1; CHY 8/68-1; SHE 8/68-1; SHE 6/69-4; SHE 8/69-1. (51)

FC-AFC SIR MIKE OF ORCHARDVIEW SA-46220 1/13/59 Roger Vasselais—By Tugney of Oakview (Austin of Avandale - Amber) ex Red Lady's Cinderella (Mississippi King - Red Lady)

OPEN—3/64-2; WNY 9/64-2; WOL 9/64-1; MAR 10/64-4; DEL 10/64-4; ALM 2/65-2; PTA 3/65-1; LIR 4/65-3; DUL 6/65-4; WOL 9/65-2; LIR 10/65-2; NFL 2/66-3; MOB 2/66-4; WOM 4/66-3; MNS 5/66-2; TRI 6/66-1; BUK 6/66-2; LIR 10/66-3; SWA 11/66-1; MAI 5/67-3; MAI 9/67-3. (49)

AMATEUR—BUK 9/62-4; LST 3/63-1; NUT 5/63-2; CNY 5/63-2; BUK 9/63-3; MAR 10/63-2; TAL 3/64-2; NEB 4/64-4; LAB 4/64-4; WOL 5/64-1; MAD 8/64-2; WOL 9/64-4; MAR

10/64-4; LST 3/65-1; SWA 3/65-1; TAL 3/65-4; WOM 4/65-2; LAB 4/65-2; SHR 5/65-1; NUT 5/65-1; DUL 6/65-3; BUK 9/65-1; LIR 10/65-3; SLA 2/66-2; MOB 2/66-2; MEM 3/66-4; SWA 3/66-2; TAL 3/66-1; LAB 4/66-3; MII 5/66-4; MNS 5/66-2; CMI 5/66-2; TRI 6/66-1; BHB 6/66-4; BUK 9/66-1; WOL 9/66-1; OHV 9/66-1; SWA 11/66-1; CMI 5/67-3; TRI 6/67-1; MIL 6/67-3; FRR 8/67-1; WNY 9/67-1; COL 9/67-2.　　　　(129½)

SKOOKUM BINGO SA-476150 5/8/66 Virginia T. Wylie — By Nodrog Nike* (Mainliner Mike - Beautywood's Rebel Queen) ex Skookum Scooter (Castlemore Shamus - Birdie's Misty)
OPEN—LIR 5/72-3.　　　　(1)
AMATEUR—COL 9/69-3; LAB 11/69-3; WCH 5/70-3; SHO 9/70-2; SWA 11/70-2; LIR 5/71-2; DEL 10/71-3.　　　　(13)

FC SKOOKUM DALE'S NIKE MARK X SA-595928 5/8/66 Dr. Richard C. Greenleaf—By Nodrog Nike* (Mainliner Mike - Beautywood's Rebel Queen) ex Skookum Scooter (Castlemore Shamus - Birdie's Misty)
OPEN—COL 9/69-3; MAI 9/69-2; WCH 5/70-4; FTP 6/70-4; TAL 4/71-3; WOM 4/71-1; MAR 10/71-3; SRZ 2/72-3; CSC 2/72-4.　　　　(13½)

AFC SMOKE TAIL'S CHICO SA-46197 4/18/60 Howard A. Jacobs—By Dolobran's Smoke Tail (Dolobran's Spook - Dolobran's Mitghy Mite) ex Shady Haven Farm Lady (Smudge of Prairie Creek Farm - Random Lake Black Ghost)
OPEN—MTR 9/63-3; MON 9/65-1; MON 6/66-4; SHE 9/66-3; MTR 9/66-4; MTR 5/68-3; SHE 8/68-4.　　　　(9½)
AMATEUR—CHY 5/63-4; BHB 6/64-1; CHY 8/64-2; MIT 8/65-2; CHY 8/65-1; MTR 9/66-1; MTR 5/67-1; MON 6/67-3; MTR 5/68-2; MTR 5/70-4.　　　　(31)

SMOKEY OF JETCIN SA-231876 6/18/62 Donald E. Mann—My Jet of Spook (Spook of Granton - Cymro Queen) ex Nodak Tar Pride (Bigstone Tar Gum - Stonegate's Trixie)
AMATEUR—NWR 9/69-1; SAM 3/70-1; PUG 4/70-2; PUG 4/71-4.　　　　(13½)

FC SMOKY'S BLACK JET SA-386598 8/17/65 John M. Olin — By Martens' Little Smoky* (Crowder - Martens' Little Bullet) ex Hunt's Charming Annebelle (Del-Tone Buck* - Jac-Lor Miss Cindy)
OPEN—WIS 5/70-2; MNS 9/70-1; LIT 4/71-2; MIC 8/71-3; MNS 9/71-1; MIV 10/71-4; MIW 4/72-2; WIS 4/72-4; MII 6/72-4; MIW 10/72-1.　　　　(26½)

SNOOPY OF DICKINSON SA-376353 12/21/65 J. T. Montgomery—By Cher Te Beau of Repmen (Cher Te Neg - Calcasieu Queen) ex Cathy-Chris' Yellow Sue (Colonel's Mr. Chips - Barnes Sugar Bee)
OPEN—LST 10/71-3.　　　　(1)

SPIRIT'S BLACK PEPPER SA-190899 7/7/62 J. D. Rankin, Jr. — By Rowdy Dow of Minyok (Trevrchamp Minyok - Highland Jet's Queen Sheba) ex Ivanhoe Sally (Crowder - Little Magic Lady)
OPEN—MTR 5/68-4.　　　　(½)

SPOOK OF JETCIN SA-238101 6/18/62 Gordon Lindemere—By My Jet of Spook (Spook of Granton - Cymro Queen) ex Nodak Tar Pride (Bigstone Tar Gum - Stonegate's Trixie)
OPEN—SAM 3/68-4.　　　　(½)

SPOOK OF MARIAN'S TIM S-986489 11/23/58 Don Hutt—By Marian's Timothy (Rip of Holly Hill - Shady of Spanaway Creek) ex Beautywood's Lady Fair (Webway's Crusader - Gilmore's Peggy)
OPEN—BHB 6/64-3; TAC 8/66-3; MON 6/67-3.　　　　(3)
AMATEUR—BHB 6/65-3; MON 6/66-1.　　　　(6)

SPORT OF UPLAND FARM SA-437645 5/24/66 Roger Vasselais—By
Glengarven's Mik* (Glengarven's Kim - Gordon's Black Babe) ex
Sister Kate of Upland Farm (Skeeter of Upland Farm - Belle of Upland
Farm)
    OPEN—MIL 6/70-4.   (½)

SPRING FARMS LUCKY SA-411762 7/18/66 Rex V. Carr—By Paha
Sapa Chief II (Freehaven Muscles - Treasure State Be Wise) ex Ironwood Cherokee Chica (Cherokee Buck - Glen-Water Fantom)
    OPEN—LAS 2/72-3.   (3)
    AMATEUR—SCA 3/72-2.   (3)

SPRING FARM'S SMOKEY SA-553356 3/5/68 Mrs. George Schellinger
    —By Spring Farm's Lucky* (Paha Sapa Chief II - Ironwood Cherokee
Chica) ex Midnight Star of Ruslyn (Ace-Hi's Lone Star - Opal of
Ramapo Valley)
    OPEN—MAI 9/72-4; LIR 10/72-3.   (1½)
    AMATEUR—WOM 4/71-3; COL 10/71-4; COL 9/72-3.   (2½)

AFC SQUIRE OF REO RAJ SA-261820 6/1/63 John R. Cross — By
Yankee Clipper of Reo Raj (Stonegate's Captain - Little Peggy Black
Gum) ex Duchess of Miller's Haven (Duke of Ashton - Prana's
Replica of Bingo)
    OPEN—WIS 9/69-4; NOI 9/69-2; DUL 8/70-4; NDK 8/71-2;
    MNS 5/72-2.   (10)
    AMATEUR—NDK 8/68-1; DUL 8/70-1; NDK 8/70-1; MAN
    8/70-1.   (20)

ST. HUBERT OF TEWKESBURY KNOB SA-544926 11/12/68 S. M.
Pound—By Tanker of Los Altos Hills (Rip of Mountain Lake - Sara-
Lee) ex Kashpureff Lady Fats (Kashpureff Tiger - Kashpureff Blackie)
    AMATEUR—SAG 3/72-4.   (½)

STILLWATERS CARRY BACK SA-288918 8/28/64 Harvey E. Peterson
    —By Carr-Lab Hilltop (Marian's Duke of Bendick - Carr-Lab Pride's
Ad Lib) ex Stillwaters Lady Jeep (Spook of Delta - Sunnyway's Lady
Diana)
    OPEN—HEL 9/70-4.   (½)

STONE CASTLE'S YELLOW JACKET SA-374692 4/21/65 James
Anderson — By Stone Castle Jack (Staindrop Ringleader - Bigstone
Sugar) ex Stone Castle Gypsy (Marshwise Snapshooter - Tam Beau's
Belle Lady)
    AMATEUR—MTA 10/68-4.   (½)

FC-AFC STONEGATE'S ARROW SA-15715 6/22/59 John Wilson Kelsey
    —By Stonegate's Brazen Beau (Marvadel Black Gum - Comay Classy
Chassis) ex Cormats Pam (Rip's Bingo - Nodak Topps)
    OPEN—MIT 8/63-3; CSC 2/64-2; MON 5/64-2; NDK 8/64-1;
    ALM 11/64-3; SRZ 2/65-4; SCA 3/65-4; MII 5/65-2; PIK 8/65-2;
    CHY 8/65-4; SHE 9/65-3; MOV 9/65-2; PTA 3/66-4; NTX
    3/66-4; MIV 4/66-1; BHB 6/66-4; MAN 8/66-1; KAN 10/66-1;
    LST 3/67-4; MIV 4/67-2; CNB 5/67-4; MII 5/67-2; RKM 5/67-1;
    MTR 5/67-3; MON 6/67-4; MOV 9/67-4; NOI 9/67-4; MIW
    10/67-2; NTX 3/68-3; PTA 3/69-1.   (64½)
    AMATEUR—WMO 5/64-2; SXV 9/64-1; MON 9/64-1; MEM
    10/64-4; ALM 11/64-4; CSC 2/65-2; LST 10/65-2; ALM 11/65-1;
    LST 3/66-3; NOI 10/66-2; MIW 10/66-2; NFL 2/67-2; NTX
    3/67-4; MIV 4/67-4; MII 5/67-1; BHB 6/67-4; MIV 10/67-1;
    CNB 5/68-2; PIK 5/69-3.   (50½)

189

STORM'S EBONY ECHO SA-244739 2/13/63 James K. Shruell — By
Ace's Storm of Winniway (Ardyn's Ace of Merwalfin - Black Pantheress
of Ming) ex Kristin's Liz of Timber Town (Comus of Timber Town -
Black Mammie of Timber Town)
AMATEUR—SHR 4/67-4; COL 9/68-3.   (1½)

STRAW HOLLOW'S ROWDY CRUSADER SA-253640 4/4/64 Douglas
Allen — By Straw Hollow's Ceb (Straw Hollow's Captain Bruin - Straw
Hollow Merganser) ex Straw Hollow's Plover (Black Brooks Beaver -
Petra of Avandale)
AMATEUR—SHO 9/71-3.   (1)

STRIPER OF RAMAPO VALLEY SA-210682 2/1/63 Rosanne R. and
L. Larkin—By Angus of Wayland (Whygin Poppitt - Diamond Jet of
Greenhill) ex Opal of Ramapo Valley (Cash 'N' Carry - Roney Beauty)
OPEN—NUT 5/67-2.   (3)

NRFC '68-NARFC '67 & '68 SUPER CHIEF SA-153347 6/27/62 August
Belmont—By Paha Sapa Chief II (Freehaven Muscles - Treasure State
Be Wise) ex Ironwood Cherokee Chica (Cherokee Buck - Glen-Water
Fantom)
OPEN—LIR 10/64-4; NCA 3/66-3; SRN 5/66-1; RED 7/66-3;
COL 9/66-3; SWA 11/66-2; SAG 3/67-2; LIR 4/67-1; LAB
4/67-1; NUT 5/67-4; SAG 9/67-2; WNY 9/67-2; BUK 9/67-1;
MAI 9/67-2; MAR 10/67-1; NCA 3/68-3; WOM 4/68-2; GOL
7/68-1; GSL 8/68-3; PIK 8/68-1; SAG 8/68-1; COL 9/68-4;
NST 11/68-1; SAG 3/69-4; DEL 3/69-2; WCH 5/69-3; NCA
9/69-3; LIR 10/69-3; SCA 3/70-2; SAG 3/70-3; TAL 4/70-3;
LAB 5/70-3; SHO 9/70-3; WOM 10/70-1; SCA 3/71-1; NCA
3/71-2; JAM 3/71-4; SHR 4/71-4; TAC 8/71-4; SRZ 2/72-1;
MAR 5/72-4; IDA 8/72-4; SHO 9/72-2; DEL 10/72-1.   (112½)
AMATEUR—MAI 9/64-1; MAR 10/65-3; WOM 10/65-3; SWA
11/65-1; LIR 4/66-3; WOM 4/66-4; SAG 9/66-2; MAI 9/66-1;
MAR 10/66-1; DEL 10/66-1; WOM 10/66-3; SWA 11/66-3; SCA
3/67-1; TAL 4/67-1; LIR 4/67-3; SHR 4/67-1; NUT 5/67-1;
MAI 5/67-1; NAM 6/67-1; RED 7/67-2; SAG 9/67-1; BUK 9/67-
2; OHV 9/67-2; MAR 10/67-2; LIR 10/67-1; SCA 3/68-1; NCA
3/68-1; SAG 3/68-4; DEL 3/68-1; TAL 3/68-4; LIR 4/68-1;
WOM 4/68-3; SHO 5/68-1; NAM 6/68-1; GOL 7/68-1; GSL
8/68-1; SAG 8/68-1; DEL 10/68-4; SCA 2/69-2; NCA 3/69-2;
SAG 3/69-2; DEL 3/69-1; TAL 3/69-2; SHR 4/69-1; WCH 5/69-
4; PIK 8/69-1; NCA 9/69-4; COL 9/69-1; LIR 10/69-1; NCA
3/70-4; SAG 3/70-4; SHR 4/70-3; MAR 5/70-2; GSL 8/70-3;
IDA 8/70-2; SHO 9/70-3; WNY 9/70-1; WOM 4/70-1; SCA
3/71-2; SAG 3/71-4; JAM 3/71-1; TAL 4/71-4; SHR 4/71-1;
WCH 5/71-1; MAR 10/71-4; DEL 10/71-1; SHR 4/72-1; WOM
4/72-4; TAL 4/72-2; MAR 5/72-1; SNA 8/72-2; MAI 9/72-2;
MAR 10/72-3; DEL 10/72-1.   (242)

FC SWEET WILLIAM II SA-688152 3/27/68 H. V. P. Lewis—By Tyker
Baby* (Tar Baby's Little Sweet Stuff - Dessa Rae) ex Duxbak Vronce
(Carnmoney Carbon Copy - Duxbak Trixie)
OPEN—MIV 10/71-1; MIW 4/72-4; WIS 4/72-3; SXV 9/72-1.   (11½)

FC SWING TARZAN SWING SA-413002 5/26/66 J. J. Heneghan—By
Tar Baby's Little Sweet Stuff (Tar Baby of Holly Hill - Debbie of Holly
Hill) ex Dessa Rae* (Odessa's King - Jerry)
OPEN—WIL 8/69-2; SAM 8/69-1; NWR 9/69-2; SCA 3/70-3;
WIL 8/70-2; SHA 9/70-4; LAS 2/71-3; WIL 8/71-3; LAS 2/72-3;
NCA 3/72-4; SAM 9/72-2; SHA 9/72-1.   (27)
AMATEUR—NWR 4/71-2; SPO 10/71-1; CSC 2/72-3.   (9)

SYLDONNEL'S CAPTAIN JACK SA-455275 6/13/66 Jack Rautiainen—
By Tar Baby's Little Sweet Stuff (Tar Baby of Holly Hill - Debbie of
Holly Hill) ex Country Club's Little Bullet (Craigend Rock - Flirt of
Timbershed)

    AMATEUR—ORE 4/71-3; ORE 3/72-4; MON 6/72-3.   (2½)

AFC TALIAFERRO'S TRACER SA-144780 4/1/62 Howard T. Jones—
By Cajun Smut (Brook Ben - Cajun Chloe) ex Chiro's Lady Bee
(Tuck's Flash - Lurry's Traveling Trixie)

    OPEN—SLA 9/68-3; MOB 11/68-1.   (6)

    AMATEUR—SLA 9/66-2; MEM 10/68-1; MEM 10/69-1; MOB
10/69-4.   (13½)

FC-AFC TARBLOOD OF ABSARAKA S-898245 7/15/57 John A. Love
and Bruce Bridgeford—By Tarblood Buffalo Chief (Tarblood Spider-
creek King - Tarblood Favor Sweep) ex Lady Gretchen of Buffalo
(Shaduf - Black Deborah of Whitmore)

    OPEN—CNB 5/60-3; MOV 5/60-3; MNS 5/60-1; GSL 8/60-1;
RKM 8/60-4; NEB 4/61-4; MIW 4/61-3; CNB 5/61-4; GOL 5/61-1;
PIK 8/61-2; GSL 8/61-3; MON 9/61-1; NOI 9/61-4; NEB 5/62-4;
CNB 5/62-3; SHE 6/62-1; BHB 6/62-3; RKM 8/62-2; MON
9/62-3; MTR 9/62-2; MOV 9/62-2; LST 3/63-4; PTA 3/63-1;
MIV 4/63-1; RKM 5/63-3; CHY 5/63-1; GSL 5/63-2; CHY
8/63-2; MON 9/63-2; KAN 3/64-3; MIV 4/64-2; CHY 5/64-2;
MON 5/64-4; RKM 5/64-3; MAD 8/64-3; RKM 8/64-1; MON
9/64-4; MOV 9/64-1; HEL 9/64-3; SHE 9/64-1; NOI 10/64-4;
MIW 10/64-4; ALM 2/65-4; LST 3/65-2; PTA 3/65-2; KAN
4/65-4; NEB 4/65-4; CHY 5/65-1; LST 10/65-1; SLA 2/66-2;
ALM 2/66-1; LST 3/66-3; KAN 4/66-4; JAY 4/66-4; MIW
4/66-2; GSL 5/66-3; CHY 5/66-3; SHE 6/66-3; PIK 8/66-2;
MTR 9/66-3; RKM 5/67-4; BHB 6/67-3; SHE 6/67-2; RKM
8/67-2; SHE 9/67-2; MON 9/67-4; WMO 9/67-3; NLA 10/67-4;
ALM 11/67-1; GSL 5/68-1; MTR 5/68-1; SHE 6/68-4.   (165)

    AMATEUR—WMO 5/60-4; PIK 8/60-3; SHE 9/60-4; PTA
3/61-3; KAN 3/61-3; WMO 5/61-1; MON 6/61-4; PIK 8/61-4;
NTX 10/61-2; LST 3/62-3; TAL 3/62-2; SHE 6/62-2; MON
9/62-3; MTR 9/62-4; GSL 8/62-3; NEB 4/63-3; MIW 4/63-3;
SHE 8/63-4; MON 9/63-2; PTA 3/64-1; RKM 5/64-4; MON
5/64-4; PIK 8/64-2; SHE 9/64-2; MON 9/64-4; MTR 9/65-3;
ALM 2/66-2; MON 6/66-4; BHB 6/66-1; SHE 6/66-1; RKM
8/66-2; PIK 5/67-3; RKM 8/67-4; MON 9/67-1; SHE 6/68-2.   (67½)

TAR DESSA'S COMANCHE MIKE SA-613145 7/8/62 Wm. and Peggy
Morton—By Tar Dessa Venture* (Tar Baby's Little Sweet Stuff - Dessa
Rae*) ex Corona's Miss Consistency (Martens' Little Smoky* - Vans-
pride Ebony Shadow*)

    AMATEUR—MIV 4/72-2.   (3)

FC TAR DESSA VENTURE SA-246855 10/28/63—John M. Preston—
By Tar Baby's Little Sweet Stuff (Tar Baby of Holly Hill - Debbie of
Holly Hill) ex Dessa Rae* (Odessa's King - Jerry)

    OPEN—NCA 9/66-4; SHA 4/67-4; MON 6/67-1; SHE 6/67-4;
IDA 8/67-2; LAS 2/68-2; TAC 4/68-1; SHA 4/68-1; RED 7/68-2;
SAM 8/68-4; SHA 9/68-3; ORE 9/68-1; CSC 2/69-3; SAG
3/69-1; ROV 3/69-1; ORE 3/69-1; TAC 4/69-2; NWR 4/69-3;
IDA 5/69-1; IDA 8/69-1; SAM 8/69-4; SHA 9/69-1; NWR
9/69-1; CSC 2/70-1; ROV 3/70-1; ORE 4/70-3; TAC 4/70-4;
PUG 4/70-3.   (85)

    AMATEUR—NCA 9/66-4.   (½)

AFC TARGHEE SAM SA-208308 3/7/63 Blaine Murray—By Tim Dugan
of Ogden (Woldgate Valcour - Lady of Gold) ex Cinder Toni of
Sunnymede (Butch's Bitterroot Smoky - Navajo Toni of Sunnymede)

Shamrock Acres Drake

Sir Mike of Orchard View

Stonegate's Arrow

Tarblood of Absaraka

OPEN—PTA 10/67-2; LST 10/68-2. (6)

AMATEUR—ALM 11/67-1; PTA 10/68-2; NTX 10/68-1; KAN 10/69-1. (18)

TARRNOF OF V & C CHIP SA-646025 1/1/69 Chas. S. Polityka—By V & C Chip (Larry's Lasser* - Silent Susie) ex Smokey's Black Chrystal (Martens' Little Smoky - Shamrock Acres Simmer Down)
OPEN—SAM 3/72-1; WIL 8/72-4; SAM 9/72-4. (6)

TELSTAR OF ZENITH SA-540688 10/7-67 Carnation Farm Kennels— By Anzac of Zenith* (Black Mike of Lakewood - Jezebel of Normandy) ex Happy's Twinkle* (Night Cap Again - Miss Behavior)
OPEN—SPO 10/71-3. (1)

AFC THE BALLAD OF TEALBROOK SA-210659 5/7/63 Marshall Simonds—By Duxcross Chemo (Brigand of Timber Town - Sebasticook Lady) ex Danny's Joy of Tealbrook (Chino's Wildflower - Pride and Joy of Random Lake)
OPEN—MAI 5/66-4; LAB 4/68-3; LST 2/69-3; NTX 3/69-3; DEL 10/69-4. (4)
AMATEUR—WNY 9/67-3; MAI 9/68-2; LAB 11/68-1; LAB 4/69-2; SHO 5/69-1; WCH 5/69-2; LAB 11/69-4; LAB 5/70-2. (23½)

THE BAMBOO BANDIT SA-361242 11/18/64 Barry Coletti — By Duxcross Chemo (Brigand of Timber Town - Sebasticook Lady) ex Danny's Joy of Tealbrook (Chino's Wildflower - Pride and Joy of Random Lake)
AMATEUR—COL 9/69-4; NFL 2/70-3; SHO 9/70-4. (2)

THUNDER OF REBEL'S GYPSY SA-663159 1/22/69 Peter T. Brown— By Dakota Duke II (Radar Pal - Lee of Chic O'Swami) ex Rebel's Gypsy (My Rebel* - Brown's Duchess)
AMATEUR—NOI 7/72-2; SXV 9/72-4. (3½)

TIGER'S LUCKY BUCK SA-718792 3/27/69 William K. Laughlin— By Guy's Bitterroot Lucky* (Beavercrest's Toreador - Pickrel's Ebony Babe) ex Jilly's Tiger Lil (Duxbak Scooter - Jilly Girl*)
OPEN—WOM 4/72-4; RED 7/72-3; EID 7/72-2; SPO 9/72-2. (7½)

AFC TIMCIN'S BLACK DOMINO SA-231115 9/5/63 Mrs. Lorraine Hill By Namahbin of Oakridge (Nilo Possibility - Jet of Oakridge) ex Grace-Art's Bouncing Baby (Nascopie Dark Destroyer - Grace-Art's Classy Boots)
OPEN—MAD 8/68-4; NOI 9/68-4; WIS 9/70-4; MIW 10/70-3; MII 6/72-2. (5½)
AMATEUR—NFL 2/68-4; MAD 5/68-3; MAN 8/68-1; MIC 8/68-1; MAD 5/69-4; MAN 8/70-3; GOL 5/71-4; MNS 5/71-2. (16½)

TIME OF FRONTIER SA-278640 1/9/64 Don H. Gearheart—By Duxbak Scooter* (Baker's Jerry - Carnmoney Moira) ex Nilo Ida's Pretender (Pomme de Terre Pete - Staindrop Isla)
OPEN—MIL 6/67-1; MIW 10/68-3; JAX 1/69-2. (9)
AMATEUR—FTP 5/69-2; MAR 10/69-3; MOB 2/70-3; MOB 3/71-2. (8)

TINA'S BLACK CHIP SA-386845 3/30/66 Mrs. Emily F. Bisso — By Ebony Moods Bingo* (Dutchmoor's Black Mood* - Bigstone Lady B) ex Tina of Grey Summit (Black Watch Horseshoe - Purina's Black Magic)
AMATEUR—MOB 3/71-4. (½)

AFC TOGOM'S TIGER OF ABILENA SA-607026 5/12/68 Stanley Gacek —By River Oaks Corky* (Martens' Mister Nifty* - Don's Ginny Soo) ex O'Torq's Kimberly (Black Squeek of Netley Creek - Highlander's Fancy)

OPEN—FRR 8/71-4; MIW 10/72-3. (1½)

AMATEUR—AAR 5/71-2; MIL 6/71-2; FRR 8/71-1; WIS 4/72-2; WOL 5/72-4; AAR 9/72-4; WOL 9/72-2. (18)

TOM'S THADIUS SA-568715 3/2/68 John Boyer — By Moby Dick* (Stiillwater's Royal Rick - Navajo Toni of Sunnymede) ex Peterson's Pretty Penny (Baden's Rebel of Chipsdale - Sue San)
AMATEUR—GSL 8/71-3. (1)

FC TONI'S BLAINE CHILD SA-700112 6/17/69 E. R. Leatherbury—By Anzac of Zenith* (Black Mike of Lakewood - Jezebel of Normandy) ex Dessa Baby (Tar Baby's Little Sweet Stuff - Dessa Rae*)
OPEN—NFL 3/72-4; MTA 4/72-1; MEM 4/72-4; MNS 5/72-1; MII 6/72-1; MTA 10/72-4; MEM 10/72-4. (17)

AFC TONI'S TAR SA-157123 4/28/62 John T. Fotheringham — By Hyde's Black Splash (Sunday Shoes - Belle of Bear River) ex Navajo's Toni of Sunnymede (Navajo Tar of Sunnymede - Navajo Corkey of Bigstone)
OPEN—GSL 5/65-4; GSL 5/69-4. (1)

AMATEUR—GSL 8/67-1; GSL 5/69-1; GSL 8/69-1; GSL 8/70-2. (18)

FC-AFC TORQUE OF DAINGERFIELD SA-238006 10/1/62 Joan Shoemaker—By Man of Night (Butchboi - Ruth of Avandale) ex Dixie Bell (Tug O'Mike - Mother Fletcher's Black Lady)
OPEN—NWR 9/65-4; TAC 4/66-3; RKM 5/66-1; SHA 9/66-4; PTA 10/66-4; SCA 3/67-2; SAM 3/67-4; ORE 3/67-1; WIL 8/67-4; NWR 9/67-4; ORE 9/67-2; SAM 9/67-1; CSC 2/68-4; SAM 3/68-2; SHA 4/68-2; IDA 5/68-1; WIL 8/68-4; SHA 9/68-1; NWR 9/68-4; SPO 9/68-4; SAM 3/69-4; ROV 3/69-2; SPO 5/69-4; EID 7/69-1; ORE 9/69-3; SAM 3/70-4; SHA 5/70-3; GOL 5/70-3; SPO 5/70-4; NWR 9/70-3; SPO 10/70-4. (57½)

AMATEUR—ORE 4/66-3; IDA 8/66-2; SAM 3/67-4; ORE 3/67-2; NWR 4/67-3; PUG 8/67-1; SHA 9/67-3; ORE 9/67-3; SPO 9/67-3; CSC 2/68-1; SCA 3/68-2; SAM 3/68-2; PUG 4/68-1; NWR 4/68-1; SHA 4/68-1; SHA 9/68-4; NWR 9/68-2; ORE 9/68-2; SPO 9/68-1; ORE 3/69-2; PUG 4/69-3; SHA 4/69-3; GSL 8/69-4; PUG 8/69-4; ORE 9/69-2; SPO 5/70-3; RED 7/70-4; WIL 8/70-4; ORE 9/70-1; SPO 10/70-3. (71)

TRAPPERS PAHA CORK SA-78491 12/25/60 Mr. and Mrs. M. B. Wallace, Jr.—By Paha Sapa Chief II (Freehaven Muscles - Treasure State Be Wise) ex Penny Girl (Cork of Oakwood Lane - Min-A-Jet of Reo Raj)
OPEN—WOL 5/65-1; AAR 9/65-2; MEM 3/66-4; WOL 5/67-3; AAR 5/67-4. (10)

FC TROUBLEMAKER OF AUDLON II SA-313146 8/10/64 Mr. and Mrs. M. B. Wallace, Jr. — By Beautywood Rare Trouble (Roy's Rowdy - Beautywood's Repeat) ex Trouble's Double of Audlon (Pierrot of Stonegate - Little Trouble of Audlon)
OPEN—MAD 5/69-4; MEM 10/70-1; NFL 3/71-4; WIS 4/71-4; MEM 10/71-1; NLA 10/72-3. (12½)
AMATEUR—JAX 1/69-3; MOB 10/69-2. (4)

FC-AFC TWEET'S BEBE SA-525090 11/8/66 Oscar S. Brewer — By Beavercrest Ripper (Paha Sapa Chubby Brave - Beavercrest Black Cinder) ex Tweet's Taffy (Paha Sapa Brave - Mimi's Miss Blitz)
OPEN—SRZ 2/70-4; JAY 3/70-4; ALB 5/70-2; MTR 5/70-4; GSL 8/70-1; CHY 8/70-4; NTX 11/70-1; RKM 5/71-3; MON 6/71-1; MON 9/71-3; HEL 9/71-2; NTX 10/71-3; KAN 10/71-2; ALB 5/72-3; CHY 8/72-2. (33)
AMATEUR—LST 3/71-4; NTX 3/71-1; JAY 3/71-4; KAN 4/71-1; MII 5/71-2; BHB 6/71-4; MOV 9/71-4; KAN 10/71-3; NEB 4/72-1; ALB 5/72-3; NOI 7/72-3; PIK 8/72-1; KAN 10/72-2. (31)

TYCOON OF RALSTON VALLEY SA-219685 9/9/63 Guy A. Coburn
—By Ralston of Shamrock Acres (Whygin Poppitt - Whygin Campaign
Promise) ex Prim Pat of Ralston Valley (Shamrock Acres Jim Dandy -
Lady Ginger of Shady Lane)
OPEN—ALB 5/68-4.   (½)

TYKER BABY SA-222730 10/28/63 Toni Carpenter — By Tar Baby's
Little Sweet Stuff (Tar Baby of Holly Hill - Debbie of Holly Hill) ex
Dessa Rae* (Odessa's King - Jerry)
AMATEUR—WIL 8/67-2; SPO 5/69-3.   (4)

TYKER'S FLECK OF CORK SA-584122 6/6/68 Robert H. Bain — By
Tyker Baby* (Tar Baby's Little Sweet Stuff - Dessa Rae*) ex Ripco's
Little Bit of Cork (Ripco's Peter Pan - Whidbey's Penny O'Cork)
OPEN—ALK 8/71-1; ALK 8/72-2.   (8)
AMATEUR—ALK 8/71-3.   (1)

VALHALLA BONEFISH SAM SA-660966 1/30/69 Dr. J. Byron Beare
—By Geechee* (Ridgewood Playboy - Grace-Art's Smart Lady) ex
Valhalla Trooper's Persimmon (Medlin's Texas Trooper - Betsy's
Copy Kat)
OPEN—NLA 10/72-4.   (½)

FC V AND C CHIP SA-523993 6/23/67 Dr. Armand Jacques—By Larry's
Lasser* (Ripco's Western Blend - Morgan's Anne) ex Silent Susie
(Duke of Billmar - Pat's Black Rose)
OPEN—SNA 8/70-4; WMO 9/70-2; NTX 3/71-3; PTA 10/71-1;
ALM 11/71-3; PTA 3/72-2; CHY 8/72-4; SLA 9/72-3.   (15)
AMATEUR—IDA 8/70-4; SLA 3/72-1.   (5½)

VAN'S BOMBER SA-358225 11/15/65 Harry J. Van Arsdale — By
Crook's El Toro (Crook's Tahoe Pat - Black Rapids of Baranof) ex
Rimrock Briquet (Rimrock Rufus - Rubino's Silk)
AMATEUR—SAG 7/69-4.   (½)

FC V-JAY'S BLACK PADDLE SA-70891 6/25/60 Joe S. and Verna
Simpson—By Nodak Ar-Dee (Cork of Oakwood Lane - Spider Wise) ex
Lucifer's Lady* (Bracken's High Flyer - Shasta Stormy)
OPEN—NCA 9/63-2: LAS 10/64-1; ORE 4/65-2; SRN 5/65-4;
CSC 2/66-1; SCA 3/66-2: ROV 3/66-4; ACC 8/66-4; SCA 9/66-1;
ORE 3/67-4; SAG 9/67-3; NCA 9/67-1; CSC 9/67-1.   (37)

AFC WACCAMAW'S TINKER SA-274302 1/24/64 William A. Chandler
—By Mycur Bimbo (Hiwood Benjamin - Queen O' The Carse) ex
Jo-Ann of Avandale II (Zelstone Sparkle - Minstrel Girl of Avandale)
OPEN—PTA 10/67-1; LST 10/67-4; ALM 11/68-2.   (8½)
AMATEUR—ALM 2/67-1; LST 3/67-3; NLA 3/67-1; ALM
2/68-1; LST 3/68-2; SLA 9/68-4; LST 10/68-1.   (24½)

WALLACE'S PLAYBOY'S TOPSY TAR SA-304348 1/22/65 Elizabeth
Wallace—By Ridgewood Playboy (La Sage's Smoky - Nelgard's Counter
Point) ex Topsy Turvy Tar Baby (Nigger of Dacity - Glen-Water
Fal-Lal)
OPEN—SNA 5/70-3; GSL 5/70-4.   (1½)
AMATEUR—GSL 5/69-3.   (1)

WANAPUM LUCKY YO YO SA-769753 5/9/69 August Belmont — By
Spring Farms Lucky* (Paha Sapa Chief II - Ironwood Cherokee
Chica) ex Toni of Wanapum (Pepper's Jiggs - Ar-Dee's Sassy Holly)
OPEN—SHA 4/72-4; SPO 5/72-2.   (3½)
AMATEUR—NCA 3/72-2; TAC 4/72-3; SPO 5/72-1.   (9)

WANDARIN HEIGHTS VENTURE SA-389901 8/13/65 William C. Last
—By Tar-Dessa Venture* (Tar Baby's Little Sweet Stuff - Dessa Rae*)
ex Wandarin Heights Williwaw (Wandarin Heights Diogenes - Cinders
Lady of Journey's End)
OPEN—ROV 3/71-3. (1)
AMATEUR—SHA 9/69-3. (1)

WARPATH COWBOY JOE SA-417753 7/23/66 Jere Bogrett — By
Middlespunk Scamper (Beautywood Rare Trouble - Glen-Water Fury)
ex Paha Sapa Jet Stream (Paha Sapa Chief II - Paha Sapa Princess)
OPEN—LST 10/71-4. (½)
AMATEUR—IDA 5/71-1; SNA 5/71-3. (6)

WARPATH JUST IN CASE SA-631769 10/25/68 Ed and Mary Case—
By Warpath Tuff* (Del-Tone Colvin - Paha Sapa Wacincala) ex
Cricket of Ralston Valley (Zelstone Sparkle - Spirit of Avandale)
AMATEUR—CHY 8/71-3; JAY 3/72-4. (1½)

FC-AFC WARPATH RIP SA-390594 11/17/64 Mr. Oscar S. Brewer—By
Middlespunk Scamper (Beautywood Rare Trouble - Glen-Water Fury)
ex Paha Sapa Jet Stream (Paha Sapa Chief II - Paha Sapa Princess)
OPEN—ALM 2/68-2; LST 3/68-2; JAY 3/68-3; RKM 5/68-1;
NEB 4/69-3; CNB 5/69-3; CHY 8/69-3; MON 9/69-
1; HEL 9/69-1; ALM 2/70-3; MON 6/70-1; SHE 9/70-4; NTX
11/70-2; LST 3/71-1; NTX 3/71-4; MTA 5/71-1; SHE 9/71-2;
MTR 5/72-2; MIV 10/72-3; KAN 10/72-4; LST 10/72-3. (58½)
AMATEUR—MOV 9/69-3; MIV 10/69-4; SAG 3/70-3; JAY
3/70-4; MII 5/70-4; MOV 9/70-3; NTX 3/71-2; BHB 6/71-2;
KAN 10/71-1; LST 3/72-2; NTX 3/72-2; JAY 3/72-3; KAN
3/72-1; RKM 5/72-2; CWY 8/72-4; SHE 9/72-3; MIV 10/72-3. (33)

FC-AFC WARPATH TUFF SA-272597 7/8/64 Orus J. Matthews Jr. —
By Del-Tone Colvin (Cork of Oakwood Lane - Del-Tone Bridget) ex
Paha Sapa Wacincala (Freehaven Muscles - Treasure State Be Wise)
OPEN—RKM 5/68-4; ALM 2/69-2; PTA 3/69-3; MIV 4/69-3;
MII 5/69-2; MTR 5/69-1; KAN 10/69-1; LST
3/70-3; ALB 7/71-3; PIK 8/71-2; RKM 8/71-3; LST 3/72-4;
NTX 3/72-2; PIK 8/72-1. (33½)
AMATEUR—PIK 5/68-4; RKM 5/68-4; HEL 9/68-1; ALM
2/69-4; LST 2/69-4; CNB 5/69-2; RKM 8/69-3; RKM 8/70-2;
CWY 8/70-3; NCA 3/71-2; JAY 3/71-2; CNB 5/71-2; RKM
5/71-3; MTR 5/71-3; CHY 8/71-1; RKM 5/72-1; ALB 7/72-3;
PIK 8/72-2. (40)

WAYSIDE BLACK BUSTER SA-366371 8/11/65 Jon W. Morar — By
Hoppy of Jefferson Lane (Cork of Oakwood Lane - Beautywood's Creole
Jane) ex Martens' Little Rocket (Royal of Garfield - Martens' Lady
Jane)
OPEN—LST 10/69-1. (5)
AMATEUR—PTA 10/69-2. (3)

WHISKEY CREEK BLUE SAHIB SA-296852 11/30/64 Richard L. White,
M.D.—By Ar-Dee's Smorgasbord (Marian's Timothy - Beautywood's
Lady Fair) ex Sauk Trail Black Starlight (Comanche of Thunderbolt -
Sauk Trail Black Fox)
OPEN—WOL 9/69-4. (½)

AFC WHITE RIVER DUKE SA-410334 7/17/66 David J. Wirth—By Zip
of Geneva Lake* (Shady Haven Farm Smudge - Last Chance Spice
Queen) ex Happy of Broadway (Top Gun of Random Lake - Red
Cedar Lake Bimba)
OPEN—TRI 6/72-2. (3)
AMATEUR—MNS 5/71-3; AAR 5/71-1; DUL 8/71-2; AAR
5/72-1; TRI 6/72-2. (17)

FC-AFC WHITE'S MAR-KE-TAM NERRO SA-461391 4/2/66 Ben F. Mitchell, M.D.—By Jagersbo Claim Jumper (Silvertown Treve - Jagersbo Ginger Miss) ex Cathy-Chris' Black Bess (Colonel's Mr. Chips - Frosty)

    OPEN—ALM 10/69-2; SLA 10/70-3; LST 10/70-3; SLA 4/71-1. (10)

    AMATEUR—SLA 9/68-3; LST 10/69-4; RKM 5/70-2; CAS 10/70-2; PTA 3/71-3. (8½)

NRFC '66 & '69 WHYGIN CORK'S COOT SA-157920 6/12/62 Mrs. Geo. Murnane — By Cork of Oakwood Lane (Coastal Charger of Deer Creek - Anoka Liza Jane of Kingdale) ex Whygin Dark Ace (Whygin Poppitt - Whygin Cricket)

    OPEN—SWA 3/65-2; TAL 3/66-1; SHR 4/66-2; LAB 4/66-1; CNY 5/66-4; FTP 6/66-1; MAR 10/66-4; DEL 10/66-3; WOM 10/66-2; NST 11/66-1; MTA 3/67-1; CNY 5/67-1; BUK 9/67-2; OHV 9/67-2; LIR 10/67-2; WOM 10/67-4; SWA 11/67-1; LAB (S) 11/67-4; SHO 5/68-1; CNY 5/68-2; FTP 5/68-4; MIT 8/68-1; DUL 8/68-1; NDK 8/68-3; WNY 9/68-1; COL 9/68-3; MAR 10/68-2; SWA 11/68-3; LAB 11/68-1; NLA 3/69-1; WCH 5/69-2; SLA 9/69-2; NLA 10/69-4; NST 11/69-1; LAB 11/69-2; LAB 5/70-1; MAD 8/70-1; SXV 4/70-1; OHV 10/70-3; LIR 10/70-1; DEL 10/70-3; CWY 8/71-1. (137)

WHYGIN WELLMET ANGUS SA-504268 6/24/67 David B. Bandler— By Whygin The Tarboy (Cork of Oakwood Lane - Whygin The Bedford Brat) ex Misty Velvet (Dark Calli - Miss Velvet Mist)

    OPEN—WOM 10/72-2. (3)

    AMATEUR—LAB 4/72-4; WNY 9/72-4; WOM 10/72-4. (1½)

WILD JOKER OF NAPI SA-866789 2/8/70 Mr. & Mrs. Richard Bartlett —By Anzac of Zenith* (Black Mike of Lakewood - Jezebel of Normandy) ex Toni of Wanapum (Pepper's Jiggs - Ar-Dee's Sassy Holly)

    AMATEUR—SHE 9/72-2; WMO 9/72-1. (8)

FC WILLOWMOUNT EL DIABLO SA-804280 12/11/68 Charles E. Cooney—By Highlander's Bojangles (Salty of Sugar Valley - Highlander's Diana) ex Willowmount Honey Bunny (Don Head Barley Sugar - Burnham Breeze)

    OPEN—BUK 4/72-1; GOL 5/72-3; WOL 5/72-1; MAN 8/72-2; BUK 9/72-1; MTA 10/72-3; MOB 11/72-4. (20½)

    AMATEUR—WOL 5/72-2. (3)

WINGFORD'S BIG FLINTSTONE SA-490799 6/4/67 Laura Ford Winans —By Bigstone Flint* (Martens' Mister Nifty* - Dick's Black Scamp) ex Wingford's Dinah Soar (Highlander's Bucaneer - Blue Dawn of Sunway)

    OPEN—WOL 9/71-3. (1)

    AMATEUR—WOL 5/71-3; WOL 5/72-3; MIC 8/72-2; AAR 9/72-2. (8)

WINGOVER CHEROKEE CHIEF SA-364671 6/29/65 Elizabeth P. Millikin—By Caesar of Great Meadows (Bobbs Black Knight - Wilson's Cricket) ex Ballybrook Lil (Strokestown Deuce - Ballybrennan Deborah)

    AMATEUR—MAI 9/70-1; WOM 4/71-2. (8)

AFC WINROC'S RIPPER SA-550579 1/14/68 John H. Anderson, D.V.M. —By Crook's El Toro (Crook's Tahoe Pat - Black Rapids of Baranof) ex Shamrock Acres P.D.Q. (Martens' Little Smoky* - Whygin Gentle Julia of Avec)

    OPEN—ACC 8/71-2; ORE 9/71-1; SAG 3/72-4. (8½)

    AMATEUR—RED 7/71-4; NCA 9/71-1; ORE 9/71-2; ROV 3/72-2. (11½)

Tar-Dessa Venture

Torque of Dangerfield

Warpath Rip

Whygin Cork's Coot

FC WIN-TOBA'S BLACK HIGH POINT SA-365050 8/21/64 Wm. E. Jamieson—By Stonegate's Knight of Roslyn (Treveilyr Commander - Cormat's Pam) ex Sprucelane's Ember (Black Squeek of Netley Creek - Nilo Mark's Beth)
OPEN—NFL 2/68-3; MAD 8/68-1; MIT 8/68-4; DUL 8/68-3; BUK 9/68-2; MAR 10/68-4; MAR 5/69-3; CNY 5/69-3; WCH 5/69-4. (13½)

YANKEE BLACK POWER SA-542085 1/11/67 Carl Pearson—By Squire of Reo Raj* (Yankee Clipper of Reo Raj - Duchess of Miller's Haven) ex Lady Schrintza (King Daniel - Princess Robbie)
OPEN—MEM 4/71-3; NDK 8/71-3. (2)
AMATEUR—MAD 5/72-4; CMI 5/72-2. (3½)

YAZ RAZZMATAZZ SA-197896 3/25/63 Dr. Darrell Willerson — By Raven Mike of Stonegate (Stonegate's Brazen Beau - Midge of Stonegate) ex Nilo Lulubelle (Freehaven Muscles - Nilo Lady Pam)
OPEN—FTP 8/67-4; CMI 5/69-1; PTA 3/70-2. (8½)

YOGI II SA-636382 3/17/67 Carl W. Jones — By Captain of Lomac* (Spook of Manhattan - Country Club's Little Deb) ex Mandy of Jet (Jet of Spook - Peggy of Greentimbers)
OPEN—TAC 8/69-2. (3)

FC YOUR SHOT MINNESOTA FATS SA-486728 4/27/67 Thomas J. Tracy — By Bigstone Flint* (Martens' Mister Nifty* - Dick's Black Scamp) ex Bigstone Black Liberty (Bigstone Butch - Martens' Black Dot)
OPEN—SLA 10/70-2; NLA 10/70-4; NLA 3/71-4; RKM 5/71-4; MTR 5/71-2; PIK 8/71-3; CHY 8/71-3; NFL 11/71-1; MEM 4/72-2; RKM 8/72-1; NTX 10/72-3. (23½)
AMATEUR—NTX 11/70-4; NTX 10/72-3. (1½)

ZIP OF GENEVA LAKE SA-200328 6/5/63 Mr. and Mrs. George Stebbins—By Shady Haven Farm Smudge (Smudge's Magic - Shady Haven Farm Lady II) ex Last Chance Spice Queen (Last Chance Shed - Last Chance Duchess)
AMATEUR—MNS 5/67-2. (3)

FC ZIPPER DEE DO SA-464617 2/16/67 Timber Town Kennels — By Ridgewood Playboy (La Sage's Smoky - Nelgard's Counter Point) ex Grady's Shadee Ladee* (Black Mike of Lakewood- Jezebel of Normandy)
OPEN—GSL 8/69-3; ACC 8/69-4; WOM 10/69-3; MEM 3/70-1; TAL 4/70-2; COL 10/70-4; MAR 10/70-2; NFL 3/71-1; TAL 4/71-1; WCH 5/71-4; MAR 5/71-1; SHO 9/71-2; WNY 9/71-3; COL 10/71-1; DEL 10/71-1; JAX 3/72-4; NFL 3/72-1; CNY 5/72-2; WNY 9/72-2; COL 9/72-3; MAR 10/72-1; DEL 10/72-2; SWA 11/72-3; LAB (S) 11/72-4. (65½)

LABRADOR RETRIEVERS - BITCHES

AFC ACUTE ACCENT, SA-323175 1/10/65 R. Patopea—By Ripco's Peter Pan (Rip of Holly Hill - Whitmore's Rowdy Lady) ex Shoe's Del-Tone Femme (Del-Tone Colvin - Bridget Sue of Mercer)
OPEN—PUG 4/69-4; PUG 8/69-2. (3½)
AMATEUR—SAM 3/68-1; NWR 9/68-4; TAC 4/69-2; NWR 9/71-2. (11½)

AERCO'S BIT O'HONEY, SA-398226 10/4/65 Sig Vilagi—By Admiral of the Fleet (Audubon Gold Chip - Kmo's Merry Maid) ex Skip to My Lou (Ainville's Mister Chips - Kmo's Duchess)
OPEN—MAD 8/71-2; MAD 5/72-4. (3½)
AMATEUR—TRI 6/71-1. (5)

ALLO DERE LOUISE, SA-310830 10/1/64 Dr. J. Knudson and Dr. M. D. Hoffman—By Valentine's Cork (Massie's Sassy Boots - Judy of Valentine) ex Rosehill's Little Dutch Boots* (Nodak Boots - The Duchess of Rose Hill)

OPEN—SXV 9/70-3. (1)

AMATEUR—MIT 8/67-4; NDK 8/68-4; MIT 8/69-4; MON 9/72-3. (2½)

ANGELIQUE SA-699633 1/6/69 Jerry D. Patopea—By Tyker Baby* (Tar Baby's Little Sweet Stuff - Dessa Rae*) ex Acute Accent* (Ripco's Peter Pan - Shoes Del-Tone Femme)

OPEN—SAM 9/72-1; PHO 10/72-2. (8)

AQUARIAN LADY O' THE AUTUMN MOON SA-731579 11/6/69 Donald Des Jardin—By Shamrock Acres Super Drive* (Super Chief* - Could Be's Miss Erable) ex Juste's Velvet Mist (Tar of Ralston Valley - Ironwood Two-Bits)

OPEN—PIK 8/72-2. (3)

FC-AFC BALSOM'S MANDY SA-971964 10/21/58 B. B. Baker D.V.M. —By Alpine Black King (Cherokee Buck - Nelgard's Madam Queen) ex Bonnie Jay of Krisday (Freehaven Muscles - Treasure State Be Wise)

OPEN—SHA 9/64-4; TAC 9/65-1; SHA 9/65-1; CSC 10/65-4; SCA 3/66-4; RED 7/66-2; ACC 9/66-1; PUG 8-67-4; SAG 9/67-1; SHA 9/67-1; SRN 5/68-3. (26½)

AMATEUR—ORE 9/64-2; TAC 4/65-3; SRN 5/65-3; WIL 8/65-2; NCA 9/65-4; ORE 9/65-1; SCA 3/66-1; ORE 4/66-1; PUG 4/66-4; SRN 5/66-4; NCA 3/67-2; LAS 2/68-4. (23½)

FC-AFC BEAN BALL SA-72441 4/18/60 Richard H. Hecker — By Dolobran's Smoke Tail (Dolobran's Spook - Dolobran's Mighty Mite) ex Shady Haven Farm Lady (Smudge of Prairie Creek Farm - Random Lake Black Ghost)

OPEN—ALM 11/66-3; BHB 6/67-1; NTX 10/67-4; ALB 5/68-2; NTX 10/68-4. (10)

AMATEUR—MIW 4/64-4; WOL 5/64-4; AAR 5/64-3; BUK 4/65-2; NLA 10/66-3; NTX 10/66-1; MON 6/67-2; BHB 7/67-3; PTA 10/67-2; LST 10/67-1; ALM 11/67-4; ALB 5/68-1; IDA 8/68-3; SNA 8/68-2. (32½)

FC BEAUTYWOOD'S TINGLER SA-38571 2/5/60 Mrs. R. M. Lewis— By Del-Tone Sam (Stonegate's Rip II - Del-Tone Bridget) ex Beautywood's Sugar Pill (Webway's Crusader - Gilmore's Peggy)

OPEN—AAR 5/64-2; CMI 6/64-4; SUP 6/64-3; GOL 5/65-3; WOL 5/65-3; MAI 9/65-4; LIR 10/65-1; DEL 10/65-4; WNY 9/66-4; TAL 3/67-1; BUK 9/67-4. (18½)

AMATEUR—MAR 10/65-1; DEL 10/65-3; WOM 10/65-2; WOM 10/66-1. (14)

AFC BEAVERCREST SASSY SIOUX SA-188391 11/10/61 Wayne Mahan—By Tarblood of Absaraka* (Tarblood Buffalo Chief - Lady Gretchen of Buffalo) ex Beavercrest Starlet (Smudge's Bingo - Burrill's Black Sheba)

OPEN—BHB 5/68-2; SHE 6/69-4; WMO 5/70-4. (4)

AMATEUR—MON 6/67-4; MON 5/69-4; SHE 6/69-1; EID 6/69-1; EID 7/69-3. (12)

BEL-AIRE DAM SA-192814 12/17/62 Leland Hirt—By Ace Bingo (Bingo Again - Bigstone Dinah Girl) ex Green Ridge Sally (Del-Tone Colvin - Shady Haven Farm Jet)

AMATEUR—CNB 5/67-2. (3)

BELLATRIX OF HICKORY GLEN SA-527564 8/8/67 Dr. John De Garmo — By Butte Blue Moon* (Beavercrest Storm Cloud - Macushla of Rockmont) ex Typhoon of Audlon (Duxbak Scooter* - Trouble's Double of Audlon)
OPEN—MIV 10/72-2. (3)
AMATEUR—MIV 4/72-3; KAN 10-72-1. (6)

BELLE RINGER SA-657442 8/19/68 Harvey and Nancy Peterson — By Washington's Tater Tate (Katanga Pepper - Black Diamond Liz) ex Jezebel of Normandy (Yankee Clipper of Reo-Raj - Belle of Zenith)
AMATEUR—PUG 8/72-4; NWR 9/72-1. (5½)

BIGSTONE BLACK LONGSHOT II SA-311146 8/21/64 M. J. Thompson —By Bigstone Chief (Royal of Garfield - Martens' Lady Jane ex Bigstone Belle (Martens' Hi Style Buck - Bigstone Bang)
OPEN—DEL 3/69-4; LIR 5/69-3. (1½)
AMATEUR—SHR 3/68-2; LAB 4/68-2; MAR 5/68-1. (11)

BIGSTONE PRAIRIE WIND SA-231365 5/14/63 Dr. K. W. Vandersluis —By Bigstone Bounty (Crowder - Bigstone Ricky) ex Magi Gal of Christ Lac (Cork of Oakwood Lane - Min-A-Jet of Reo Raj)
OPEN—MEM 3/70-2; BUK 4/70-3; WOL 5/70-2. (7)
AMATEUR—MAD 8/70-2. (3)

BLACK IRISH KELLY SA-399234 3/6/66 Robert and Dolores Mesch— By Shamrock Acres Gun Away* (Beautywood Rare Trouble - Marlab's Gypsy) ex Personality Plus (Greatford Glenfarg Bragg - West Island Cleopatra)
OPEN—LAB (S) 11/70-1; LAB (S) 11/71-4; SHO 9/72-3. (6½)
AMATEUR—LAB 4/71-3; LIR 10/71-1; SWA 11/71-4; CNY 5/72-2; DEL 10/72-4. (10)

BLACK SUSAN OF POLHEMUS SA-255118 3/29/64 Alfred M. Pauli— By Bat-Jac's Tinny Tim (Cumshaw Batjac Boy - Ademala's Fay) ex Wandarin Heights Shannon (Black Monk of Roeland - Manzanal Lilac)
AMATEUR—SHA 9/68-3; SCA 9/68-3; NCA 9/70-3; SCA 3/71-4. (3½)

BRANDI OF CAYNE SA-406484 6/17/66 Robert and Lynn Knox—By Huracan of Vulcan Crest (Nelson's Vulcan Storm of Wake - Black Snow of Vulcan Crest) ex Nelson's Vulcan Wind (Black Diamond of Liberty - Dahl's Dixie)
AMATEUR—CSC 10/71-3. (1)

BRANDYWINE STAR SA-97577 1/19/61 William T. Reardon, M.D.—By Di Mondi's Danny (Alvaleigh's Shiner - Zelstone Kate) ex Lockerbie Bally (Ballyduff Treesholme Terrybog - Ballyduff Candy)
OPEN—COL 10/65-3; SWA 11/65-4; SWA 3/66-4; LAB(S) 11/66-4. (2½)
AMATEUR—WNY 9/65-4; WOM 10/65-4; TAL 3/67-4; BUK 4/67-4; DEL 10/67-4; WOM 10/67-4; LAB 5/68-4; SHO 5/68-3; LAB 11/68-3. (5½)

BRECKONHILL ERIN'S KELLI SA-295745 2/4/64 Barbara T. Yanick —By Breckonhill's Sean O'Moore* (Breckonhill Ben - Erin O'Moore) ex Erin O'Moore (Ripco's Peter Pan - Lady Coleraine's Velvet)
AMATEUR—SAM 3/67-2; SAM 3/68-4; PUG 9/68-2; SAM 3/69-3. (7½)

BRIDGITS BLACK KARGO SA-331922 6/24/65 James Marth — By Hauser's Last Chance (Yankee Bob - Middle Spunk Lady) ex John's Bridgit (Stonegate's Lad of Hi-Taffey - Ree of Brookdale)
AMATEUR—MTA 10/69-3. (1)

BROCK'S LIVELY LARK SA-516161 12/9/66 J. T. S. Brock — By Shamrock Acres Jim Dandy (Brodhead's Bar Booze - Whygins Gentle Julia of Avec) ex Ralston Valley's Lady Luck (Ralston of Shamrock Acres - Spirit of Avandale)
AMATEUR—LST 10/71-4. (½)

CALAMITY JANE OF ROCKMONT SA-397711 12/16/65 William Horn —By Beavercrest Storm Cloud (Del-Tone Colvin - Beavercrest Shore Leave) ex Macushla of Rockmont (Beavercrest Toreador - Apache Teardrop)
AMATEUR—SPO 4/71-2. (3)

FC CANUCK-CREST CUTTY SARK SA-187048 11/11/61 Mrs. A. P. Loening—By Jet of Zenith* (Massie's Sassy Boots - Thornwood Rhea) ex Canuck-Crest Tami O'Churchlee (Beautywood's Carbon Copy - Twink of Belle Isle)
OPEN—SWA 11/64-2; DUL 8/64-4; DUL 8/65-4; COL 10/65-4; TAL 3/66-4; SHR 4/66-1; MAI 5/66-3; CNY 5/66-2; BUK 9/66-3; MAI 9/66-1; COL 9/66-1; TAL 3/67-2; SHR 4/67-2; CNY 5/67-3; FTP 5/67-1; WNY 9/67-1; MAR 10/67-3; SWA 11/67-3; DEL 3/68-2; LIR 4/68-2; SHO 5/68-3; CNY 5/68-1; WOM 10/68-2; SWA 11/68-1; MEM 2/69-3; MTA 3/69-4; DEL 3/69-1; TAL 3/69-2; MAI 9/69-3; WOM 10/69-1; SWA 11/69-3; CNY 5/70-1; WNY 9/70-3; COL 10/70-2; MAR 10/70-3; WOM 10/70-2; JAM 3/71-1; SHR 4/71-3; MAR 5/71-2; CNY 5/71-3; SHO 9/71-1; DEL 10/71-4. (109)

CANUCK-CREST SALLY SA-178825 11/11/61 Del Phinney—By Jet of Zenith* (Massie's Sassy Boots - Thornwood Rhea) ex Canuck-Crest Tami O'Churchlee (Beautywood's Carbon Copy - Twink of Belle Isle)
OPEN—MAI 9/68-4. (½)
AMATEUR—MAI 9/64-4. (½)

CAPTAIN'S MISS SA-548811 5/14/67 G. D. Devey—By Captain Kid (Kipper of Alder - Holaday Smoke) ex Talaka's Mist (Velvet's Bimbo - Misty Mist Tu II)
AMATEUR—ORE 9/71-4. (½)

CARR-LAB SPIRIT SA-351217 9/24/65 Mr. and Mrs. T. E. Fajen—By Del-Tone Buck* (Martens' Hi Style Buck - Glen-Water Fan Fare) ex Miss Chief Cherokee (Paha Sapa Chief II - Ironwood Cherokee Chica)
OPEN—NCA 3/70-3. (1)

FC CASCADE CHARADE SA-328791 5/22/65 Mrs. R. M. Lewis—By Jigaboo of Mountaindale (Jet of Beaver Hill - Belle of Mountaindale) ex West Island Hortense (Roy's Rowdy - West Island Salome)
OPEN—FTP 5/68-2; LIR 10/68-2; WOM 4/69-1; MAR 5/69-2; LIR 5/69-1; MAR 10/69-1; DEL 10/69-2; WOM 10/69-4; LAB (S) 11/70-2; TAL 4/71-2; LIR 5/71-3; CNY 5/71-4; LIR 10/71-2; WOM 10/71-2. (41)
AMATEUR—MAI 9/68-3; WOM 10/68-3; MAI 9/72-4. (2½)

CHA-CHA-CHA OF DISTRICT TEN SA-85858 9/2/60 H. Fleishhacker, Jr.—By Whincovert Tango (Greatford Pettistree Shadow - Whincovert Kate) ex Peep of Beau (Beau of Zenith - Miss Sandals)
OPEN—SAG 9/65-3; LAS 10/65-4; LAS 2/66-4; ROV 3/66-3; LAS 2/67-2; SCA 9/67-3; LAS 2/68-4. (7½)
AMATEUR—SAG 3/66-2; SAG 3/67-2; ROV 3/68-3. (7)

CHAIN'S PRINCESS PET SA-101858 11/4/60 Marjorie Banks—By Nodak Surprise (Nodak Ever Rest - Nodak Theta) ex Siskiyou Chain (Ardyn's Ace of Merwaljin - Jibodad Velvet)
AMATEUR—SHA 4/67-3. (1)

CHOPPY BABE SA-395018 7/22/65 Dr. A. L. Ryan—By Colonel Smokey Squirrel* (Dyke - Nilo Smoky's Cassandra) ex Arkansas Lady (Arkansas Traveler - Ebony Maiden of Windsor)
OPEN—PHO 10/70/3; SNA 5/71-3. (2)
AMATEUR—SRZ 2/68-4; SNA 8/69-1; CSC 9/69-4; SNA 5/71-2; ACC 8/71-3. (10)

CINDER OF COLE SA-300366 12/18/64 Gary D. and Dell M. Jones— By Roman's Tar Boy (Scotsdale's Black Shadow - Bittersweet's Black Velvet) ex Roman's Second Lady (Big Oaks Black Rip - Brenner's Canadian Grenadier)
AMATEUR—CSC 2/70-3. (1)

COLL-A-DENE'S KELLY SA-506870 7/21/67 Thomas R. Hellwig—By Caliph Obsidian Hobii* (King Cole of Menomin - Jinjo Black's Jet Jewel) ex Melissa of Oakridge (Nilo Possibility - Jet of Oakridge)
AMATEUR—CAS 9/71-2. (3)

FC COPY CAT DEL NORTE SA-532168 9/20/67 Michael Murray—By My Rebel* (Yankee Clipper of Reo-Raj - Duchess of Miller's Haven) ex Martens' Little Susie (Martens' Mister Nifty* - Martens' Black Doll)
OPEN—LST 11/71-1; NLA 3/72-3; NLA 10/72-1; PTA 10/72-2. (14)

FC CREAM CITY COED SA-406 5/10/59 C. H. Morgan—By LaSage's Smoky (Oakcreek Monarch - Princess Pat of Tanca Moor) ex Cream City Clipper (Deer Creek's Do It Now - Hullabaloo of Audlon)
OPEN—LST 3/61-3; PTA 3/62-4; NLA 3/62-1; WIS 4/62-2; AAR 9/62-3; MOV 10/62-4; ALM 2/63-1; LST 3/63-1; MNS 5/63-1; MNS 9/64-2; OHV 10/64-1; MOV 10/64-2; GOL 5/65-2; BHB 6/65-4; MAD 8/65-3; WIS 4/66-1; TRI 6/66-2; AAR 9/66-3; JAY 3/67-1; MOV 4/67-4; MNS 9/67-2. (59)
AMATEUR—WIS 9/65-3; WIS 4/66-3; MAN 8/66-4; WIS 9/66-1; OHV 9/67-1; ALB 5/68-4. (13)

NRFC '70-AFC CREOLE SISTER SA-124779 12/13/61 Donald P. Weiss —By Bob of Random Lake II (The Black Mambo of Kingswere - Cream City Clipper) ex Lady of Allan-A-Dale (Herr Thor Von Tam Beau - Connecticut Lady)
OPEN—PTA 10/66-2; NLA 3/67-4; GSL 8/67-2; ALM 2/68-1; NLA 3/68-2; CHY 8/68-1; SLA 9/68-1; NLA 10/68-4; PTA 10/68-3; MOB 2/69-1; ALM 2/69-1; NTX 3/69-2; RKM 5/69-3; MTR 5/69-3; MON 5/69-1; PIK 8/69-3; NTX 10/69-1; ALM 11/69-1; NFL 2/70-4; PTA 3/70-4; NLA 3/70-2; KAN 4/70-1; MON 6/70-3; EID 7/70-2; MON 9/70-1; NLA 10/70-3; ALM 11/70-1; NAM 11/70-1; NLA 3/71-2; SLA 4/71-3. (88)
AMATEUR—NLA 10/65-1; LST 3/66-4; MOB 2/67-4; SLA 2/67-2; PTA 3/67-4; NLA 9/67-1; PTA 10/67-1; LST 10/67-2; MOB 2/68-2; ALM 2/68-2; NLA 10/68-1; LST 10/68-4; NTX 10/68-3; ALM 11/68-1; ALM 2/69-3; LST 2/69-2; NLA 3/69-4; ALB 5/69-1; RKM 8/69-2; PIK 8/69-2; PTA 10/69-1; NTX 10/69-1; ALM 10/69-2; PTA 3/70-1; NTX 3/70-2; NLA 3/70-1; BHB 6/70-3; CWY 8/70-1; CHY 8/70-2; SHE 9/70-1; SLA 10/70-3; NLA 10/70-2; PTA 10/70-3; LST 10/70-1; ALM 10/70-1; NTX 3/71-3; NLA 3/71-1; SLA 4/71-1; CAS 9/71-1; PTA 10/71-4; NLA 3/72-2. (130)

FC-AFC DAIRY HILL'S MICHIKINIQUIA SA-626535 4/25/68 A. A. Jones—By Super Chief* (Paha Sapa Chief II - Ironwood Cherokee Chica) ex Dairy Hill's Toddy Tot* (Dairy Hill's Night Cap - Carr-Lab Babe)
OPEN—SCA 9/71-2; SAG 3/72-2; ACC 7/72-3; SNA 8/72-3; PHO 10/72-1. (13)
AMATEUR—GSL 5/71-2; ALK 8/71-2; CSC 10/71-4; CSC 2/72-1; MIV 4/72-4; ACC 7/72-2; SAG 7/72-3; RED 7/72-4; SNA 8/72-3. (17½)

Zipper Dee Do

Canuck-Crest Cutty Sark

Cream City Co-Ed

Creole Sister

DAIRY HILLS TODDY TOT SA-122318 12/6/60 A. A. Jone---By Dairy
Hill's Night Cap (Slo Poke Smokey of Dairy Hill - Dairy Hill's Flame's
Fury) ex Carr-Lab Babe (Black Demon of Granton - Carr-Lab Ditto's
Guide)
OPEN—CSC 2/65-4; IDA 8/65-4. (1)
AMATEUR—SRN 5/64-3; CSC 2/65-4; GSL 5/65-4; IDA 8/65-2;
CSC 10/65-2; CSC 9/66-3; RED 7/67-4; NCA 9/67-2. (12½)

DAIRY HILL'S WAMPUM SA-569645 9/25/67 Robert P. Ernaut—By
Super Chief* (Paha Sapa Chief II - Ironwood Cherokee Chica) ex
Dairy Hill's Toddy Tot* (Dairy Hill's Night-Cap - Carr-Lab Babe)
OPEN—ACC 7/72-2; NCA 9/72-3. (4)

AFC DAWN OF ALADON SA-288129 2/16/63 Virginia Wylie—By Del-
Tone Buck* (Martens' Hi Style Buck - Glen-Water Fan Fare) ex
Valgaard Lady of Shady Lane (Yankee Clipper of Reo Raj - Rock
Haven's Black Angel)
OPEN—LIR 10/68-3; WCH 5/69-1; BUK 9/69-4; CSC 2/70-3;
LIR 5/70-3. (8½)
AMATEUR—DEL 10/67-2; NCA 3/68-4; LIR 4/68-4; CNY
5/68-2; WOL 9/68-3; LAB 11/68-4; CSC 2/69-3; WCH 5/69-3;
MAR 10/69-4; WCH 5/70-4; TAL 4/71-1; MAI 9/71-1; CNY
5/72-4; SHO 9/72-2. (25)

FC-AFC DEERWOOD SHANTOO SA-295377 9/23/64 Daniel M. Mahoney—By Cochise Renegade (Cork Wingdinger - Wing-Foot's Judy)
ex Diablo De Norte (Blackie of Sunnymede - Satana)
OPEN—MII 5/68-3; KAN 10/68-3; KAN 3/69-3; MOV 10/69-3;
NTX 10/69-2; RKM 8/70-1; NTX 11/70-4; LST 3/71-3; ALB
5/71-2; NLA 10/71-3; MII 5/72-2; MTR 5/72-3; LST 10/72-1. (26½)
AMATEUR—MON 9/68-2; KAN 3/69-1; JAY 3/70-2; ALB
5/70-1; KAN 10/70-1; KAN 4/71-2; BHB 6/71-3; NTX 3/72-4;
MON 6/72-1. (30½)

DEL-TONE MAC'S BELLE SA-309155 1/10/65 S. Buford Scott — By
Del-Tone Buck* (Martens' Hi Style Buck - Glen-Water Fan Fare) ex
Rill Shannon Dark Dell* (Del-Tone Colvin - Glengarven's Black Bess)
OPEN—MAR 10/70-4. (½)

DESERT GYPSY II SA-545202 10/5/67 Wayne D. Nygaard—By Singing
Woods War Cloud (Paha Sapa II - Fallwood's Hi Top Boots) ex Redd
(Crowder - Bigstone Ricky)
OPEN—SCA 9/71-3; CSC 10/71-4; SAD 9/72-2. (4½)

FC-AFC DESSA RAE SA-34521 2/6/60 A. John Scharwat—By Odessa's
King (Ardyn's Ace of Merwalfin - Lady Cinder Mattausch) ex Jerry
(Bingo - Black Eyed Susan)
OPEN—SPO 9/62-1; SAM 3/63-3; NWR 4/63-2; WMO 5/63-3;
ORE 9/63-2; SPO 9/63-2; NWR 4/64-2; WMO 5/64-2; TAC
8/64-4; NWR 9/64-1; NWR 3/65-1; SPO 5/65-1; NWR 9/66-1;
TAC 4/67-3; NWR 4/67-3; TAC 8/67-1; ORE 3/68-3; PUG
4/68-2; NWR 4/69-4; SPO 5/69-1. (59)
AMATEUR—TAC 4/62-4; SPO 5/62-1; TAC 8/62-2; IDA
8/62-1; NWR 9/62-1; SPO 9/62-4; IDA 8/63-4; NWR 9/63-3;
ORE 9/63-2; TAC 4/64-1; NWR 4/66-3. (29½)

DESSA SWEET SA-233505 10/28/63 A. John Scharwat — By Tar Baby's
Little Sweet Stuff (Tar Baby of Holly Hill - Debbie of Holly Hill) ex
Dessa Rae* (Odessa's King - Jerry)
OPEN—SPO 10/70-3. (1)
AMATEUR—SPO 5/68-4. (½)

DILLY BE WISE SA-182043 12/22/62 Sandy MacKay—By Ahab's Mack The Knife (Freehaven Muscles - Heather Sweep of Audlon) ex Frisky Lou (Zoro II - Dixie Queen Lee)
AMATEUR—MON 5/68-4; SNA 8/68-4. (1)

FC DINK'S GINGER GUINESS STOUT SA-481043 1/31/67 Dr. John D. Ramsey—By Mister Zan Sun (Medlin's Texas Buckshot - Lady Ann Taylor) ex Eason's Nikie (Koncak's Jet - Edwards' Black Gypsy)
OPEN—PTA 10/71-2; MTA 10/72-2; ALM 11/72-1. (11)
AMATEUR—LST 10/72-4. (½)

FC-AFC DOBE'S DESDEMONA SA-78083 12/7/60 Rupert A. Dobesh—By Salt Valley Ottie (Butch's Bitterroot Smokey - Fenbroke's Meath) ex That's Mandy (Freehaven Muscles - Treasure State Be Wise)
OPEN—GSL 5/64-2; IDA 8/64-4; SNA 8/64-1; GSL 8/64-1; SNA 5/65-2; SRN 5/65-3; GSL 5/67-4; SNA 8/67-2; GSL 5/68-3; GSL 8/68-2; ACC 8/68-1. (30)
AMATEUR—IDA 5/64-3; GSL 5/64-2; ACC 7/64-2; GSL 8/65-1; HEL 9/65-1; SNA 5/66-4; SNA 8/64-2; SNA 5/67-1; GSL 5/68-1; SRN 5/68-4; GSL 8/68-3. (32)

DOVE OF LITTLE DUTCH BOOTS SA-288080 10/1/64 Alex Przymus—By Valentine's Cork (Massie's Sassy Boots - Judy of Valentine) ex Rosehill's Little Dutch Boots* (Nodak Boots - The Duchess of Rose Hill)
AMATEUR—LST 3/68-3; MIT 8/68-3; MIT 8/70-3; CMI 5/71-2. (6)

DUCKY O'CEDAR SA-547972 6/16/67 Mrs. Morris W. Stroud III—By Bigstone Blaze (Martens' Mister Nifty* - Dick's Black Scamp) ex Spade O'Cedar (Lolu's Sweet Billy - Queen of Spades XIII)
OPEN—WOL 9/71-2; SLA 3/72-2; ALK 8/72-3. (7)
AMATEUR—MIC 8/71-4. (½)

DUKW-TRAX MANDEGHO SA-190162 11/8/62 Lois A. Poole — By Tarblood of Absaraka* (Tarblood Buffalo Chief - Lady Gretchen of Buffalo) ex Bob's Miss Zipper (Bigstone Sambo - Bigstone Bracken)
AMATEUR—CSC 9/67-3. (1)

DYNA-MITE-WIN SA-219412 6/16/63 Robert and Bobby Hollinger—By Pebble's Rowdy Rebel (Stonegate's Charkie - Dee Ann) ex Cindy Lou Daglo (Bingol Bengul Bouncer - Lady Carbon Daglo)
AMATEUR—MII 5/68-3. (1)

EBONY MAJOR SASSY MISS SA-157860 7/5/62 E. Rob Leatherbury—By Nodak Boots (Massie's Sassy Boots - Spider Wise) ex Glen-Water Fal-Lal (Cork of Oakwood Lane - Little Peggy Black Gum)
OPEN—WIS 4/65-3; MOB 11/66-4; MTA 10/67-4; NLA 9/68-3. (3)
AMATEUR—SLA 9/67-4. (½)

FC-AFC ERN-BARS TWINKLE BOOTS SA-530618 10/7/67 Jack T. Walker II—By Anzac of Zenith* (Black Mike of Lakewood - Jezebel of Normandy) ex Happy's Twinkle* (Night Cap Again - Miss Behavior)
OPEN—NCA 9/70-1; SHA 9/71-4; NWR 9/71-3; ORE 9/71-4; PHO 10/71-1; SHA 4/72-3. (13)
AMATEUR—ROV 3/70-4; ORE 4/70-1; SHA 5/70-1; SRN 5/70-4; ORE 9/70-4; ROV 3/71-4; ORE 4/71-1; SHA 4/71-3; SRN 3/71-1; TAC 8/71-4; WIL 8/71-3; NWR 9/71-3; TAC 4/72-1; SHA 4/72-1; SHA 9/72-1; NWR 9/72-4; ORE 9/72-1. (46)

FC-AFC FRANCES FISHTAIL S-820403 6/5/56 Richard H. Hecker—By Dolobran's Smoketail (Dolobran's Spook - Dolobran's Mighty Mite) ex Princess Patricia Stieg (Black Prince of Holly - Arodle Peggy)

OPEN—NCA 3/59-3; CHY 8/59-3; SRN 5/60-2; WMO 9/60-3;
SCA 3/61-1; AAR 5/61-3; TRI 6/61-2; SUP 6/61-2; CSC
9/61-3; SWA 11/61-4; ALM 3/62-4; GSL 5/62-4; MON 6/62-1;
BHB 6/62-4; SHA 9/62-1; SCA 9/62-4; CSC 9/62-2; ALM 10/62-4;
CSC 2/63-1; NCA 3/63-4; WOL 9/63-1; MIW 10/63-3; WOL
5/63-3; AAR 5/63-4; NTX 10/66-2; PTA 10/66-1; ALM 11/66-2;
ALB 5/67-1. (64)

AMATEUR—OHV 9/58-2; NCA 3/59-4; KAN 4/60-1; MIV
4/60-3; SNA 5/60-3; MON 9/60-3; WMO 9/60-2; KAN 10/60-4;
SCA 3/61-1; SAG 3/61-1; AAR 5/61-2; HEL 9/61-3; DEL
10/61-1; SWA 11/61-2; LAB (S) 11/61-1; NTX 3/62-1; ACC
8/62-2; SHA 9/62-1; CSC 9/62-1; ALM 10/62-1; SAG 3/63-2;
WMO 5/63-3; OHV 9/63-4; OHV 10/64-2; NLA 10/66-1; NTX
10/66-2; SCA 3/67-3; WMO 5/67-3. (82½)

GAHONK'S TYENDINAGA TOTOM SB-33653 10/6/68 John F. White
—By My Rebel* (Yankee Clipper of Reo-Raj - Duchess of Millers
Haven) ex Canvasback Dee (Ace-Hi Royal Flush - Duxbak Dandy)
OPEN—MIT 8/72-2. (3)
AMATEUR—SLA 9/72-2. (3)

GILJO'S NIKKI OF BOW MAR SA-499350 5/2/67 Robert F. Johns—
By Sir Knight Falcon* (Patch of Bonniehurst - Faindi Kalp Asswad)
ex Sumi No Kodomo (Jet Black Cinder - Sumi San)
AMATEUR—RKM 5/71-4. (½)

FC-AFC GRADY'S SHADEE LADEE SA-235270 3/24/63 Wm. K.
Chilcott Jr.—By Black Mike of Lakewood (Vicky's Duffy Boy - Thorn-
wood Bracken Sweet) ex Jezebel of Normandy (Yankee Clipper of Reo
Raj - Belle of Zenith)
OPEN—SCA 3/66-1; NWR 4/66-2; TAC 8/66-1; PUG 8/66-2;
SAM 9/66-3; SPO 10/66-3; PUG 4/67-2; SPO 5/67-3; SRN
5/67-2; WIL 8/67-1; NWR 4/68-2; SPO 5/68-2; TAC 8/68-4;
LAS 2/69-3; CSC 2/69-4; NWR 4/69-2; MON 5/69-4; IDA
8/69-3; NWR 4/70-1; IDA 5/70-3; SNA 5/70-1; GSL 5/70-2;
WMO 5/70-2; WMO 9/70-4. (60)
AMATEUR—SPO 10/65-3; TAC 8/66-3; IDA 8/67-2; NWR
9/67-4; SPO 9/67-1; RED 7/68-3; PUG 8/68-1; LAS 2/69-1;
CSC 2/69-2; PUG 4/69-1; NWR 4/69-3; MON 5/69-2; IDA
8/69-3; PUG 8/69-2; SCA 3/70-1; WMO 5/70-1. (47½)

GRANT'S LADY BIRD SA-498443 8/15/65 Grant Haug — By Burr
(King High Siam - Cindy of Gourd) ex Rille Ann's Lady (Del-Tone
Colvin - Oma's Sassy)
AMATEUR—DUL 8/70-3. (1)

GREENLIEF'S BLACK IMP SA-220740 6/2/63 Donald Greenlief—By
Beavercrest Storm Cloud (Del-Tone Colvin - Beavercrest Shore Leave)
ex Macushla of Rockmont (Beavercrest Toreador - Apache Teardrop)
OPEN—WMO 9/69-4. (½)
AMATEUR—HEL 9/68-4. (½)

AFC GWEN'S RINGTAIL VELVET SA-190997 9/2/62 Will C. Carraway
—By Robbet's Black Hope (Staindrop Murton Marksman - Ebony
Duchess) ex Gwen's Missie (Haroland's Black Joker - Belle's Baby)
AMATEUR—NLA 3/68-2; SLA 9/68-2; PTA 10/68-3; MOB
11/68-3; SLA 9/69-2; MOB 10/69-1; MTR 5/70-3; MON 6/70-3. (18)

AFC GWEN'S TROUBLE SA-191291 9/2/62 Mrs. Gwen L. Carraway—
By Robbet's Black Hope (Staindrop Murton Marksman - Ebony
Duchess) ex Gwen's Missie (Haroland's Black Joker - Belle's Baby)
OPEN—NFL 11/70-2. (3)
AMATEUR—NLA 3/68-1; MEM 10/68-2; MOB 11/68-1; MII
6/69-3; MEM 10/69-2; MEM 10/70-1; SLA 10/71-4. (25½)

207

HAL'S CHULA PRIETA SA-475914 1/27/67 Richard Otis Halligan—By
Ridgewood Playboy (La Sage's Smoky - Nelgard's Counter Point) ex
Jac-Lor Miss Cindy (Manzanal Duffer - Savage Sue)
AMATEUR—WMO 5/71-2. (3)

HAPPY PLAYBOY'S PEARL SA-700534 7/20/69 Clinton Swingle—By
Happy Playboy* (Castlemore Shamus - Suzie) ex Duxbak Betty
(Baker's Jerry - Carnmoney Moira)
OPEN—LIR 5/72-4. (½)
AMATEUR—SWA 11/72-1. (5)

HAPPY'S TWINKLE SA-326114 5/23/65 Del Bergman—By Night Cap
Again (Dairy Hill's Night Cap - Jig's Moonbeam) ex Miss Behavior
(Git 'N' Go Ace - Purty Sure Judy)
OPEN—WIL 8/70-4. (½)
AMATEUR—RED 7/69-4; ORE 4/70-3; SHA 5/70-3; NWR
9/71-4. (3)

HIGHLANDER'S DAME SALLY SA-567433 10/21/67 Joseph and Mary
C. Hall—By Hoss Wright of Ponderosa (Mountain View's Buff - Brandy
Gold of Ibaden) ex Midge of Barbie Town (Alta's Duke of Rich-
mond - Buff's Cinder Ella)
AMATEUR—SAD 9/72-3. (1)

HIGH BRASS SASSY SA-437653 5/12/65 Marie E. Redefer—By Billy Be
Good (Paha Sapa Chief II - Ironwood Cherokee Chica) ex High Brass
Bama (Ace's Storm of Winniway - Invail's Anise of South Bay)
AMATEUR—SHR 4/71-4. (½)

FC HOWIE'S HAPPY HUNTER S-967930 6/30/57 Mr. and Mrs. D. H.
Gearheart—By Bigstone Tar Gum (Marvadel Black Gum - Ducklore
Black Mallard) ex Bigstone Jumper (Cork of Oakwood Lane - Frank's
Christy Girl)
OPEN—BUK 9/61-4; MAR 10/61-1; LR 10/61-3; WOM 9/61-3;
MOB 2/62-4; TAL 3/62-4; SWA 3/62-2; COL 9/62-3; MAR
10/62-1; LIR 10/62-2; LIR 4/63-1; NUT 5/63-4; CNY 5/63-1;
WNY 9/63-1; BUK 9/63-4; COL 9/63-4; LIR 10/63-3; LAB
4/64-4; MAI 5/64-4; CNY 5/64-2; BUK 9/64-2; COL 10/64-3;
MOB 2/65-4; SWA 11/65-1; NFL 2/66-4; MOB 2/66-2; SWA
3/66-3; TAL 3/66-3; WOL 9/66-1; OHV 9/66-2; LAB (S)
11/66-1; SLA 2/67-1. (72½)

AFC HUNT'S CLOUD OF SMOKE SA-476047 3/3/67 Thomas S. Flug-
stad—By Martens' Little Smoky* (Crowder - Martens' Little Bullet) ex
Hunt's Charming Annabelle (Del-Tone Buck* - Jac-Lor Miss Cindy)
OPEN—ALB 7/72-1. (5)
AMATEUR—NEB 5/71-3; RKM 5/71-3; CNB 5/72-4; PIK
5/72-1; MTR 5/72-2; ALB 7/72-2. (13½)

HUNT'S DIGGER BY LITTLE SMOKEY SA-397873 8/10/65 Mrs.
M. R. Flannery—By Martens' Little Smoky* (Crowder - Martens' Little
Bullet) ex Hunt's Charming Annabelle (Del-Tone Buck* - Jac-Lor Miss
Cindy)
AMATEUR—BUK 4/70-1; FTP 6/70-1; BUK 4/71-3. (11)

FC I LOVE LUCY OF AUDLON SA-221742 5/22/63 Tim Treadwell III
—By Oak View's Mill Pond Duster (Tugney of Oak View - Bonnie's
Ginger) ex Little Doll Face of Audlon (Pierrot of Stonegate - Miss
Maggie of Audlon)
OPEN—DUL 8/67-1; MTA 10/67-2; NDK 8/68-2; MIW 4/69-3;
GOL 5/69-1; MIV 4/70-4; ATL 5/70-3. (18½)
AMATEUR—SLA 2/68-2. (3)

IMPERIAL CREST MAGGY SA-249858 2/26/64 Mr. and Mrs. D. H. Gearheart—By Sprucelane's Chippewa Chief (Paha Sapa Chief II - Lady of Sandy Hill) ex Canuck-Crest Sally* (Jet of Zenith - Canuck-Crest Tami O'Churchlee)

OPEN—MOB 2/68-2. (3)

AMATEUR—LAB 5/70-3; LAB (S) 11/70-2. (4)

JAC-LOR'S LAJA SA-301339 3/6/64 Roy M. Hutchinson, M.D. — By Del-Tone Buck* (Martens' Hi Style Buck - Glen-Water Fan Fare) ex Jac-Lor Miss Cindy (Manzanal Duffer - Savage Sue)

AMATEUR—MIT 8/69-2. (3)

J.J.'s LADY EBONY SA-593789 3/4/68 J. T. Janicki—By Tar of Pintail (Inca of Donbeth - Wing of Pintail) ex Ralston Valley's Kitty (Shamrock Acres Jim Dandy - Shadow of Ralston Valley)

AMATEUR—BUK 4/72-4. (½)

J.A.M.'s STEAMIN' DEMON SA-387713 7/24/65 Mr. and Mrs. Byron B. Grunwald—By Martens' Mister Nifty* (Royal of Garfield - Martens' Black Badger) ex Pre Don Jacky (La Sage's Smoky - Jet Doubledot's Trade)

OPEN—NOI 9/68-2; ALM 2/69-3; MNS 5/69-4. (4½)

AMATEUR—MIV 10/69-3. (1)

AFC JILLY GIRL SA-128986 12/25/60 Frank W. Miller—By Paha Sapa Chief II (Freehaven Muscles - Treasure State Be Wise) ex Penny Girl (Cork of Oakwood Lane - Min-A-Jet of Reo Raj)

OPEN—SXV 9/66-1; NOI 10/66-2; TRI 5/68-4. (8½)

AMATEUR—DUL 8/64-4; AAR 9/64-3; MII 5/65-3; MNS 5/65-3; DUL 8/65-4; MAD 5/66-3; MNS 5/66-3; DUL 8/66-2; WIS 9/66-3; MNS 5/67-3; MNS 9/68-1. (16)

JINGLES' BITTER TRACE SA-687477 5/11/69 Jimmy Paul Shahan—By Homestead's Beau Jingles (Kranwood's Charlie of Falcona - Homestead Clinty) ex Homestead's Sweet Pixie (Kranwood's Charlie of Falcona - Sutton Ash)

AMATEUR—CSC 10/71-4. (½)

JOHNNY'S HIGH YELLOW SA-461039 11/1/66 Johnny Pair — By Black Baron of Cajunland (Daring Topper of Swampland - Black Beauty of Swampland) ex Don's Princess Peg (Medlin's Texas Jack-Tar - Jethaven Black Lucky)

AMATEUR—PTA 3/71-4. (½)

FC JOHN'S MINNIE SA-314419 7/5/64 Glen Stewart — By Mark of Hidden Springs (Staindrop Murton Marksman - Peggy of Sugar Valley) ex Nilo Storm's Peggy (Hiwood Storm - Nilo Tammy)

OPEN—PIK 5/68-2; NTX 3/69-4; CNB 5/69-1; SXV 8/69-2; CNB 5/70-2; MTR 5/70-3; EID 7/70-4; NOI 10/70-4. (16½)

AMATEUR—SHE 6/68-4. (½)

FC JULIE COLE OF MENOMIN SA-187349 2/1/63 Dr. Paul Hanahan —By King Cole of Menomin* (Black Gum Gus - Rushmore's Black Shaw) ex Jinjo Black's Jet Jewel (West Island Pons' Pride - Rodney's Pitch Black)

OPEN—BUK 4/68-3; WIS 4/68-4; LAB 11/68-3; TAL 3/69-3; BUK 4/69-3; FTP 5/69-3; NFL 11/69-1; BUK 4/70-1; MIC 8/70-1. (20½)

FC KNIGHT'S NOEL SA-191865 12/25/61 Mrs. Charles R. Hook, Jr.— By Bigstone Tar Gum (Marvadel Black Gum - Ducklore Black Mallard) ex Bigstone Jumper (Cork of Oakwood Lane - Frank's Christy Girl)

OPEN—MAI 9/67-4; LIR 10/67-1; WOM 10/67-3; SHR 3/68-2; LAB 4/68-1. (14½)

LADY VI SA-314138 2/27/65 John Nydegger — By MacGene's Ripco Zipper (Ripco's Peter Pan - MacGene's Highland Lass) ex Whisk of Gin (Black Boots of Zenith - Buchanan's Lady Gin)
OPEN—NWR 9/69-3. (1)

LADY OF WAKE SA-443371 1/23/66 Warren R. Grimsby—By Tornado of Vulcan Crest (Nelson's Vulcan Storm of Wake - Black Snow of Vulcan Crest) ex Miller's Susie Q (Nigger of Dacity - Glen-Water Fal-Lal)
OPEN—GSL 5/71-2; GSL 8/71-1; GSL 5/72-4. (8½)

LAKE RIPLEY POOKA SA-348609 8/21/65 Norman W. Olson — By Black Mike of Lakewood (Vicky's Duffy Boy - Thornwood Bracken Sweet) ex Kemper's Sassy Sue (Massie's Sassy Boots - Thornwood Rhea)
AMATEUR—SNA 5/70-4; IDA 5/71-3; IDA 5/72-4; IDA 8/72-3. (3)

LIL'S LUCKY LINDA SA-560303 11/3/67 M. L. Darling — By Guy's Bitterroot Lucky* (Beavercrest Toreador - Pickrel's Ebony Babe) ex Jilly's Tiger Lil (Duxbak Scooter* - Jilly Girl*)
OPEN—MON 6/71-2; EID 7/71-3; MON 6/72-2; CSC 9/72-2. (10)
AMATEUR—GSL 8/72-2. (3)

LISA'S PET SA-352850 4/22/62 Charles W. Cox—By Braemar Bounce Of Willowmount (Don Head Barley Sugar - Golden Bess) ex Hylands Black Rex (Ballyduff Poacher - Black Mina)
OPEN—FRR 8/68-4; MAN 8/70-1; BUK 9/70-3; WOL 5/71-3. (7½)

LITTLE BILLIE JO SA-465207 11/25/66 Tomie Voigt — By Billy Pawlesta* (Robbet's Black Hope - Toto of Audlon) ex Matilda II (Paha Sapa Chief II - Jumper)
OPEN—ALM 10/69-4; NLA 3/70-4; PTA 3/71-4; ALM 2/72-4; PTA 3/72-4. (2½)
AMATEUR—ALM 2/71-4; SLA 4/71-3; PTA 10/71-1; PTA 3/72-3; LST 3/72-4; NLA 3/72-4. (8½)

FC-AFC LITTLE MISS SAMANTHA SA-430697 1/2/66 Wm. G. Wilson —By Glor-Loral Watch My Smoke (Annwyn's Shedrow - Glor-Loral Lightning Ebony) ex Topsy Turvy Tar Baby (Nigger of Dacity - Glen-Water Fal-Lal)
OPEN—MIW 4/71-1; TRI 6/72-4; MAD 8/72-1. (10½)
AMATEUR—MAD 5/69-2; NOI 9/69-1; WIS 5/70-3; MNS 5/70-2; AAR 5/70-1; AAR 9/70-4; WIS 9/70-2; OHV 10/70-4; LIT 4/71-1; TRI 6/71-2; MII 6/71-3; MNS 9/71-3; MAN 8/72-3; MNS 9/72-2. (35)

FC-AFC LUCIFER'S LADY S-944958 3/6/58 Dr. R. L. Ellis — By Bracken's High Flyer (Kingdale Shadrach - Bracken's Flight) ex Shasta Stormy (Black Demon of Granton - Robbin of South Pass)
OPEN—SRN 5/62-3; LAS 10/62-1; IDA 5/63-3; SRN 5/63-2; WIL 8/63-2; ACC 8/63-1; SAG 8/63-1; SAG 3/65-3; ROV 3/65-1; ORE 4/65-1; SPO 5/66-2; RED 7/66-1; ROV 3/67-2; SHA 4/67-1; SRN 5/67-3. (51)
AMATEUR—LAS 10/60-1; LAS 10/61-2; IDA 5/62-1; SRN 5/62-1; RED 7/62-1; SAG 8/62-2; LAS 10/62-2; WIL 8/65-3; IDA 5/66-1; WIL 8/66-3; LAS 2/67-3. (37)

AFC LUCKY'S LADY IN RED SA-671729 12/28/68 Dr. C. W. Erwin - —By Guy's Bitterroot Lucky* (Beavercrest Toreador - Pickrel's Ebony Babe) ex Lady of Wake* (Tornado of Vulcan Crest - Miller's Susie Q)
OPEN—NTX 10/72-4. (½)
AMATEUR—ATL 10/71-3; NFL 11/71-2; ATL 4/72-3; CNY 5/72-1; NLA 10/72-4; FRR 8/72-1. (15½)

FC-AFC LUKA OF CASEY'S ROCKET SA-221876 5/19/63 R. J. Doyle,
Jr.—By Cougar's Rocket* (Black Cougar - Bay City Katie Jane) ex
Pacific Mo Kee (Shasta Swede of Bracken · Mistletoe Meadow Lark)
OPEN—SCA 3/68-4; SCA 9/68-2; LST 10/68-1; PTA 10/68-4;
SHA 4/69-3; SAG 7/69-2; SCA 9/69-3; SRZ 2./70-1; SNA 5/70-4;
GSL 8/70-4; SCA 9/70-1; ACC 8/71-1; PHO 10/71-3.   (31)
AMATEUR—LAS 2/69-4;LAS 2/70-3; SCA 9/70-1; SAG 3/72-2.   (9½)

FC MARTENS' BLACK POWDER KATE SA-342479 6/29/65 James J.
Doherty—By Martens' Mister Nifty* (Royal of Garfield - Martens' Black
Badger) ex Dick's Black Scamp (Yankee Bob - Glen-Water Fan Fare)
OPEN—SHA 5/70-1; IDA 5/70-2; NWR 9/70-4; ORE 9/70-3;
SPO 10/70-1; TAC 8/71-3; PUG 8/71-4; MIV 4/72-4; SNA
5/72-4; SNA 8/72-2; SHA 9/72-2; CSC 9/72-4.   (23½)

McCLINTOCK'S EBONY BELLE SA-251804 4/21/63 M. E. McClintock
—By Black Jack Sambo (Bigstone Sambo - Bigstone Christie) ex
Avalanche Mitzie (Satan III - Buttons of Avalanche)
AMATEUR—BHB 6/68-3.   (1)

McKEMIE'S POLA SA-217535 3/16/63 Jack K. McKemie—By Wingford's
Water Witcher (Wingford's Leader Bill - Blue Dawn of Sunway) ex
Kelly of Country Acres (Bourbon of Ibaden - Clappersmead Skylark)
AMATEUR—NTX 3/67-2; NTX 10/67-3; NTX 3/68-1.   (9)

MEDLIN'S GAY TEAL OF CASTAWAC SA-287780 9/9/64 Dr. and
Mrs. Roy J. Brinkman—By Robbet's Coaldust (Staindrop Murton
Marksman - Ebony Duchess) ex Medlin's Texas Happy Time (Medlin's
Cork of Grapevine - Medlin's Cricket)
OPEN—NFL 11/70-4.   (½)
AMATEUR—ATL 4/71-2; ATL 4/72-4.   (3½)

MEL'S YULTIDE HONEY SA-372588 12/21/65 Melanie Pennington—
By Cher Te Beau of Repmen (Cher Te Neg - Calcasieu Queen) ex
Cathy-Chris' Yellow Sue (Colonel's Mr. Chips - Barnes Sugar Bee)
OPEN—CAS 10/70-2.   (3)
AMATEUR—LST 3/70-2; LST 10/70-3.   (4)

FC MICHELLE SA-246304 1/29/63 Ed Minoggie—By Black Mike of
Lakewood (Vicky's Duffy Boy - Thornwood Bracken Sweet) ex Kemp-
er's Sassy Sue (Massie's Sassy Boots - Thornwood Rhea)
OPEN—SRZ 2/65-1; NWR 4/65-4; TAC 8/65-1; IDA 8/65-3;
WIL 8/65-1; SAM 9/65-1; NCA 9/65-3; ORE 9/65-2; LAS
10/56-3; SCA 3/66-3; SAG 3/66-1; SHA 4/66-1; RED 7/66-4;
TAC 8/66-2; IDA 8/66-1; WIL 8/66-1; SAM 9/66-1; ORE 9/66-1;
LAS 2/67-3; NCA 3/67-3; TAC 4/67-2; NWR 4/67-1; IDA
5/67-1; SNA 5/67-3; WMO 5/67-2; SHE 6/67-1; RED 7/67-2;
LAS 2/68-3; SCA 3/68-1; ORE 3/68-2; IDA 5/68-3; SNA 5/68-2;
GOL 7/68-2; RED 8/68-3; SAM 8/68-2; NWR 9/68-1; NCA
3/69-3; SAG 3/69-2; ORE 3/69-4; TAC 5/69-1; PUG 4/69-2;
SHA 5/69-4; SRN 5/69-3; RED 7/69-3; TAC 8/69-4; ORE 4/70-1;
SAG 7/70-1; PUG 8/70-2; SAM 9/70-4; LAS 2/71-4; SRZ 2/71-1;
SAM 9/71-1.   (152½)

FC MI-CRIS OF HAYDEN SA-272601 12/12/63 Ausey H. and Elizabeth
F. Robnett — By Highlander's Bojangles (Salty of Sugar Valley -
Highlander's Diana) ex Twink of Belle Isle (Yankee Clipper of Reo
Raj - Fallwood's Lucky Lady)
OPEN—SPO 10/66-2; TAC 4/67-1; SRZ 2/68-2; IDA 5/68-4.   (11½)

FC-AFC MIDGE OF GREENWOOD SA-439323 10/20/66 Joe Boatright
—By Grand Street Duck (Big Meadow Mike - Grand Street Gypsy)
ex Thunder Cloud's Shadow (Deacon of Cochise - Clares' Patty)

Frances Fishtail

Grady's Shadee Ladee

Howie's Happy Hunter

Michelle

OPEN—SHA 5/70-2; SAG 7/70-4; RED 7/70-3; NCA 3/71-3; SAG 3/71-2; ROV 3/71-4; NCA 9/71-1; SAG 7/72-4; RED 7/72-2. (17½)

AMATEUR—NCA 9/69-3; NCA 3/70-1; SHA 5/70-2; SAG 7/70-2; LAS 2/71-1; RED 7/71-1; NCA 3/72-4; ACC 7/72-3; RED 7/72-1. (28½)

MIKE'S LIZZIE ODOM SA-286084 9/12/64 James R. Leonard — By Gee Baby* (Riefler's Dutch - Pretty Nifty) ex Dee Dee Baby (Riefler's Sprig - Pretty Nifty)
AMATEUR—ALM 2/67-2; NLA 10/67-2. (6)

MISS FORTUNE SA-482195 1/29/67 Hank Tullis—By Nyrobie Playboy (Dolobran's Smoketail - Shady Haven Farm Lady) ex Maiden Margaret (Jet of Zenith - Stormy Snowy)
OPEN—ALB 5/71-4. (½)

MISS NYX SA-687124 6/10/69 Dr. John L. Baumann—By Martens' Little Smoky* (Crowder - Martens' Little Bullet) ex Happy Rajah of Jumpsville (Little Joe of Duckmaster - Deacon's Warbonnet)
AMATEUR—SHA 9/72-4. (½)

FC-AFC MISTY OF OTTER CREEK SA-249760 3/6/64 Robert Rovelstad—By Ridgewood Playboy (La Sage's Smoky - Nelgard's Counter Point) ex Black Beauty of Random Lake (Marshland's Cooley - Marshland's Cindy)
OPEN—WOL 5/67-4; AAR 5/67-3; FRR 8/67-3; AAR 9/67-2; WOL 9/67-1; MIC 8/68-1; MOB 11/68-4; MAD 5/69-1; MIW 10/69-3; MEM 10/69-1; MIW 4/70-1; LIT 4/71-3. (33)
AMATEUR—AAR 9/67-2; GOL 5/69-1; MIC 8/69-3; AAR 9/70-3; LIT 4/71-2; TRI 6/71-3. (14)

MONTINA LADY SA-213644 8/28/63 Dale M. Johnson—By Del-Tone Buck* (Martens' Hi Style Buck - Glen-Water Fan Fare) ex Lakewood's Resolution (Del-Tone Colvin - Virginia Lady)
AMATEUR—MNS 9/67-2. (3)

MOOSE'S LOUISE SA-556389 1/7/67 Mary S. Wilbor — By Royal's Moose's Moe* (Royal's Moose - Spirit Lake Gal) ex Duke's Sheba (Spirit Lake Duke - Dee Ann)
OPEN—CMI 5/72-1. (5)
AMATEUR—MNS 9/71-4; SXV 9/72-1. (5½)

MUFFET'S TUFFET SA-744877 1/11/69 Ross Eggestein—By Del-Tone Lad (Del-Tone Buck* - Cherokee's Lucky Lady) ex Rebel's Miss Muffet (My Rebel* - Merlin of Roselawn)
OPEN—NOI 7/72-3; NDK 8/72-4. (1½)

MUSE'S BONNIE GIRL SA-224383 5/17/63 M. H. Muse—By Bigstone Crowder's Cap (Crowder - Bigstone Goldie) ex Cimaroc Lady Jean (Nodak Boots - Hull's Oma)
AMATEUR—MIL 6/69-3. (1)

NASCOPIE CINDER OF LUCIFER SA-612902 6/5/65 Dr. and Mrs. Wm. N. Bernard—By Stormy of Spirit Lake Gal (Ace Bingo - Spirit Lake Gal) ex Nascopie Little Aggie (Timbershed Totem of Nascopie II - Nascopie Bess's Corkette)
OPEN—COL 10/70-1; LIR 10/70-2. (8)
AMATEUR—MAI 9/69-2; SWA 10/69-4; LAB 11/69-2; MAR 10/70-2. (9½)

NEFERTITI SA-287608 3/2/64 Mrs. Reginal M. Lewis — By Parky* (Pepper's Jiggs - Jibodad Velvet) ex Lilli of Corfu (Fenbroke Cottesmore - Mueller's Havenhurst Dilly)
OPEN—SHA 9/66-2; SCA 9/67-4; CNY 5/68-4; MAR 10/69-4; LIR 5/70-4. **(5)**
AMATEUR—SNA 8/66-4. (½)

NEMO'S DELL-GIN SA-551395 9/21/67 David V. Schaaf—By Nethercroft Nemo of Nascopie* (Timbershed Totem of Nascopie II - Nimrod's Wendy of Windy Mains) ex Bit O' Ginger (Del-Tone Colvin - Cloe of Endo Trail)

    AMATEUR—DUL 8/70-4. (½)

NETLEY CREEK'S CHICKADEE SA-338527 10/24/63 John White— By Black Squeek of Netley Creek (Stonegate's Brazen Beau - Cormat's Pam) ex Del-Tone Colvinette (Del-Tone Colvin - Fallwood's Lucky Lady)

    OPEN—MTA 10/68-2. (3)

NILO GYPSY SA-406761 5/30/66 Nancy and Dr. Norman Bone — By Staindrop Talent (Scotney Dusty - Staindrop Cindy) ex Nilo Ida's Pretender (Pomme de Terre Pete - Staindrop Isla)

    OPEN—RKM 8/70-3; CWY 8/70-2; MON 9/70-3; ALM 2/71-4; MII 5/71-4; PIK 8/71-4; RKM 8/71-4; CHY 8/71-4; HEL 9/71-3; MII 5/72-4. (9)

    AMATEUR—MII 5/69-2; MOV 9/71-4; NOI 7/72-4. (4)

FC-AFC NODROG PENNY SA-94360 3/26/60 Gordon B. Olinger—By Mainliner Mike (Skipper of Rodall II - Wendy of Candlewood) ex Beautywood's Rebel Queen (Roy's Rowdy - Beautywood's Repeat)

    OPEN—PIK 8/63-3; SHE 6/64-1; RKM 5/65-2; RKM 8/65-4; RKM 5/66-3; CHY 5/66-1; PIK 8/66-4; CHY 8/66-2; MTR 5/67-2; RKM 8/67-4; CHY 8/67-4; PIK 5/68-4; RKM 8/68-1; CHY 8/68-2; ALB 5/69-1; MTR 5/69-2; PIK 8/69-1; SHE 8/69-2; BHB 6/70-1. (52½)

    AMATEUR—BHB 6/64-2; PIK 8/64-1; RKM 8/64-1; CHY 5/65-3; PIK 8/65-1; RKM 5/66-2; PIK 5/67-2; RKM 5/67-2; SHE 6/67-2; PIK 8/67-1; CHY 8/67-3; PIK 5/68-1; PIK 8/68-3; RKM 8/68-1; CHY 8/68-2; ALB 5/69-4; PIK 5/69-1; RKM 5/69-1; MTR 5/69-2; BHB 6/70-2; PIK 8/70-1. (72½)

NODROG PIXIE SA-442553 3/29/66 Gordon and Joyce Olinger — By Sir Knight Falcon* (Patch of Bonniehurst - Faindi Kalp Asswad) ex Nodrog Penny* (Mainliner Mike - Beautywood's Rebel Queen)

    OPEN—CNB 5/71-4. (½)

    AMATEUR—MTR 5/69-4. (½)

ORION'S LADY DART SA-567867 4/19/68 Mrs. John W. Martin—By Super Chief* (Paha Sapa Chief II - Ironwood Cherokee Chica) ex Dart of Netley Creek (Netley Creek Sugar - Stonegate's Susie Q)

    OPEN—FTP 6/72-3. (1)

    AMATEUR—AAR 5/71-4; BUK 9/71-2; AAR 9/72-3; WNY 9/72-2; BUK 9/72-1. (12½)

AFC OSCAR'S PETITE LIGHTNING SA-311676 2/1/62 Mrs. R. M. Lewis —By Gerwin's Chocolate Coko (Gerwin's Stormy - Gerwin's Cindy) ex Gerwin's Petite Viking (Kimbow General Monty - Gerwin's Lucy Lenora)

    AMATEUR—ROV 3/66-2; SHA 9/66-4; NWR 9/66-1; WMO 9/66-1; LAB 4/67-3; MAR 10/67-3; WOM 10/67-1; MAR 10/68-1; CNY 5/69-1; MAR 10/69-2. (33½)

AFC PAT'S PENNY JO SA-471112 3/28/67 Leonard D. Ferucci, M.D.— By Dessa's Little Tar Baby* (Tar Baby's Little Sweet Stuff - Dessa Rae*) ex Missy of Big Bend (Buck of Merry Meeting Wood - Camelsback Miss)

    OPEN—ALK 9/70-1; ORE 4/71-4; WMO 5/71-4; WMO 9/71-2. (9)

    AMATEUR—ORE 4/71-2; SPO 5/71-4; WMO 5/71-1; ALK 8/71-1; WMO 9/71-2; SAM 3/72-3. (17½)

FC PEG OF TURKEY RUN SA-92531 3/26/61 Gilbert Schaefer — By
Ace's Storm of Winniway (Ardyn's Ace of Merwalfin - Black Pantheress
of Ming) ex Invail's Anise of South Bay (Salty of Sugar Valley -
Martens' Jumper)
OPEN—WMT 6/65-4; MAR 10/65-1; MOB 11/65-4; SHR 4/66-4;
WOL 5/66-4; FRR 8/66-1; WOL 9/66-2; OHV 9/66-3; WOL
9/67-4; WOL 5/68-2; FRR 8/68-2; WOL 9/68-2; MIV 10/68-1;
DEL 10/68-3; DEL 3/69-3; WOL 9/69-2; MOB 8/70-3; SLA
2/70-4; MAD 5/70-2; CNY 5/70-4; OHV 10/70-4; MOB 3/71-4;
OHV 10/71-2.   (44)

FC-AFC PELICAN LAKE PEGGY SA-415176 1/24/64 Scotty Gillespie
—By Castlemore Shamus (Strokestown Duke of Blaircourt - Hilldown
Sylver) ex Birdie's Misty (Crozier's Cinco' Cork - Rockwell's Birdie)
OPEN—MIT 8/67-3; NDK 8/67-3; MIT 8/68-2; MIT 8/69-1.   (10)
AMATEUR—MIT 8/67-2; MIT 8/68-2; NDK 8/68-3; MIT 8/69-1.   (12)

AFC PENNY OF EVERGREEN SA-352451 7/24/65 Mrs. Warner L.
Atkins—By Martens' Mister Nifty* (Royal of Garfield - Martens' Black
Badger) ex Pre Don Jacky (La Sage's Smoky - Jet Doubledot's Trade)
OPEN—CHY 8/68-3; JAY 3/69-3; ATL 5/70-2; ATL 4/71-4.   (5½)
AMATEUR—NTX 3/69-2; NTX 3/70-1; MIW 4/70-4; ATL
5/70-1; JAX 3/72-2.   (16½)

PIEGAN'S CRYSEYDE SA-652932 3/7/69 Sheila A. Sabbag — By Super
Chief* (Paha Sapa Chief II - Ironwood Cherokee Chica) ex Smoky's
Miss Tremendous (Martens' Little Smoky* - Hunt's Charming
Annabelle)
OPEN—EID 7/72-1; GSL 7/72-4.   (5½)
AMATEUR—IDA 8/72-4; PTA 10/72-1.   (5½)

PIXIE IV SA-498805 2/3/67 G. W. Bradford—By MacGene's Fall Guy
(Ripco's Peter Pan - MacGene's Highland Lass) ex Washington's
Tootie Kazootie (Katanga Pepper - Black Diamond Liz)
OPEN—OHV 10/69-3; ATL 10/71-1; NFL 11/71-4.   (6½)
AMATEUR—MTA 10/71-3; MEM 10/71-3; JAM 3/72-4.   (2½)

RAVENHILLS LUCKY LADY SA-730753 3/8/68 Irvin Reid—By Netley
Creek Sugar (Sambo of Somonauk II - Nelgard's Madam Queen) ex
Ravenhill's Char* (Pepper's Jiggs - Dart of Netley Creek)
AMATEUR—MIT 8/71-3.   (1)

RAVEN'S GINGERBREAD GIRL SA-379507 1/28/66 Bachman Doar, Jr.
—By Raven of Tredinnock (Ace Bingo - Nelsen's Dixie Coffee Pot) ex
Belle of Curles Neck (Beautywood's Best Effort - Midge of Treveilyr
Swift)
AMATEUR—TAL 4/70-3.   (1)

REGINA DI CAMPI SA-93712 2/18/61 John D. Fields—By Marshwise
Snapshooter (Freehaven Muscles - Dark Discovery of Franklin) ex
Stormy Cindy (Pawlesta Stormy Weather - Bob's Black Babe II)
AMATEUR—SXV 9/64-4; KAN 10/64-1; SXV 9/65-3; NTX
10/65-3; SXV 9/66-2; CNB 5/67-3; MOV 9/67-2.   (14½)

FC-AFC RILL SHANNON'S DARK DEL SA-149551 10/24/60 Michael
R. Flannery—By Del-Tone Colvin (Cork of Oakwood Lane - Del-Tone
Bridget) ex Glengarven's Black Bess (Galleywood Shot - Templegrove
Jill)
OPEN—MEM 10/64-4; MEM 3/65-1; NLA 3/65-2; MAD 8/65-4;
MTA 3/66-2; AAR 5/66-2; FTP 6/66-4; MNS 9/66-2; SLA
9/66-1; MEM 10/66-2; NLA 3/67-1; MAD 5/67-3; WOL 5/67-2;
NLA 10/67-1; MIV 10/67-4; WIS 4/68-2; MTA 10/68-1; GOL
5/69-4.   (49½)

AMATEUR—WOL 9/63-3; MEM 2/64-2; MIW 4/64-2; MAD 8/64-3; MAN 8/64-4; AAR 9/64-4; MNS 9/64-3; MIV 10/64-2; KAN 4/65-2; MAD 8/65-2; FRR 8/65-2; AAR 9/65-2; SWA 11/65-3; MTA 3/66-3; SWA 3/66-3; BUK 4/66-1; WIS 4/66-2; GOL 5/66-3; WOL 5/66-1; FRR 8/66-2; AAR 9/66-1; MEM 10/66-2; MOB 11/66-1; MTA 3/67-1; NLA 3/67-3; KAN 3/67-1; MIV 4/67-3; BUK 4/67-1; MAD 5/67-2; WOL 5/67-1; MAD 8/67-2; WOL 9/67-2; OHV 9/67-4; MEM 3/68-4; MTA 3/68-2; DEL 3/68-4; TAL 3/68-3; MIV 4/68-3; BUK 4/68-3; WIS 4/68-1; FTP 5/68-2; MIL 6/68-2; DUL 8/68-1; NDK 8/68-1; MTA 3/69-3.   (118½)

NRFC '64-AFC RIPCO'S V C MORGAN SA-37521 10/29/59 J. D. Ott —By Ripco's Peter Pan (Rip of Holly Hill - Whitmore's Rowdy Lady) ex Peppy of Lopez (Chanbar Shadow - Pepper's Maggie)
OPEN—SPO 9/63-3; ROV 3/64-2; TAC 4/64-3; WMO 5/64-1; MON 5/64-1; TAC 8/64-3; WIL 8/64-2; NWR 9/64-3; ORE 9/64-3; SPO 10/64-2; NAT 11/64-1; SAM 3/65-1; ROV 3/65-4; PUG 4/65-4; WIL 8/65-4; HEL 9/65-4; PUG 8/66-4; SAM 9/66-2; ORE 9/66-2.   (42½)
AMATEUR—PUG 4/62-4; SAM 3/63-3; ROV 3/65-4; SAM 3/66-3; ORE 9/66-1; SPO 10/66-4; TAC 4/67-4; PUG 4/67-1.   (14)

RIVER OAKS BLACK FROST SA-603598 7/24/68 Harry Crumley—By River Oaks Corky* (Martens' Mister Nifty* - Don's Ginny Soo) ex Random Rapscallion (Duxbak Scooter* - Random Shot)
OPEN—CMI 5/72-3; ATL 10/72-3.   (2)

RIVER OAKS CREAM CADETTE SA-603597 9/16/68 John Trzepacz— By River Oaks Corky* (Martens' Mister Nifty* - Don's Ginny Soo) ex Sandy's Black Mahria (Winnebago Yankee - Shadow of Silhouette)
OPEN—TRI 6/72-3.   (1)
AMATEUR—FRR 8/70-4; MAD 8/71-2; AAR 9/71-2.   (6½)

FC-AFC ROSEHILL'S LITTLE DUTCH BOOTS SA-122448 3/19/61 Michael R. Flannery—By Nodak Boots (Massie's Sassy Boots - Spider Wise) ex Duchess of Rose Hill (Jet Black Sin - Peggy Gervain)
OPEN—MOB 11/66-3; MTA 3/68-2; DEL 3/68-3; DUL 8/68-2; BUK 9/68-4; OHV 9/68-1; GOL 5/69-3.   (14½)
AMATEUR—SHR 4/66-3; WIS 4/66-1; MAD 5/66-2; GOL 5/66-1; AAR 5/66-1; AAR 9/66-3; MNS 9/66-2; WOL 9/66-3; MEM 10/66-4; MOB 11/66-3; KAN 3/67-4; BUK 4/67-3; WIS 4/67-1; WOL 5/67-3; MEM 3/68-2; DEL 3/68-2; TAL 3/68-2; BUK 4/68-1; FTP 5/68-4: AAR 8/68-1; BUK 9/68-1; WOL 5/69-2; MIL 6/69-4; BUK 9/69-1; WOM 10/69-4; BUK 4/70-3; AAR 5/70-2.   (70½)

ROXIE OF MERCER LAKE SA-173420 11/29/61 E. R. McGraw—By Git 'N' Go Ace (Ardyn's Ace of Merwalfin - Hot Toddy's Mindy) ex Purty Sure Judy (Larry's King Kole - Larry's Stormy)
OPEN—WIL 8/66-3.   (1)
AMATEUR—ORE 9/65-3; SCA 9/69-2.   (4)

ROYAL OAKS HAVOC'S HAZE SA-605040 9/25/68 W. and M. L. Daley —By Super Chief* (Paha Sapa Chief II - Ironwood Cherokee Chica) ex Shamrock Acres Whygin Tardy (Del-Tone Buck* - Whygin Ink of Shamrock Acres)
AMATEUR—SCA 9/72-1.   (5)

AFC ROYAL OAKS JILL OF BURGUNDY SA-601255 9/25/68 Alanson C. Brown III—By Super Chief* (Paha Sapa Chief II - Ironwood Cherokee Chica) ex Shamrock Acres Whygin Tardy (Del-Tone Buck* - Whygin Ink of Shamrock Acres)
OPEN—SAG 7/71-3.   (1)
AMATEUR—SWA 11/71-3; KAN 3/72-4; WOM 4/72-1; WIS 4/72-1; COL 9/72-4; MAR 10/72-1.   (17)

SAGE BRANDY OF SUNNY SLOPE SA-447609 12/4/66 Marge and
Gene Poppendorf — By Kim O'Sage* (Avalanche Burnt Sage - Hull's
Oma) ex Simmers' Shot of Brandy* (Brandy Spirit of Netley* - Sham-
rock Acres Simmer Down*)

OPEN—MNS 5/71-4. (½)

AMATEUR—MAD 5/71-1; MIC 8/71-3; WIS 9/71-3; MAD
5/72-3. (8)

FC-AFC SAND GOLD KIM SA-52832 4/16/60 Jerome Bernstein — By
La Sage's Smoky (Oakcreek Monarch - Princess Pat of Tanca Moor)
ex Nelgard's Counter Point (Freehaven Muscles - Ladies Day at Deer
Creek)

OPEN—MIW 10/62-4; NFL 2/64-1; WMT 6/64-2; AAR 9/64-2;
MIW 10/64-3; MEM 10/64-3; MOB 2/65-1; SLA 5/65-1; SLA
2/66-1; NLA 3/66-4; MAD 5/66-3; WIS 9/66-1; SLA 9/66-4;
NLA 10/66-4; MIV 10/66-2; MTA 10/66-1; MOB 11/66-2; SLA
2/67-4; WIS 9/67-2; SLA 9/67-3; MOB 11/67-1. (59½)

AMATEUR—MEM 3/62-4; WOL 9/63-1; MIW 10/63-1; MEM
10/63-2; OHV 10/64-1; MAD 5/64-2; GOL 5/64-1; FRR 8/64-4;
MEM 10/64-3; MIW 4/65-2; WIS 5/65-2; WMT 6/65-3; MTA
3/66-1; MIV 4/66-1; MIS 10/66-1; MEM 3/67-2; MIL 6/67-4;
WIS 9/67-2; MIV 4/68-2; MAD 5/68-4. (60)

SAND GOLD VENUS SA-530 2/10/59 J. W. Whitehill — By Nodak
Never Again (Deer Creek Black Ace - Stonegate's Trixie) ex Gypsy
Queen of Random Lake (Treveilyr Swift - Comay Classy Chassis)

OPEN—MAD 8/63-3; MAD 8/67-4. (1½)

AMATEUR—MIW 4/63-1; WIS 9/65-4; WIS 9/66-2; MAD
8/68-3. (9½)

SASSY SIOUX OF TUKWILA SA-567865 4/20/68 Forrest E. Mars—By
Super Chief* (Paha Sapa Chief II - Ironwood Cherokee Chica) ex
Dart of Netley Creek (Netley Creek's Sugar - Stonegate's Suzie Q)

OPEN—NWR 9/71-4; WMO 9/71-3; SHR 4/72-3; TAL 4/72-3;
MAR 5/72-2; SWA 11/72-4. (7)

AMATEUR—NWR 9/70-4; SPO 10/70-2; SPO 10/71-2. (6½)

FC SASSY SIOUX OF WILLOW CREEK SA-294094 3/14/64 Mary Ford
Eddy—By Stillwaters Royal Rick (Carr-Lab Hilltop - Stillwaters Lady
Jeep) ex MacKenzie's Di Dee Dee (Dapper Dan of Holly Hill - Nettion
of Honey Lake)

OPEN—HEL 9/67-1; SAM 3/68-1. (10)

SAUK TRAIL BLACK PEPPER SA-305899 1/29/65 C. H. Nicholson—
By Dutchmoor's Etaoin Shrdlu (Calypso Clipper - Jet's Tammy) ex
Sauk Trail Black Pine (Comanche Thunderbolt - Sauk Trail Black Fox)

OPEN—MIW 4/69-4. (½)

SCIOTO BLACK LIBBY SA-180465 9/19/62 John and Eva Wilson—By
Robinson's Blackbird (Haroland's Ace High - Blacksmith Bass Girl) ex
Buckeye Black Princess (Prince William of Erie - Taffy of Buckeye
Lake)

OPEN—OHV 9/68-2; MIV 10/68-4; FRR 8/69-4; OHV 9/69-2. (7)

FC-AFC SERRANA SOOTANA OF GENESEE SA-192717 1/5/63 Ray E.
and Joan Bly—By Paha Sapa Chief II (Freehaven Muscles - Treasure
State Be Wise) ex Princess Sootana of Buffalo (Tarblood Buffalo
Chief - Lady Gretchen of Buffalo)

OPEN—ALB 5/68-1; PIK 8/68-3; LST 2/69-1; PIK 5/69-3;
BHB 6/69-1; SLA 9/69-4; NTX 10/69-3; ALB 5/70-1; PIK
5/70-3; RKM 5/70-1; MTR 5/70-2; PIK 8/70-4; RKM 8/70-2;
SHE 9/70-3; ALM 11/70-4; CAS 9/71-1; SLA 10/71-3; ALM
11/71-4; SOO 4/72-1; RKM 5/72-3. (50)

Nodrog Penny

Rill Shannon's Dark Del

Rosehill's Little Dutch Boots

Sand Gold Kim

218

AMATEUR—RKM 5/66-3; SXV 9/67-2; NEB 4/68-1; MTR 5/68-3; NOI 9/68-4; LST 2/69-1; ALB 5/69-2; PIK 5/69-2; CHY 8/69-4; SHE 8/69-4; ALB 5/70-3; PIK 8/70-3; MON 9/70-1; NEB 4/71-2; PIK 5/71-4; MTR 5/71-1; PIK 5/72-4.   (38½)

SEYMOUR'S BLACK DIAMOND SA-451756 9/21/65 Marjorie C. and Allison Bishopric—By Ace Hi Cherokee Reb (Paha Sapa Chief II - Tammi) ex Gambler's Rosie (Prince William of Erie - Gambler's Lady)
OPEN—LAB 4/72-4.   (½)

SEYMOUR'S HOT LINE PEPPER SA-519949 10/12/67 R. D. Seymour—By Super Chief* (Paha Sapa Chief II - Ironwood Cherokee Chica) ex Could Be's Miss Erable (Mighty Manfred of Maryglo - Beer's Mug)
OPEN—OHV 4/72-4; WOL 5/72-4; AAR 9/72-2.   (4)
AMATEUR—OHV 4/72-3; MIC 8/72-3; OHV 9/72-3.   (3)

SHAMROCK ACRES LUCKY LADY SA-640266 1/14/69 M. J. Thompson—By Super Chief* (Paha Sapa Chief II - Ironwood Cherokee Chica) ex Shamrock Acres Smoky Cinder (Martens' Little Smoky* - Shamrock Acres Miss Cinders)
OPEN—COL 9/72-2.   (3)

AFC SHAMROCK ACRES SIMMER DOWN SA-99844 5/6/61 Jean and James F. Marth—By Brodhead's Bar Booze (Loafden's Trigger - Dela-Winn's Blonde) ex Whygin Gentle Julia of Avec (Whygin Gold Bullion - Whygin Black Gambit of Avec)
OPEN—MTA 10/67-3; AAR 5/68-1; MIL 6/68-4; AAR 8/68-2.   (9½)
AMATEUR—MIW 10/63-3; GOL 5/64-3; MAD 8/64-4; WIS 9/64-4; WMT 6/65-1; AAR 9/65-4; MEM 10/65-1; MIW 4/66-2; MAN 8/66-1; FRR 8/66-3; AAR 9/66-4; MTA 10/66-1; GOL 5/67-2; MAN 8/67-3; AAR 9/67-3; MIW 10/67-3; MTA 10/67-1; MIL 6/68-1; FRR 8/68-1; MOB 11/68-4; WOL 5/69-3; AAR 5/69-3; MTA 2/69-2.   (54½)

SHAMROCK ACRES WINNIE POOH SA-771320 1/14/69 John L. and Janet T. Boyer—By Super Chief* (Paha Sapa Chief II - Ironwood Cherokee Chica) ex Shamrock Acres Smoky Cinder (Martens' Little Smoky - Shamrock Acres Miss Cinders)
OPEN—GSL 8/72-3.   (1)

SHANNON'S TERROR SA-481451 7/2/66 L. Y. Dyrenforth, Jr. — By Taliaferro's Tracer* (Cajun Smut - Chiro's Lady Bee) ex Pontchippi Matrix (Harrowby Ajax - Black Minx of Franklin)
AMATEUR—MOB 11/70-4.   (½)

SHAR-LOY'S MISS MIDNIGHT SA-307503 1/4/65 Mark and Roberta Grove — By Floodbay's Baron O' Glengarven* (Beautywood Rare Trouble - Glengarven's Black Shadow) ex Duchess of Rankin (Paha Sapa Chief II - Black Lady of Valentine)
AMATEUR—HEL 9/71-4.   (½)

FC SHEBA'S WESTMOOR CLEOPATRA SA-285108 3/6/64 Mrs. Wm. K. Laughlin—By Ebbanee's Ricochet* (Blair's Black Victory - Ebbanee's War Dancer) ex Ace's Sheba of Ardyn (Ardyn's Ace of Merwalfin - Chanbar Christmas Holly)
OPEN—SHO 5/68-4; BUK 9/68-3; SRZ 2/69-3; NCA 3/69-4; SNA 8/69-4; WNY 9/69-4; COL 9/69-1; LAB 4/71-3.   (10)
AMATEUR—WOM 4/67-3; MAI 5/67-4; LIR 5/69-2; LAB (S) 11/70-1.   (9½)

FC SHEBA'S WESTMOOR CONTESSA SA-221476 2/16/63 Mrs. S. G. B. Tennant—By Glengarven's Kim (Yankee Clipper of Reo Raj - Burndale's Cedar Lass) ex Ace's Sheba of Ardyn (Ardyn's Ace of Merwalfin - Chanbar Christmas Holly)

OPEN—ALM 2/66-2; NTX 3/67-1; LST 10/67-2; ALM 11/67-4;
PTA 3/68-2; PTA 10/68-2; ALB 5/69-2; GSL 5/69-1. (25½)
AMATEUR—LST 3/68-4; NLA 3/68-3; NLA 10/68-3. (2½)

FC SHERWOOD'S MAID MARION SA-320722 12/23/63 Bill Keyes—By
Sun Beau of Franklin (Beau of The Lark - Pitch of Franklin) ex Sandy
of Danville (Monterey Jack - Rusty Rogue)
OPEN—SPO 9/69-2; IDA 5/70-1; NWR 9/70-1. (13)

AFC SIMMER'S SHOT OF BRANDY SA-266820 11/15/63 Jean and
James F. Marth—By Brandy Spirit of Netley* (Crozier's Silver Lance -
Bonnie Star of Netley) ex Shamrock Acres Simmer Down* (Brodhead's
Bar Booze - Whygin Gentle Julia of Avec)
OPEN—MEM 10/67-4; AAR 5/68-3. (1½)
AMATEUR—AAR 5/67-1; MTA 10/67-4; MIV 4/68-4; AAR
5/68-2; MIL 6/68-3; MAD 8/68-4; MIC 8/68-2; AAR 8/68-3;
WIS 9/68-2; MAD 8/69-4; OHV 9/69-2; MIV 10/69-2. (24)

SKOOKUM REDWING SA-531776 3/29/67 C. L. Phinney — By Raven
Mike of Stonegate (Stonegate's Brazen Beau - Midge of Stonegate) ex
Skookum Scooter (Castlemore Shamus - Birdie's Misty)
AMATEUR—EID 7/70-4; IDA 5/71-2; EID 7/71-1. (3½)

FC-AFC SMOKEY OF PARK AVENUE SA-245034 1/7/64 Dick and
Dorothy Borden — By Alpine Cherokee Rocket (Cherokee Buck -
Nelgard's Madam Queen) ex Long Lake Duchess (Lone Lake's Play-
boy - Bridget of Tamarack Lake)
OPEN— NOI 9/67-3; JAY 3/68-2; DUL 8/69-3; NDK 8/69-4;
MNS 9/69-1; MOV 9/69-1; NOI 9/69-3; MNS 5/70-1; CMI
5/70-1; SXV 9/70-4; MOV 9/70-4; NOI 10/70-3. (28½)
AMATEUR—DUL 8/67-3; NOI 9/67-4; PTA 3/68-3; MNS
5/68-3; WIS 4/69-2; MII 5/69-3; MNS 5/69-1; TRI 5/69-3; DUL
8/69-4; NDK 8/69-4; SXV 8/69-1; MNS 9/69-1; NOI 9/69-2;
MNS 5/70-1; CMI 5/70-2; SXV 9/70-2; MNS 9/70-2; NOI
10/70-2; MII 5/71-1; DUL 8/71-4; MNS 9/71-2. (53)

TAFFY OF JANIE LANE SA-614223 4/11/68 Philip D. Baker — By
Pecan Island Clipper (Black Rascal of Reo Raj - Debbie Lee of Reo
Raj) ex Jemima's Blue Maxine (Cal-Vada's Charky - Jemima of Big
Horn)
AMATEUR—NLA 3/71-3; NLA 10/72-2. (4)

TEALWOOD TAMMY SA-553422 7/19/67 W. E. and Joy A. Bowen—By
Martens' Little Smoky* (Crowder - Martens' Little Bullet) ex Sham-
rock Acres Black Button (Shamrock Acres Sonic Boom - Whygin
Campaign Promise)
OPEN—NLA 3/72-4. (½)

FC-AFC TIGATHOE'S MAINLINER MARIAH SA-370868 8/23/65
Alanson C. Brown III — By Mainliner Mike II (Mainliner Mike -
Semloh's Black Buttons) ex Black Brook's Bartered Bride (Ridgewood
Playboy - Black Brook's Miss Chief)
OPEN—AAR 8/68-4; MAI 9/68-3; NFL 2/69-2; SLA 2/69-4;
MAD 8/69-2; MAN 8/69-2; NFL 11/69-3; FRR 8/70-4; MAR
10/70-1; SWA 11/70-2; TAL 4/71-4; CNY 5/71-2; MAN 8/71-3;
SHR 4/72-2; WIS 4/72-2; WCH 5/72-2; HEL 9/72-1; WMO
9/72-2; SPO 9/72-4. (42½)
AMATEUR—FRR 8/68-3; MTA 3/69-2; DEL 3/69-2; TAL
3/69-4; NEB 4/69-4; WOM 4/69-4; WCH 5/69-1; MAD 8/69-3;
MAN 8/69-2; MIC 8/69-2; WNY 9/69-1; BUK 9/69-4; MAI
10/69-1; LIR 10/69-2; DEL 10/69-4; NFL 11/69-4; JAX 2/70-3;
NFL 2/70-1; LAB 5/70-1; WCH 5/70-2; LIR 5/70-1; CNY
5/70-2; BUK 9/70-1; WOM 4/70-2; FRR 4/70-2; LIR 10/70-2;
DEL 10/70-1; WOM 10/70-3; CSC 3/71-3; TAL 4/71-3; SHR

4/71-3; LAB 4/71-1; LIR 5/71-1; SAG 7/71-4; MAN 8/71-4; KAN 3/72-3; SHR 4/72-3; WOM 4/72-2; WIS 4/72-4; MAR 5/72-3; WCH 5/72-1; LIR 5/72-1; TAC 8/72-2; PUG 8/72-1; MON 9/72-1; WMO 9/72-2; SPO 9/72-2.   (126½)

AFC TIMBERLAKE FLYING MUFFIN SA-149204 1/7/62 Ronald R. Pfister, M.D. — By Tarblood of Absaraka* (Tarblood Buffalo Chief - Lady Gretchen of Buffalo) ex Nyssa's Tanagra of Zenith (Beau of Zenith - Countess Diane of Marshland)
OPEN—CHY 8/65-3.   (1)
AMATEUR—PIK 5/68-2; BHB 6/68-2; SHE 8/68-3; HEL 9/68-2; RKM 5/69-4; MTR 5/69-1.   (15½)

TWINKLE'S MANDY SA-628860 11/28/68 Jack T. Walker II — By Anzac of Zenith* (Black Mike of Lakewood - Jezebel of Normandy) ex Happy's Twinkle* (Night Cap Again - Miss Behavior)
OPEN—PUG 4/71-3; LAS 2/72-2; SAM 3/72-2; ORE 9/72-3.   (8)
AMATEUR—SAM 3/71-3; SAM 3/72-1; NWR 4/72-2.   (9)

TWINK'S TINKER BELL SA-531197 10/7/67 Tom Rickard — By Anzac of Zenith* (Black Mike of Lakewood - Jezebel of Normandy) ex Happy's Twinkle* (Night Cap Again - Miss Behavior)
AMATEUR—SRN 5/70-1.   (5)

TYKER'S LUCKY PENNY SA-457562 12/1/66 Bob Crapo—By Tyker Baby* (Tar Baby's Little Sweet Stuff - Dessa Rae*) ex Halroy's Christmas Carol (Black Mike of Lakewood - Halroy's Tarina Zarina)
OPEN—SAM 3/71-4.   (½)
AMATEUR—ALK 9/70-4; CSC 2/71-4; SAM 3/71-2; EID 7/71-3.   (5)

FC VAN'S PRIDE EBONY SHADOW SA-152054 1/14/62 W. E. Van Sickle—By Stone Castle Jack (Staindrop Ringleader - Bigstone Sugar) ex Jet Firefly of Dacity (Marshwise Snapshooter - Jigger of Dacity)
OPEN—KAN 4/65-2; MIV 4/65-3; CNB 5/65-1; WMT 6/65-1; NFL 2/66-2; MIL 6/60-1; PIK 8/66-1; MNS 9/66-1; MIV 10/66-3; LST 3/67-2; MNS 5/67-2; CHY 8/67-1; SXV 9/67-3; SLA 2/68-2; LST 3/68-4; KAN 4/68-4; CNB 5/68-3; PIK 5/68-3; PIK 8/68-4; SXV 8/68-1; MOV 9/68-1; PTA 3/69-2; MAN 8/69-3; RKM 8/69-2; CHY 8/69-2; LST 10/69-2; KAN 4/70-3; PIK 5/70-2; SXV 9/70-2; PTA 10/70-1.   (34½)

FC-AFC VELVET'S JEZEBEL SA-130191 12/18/62 Frank L. Fletcher, M.D.—By Pepper's Jiggs (Ardyn's Ace of Merwalfin - Black Magic of Van Nola View) ex Jibodad Velvet (Rip of Holly Hill - Jibodad Gypsy)
OPEN—SHA 4/68-3; WMO 5/68-3; SRZ 2/69-1; SNA 8/69-1.   (12)
AMATEUR—HEL 9/65-3; IDA 8/67-3; WMO 9/67-1; ORE 3/68-3; SHA 4/68-2; SNA 5/68-3; WMO 5/68-1; EID 7/68-1; EID 7/69-1; HEL 9/69-4.   (27½)

WACAP'S WINDY SA-661895 6/16/67 Carl L. Peck—By Wacap's Geritol (Wacap's Rook - Harmony Jill's Peggy) ex Wacap's Breeze (Webway's Hurricane - Wacap's Peppy Papoose)
AMATEUR—CSC 10/71-2.   (3)

AFC WANAPUM DART'S DANDY SA-827919 3/1/70 Charles L. Hill— By Super Chief* (Paha Sapa Chief II - Ironwood Cherokee Chica) ex Dart of Netley Creek (Netley Creek's Sugar - Stonegate's Suzie Q)
OPEN—WIL 8/72-2; ORE 9/72-1.   (8)
AMATEUR—RED 7/72-2; TAC 8/72-4; ORE 9/72-2; SPO 9/72-1.   (11½)

Van's Pride Ebony Shadow

Tigathoe's Mainliner Mariah

Serrana Sootana of Genesee

WANAPUM SHEBA SA-565263 4/20/68 Kay DeWitt—By Super Chief*
(Paha Sapa Chief II - Ironwood Cherokee Chica) ex Dart of Netley
Creek (Netley Creek's Sugar - Stonegate's Suzie Q)
OPEN—SPO 5/72-3; WMO 5/72-2; NWR 9/72-3. (5)
AMATEUR—WMO 5/72-1. (5)

WARPATH KITTY SA-411130 4/27/66 Robert D. Ackles—By Middle-
spunk Scamper (Beautywood Rare Trouble - Glen-Water Fury) ex Blue
River Genie III (Paha Sapa Chief II - Semloh's Deb of Walden Pond)
AMATEUR—NEB 4/70-2. (3)

WASHINGTON'S TIZZY L'ZZY SA-662472 3/1/69 Mr. and Mrs. A.
Starke Taylor III — By Guy's Bitterroot Lucky* (Beavercrest's
Toreador - Pickrel's Ebony Babe) ex Jilly Girl* (Paha Sapa Chief
II - Penny Girl)
OPEN—MOV 9/72-2. (3)
AMATEUR—NTX 10/72-4. (½)

WHITTAKER'S FIREFLY SA-229940 4/27/63 Robert Ladwig — By
Ebony's Jet Rebel (Dela-Winn's Hot Rod - Dela-Winn's Bonnie Queen)
ex Gramp's Joy (Gramp's King - Lady Rolande)
AMATEUR—GOL 5/66-2; MIW 10/68-3; AAR 8/69-4; WIS
9/69-1; WOL 9/69-3; WOL 5/70-3. (11½)

WILDHEARTED DINAH SA-625632 9/8/68 John H. Anderson DVM—
By Carnmoney Brigadier* (Bandit of Carnmoney - Castlemore Sheila
of Cordova) ex Midge of Greenwood* (Grand Street Duck - Thunder
Cloud's Shadow)
AMATEUR—SHA 9/71-4. (½)

WILLOWMOUNT EL DIABLO SA-804280 11/12/68 Charles E. Cooney
—By Highlander's Bojangles (Salty of Sugar Valley - Highlander's
Diana) ex Willowmount Honey Bunny (Don Head Barley Sugar -
Burnham Breeze)
OPEN—MEM 10/71-3. (1)

AFC WILLOW'S BOE LONGSHOT SA-333664 2/28/65 Mr. and Mrs.
Don H. Gearheart — By Del-Tone Buck* (Martens' Hi Style Buck -
Glen-Water Fan Fare) ex Don's Ginny Soo (Don-El's Doo Lee - Beauty-
Wood's Creole Jane)
OPEN—LAB 11/68-4. (½)
AMATEUR—SHR 3/68-1; MOB 2/69-3; JAX 2/70-1; SHR
4/70-2; FTP 6/70-3; DEL 10/70-3. (16)

ZOE OF SANDY PORT SA-392795 1/22/66 Jeffrey Goodman — By
Othello of Parsonage Point (Matador of Maryglo - Smudge of Farrior
Place) ex Black Brant's Marylin M. (Black Brant's Treble Pebble - Pipe
Dream of Upland Farm)
AMATEUR—SHR 3/68-4; WNY 9/68-4; PTA 3/69-4. (1½)

GOLDEN RETRIEVERS - DOGS

ANGUS OF STILROVIN SA-275874 8/20/64 Sara and R. H. Harman
—By Gunnerman's Coin of Copper (Cedarburg Joe - Gunnerman's
Proper) ex Stilrovin Kathy K (Stilrovin Bearcat - Pink Lady of Audlon)
AMATEUR—PUG 4/72-4. (½)

BONNIE BROOKS BARNEY SA-711557 7/1/68 Helen Kerns—By Jolly
Again of Ouilmette* (Holway Stubblesdown Jolly - Gunnerman's
Copper Penny) ex Nancy's Golden Dawn (Steitz's Golden Nugget -
Gold Dust of Scotwell)
AMATEUR—MIW 4/72-4. (½)

BONNIE BROOKS COPPER SA-379862 12/31/65 Brocker R. and Diane Voigt—By Jolly Again of Ouilmette* (Holway Stubblesdown Jolly - Gunnerman's Copper Penny) ex Bonnie Brook's Honey (Hot Toddy - Golde Arbor Vita's)
    OPEN—GOL (S) 9/71-2; OHV 4/72-2. (6)

BONNIE BROOKS DANNY SA-486567 3/27/67 Mrs. Richard Carlsen—By Jolly Again of Ouilmette* (Holway Stubblesdown Jolly - Gunnerman's Copper Penny) ex Bonnie Brooks Honey (Hot Toddy - Golde Arbor Vita's)
    OPEN—AAR 5/71-3; FRR 8/71-3. (2)
    AMATEUR—AAR 9/71-3; WIS 9/71-4; WIS 9/72-4. (2)

AFC BONNIE BROOKS ELMER SA-297157 1/27/65 Mrs. Geo. H. Flinn, Jr.—By Jolly Again of Ouilmette* (Holway Stubblesdown Jolly - Gunnerman's Copper Penny) ex Nancy's Golden Dawn (Steitz's Golden Nugget - Gold Dust of Scotwell)
    OPEN—LST 2/69-2; SHE 9/70-1; NTX 3/72-4. (8½)
    AMATEUR—MIV 4/69-3; SHO 5/69-3; CNY 5/69-4; RKM 8/69-4; FTP 6/70-2; LAB 4/71-4; WCH 5/72-3; COL 9/72-1; MOB 11/72-4; NFL 11/72-2. (16)

BONNIE BROOKS MIKE SA-306961 3/16/65 Walter K. Scherer, Jr.—By Jolly Again of Ouilmette* (Holway Stubblesdown Jolly - Gunnerman's Copper Penny) ex Indian Knoll's Memengwa (Indian Knoll's Roc-N-Rye - Heiress Adelle of Hillcrest)
    OPEN—GOL (S) 9/68-4; SPO 9/69-3; GOL (S) 10/69-3; TRI 6/71-3; MAD 8/71-4; AAR 9/71-2; ATL 10/71-2; MIC 8/72-4; FLR 8/72-4; GOL (S) 10/72-4; ATL 10/72-2. (14½)
    AMATEUR—GOL 5/69-4; JAX 3/72-3; MIW 4/72-3; FLR 8/72-2; MIW 10/72-4. (6)

FC BONNIE BROOKS TUFF & A HALF SA-297155 1/27/65 Charles E. Cooney—By Jolly Again of Ouilmette* (Holway Stubblesdown Jolly - Gunnerman's Copper Penny) ex Nancy's Golden Dawn (Steitz's Golden Nugget - Gold Dust of Scotwell)
    OPEN—MIC 8/69-4; SHR 4/70-3; MAR 5/70-4; AAR 9/70-3; GOL (S) 9/70-4; BUK 9/70-4; OHV 10/70-1; MEM 10/70-3; MOB 11/70-2; WIS 4/71-1; MIC 8/71-2; MOB 11/71-1; GOL 5/72-2; MIL 6/72-3; WOL 9/72-3; GOL (S) 10/72-3; MOB 11/72-2. (35)
    AMATEUR—FTP 6/71-3; WOL 5/72-1. (6)

BRACKENHOLLOW'S SUNGOLD ROCK SA-460409 1/16/67 K. P. Fisher—By Sherrydan Tag (Pennard Golden Kerry - Tarmoon Scampi) ex Duke's Orofina (Golden Duke of Trey-C - Sun Dance's Flare)
    AMATEUR—ORE 4/71-4; PUG 8/71-3. (1½)

BRIGGS LAKE GOLDEN BOY SA-159959 7/19/62 Joseph and Elaine S. Rizzardi—By Briggs Lake Mac (Granite City Red - Briggs Lake Ginger) ex Rushmore's Little Miss Muffet (Beautywood's Tamarack - Gold Mont Pam)
    AMATEUR—WOL 5/67-4; WOL 5/68-4; AAR 5/68-3; WOL 5/69-1. (7)

AFC CHIEF SANDS SA-438222. 12/2/66 Richard Sampson — By Chief Oshkosh of Stilrovin—Gunnerman's Coin of Copper - Stilrovin Kathy-K) ex Echo of Sands (Riffwood Sand - Goldie of Merry Jewel)
    OPEN—GOL (S) 9/70-1; GOL (S) 9/71-3; NOI 10/71-4; MIW 4/72-3; AAR 9/72-3. (8½)
    AMATEUR—WIS 4/71-3; MAD 8/71-3; MAN 8/71-1; MAD 5/72-1; GOL 5/72-2; DUL 8/72-4; WIS 9/72-2. (18½)

FC-AFC CLICKETY CLICK SA-263912 11/12/63 L. Floberg—By Bishops Golden Pet (Kingdale's Rusty VI - Steven's Goldrush Judy) ex Way-farer's Annette (Kathmar Pepper Boy's Drake - Braconlea Sorrel)

OPEN—GOL 9/68-3; CMI 5/69-3; NDK 8/69-1; SRZ 2/70-2;
MIT 8/70-3; NDK 8/70-4; GOL (S) 9/70-3; HEL 9/70-1; JAY
3/71-2. (20½)
AMATEUR—WMO 5/67-4: MIT 8/68-4; NDK 8/69-2; SXV
8/69-3; NDK 8/70-3; HEL 9/70-1; SRZ 2/71-4. (11½)

DUKE OF HANDJEM SA-403209 3/9/66 Ted R. Hottel — By Poika of
Handjem (Brandy Snifter - Torch of Handjem) ex Shenandoah of
Stilrovin (Gunnerman's Coin of Copper - Stilrovin Kathy-K)
AMATEUR—PIK 8/71-4; GSL 5/72-3; SHE 9/72-4. (2)

DUTCH'S RED SA-330352 7/25/64 Albert E. Butcher—By Lucky Star
Duke (Happy Go Lucky - Tammy Bright Star) ex Jolly's Justi-Nuff
(Sir Charles of Mt. Whitney - Webkap Sally)
OPEN—LAS 2/69-4. (½)
AMATEUR—RED 7/68-4; WIL 8/69-2. (3½)

GIGI'S GOLDEN PRINCE SA-560153 7/18/67 Ted R. Hottel — By
Goldenloe's Aces High (Reo Raider - Woodlawn's Golden Calamity)
ex Golden Girl of Gigi (Chipper's Gold Brick - Gigi Genger of
Chances)
AMATEUR—RKM 8/71-4. (½)

FC-AFC GOLDEN ROCKET'S MISSILE SA-175930 7/29/61 Bud
Shearer—By Golden Rocket VI (Sir Charles of Mt. Whitney - Thorn-
wood's Roxana) ex Bonny Lucy Loch (Owen's Golden Ted - Oakcreek's
Spooks)
OPEN—SAM 3/65-2; IDA 5/65-4; TAC 8/65-3; SHA 9/65-4;
SAM 9/65-3; ORE 4/66-3; IDA 8/66-3; PUG 8/67-1; ROV
3/68-4; TAC 4/68-3; GOL 7/68-3; TAC 8/68-2; IDA 8/68-2;
ORE 9/68-2; SAM 3/69-2; GOL (S) 10/69-4. (28)
AMATEUR—SHA 9/64-3; ROV 3/65-1; TAC 4/65-2; SHA
5/65-4; TAC 8/65-2; SHA 9/65-4; TAC 4/66-4; SPO 5/66-1;
WIL 8/66-2; NWR 9/66-2; ROV 3/67-4; TAC 4/67-2; SHA
4/67-1; TAC 8/67-2; PUG 8/67-3. (37)

GOLDEN ROCKET'S RAINCHECK SA-356564 7/5/64 Jack and Georgia
Vallerius—By Golden Rocket VI (Sir Charles of Mt. Whitney - Thornwood's Roxanna) ex Metolius Miss (Patrick Shane of Ptarmilyn - Skoal
of Laketree)
OPEN—LAS 2/69-2. (3)

GOLDEN ROCKET'S RUFF BOY SA-308729 7/5/64 Don Pryor—By
Golden Rocket VI (Sir Charles of Mt. Whitney - Thornwood's Rox-
anna)) ex Metolius Miss (Patrick Shane of Ptarmilyn - Skoal of
Laketree)
AMATEUR—ORE 9/67-4. (½)

HONOR'S DARADO OF SPINDRIFT SA-704435 7/9/69 John J. and
Bonnie D. Sprude—By Beckwith's Tallyho (Milaur's Baal Benefactor -
Beckwith's Wildwing Feather) ex Honor's Chances Are (Briggs Lake
Windy - Norton's Golden Queen)
AMATEUR—MIV 10/72-4. (½)

JOLLY AGAIN OF OUILMETTE SA-159661 10/12/61 Richard and
Helen Kerns—By Holway Stubblesdown Jolly (Holway Leo - Stubbles-
down Kandy) ex Gunnerman's Copper Penny (Cedarburg Joe - Gun-
nerman's Proper)
OPEN—GOL (S) 9/67-1; MIW 10/67-4. (5½)
AMATEUR—WOL 5/65-4; OHV 8/67-3. (1½)

KING KINIKE OF HANDJEM SA-403210 3/9/66 James T. and Sally
Venerable—By Poika of Handjem (Brandy Snifter - Torch of Hand-

jem) ex Shenandoah of Stilrovin (Gunnerman's Coin of Copper -
Stilrovin Kathy-K)
OPEN—MIW 4/70-4.   (½)
AMATEUR—MIW 5/70-3; MAD 5/70-1.   (6)

KINIKE CHANCELLOR SA-708517 8/20/69 C. I. and J. W. Rogers—
By Poika of Handjem (Brandy Snifter - Torch of Handjem) ex Shen-
andoah of Stilrovin (Gunnerman's Coin of Copper - Stilrovin Kathy K)
OPEN—MAR 10/72-3; MEM 10/72-3; NFL 11/72-2.   (5)

FC MACOPIN MAXIMUM S-836811 10/26/56 Mrs. Geo. Murnane—
By Harbor City Shadrach (Harbor City Jaabo - Virginia Dare of Boot
Lake) ex Featherquest Golden Quill (Gunner of Featherquest - Feather-
quest Golden Sprite)
OPEN—SWA 3/59-2; SWA 3/60-3; LIR 4/60-1; NUT 4/60-1;
CNY 5/60-3; WNY 9/60-4; COL 9/60-1; MAR 10/60-2; LIR
10/60-4; DEL 10/60-2; NUT 5/61-2; MAI 5/61-1; DEL 10/61-3;
LIR 10/61-2; LIR 4/62-3; WOM 4/62-2; CNY 5/62-3; BUK
9/62-1; MOB 2/63-3; TAL 3/63-2; WOM 4/63-1; SWA 3/63-4;
MAI 5/63-3; LAB 4/64-2; SHR 5/64-2; MAI 5/64-2; WOM
10/64-1; MAI 5/65-2; SWA 3/66-2; MAI 9/66-2; COL 9/66-4;
WOM 4/67-2.   (86)

MARSHALL'S TEXAS DUKE SA-354588 9/17/65 James M. Simpson—
Widgeon's Dusty Traveler (Golden Star of Oak Ridge - Aureal Wood's
Widgeon) ex Princess Grace Ann (Nelson's Only - Princess Florene Lee)
OPEN—NLA 3/71-3.   (1)

FC-AFC MISTY'S SUNGOLD LAD SA-327277 4/5/65 K. P. and Valerie
Walker — By Sherrydan Tag (Pennard Golden Kerry - Tarmoon
Scampi) ex Luke's Golden Misty (Dustrack's - Easy Able Rusty)
OPEN—ORE 3/68-4; PUG 4/68-1; PUG 8/68-2; SAM 3/69-1;
SPO 9/69-1; GOL (S) 10/69-1; SAM 3/70-2; ORE 4/70-4; TAC
9/69-1; GOL (S) 10/69-1; SAM 3/70-2; ORE 4/70-4; TAC
4/70-3; SPO 5/70-3; WIL 8/70-3; PUG 8/70-1; ORE 10/70-4;
LAS 2/71-1; NWR 4/71-2; SRN 5/71-2; RED 7/71-4; ROV
3/72-3; TAC 4/72-2; PUG 8/72-4; NWR 9/72-1.   (56½)
AMATEUR—ORE 9/67-1; LAS 2/68-3; TAC 4/68-2; WIL 8/68-4;
PUG 8/68-2; SAM 3/69-1; NWR 4/69-1; IDA 8/69-1; NWR
9/69-3; SPO 9/69-1; SAM 3/70-4; ROV 3/70-1; ORE 4/70-4;
TAC 4/70-1; GOL 5/70-4; TAC 8/70-3; SAM 3/71-1; ROV
3/71-3; TAC 4/71-1; NWR 4/71-1; SPO 5/71-3; TAC 8/71-2;
WIL 8/71-1; SHA 9/71-3; LAS 2/72-1; SAM 3/72-2; ROV
3/72-3; ORE 3/72-3; TAC 4/72-2; TAC 8/72-1; WIL 8/72-1;
SHA 9/72-3; NWR 9/72-2.   (104)

FC-AFC MOLL-LEO CAYENNE SA-182290 11/7/62 James D. Browning
—By Holway Leo (Stubblesdown Larry - Musicmaker of Yeo) ex Molly
of Crooked River (Oakcreek's Fremont - Craigmar's Missile)
OPEN—WIL 8/67-2; SHA 9/67-2; PUG 8/68-1; ORE 9/69-1.   (16)
AMATEUR—ORE 4/66-4; RED 7/66-2; WIL 8/66-1; ORE
9/66-3; ORE 3/67-4; SRN 5/68-3; RED 7/68-1; RED 7/69-1.   (21)

MOLLY'S CAYSON BEAR SA-321388 10/17/64 Gordon A. and Thea Lou
Seese—By Moll-Leo Cayenne* (Holway Leo - Molly of Crooked River)
ex Molly of Crooked River (Oakcreek's Fremont - Craigmar's Missile)
AMATEUR—WIL 8/68-2.   (3)

MR. NUGGET OF REDMOND SA-583809 6/5/68 Dr. John A. Huleen—
By Swanson's Fella (Mister Diggr - Eastgate's Golden Beauty) ex
Golden Scotch (Dustrack's Easy Able Rusty - Chamois of Poppeville)
AMATEUR—PUG 8/71-4.   (½)

Misty's Sungold Lad

Macopin Maximum

Ronaker's Novato Cain

AFC READY OF SACRAMENTO SA-224741 10/7/63 Ron and Connie Leineke—By Michael O'Destiny (Prince Patrick - Sheba of Shasta) ex Diane O'Destiny (Jolor's Peter Pan - Copper Flame)

OPEN—SHA 5/70-4; BHB 6/70-2.   (3½)

AMATEUR—SHA 4/68-4; SHA 9/68-2; SAG 7/70-4; SHA 9/70-1; ORE 9/70-2; ORE 9/71-3; LAS 2/72-4; ORE 3/72-4.   (14)

FC-AFC RIPP'N READY SA-81585 1/23/60 W. D. Connor—By Bang Away's Hay Bailer (Rusty Bang Away - Gray's Miss Tiffany) ex Goldie of Tamarack (Brick's Golden Riptide - Tammy of Tamarack)

OPEN—MAD 5/64-4; GOL 5/64-3; FRR 8/64-1; GOL (S) 9/64-3; PIK 8/65-4; GOL (S) 9/65-3; JAY 3/66-1; PIK 8/66-3; GOL (S) 9/66-3; KAN 3/67-2; CNB 5/67-3; AAR 5/67-2; PIK 8/67-4; BUK 4/68-1; CNB 5/68-4; RKM 8/68-4; KAN 10/68-1; AAR 5/69-2.   (37½)

AMATEUR—NEB 4/62-2; AAR 9/62-3; WOL 5/63-3; TRI 5/63-3; GOL 5/64-2; MIV 4/66-2; NEB 4/66-1; MOV 9/66-4; COL 9/66-3; NEB 4/67-1; MIW 4/67-3; NEB 4/68-3; BUK 4/68-4; WIS 4/68-4; NEB 4/69-2.   (29½)

DUAL-AFC RONAKERS NOVATO CAIN SA-380533 4/2/66 Desmond S. Mactavish, Jr. — By Golden Duke of Trey-C (Lakewood's Red Gold - The Duchess of Ogden Farms) ex J.'s Kate (Nickolas of Logan's End - J's Teeko of Tigathoe)

OPEN—WIL 8/69-3; SHA 9/69-4; SPO 9/69-4; GOL (S) 10/69-2; SAG 7/70-3; SHA 4/72-2; NCA 9/72-1.   (14)

AMATEUR—SRN 5/69-1; SHA 9/69-1; NCA 9/69-2; LAS 2/70-2; GOL 5/70-3; SAG 7/70-3; RED 7/70-2; WIL 7/70-2; NWR 9/70-2; SCA 9/70-4; CSC 10/70-1; RED 7/71-3; ROV 3/72-1; ACC 7/72-1; SCA 9/72-4.   (44)

SABE LO TODO OF STILROVIN SA-273256 8/20/64 Dorothy F. Ennis —By Gunnerman's Coin of Copper (Cedarburg Joe - Gunnerman's Proper) ex Stilrovin Kathy-K (Stilrovin Bearcat - Pink Lady of Audlon)

AMATEUR—NTX 10/68-4.   (½)

SIR MICHAEL ROBERT SA-541703 7/17/67 Elaine Klicker — By Charlie Brown II (Holway Leo - Braun's Taffy of Tish II) ex Tink of Golden Anno Nuevo (Ambassador of Yeo - Tish II of Golden Anno Nuevo)

OPEN—MON 9/70-4.   (½)

STILROVIN CLIPPER DELANE II SA-429014 8/28/66 Mrs. G. H. Flinn, Jr.—By Gunnerman's Coin of Copper (Cedarburg Joe - Gunnerman's Proper) ex Stilrovin Whitey Barker (Stilrovin Bear Cat - Pink Lady of Audlon)

OPEN—GOL (S) 9/70-2; GOL (S) 9/71-4; GOL (S) 10/72-2.   (6½)

AMATEUR—MAR 10/70-1; MIC 8/72-4; FRR 8/72-4.   (6)

TINK'S BEN OF PENNYWISE SA-427637 1/15/65 John F. Nash — By Elkdale's Davy Jones (Little Joe of Tigathoe - Golden Knoll's Ballerina) ex Tigerdale's Tinkerbelle (Nickolas of Logan's End - Sputnick of Tigerdale)

OPEN—GOL (S) 9/68-1.   (5)

FC-AFC TIOGA JOE SA-352221 4/8/65 Vern Weber—By Gunnerman's Coin of Copper (Cedarburg Joe - Gunnerman's Proper) ex Tigerdale's Bonnie Meg (Orchard Hill Chips Bifrenaria - Stilrovin Far Daw)

OPEN—TRI 5/69-2; MAD 5/70-3; GOL (S) 9/71-1; DUL 8/72-2; MNS 9/72-1; WIS 9/72-1.   (22)

AMATEUR—TRI 5/69-1; MNS 9/69-3; WIS 9/69-2; WIS 5/70-2; CMI 5/70-4; TRI 6/70-4; MAN 8/70-4; MIW 10/70-1; GOL 5/71-3; NOI 10/71-1; GOL 5/72-4; MAD 8/72-4; MAN 8/72-2; DUL 8/72-2; MNS 9/72-4.   (32)

WILLHAGGIN'S READY POACHER SA-561611 1/6/68 Ron Leineke—
By Ready of Sacramento* (Michael O' Destiny - Diane O' Destiny)
ex Moll-Leo Ginger Snap* (Holway Leo - Molly of Crooked River)
AMATEUR—SRN 5/71-3.   (1)

GOLDEN RETRIEVERS - BITCHES

CAZADOR'S HERMANITA SA-521851 6/17/67 Mr. and Mrs. J. R.
Blair—By Tigathoe's Brass Blade (Tigathoe's Brass Tacks - Tigathoe's
Lucky Penny) ex Golden Surprise for Xmas (Buckeye of Belle - Butter-
scotch Betsy)
AMATEUR—KAN 4/71-3; NLA 10/71-3; SOO 4/72-2; MEM
10/72-4.   (5½)

DESTINY'S READY RIPPLE SA-228062 10/7/63 W. C. and Elsie L.
Moen—By Michael O'Destiny (Prince Patrick - Sheba of Shasta) ex
Diane O'Destiny (Jolor's Peter Pan - Copper Flame)
OPEN—IDA 8/67-4; SNA 8/67-4; GSL 8/67-3; ACC 8/67-4.   (2½)
AMATEUR—SNA 8/67-2; SRN 5/68-2.   (6)

FC-AFC GERRY'S KAIWA OF ROSAMOND SA-172780 1/20/62
Geraldine Miller—By Thornwood's Rayo-De-Oro (Golden Quest of
Thornwood - Rayita De Oro) ex Jolly's Justi-Nuff (Sir Charles of Mt.
Whitney - Webkap Jolly)
OPEN—SPO 10/66-1; SHA 9/67-3; WIL 8/69-1.   (11)
AMATEUR—SHA 9/66-3; ROV 3/67-3; WIL 8/67-4; PUG
8/67-4; ORE 9/67-2; LAS 2/68-1.   (11)

JACQULINE OF ROBIN WAY SA-365753 10/30/65 David H. and
Yvonne M. Schumacher—By Lord Buff (Duke of Spring Hills - Lady
Rowena) ex Joaquin's Dixie Lee (Nickolas of Logan's End - Brandy
of Sequoia)
OPEN—CHY 8/70-2.   (3)

J'S TEEKO OF TIGATHOE SA-12754 7/4/59 Cdr. P. L. Jennings, Jr.
—By Little Joe of Tigathoe (Lorelei's Golden Rockbottom - Gold
Button of Catawba) ex Princess Kilroy (Tonkah of Kilroy - Golden
Showers)
AMATEUR—GSL 5/67-4; GSL 8/67-2.   (3½)

AFC KINIKE COQUETTE SA-378622 3/9/66 James T. and Sally
Venerable—By Poika of Handjem (Brandy Snifter - Torch of Hand-
jem) ex Gunnerman's Coin of Copper - Stilrovin Kathy-K)
OPEN—MII 6/71-4; MAN 8/71-4; MOV 9/71-2; MIW 10/71-4;
MAD 8/72-4; GOL (S) 10/72-1.   (10)
AMATEUR—AAR 9/70-2; WOL 9/70-3; GOL 5/71-1; TRI
6/71-4; WIS 9/71-2; NOI 10/71-4; NEB 4/72-2; MIW 4/72-1. (21)

MOLL-LEO GINGER SNAP SA-197628 11/7/62 Lois and Gayle Rivers
—By Holway Leo (Stubblesdown Larry - Musicmaker of Yeo) ex Molly
of Crooked River (Oakcreek's Fremont - Craigmar's Missile)
OPEN—SCA 9/69-4.   (½)
AMATEUR—CSC 2/67-3; SAG 3/69-3; RED 7/69-3.   (3)

NORTHBREAK'S PANACEA SA-586952 7/9/68 Joan G. Morter — By
Poika of Handjem (Brandy Snifter - Torch of Handjem) ex Wildwing
Abby (Orchid Hill Chips Bifrenaria - Gunnerman's Cinnamon Candy)
AMATEUR—MON 9/72-4.   (½)

AFC RIVERVIEW'S CHICKASAW THISTLE SA-96205 5/1/61 James T. and Sally S. Venerable—By High Farms Band's Clarion (Golden Band of High Farms - Little Dipper of High Farms) ex Tansy of High Farms (Dipper's Epsilon of High Farms - Golden Gal of High Farms)

    OPEN—GOL (S) 9/67-2; GOL (S) 9/68-2. (6)

    AMATEUR—WIS 4/65-1; GOL 5/66-4; MEM 10/66-3; WIS 4/68-3; MAD 5/68-2; PIK 5/68-3; MAN 8/68-4; AAR 8/68-2; WIS 9/68-3. (16)

FC-AFC STILROVIN TUPPEE TEE S-978112 12/4/57 Mrs. G. H. Flinn, Jr.—By Stilrovin Bear Cat (Stilrovin Terry Lee - Bonnie of Bear Creek) ex Pink Lady of Audlon (Lorelei's Golden Rockbottom - Masaka of Wynford)

    OPEN—PIK 8/61-4; AAR 9/61-1; PIK 8/62-3; MEM 3/63-4; PIK 8/63-4; GOL (S) 9/63-3; MTR 9/65-4; GOL (S) 9/65-4; GOL (S) 9/66-4; GOL (S) 9/67-3. (11)

    AMATEUR—PIK 8/60-2; RKM 9/60-4; COL 9/60-1; LIR 5/61-3; MAD 8/61-3; RKM 8/61-1; CHY 8/61-4; PIK 8/62-4; DEL 10/62-3; MOB 2/63-1; MEM 3/63-2; NUT 5/63-1; MAI 5/63-4; SHE 6/63-4; RKM 8/63-2; CHY 8/63-4; COL 8/63-4; WNY 9/63-3; BUK 4/64-1; NUT 5/65-2; MTR 9/65-1; WOL 9/65-3; SLA 2/66-1; LST 3/66-1; OHV 9/66-4; LIR 10/66/2; SWA 11/66-4; LST 3/67-4; NUT 5/67-3; COL 9/67-3; DEL 10/67-1. (72)

SUNBURST MISS POLARIS SA-196995 5/6/63 Curtis and Marjory Tunnel—By Rip of Wildwood (Joaquin Nugget - Dixie Belle of Wildwood) ex Golden Dipper (Baron Sunset Hue - O'Rear's Golden Penny)

    AMATEUR—NCA 9/67-4. (½)

SUN DANCE'S BABE SA-701868 7/15/69 G. C. and C. B. Branch — By Amanda's Shades of Gold (Peter Pan's Flame - Amanda of Marcel) ex Golden Purdue (Sun Dance's Dancer - Sun Dance's Picnic)

    OPEN—GSL 5/72-2; NFL 11/72-3. (4)

    AMATEUR—NWR 4/72-1; MEM 10/72-3. (6)

FC-AFC SUNGOLD SPRITE SA-382654 3/21/66 Valerie Walker — By Golden Rocket VI (Sir Charles of Mt. Whitney - Thornwood's Roxanna) ex Bracken Hollow Sherry (Sherrydan Tag - Sun Dance's Flare)

    OPEN—WIL 8/70-1; NWR 4/71-4; SPO 5/71-3; SRN 5/71-3; SAM 3/72-4; ROV 3/72-2; TAC 4/72-4. (11½)

    AMATEUR—ORE 3/69-4; PUG 4/69-4; RED 7/70-3; PUG 8/70-1; ORE 9/70-3; ROV 3/71-2; SPO 5/71-1; WIL 8/72-3; PUG 8/72-2. (20)

TIGATHOE'S CHICKASAW SA-240341 4/8/64 Mrs. Geo. H. Flinn, Jr. —By Major Drum (Golden Star of Oakridge - Goldenrod's Vixen) ex Tansy of High Farms (Dippers' Epsilon of High Farms - Golden Gal of High Farms)

    OPEN—GOL (S) 9/67-4. (½)

    AMATEUR—LIR 10/68-3. (1)

TIGATHOE'S TEETOTALER SA-131935 1/2/62 Mrs. Geo. H. Flinn, Jr. —By Nickolas of Logan's End (Sir Charles of Mt. Whitney - Little Alice) ex Stilrovin Tuppee Tee* (Stilrovin Bear Cat - Pink Lady of Audlon)

    AMATEUR—KAN 10/67-3. (1)

CHESAPEAKE BAY RETRIEVERS - DOGS

ANDY'S BULLHEADED BULLDOZER, SA-224125 2/6/63 Paul Shoemaker—By Odessa Creek Benny (Odessa Creek Radar - Bayberry Betty) ex Mount Joy's Joy (Mount Joy's Mallard - Mount Joy's Jug Ears)

    OPEN—ROV 3/67-4; ACC 7/71-4. (1)

AUBRAE'S SAND TURK, SA-227353 7/24/63 W. A. and W. A. DeBuse, Jr.—By Chesareid Donachie Topper (Baron's Tule Tiger* - Heather of Carnmoney) ex Frosty's Bold Gypsy (Chessy's Kappy Kan - Jay's Bold Ruler)

    AMATEUR—CHY 8/67-4. (½)

BARONLAND'S ALASKA BOB SA-370397 7/17/65 James Brooks—By Rocky View's Radar Duke (Odessa Creek Radar - Bayberry Betty) ex South Bay Belinda B (Bomarc of South Bay - Matilda Manorville)

    OPEN—ALK 8/71-2. (3)

    AMATEUR—ALK 9/70-3; ACC (S) 7/71-4. (1½)

FC-AFC BARON'S TULE TIGER SA-13353 4/14/59 Mrs. Walter S. Heller—By Nelgard's Baron (Rex of Rapids - Tiger of Clipper City) ex Joanie Teal (Mount Joy's Mallard - Wisconong Joe's Sandy)

    OPEN—SAG 3/64-2; PUG 4/64-2; ACC (S) 5/64-1; GSL 5/64-3; SAG 9/64-3; SCA 9/64-4; LAS 9/64-3; TAC 4/65-3; PUG 4/65-1; ACC (S) 5/65-1; SRN 5/65-2; IDA 8/65-1; NCA 9/65-2; SCO 9/65-1; LAS 10/65-1; GSL 8/66-2; ACC (S) 8/66-1; IDA 8/66-2; SAG 9/66-4; NWR 9/66-3; WMO 9/66-2; CSC 2/67-4; NCA 3/67-2; NWR 4/67-2; ACC 7/67-2; GSL 8/67-1; SCA 9/67-1; SAG 3/68-2; ORE 3/68-1; TAC 4/68-4; NWR 4/68-3; SRN 5/68-4; EID 7/68-3; ACC 7/68-2; CSC 9/68-4. (96)

    AMATEUR—ACC 5/62-2; LAS 10/63-3; LAS 2/64-3; SCA 2/64-2; SAG 3/64-3; PUG 5/64-2; ACC (S) 5/64-1; SRN 5/64-4; IDA 8/64-2; SNA 8/64-2; SNA 5/64-4; CSC 10/64-2; LAS 2/65-3; NCA 3/65-3; SAG 3/65-2; PUG 4/65-1; ACC 5/65-1; CSC 10/65-1; LAS 10/65-4; LAS 2/66-3; SCA 3/66-3; ROV 3/66-4; PUG 4/66-2; NWR 4/66-4; SHA 4/66-1; RED 7/66-1; ACC 8/66-1; SHA 9/66-1; NWR 9/66-3; WMO 9/66-4; SPO 10/66-3; SCA 3/67-2; NCA 3/67-3; SAG 3/67-1; ROV 3/67-1; NWR 4/67-1; RED 7/67-3; GRS 8/67-4; SHA 9/67-4; ORE 3/68-2; PUG 4/68-3; NWR 4/68-3; GOL 7/68-2; NCA 9/68-2; SCA 9/68-2. (111)

BOB'S ALEUTIAN TROJAN SA-107112 11/25/58 Dr. John C. Lundy—By Atom Bob (Nelgard's Riptide - Aleutian Keeko) ex Aleutian Duchess (Mount Joy's Tiger - Aleutian Water Spray)

    OPEN—ACC (S) 7/68-3; ACC (S) 8/70-4. (1½)

    AMATEUR—ACC 5/63-2; ACC (S) 7/67-3. (4)

FC-AFC CHESONOMA'S KODIAK SA-90353 10/4/59 W. E. Peltzer M.D.—By Chesonoma's Louis (Mount Joy's Mallard - Frosty Milady) ex Dinie's Miss Priss (Nelgard's Baron - Sam's Low Country Lady)

    OPEN—HEL 9/62-4; ACC 8/64-2; HEL 9/64-4; SNA 5/65-4; ACC 5/65-3; IDA 5/66-1; SNA 5/66-1; GSL 8/66-1; ACC (S) 8/66-2; ACC 8/66-2; SRN 5/68-2; ACC 8/68-3. (30½)

    AMATEUR—GSL 8/63-2; HEL 9/64-2; GSL 5/65-3; ACC 5/65-4; GSL 8/65-2; HEL 9/65-4; GSL 5/66-3; GSL 8/66-1; ACC (S) 8/66-4; ACC 8/66-2; IDA 5/67-3; SNA 8/67-4; ACC 8/67-1; SNA 5/68-4; ACC 7/68-2; ACC 8/68-2. (33½)

AFC COPPER TOPPER DER WUNDERBAR SA-717131 4/6/68 Greg and Jan McDaniel—By Hector (Shawnee Nip - Brinemixer Lucky) ex Bonnie La Bonita (Rusty Duke of Edgewater - Native Shore Ginger)

    OPEN—ACC (S) 7/71-2; ACC (S) 8/72-4; SAD 9/72-1; PHO 10/72-3. (9½)

    AMATEUR—ACC (S) 7/71-3; ACC 7/72-4; ACC (S) 8/72-1; IDA 8/72-1; PHO 10/72-2. (14½)

FC CUB'S KOBI KING SA-551686 12/9/67 Daniel Hartley—By Tiger's Cub* (Baron's Tule Tiger* - Napolitano's Lady Bug) ex Chesareid April Echoe (Chief Kamiakin - Heather of Carnmoney)

    OPEN—ACC (S) 7/71-3; ACC 8/71-4; GLS 5/72-1; MON 6/71-3; CWY 8/72-1; SHA 9/71-3; CSC 9/72-3. (14½)

Baron's Tule Tiger

Mount Joy's Louistoo

Tiger's Cub

J. J.'S HY-WYNE WILLOWS SA-218887 7/26/63 Jesse J. Mitchell—By
J. J.'s Coca Cola (Choptank Cocacola - Rip Tide Lee) ex Dyna of the
Willows (Ashby's Dynamite - Sherrie of Greenwood)
OPEN—ACC 8/68-4. (½)
AMATEUR—ACC (S) 7/68-3; ACC (S) 7/69-4. (1½)

KIMKAY TARGET SA-702466 7/19/69 C. W. Schmid — By The Big
Fellow* (Atom Bob - Wisconong Champaigne Lady) ex Chopper's
Bobbie (Aleutian Chopper - Atomalina Myrtle)
AMATEUR—ACC (S) 8/72-4. (½)

FC-AFC KOOLWATER'S COLT OF TRI CROWN SA-279418 10/1/64
Michael Paterno—By Bomarc of South Bay (Atom Bob - Aleutian
Duchess) ex Welcome of the Willows (Native Shore Dan - Dyna
of the Willows)
OPEN—NFL 11/68-3; ACC 7/69-2; MAR 10/69-3; NTX 3/70-4;
WOM 4/70-4; CWY 8/70-1; MAI 9/70-3. (12)
AMATEUR—EID 7/68-4; ACC (S) 7/68-4; GSL 8/68-4; MAI
9/68-1; NFL 11/68-4; ACC (S) 7/69-1; ACC (S) 8/70-2. (15)

FC-AFC MOUNT JOY'S LOUISTOO S-992478 11/24/57 E. C. Fleischmann—By Mount Joy's Mallard (Nelgard's King Tut - Sasnakra Sassy)
ex Frosty Milady (Willows Dime - Jacqueline)

OPEN—ACC 8/61-3; WMO 9/61-3; ROV 3/62-2; ACC 5/62-4;
RED 6/62-1; ACC 5/63-2; LAS 2/64-2; SNA 5/64-1; ACC (S)
5/64-3; SHA 5/64-4; RED 7/64-1; LAS 2/65-3; SRZ 2/65-3; IDA
5/65-3; ACC (S) 5/65-4; ACC (S) 8/65-1; SAG 9/65-2; SAG
9/66-1; SHA 9/66-3; SAG 3/67-4; ACC 7/67-1. (51)
AMATEUR—SNA 5/61-2; HEL 9/61-2; ROV 3/62-4; SHA
4/62-3; SRN 5/62-3; NCA 3/63-4; SHA 4/63-1; ACC (S) 5/63-3;
SAG 8/63-2; SHA 9/63-1; SNA 5/64-1; LAS 2/64-2; SHA 5/64-3;
LAS 2/65-2; SRZ 2/65-2; NCA 3/65-4; ACC 5/65-2; SAG 9/65-4;
ACC (S) 8/66-3; SAG 9/66-1; SHA 9/66-2; ORE 3/67-3; SRN
5/67-1; ACC 7/67-2. (60)

MOUNT JOY'S MICKEY FINN SA-399458 5/5/66 Harry W. Cosner—
By Meg's O'Timothy (Beewacker's Chester - Meg O' My Heart) ex
Mount Joy's Jug Ears (Nelgard's Captain Bob - Frosty Milady)
OPEN—ACC (S) 8/70-1. (5)
AMATEUR—EID 7/71-4. (½)

ROCKY OF CAL-PEAKE SA-648330 4/23/66 V. P. Lakusta — By
Rockyview's Radar Duke (Odessa Creek Radar - Bayberry Betty) ex
Mystic Amber of Agassiz (Chocolate's Christy Rock - Mystic Breeze of
Agassiz)
OPEN—SAM 3/71-3. (1)

STRATTE'S NORSKE SA-83356 8/26/60 Dr. Paul B. Stratte — By
Nancy's Cocoa Boy (Curly Mike of Radcliff - Beckwoods Cherokee
Maid) ex Silence of Goff's Market (Red of Los Altos - Mira Loma Pat)
OPEN—ACC (S) 5/65-2; ACC 7/67-3. (4)
AMATEUR—LAS 2/67-4. (½)

THE BIG FELLOW SA-308517 10/20/64 John C. Lundy—By Atom Bob
(Nelgard's Riptide - Aleutian Keeko) ex Wisconong Champagne Lady
(Wisconong Trigger II - Wisconong Sadie)
OPEN—ACC (S) 8/72-2. (3)
AMATEUR—ACC (S) 8/70-4; ACC (S) 8/72-3. (½)

FC-AFC TIGER'S CUB SA-360939 4/16/65 Mrs. Walter S. Heller—By
Baron's Tule Tiger* (Nelgard's Baron - Joanie Teal) ex Napolitano's
Lady Bug (Napolitano's Brown Bomber - Napolitano's Tiney Teen)

OPEN—NCA 9/68-4; SCA 9/68-1; SRZ 2/69-4; SNA 5/69-3; NCA 9/69-4; CSC 9/69-4; SAG 3/70-2; SRN 5/70-4; ACC (S) 8/70-3; NCA 9/70-3; ACC (S) 7/71-1; RED 7/72-4; ACC (S) 8/72-1.   (24)

AMATEUR—EID 7/68-3; ACC 7/68-1; IDA 8/68-1; CSC 9/68-1; SCA 2/69-1; SNA 5/69-2; ACC (S) 7/69-3; WIL 8/69-3; SCA 9/69-1; CSC 9/69-2; NCA 3/70-3; SNA 5/70-2; WIL 8/70-3; NCA 9/70-1; SNA 5/71-1; GSL 5/71-4; ACC (S) 7/71-1; IDA 8/71-2; SCA 9/71-4; SAG 3/72-1; SHR 4/72-4; GSL 8/72-3; ACC (S) 8/72-2; SPO 9/72-4.   (68)

TIGER'S TEXAS TIGER SA-536928 2/28/67 Fallon T. Gordon, M.D. —By Baron's Tule Tiger* (Nelgard's Baron - Joanie Teal) ex Napolitano's Ladybug (Napolitano's Brown Bomber - Napolitano's Tiney Teen)
OPEN—ACC (S) 7/69-4; PTA 10/69-2; PTA 10/72-3; ALM 11/72-4.   (4½)
AMATEUR—ACC (S) 8/70-3.   (1)

CHESAPEAKE BAY RETRIEVERS - BITCHES

MEG'S TAMMY O'HARA SA-25094 12/13/58 Dr. Miles E. Thomas— By Beewacker's Chester (Babe's Skipper - Pat Hand) ex Meg O' My Heart (Mueller's Nero - Lady Bush Harford)
OPEN—ACC (S) 8/66-3; ACC 7/68-1.   (6)
AMATEUR—ACC (S) 5/64-4; IDA 5/65-1; ACC (S) 7/67-4; IDA 5/68-3; WMO 9/68-3.   (8)

FC-AFC MOUNT JOY'S BIT O'GINGER SA-163900 7/30/62 Mrs. E. C. Fleischman—By Meg's O'Timothy (Beewacker's Chester - Meg O' My Heart) ex Mount Joy's Jug Ears (Nelgard's Captain Bob - Frosty Milady)
OPEN—ACC (S) 9/66-4; ACC 7/67-4; NCA 9/67-2; IDA 5/68-2; SNA 5/68-1; SRZ 2/68-2; SAG 3/69-3; IDA 5/69-3; SAG 7/69-1; ACC (S) 7/69-1.   (27)
AMATEUR—LAS 10/65-3; ACC (S) 8/66-2; SAG 9/66-4; NCA 9/66-3; SRN 5/67-2; ACC (S) 7/67-1; GSL 8/67-3; SAG 9/67-2; NCA 9/67-3; CSC 9/67-1; ROV 5/68-1; SNA 5/68-2; IDA 8/68-2; ACC 8/68-3; SAG 8/68-2; NCA 9/68-4; SCA 9/68-4; SHA 4/69-1; SRN 5/69-3; ACC (S) 7/69-2; SCA 9/69-3.   (49½)

MOUNT JOY'S DILWYNE JEZZ O'MEG SA-488380 11/26/66 Jesse J. Mitchell and R. R. M. Carpenter—By Honker of Mount Joy (Mount Joy's Mighty - Mount Joy's Holly) ex Mount Joy's Jug Ears (Nelgard's Captain Bob - Frosty Milady)
OPEN—ACC (S) 8/70-2; LIR 5/72-2; ACC (S) 8/72-3.   (7)
AMATEUR—GSL 8/69-3; ACC (S) 8/70-1; MAR 10/70-4; TAL 4/71-2; MAR 5/71-3; ACC (S) 7/71-2.   (13½)

FLAT COAT RETRIEVERS - DOGS

COPPER CALIPH OF MANTAYO SA-233214 7/19/63 Elizabeth K. and Richard E. Reed—By Bramcroft Dandy (Pencroft Prefect - Atherbram Stella) ex Claverdon Duchess (Bob of Riverglade - Claverdon Pavlova)
AMATEUR—NOI 9/67-2.   (3)

MANTAYO RAMBLIN' WRECK SA-285728 10/11/64 George C. Hinton —By Westerner (Woodlark - Blakeholme Juno) ex Claverdon Duchess (Bob of Riverglade - Claverdon Pavlova)
AMATEUR—RKM 5/70-4.   (½)

234

STOLFORD BLACK QUEEN SA-254626 12/29/63 Elizabeth Millikin—
By Stolford Whinchat (Blakeholme Jem - Claverdon Tawney Pippet)
ex Stolford Hartshorn Memory (Woodlark - Nesfield Stratton)
AMATEUR—MAI 9/69-4. (½)

WYNDHAM'S WINGOVER BRUNHILD SA-596322 5/6/68 Elizabeth P.
Milliken—By Halstock Javelin (Pewcroft Perch - Halstock Black Jewel)
ex Stolford Black Queen (Stolford Whinchat - Stolford Hartshorn
Memory)
AMATEUR—LIR 10/72-2. (3)

DOGS AND BITCHES WHOSE
PROGENY HAVE PLACED
IN OPEN AND AMATEUR STAKES

DOGS & BITCHES WHOSE PROGENY
HAVE PLACED
In Open and Amateur All-Age Stakes
1967 - 1972 Inclusive

Dogs and bitches so qualifying are credited with all their first and second generation get which placed in subject stakes during the period under review. Information with respect to get which placed in Open All-Age stakes prior to January 1, 1967 may be obtained from earlier editions of the Labrador Book and Supplements.

Sires and Dams marked with an asterisk (*) themselves placed during the period '67-'72.

First generation get placing during the period are indented with a single dash (—).

Second generation get are double indented with a double dash (=).

LABRADOR SIRES

Ace Bingo
—Bel-Aire Dam
  AFC Black Bandit
  FC-AFC Carbon Marker
    =Boatswain's Stormy Spirit
    Nascopie Cinder of Lucifer
    Raven's Gingerbread Girl
    FC-AFC Sauk Trail Deepwell
    "Doc"

Ace Hi Cherokee Reb
—Seymour's Black Diamond

Ace Hi Royal Flush
—Hermitage Hill Timberdoodle
    =Gahonk's Traveller
    Gayhonk's Tyendinaga Totom

Ace of Balboa
—FC-AFC Joy's Coal Dust
    =FC-AFC Dusty's Doctari

Ace of Garfield*
—FC Ace of Southwood
    =Rille Ann's Burr

Ace's Storm of Winniway
—FC Peg of Turkey Run
  Storm's Ebony Echo
    =High Brass Sassy

Admiral of the Fleet
—Aerco's Bit O'Honey

Ahab's Mack The Knife
—Dilly Be Wise

Alpine Black King
—FC-AFC Balsom's Mandy

Alpine Cherokee Rocket
—FC-NARFC '70 Andy's Partner Pete
  FC-AFC Smokey of Park Avenue
    =Deadly Dudley's Duxbak Coot
    AFC King Tut V
    FC Minot's Magic Marker
    FC-AFC Monster Mike
    FC-AFC Nemo's Spyder of
      Round Valley
    FC Round Valley's Lucky Tigger

Alvaleigh's Hussar
—Buck of Whittington

Angus of Wayland
—Striper of Ramapo Valley

Anzac of Zenith*
—FC Carnation Rainstar
  Ern-Bar's Andy of Anzac
  FC-AFC Ern-Bar's Twinkle Boots
  Sills Black Bandit
  Telstar of Zenith
  FC Toni's Blaine Child
  Twinkle's Mandy
  Twink's Tinker Bell
  Wild Joker of Napi

Ardee's Smorgasbord
—Whiskey Creek Blue Sahib

Avalanche Burnt Sage
—Centennial Cric
  AFC Kim O' Sage
    =Centennial Chukaluk
    Sage Brandy of Sunny Slope

Baird's Shed of Nashville
—AFC Chap

Bair's Black Sambo
—Luke of Patty Jimsue

Baker's Jerry
—FC Duxbak Scooter
    =Deadly Dudley's Duxbak Coot
    Dixieland Joe
    Duxbak Black Oak
    Fieldmarshall Heinz Guderian
    Happy Playboy's Pearl
    FC Harrowby Wheeler Dealer
    Kracken of Timber Town
    FC Minot's Magic Marker
    Time of Frontier

Bandit of Carnmoney
—FC-AFC Carnmoney Brigadier
  Carnmoney Magnum
  Carnmoney Spud
    =Ahab's Emancipator
    FC-AFC Ray's Rascal
    Wildhearted Dinah

Bat-Jac's Tinny Tim
—Black Susan of Polhemus
  Pat of Orchard Glen

Beau's Buzzsaw of Stonesthrow
—FC Cinder Feller of Stonesthrow

Beautywood's Carbon Copy
—Peter of Gaymark

=Canuck-Crest Cutty Sark
Canuck-Crest Gallant
Canuck-Crest Sally
Double Play of Audlon
FC-AFC Magic Marker of
   Timber Town

Beautywood's Rare Trouble
—Del-Tone Rex
FC-AFC Floodbay's Baron O'Glen-
   garven
FC-AFC Flood Bay Boomerang
AFC Shamrock Acres Gun Away
FC Troublemaker of Audlon II
   =Blackberry Brandy V
   Black Irish Kelly
   FC-AFC Candlewood's Little
      Lou (twice)
   Captain's Miss
   FC Carbo Computer
   Invail's Gunner
   Just Samson
   Shar-Loy's Miss Midnight
   Warpath Cowboy Joe
   Warpath Kitty
   Warpath Rip

Beavercrest's Bolo
—Beavercrest Black Tartar II

Beavercrest Kannon-Ball Kidd
—Beavercrest Goin' Gus
   =Pocatello Chief
   Rimrock Roscoe

Beavercrest Ripper
—FC-AFC Tweet's Bebe

Beavercrest Storm Cloud
—NRFC '67-AFC Butte Blue Moon
Calamity Jane of Rockmont
Greenlief's Black Imp
Bellatrix of Hickory Glen
   =Butte King of the Road
   Cirrus Sea Serpent
   Rebcha's Super Duper
   Rille-Ann's Burr

Beavercrest's Toreador
—FC-NARFC'69 Guy's Bitterroot Lucky
FC-AFC Mitch of Bitterroot
   =FC Bel-Aire Lucky Boy
   Bitterroot's Taurus
   Bruce's Happy Warrior
   NRFC '67-AFC Butte Blue Moon
   Calamity Jane of Rockmont
   Cedarhaven J. B.
   Greenlief's Black Imp
   Happy Hollow's El Champo
   Hi-M's Jake the Giant Killer
   Lil's Lucky Linda
   Lucky's Bitterroot Shasta
   AFC Lucky's Lady in Red
   Lucky's Shasta Beau
   Mitch's Dandy Bouncer
   Polaris Peter
   Tiger's Lucky Buck
   Washington's Tizzy Lizzy

Bellota Punch
—AFC Copper Cities Colliery Cal

Bewise Little Jeff
—Hi-Line King Pepper

Big Black Rippis
—FC Hank's Spook

Bigstone Blaze
—Ducky O'Cedar
FC Flint's Nifty Arrow

Bigstone Bounty
—Bigstone Prairie Wind

Bigstone Butch
—FC Bigstone Scout
FC Your Shot Minnesota Fats

Bigstone Chief
—Bigstone Black Longshot II

Bigstone's Crowder's Cap
—Bumble Buzz of Bee Sting
Lad Crowder's Ranger
Muse's Bonnie Girl
FC Nassau
   =Cimaroc Coon Willie
   FC Nassau's Nar of Minnewaska

Bigstone Flint*
—Wingford's Big Flint Stone
FC Your Shot Minnesota Fats

Bigstone Tar Gum
—FC Howie's Happy Hunter
FC Knight's Noel
   =Smokey of Jetcin
   Spook of Jetcin

Billy Be Good
—High Brass Sassy

Billy Pawlesta*
—Little Billie Jo

Bingol Bengul Bouncer
—AFC Gimp of Lakin

Bingo Again
—AFC Mallard of Devil's Garden
   =Bel-Aire Dam
   Bigstone Count Black Rip
   AFC Black Bandit
   FC-AFC Carbon Marker
   AFC Chap
   AFC Kim O' Sage
   Meto of Devil's Garden

Black Baron of Cajun Land
—Johnny's High Yellow

Black Boy of Whitmore
—FC Riskin
   =Canuck-Crest Gallant
   Morty's Ebony Magic
   Piper's Highland Drummer

Black Cougar
—FC-AFC Cougar's Rocket
   =FC-AFC Beau of Blair House
   Gunner of Gunthunder
   FC-AFC Luka of Casey's Rocket

Black Flash of Hellgate
—El Negro Sam
  Midnight in the Bighorns
    =April Fool's Yellow Jacket
    FC-AFC Rodney's Mr. M. L.
    Coon

Blackfoot's Happy New Year
—FC-AFC Lord Bomar
  =AFC Bomar's Blackfoot Wog
  Bomar's Chris
  Country's Delight Caesar
  FC-AFC Radar Rip
  FC Sauk Trail Senator

Black Gum Gus
—FC King Cole of Menomin
  =FC Caliph Obsidian Hobii
  FC Julie Cole of Menomin

Black Jack Sambo
—McClintock's Ebony Belle

Black Jack Yappee
—Gueydan of Beaumark

Black Jake of Devon*
—AFC Hawk Hill's Sam of Devon

Black Mike XVIII
—Dick's Black Duke

Black Mike of Lakewood
—FC Anzac of Zenith
  FC-AFC Grady's Shadee Ladee
  FC Michelle
  Lake Ripley Pooka
  FC-AFC Rocky Road of Zenith
    =Boise's Black Bart
    FC Carnation Rainstar
    FC-NARFC '71 Dee's Dandy
    Dude
    Ern-Bar's Andy of Anzac
    FC-AFC Ern-Bar's Twinkle Boots
    Leroy III
    Moon Rocket of Zenith
    FC-AFC Rav's Rascal
    Sills' Black Bandit
    Toni's Blaine Child
    Telstar of Zenith
    Twinkle's Mandy
    Twink's Tinker Bell
    Tyker's Lucky Penny
    Wild Joker of Napi
    FC Zipper Dee Do

Black Monk of Roeland
—Rincon Valley Jet
  =Black Susan of Polhemus
  Bomber II
  Pat of Orchard Glen

Black Nipper of Devon
—AFC Black Jake of Devon
  =AFC Hawk Hill's Sam of Devon

Black Point of Avandale
—Knots

Black Sorcerer of Sunset*
—AFC Chuk Chukar Chuk

Black Squeek of Netley Creek
—Netley Creek's Chickadee
  =Duxbak Black Oak
  AFC Togom's Tiger of Abilena
  FC Win-Toba's Black High Point

Blair's Black Victory
—FC-AFC Ebbanee's Ricochet
  =FC Invail's Cavalier Carom
  FC Sheba's Westmoor Cleopatra

Blake's Cole Black Banner
—FC Danny's Cole Black Slate

Blyth's Black Joe of Marel Van
—FC-AFC Marelvan Mike of
  Twin Oaks

Bob of Random Lake II
—NRFC '70-AFC Creole Sister
  Miss Jan's Dobie

Bo Jet II
—Knight Train

Boley's Cascade
—Cascade's Rodney St. Clair
  =FC-AFC Rodney's Mr. M. L.
  Coon

Bomar's Chris*
—Champagne El Toro

Bondill's Black Bandit
—Rolida's Stubby Bandit

Boot's and Belle's Tag-a-Long
—AFC Button Boots

Bracken's High Flyer
—FC-AFC Lucifer's Lady
  =FC V-Jay's Black Paddle

Braemar Bounce of Willowmount
—Lisa's Pet

Brandy Spirit of Netley*
—AFC Simmer's Shot of Brandy
  =Sage Brandy of Sunny Slope

Breckonhill Ben
—FC-AFC Breckonhill's Sean O'Moore
  =Ardyn's Black Bart
  Breckonhill Erin's Kelli
  FC-AFC Mackenzie's Ripco Mac

Breckonhill's Sean O'Moore*
—Breckonhill Erin's Kelli

Breckonhill's Shannon O'Moore
—Ardyn's Black Bart

Breck of Belle Isle
—Land O' Lakes Sunburst

Brodhead's Bar Booze
—AFC Shamrock Acres Simmer Down
  =Brock's Lively Lark
  AFC Ralston Valley Dandy Jake
  AFC Simmer's Shot of Brandy

Burnham's Ex
—Mike of Burrview Acres

Burr
—Grant's Lady Bird

238

Butte Blue Moon*
—Bellatrix of Hickory Glen
  Rebcha's Super Duper
  Rille-Ann's Burr

Cache Valley Drifter
—FC-AFC Beau of Blair House
  Gunner of Gunthunder

Caesar of Great Meadows
—Wingover Cherokee Chief

Cajun Smut
—AFC Taliaferro's Tracer

Caliph Obsidian Hobii*
—Coll-A-Dene's Kelly
  =Invail's Gunner

Cal-Vada's L'il Black Falcon
—AFC Gung-Ho of Granton
  =FC-AFC Ebbanee's Ricochet

Calypso Clipper
—NARFC '64 Dutchmoor's Black Mood
  =AFC Andy Black of Chestnut Hill
  Ebony Mood's Bingo
  FC Jamie's Little Tigger
  FC Mr. Lucky of Oak Hill
  FC Royl Jay
  Sauk Trail Black Mouse
  Sauk Trail Black Pepper

Camliag Pramero*
—AFC Brandy of Cortez
  Cloud Burst

Captain Kid
—Captain's Miss

Captain of Lomac*
—Yogi II

Captain's Courageous
—Glen's Lady's Casper

Carnmoney Billy Jo*
—FC Mr. Mac's Billy Boy

Carnmoney Brigadier*
—Wildhearted Dinah

Carnmoney Rockette
—FC Carnmoney Billy Joe
  =FC Mr. Mac's Billy Boy

Carnmoney Spud*
—Ahab's Emancipator
  FC-AFC Ray's Rascal

Carr-Lab Hilltop
—Stillwater's Carry Back
  =AFC Dent's Midnight Rick
  FC Moby Dick
  FC Sassy Sioux of Willow Creek

Carr-Lab Penrod*
—AFC Bellota Cacahuete
  Rockbend's Kamakura

Cascade's Rodney St. Clair*
—FC-AFC Rodney's Mr. M. L. Coon

Castlemore Shamus
—Gaylab's Gabriel
  Gaylab's Shamus

FC Happy Play Boy
Jo-Anne's Black Blade
FC Pelican Lake Boo Boo
FC-AFC Pelican Lake Peggy
FC Randy Dandy of Holly Hill
Rocky's Dartega
  =FC-AFC Carnmonev Brigadier
  Chuck of Craigend Rock
  Great Smoke Cloud
  Happy Playboy's Pearl
  Jo-Anne's Black Blade
  Martens' Mister Stubbs
  AFC Nilo Brandy Cork
  Pelican Lake Peggy
  Skookum Bingo
  FC Skookum Dale's Nike Mark X
  Skookum Redwing

Centennial Cric*
—Centennial Chukaluk

Charles of Burgundy
—FC-AFC Shadow of Provincetown

Charley of Avandale
—River Road Reho

Cherokee Chief V*
—Cherokee Peace Pipe
  Gayfeathers Domino

Cher Te Beau of Repmen
—FC-AFC Doctor Pepper of Le-Mar
  Snoopy of Dickinson
  Mel's Yuletide Honey

Chief Black Feather*
—FC-AFC Magic Marker of Timber
  Town

Cimaroc Tar Baby
—FC-AFC Cimaroc Tang
Cirrus Eclipse
—Cirrus Sea Serpent

Citation of Franklin
—Chips of Birchwood

Cochise Renegade
—FC-AFC Deerwood Shantoo
Coll-A-Dene's Royal Salute
—Coll-A-Dene's Squire
Collinwood Duke
—Nicoll's Comeback

Colonel Smokey Squirrel*
—Choppy Babe

Col-Tam of Craignook*
—Col-Tam's Stormy

Columbine Copper
—AFC Columbine Loran
Copper City Buck*
—Buckskin Torquin
  =Cirrus Sea Serpent

Cork Harbour's Princess
—Boatswain's Stormy Spirit

Cork of Oakwood Lane
—FC Ace High Scamp of Windsweep
  NRFC '66 & '69 Whygin Cork's Coot
  =Ace-Hi Indian Magic

239

FC-AFC Ace of Garfield
FC-AFC Alamo Black Jack
Alpaugh's Whistlin Jim
Attawan Pucka Sahib
Bayou Pirate
Bigstone Prairie Wind
Bigstone Scout
Carnmoney Billy Jo
FC-AFC Col-Tam of Craignook
FC-AFC Cougar's Rocket
FC Country Club's El Cid
Dakota Jake
FC Del-Tone Buck (twice)
Del-Tone Rex
Dixieland Coot's Tiger Baby
FC-AFC Duke of Crookston
Ebony Major Sassy Miss
Electricity of Audlon
Frankie of Rivernook
Harrowby Dandy
Hermitage Hill Timberdoodle
FC-AFC Hiwinds of South Bay
FC-AFC Hiwood Stormy
FC Howie's Happy Hunter
FC Invail's Cavalier Carom
Invail's Medicine Man
AFC Jilly Girl
FC Knight's Noel
FC Lakenham Paha Sun Dance
Lakeside Dean's Shadow
Mark of Gloster
NRFC '65 Martens' Little Smoky
FC Martens' Mister Nifty
FC Martens' Scrubby Giant
FC Martens' Stormy
FC Medlin's Otto of Toothachres
FC Medlin's Texas Ruff
Medlin's Texas Trooper
FC Medlin's Tiny Boom
Meto of Devil's Garden
Quien Sabe's Black Ace
FC-NARFC '65 Rebel Chief of
    Heber
FC-AFC Rill-Shannon's Dark Del
Rowdy's Sean of the Corkies
Trapper's Paha Cork
FC V-Jay's Black Paddle
FC-AFC Warpath Tuff
Wayside Black Buster
Whygin Wellmet Angus

Corks Bingo
—Old Vav

Cork's Rocket of Swinomish
—FC-AFC Black Jet XVI

Cougar's Rocket*
—FC-AFC Luka of Casey's Rocket
  Rip Von Black Winkle
    =Piegan's Bolle Blake
    FC-AFC Sauk Trail Deepwell
    "Doc"
    FC Sauk Trail Senator

Count Yurmarbles Again
—Bigstone Count Black Rip

Crook's El Toro
—Arroyo Seco Rocket

Crook's Jolly Roger
Dairy Hill's Mad Hatter
Peigan's Bolle Blake
Van's Bomber
AFC Winroc's Ripper

Crowder
—FC Ace of Garfield
  NRFC '65 Martens' Little Smoky
  FC Martens' Scrubby Giant
    =FC Ace of Southwood
    FC-AFC Balsom's Snooper
    Honker
    Bigstone Prairie Wind
    Black Nig Prince
    Bumble Buzz of Bee Sting
    FC-AFC Candlewood's
      Beau of Beaumont
    Chief Storm Cloud
    FC-AFC Cimaroc Tang
    Desert Gypsy II
    Hey You of Lake View
    AFC Hunt's Cloud of Smoke
    Hunt's Digger by Little Smoky
    Hunt's Nipper of Little Smoky
    Igo Licorice Split To
    Lad Crowder's Ranger
    Martens' Mister Lucky
    Martens' Mister Stubbs
    Miss Nyx
    Muse's Bonnie Girl
    FC Nassau
    AFC Nilo Brandy Cork
    Old Vav
    Remohcs Ebony Ace
    Rocket of Frontier
    FC Smoky's Black Jet
    Spirit's Black Pepper
    Tealwood Tammy

Crozier's Silver Lance
—FC-AFC Brandy Spirit of Netley
    =AFC Simmer's Shot of Brandy

Crozier's Sparkle
—FC-AFC Baird's Centerville Sam

Dairy Hill's Night Cap
—FC-AFC Dairy Hill's Night Watch
  Dairy Hill's Planter's Punch
  Dairy Hill's Toddy Tot
    =Ahab's Emancipator
    Dairy Hill's Mad Hatter
    FC-AFC Dairy Hill's
      Michikinquia
    Dairy Hill's Top Banana
    Dairy Hill's Wampum
    Happy's Twinkle

Dajo's Black Velvet
—Mar-Ten's Moneymaker

Dakota Duke II
—Thunder of Rebel's Gypsy

Danny's Black Mac
—Black Sorcerer of Sunset
    =AFC Chuk Chukar Chuk

David's Idaho Pete
—Archie the Cockroach

240

Del-Tone Buck*
—Bodoro's Coaley
  Buck of Woodlawn
  FC Buck's Hobo
  Carr-Lab Spirit
  FC-AFC Cork of Evergreen
  AFC Dawn of Aladon
  Del-Tone Mac's Belle
  FC-AFC Franklin's Tall Timber
  Hi Go Niki
  Jac-Lor's Laja
  Lakeshore Cowie
  Montina Lady
  Re-Mar's Black Buck
  Rille Ann's Cole Buck Blazer
  Rille Ann's Mickey
  Ringo From Happy Hollow
  FC-AFC Rover of Ramsey Place
  AFC Sir Caleb of Audlon
  AFC Willow's Boe Longshot
    =Boatswain's Stormy Spirit
    FC-AFC Candlewood's
      Beau of Beaumont
    Claymar's Crash Diver
    Corky's Ramblin Riley
    Hi-M's Jake the Giant Killer
    AFC Hunt's Cloud of Smoke
    Hunt's Digger by Little Smoky
    Hunt's Nipper of Little Smoky
    AFC Lakeland Tiger of Bruce
    Muffet's Tuffet
    River Oaks Rowdy Bear
    Rockbend's Kamakura
    Rockbend's Magic Marker
    Royal Oaks Havoc's Haze
    AFC Royal Oak's Jill of
      Burgundy
    FC Smoky's Black Jet

Del-Tone Colvin
—FC-AFC Col-Tam of Craignook
  Dakota Jake
  FC-AFC Hiwood Stormy of Alaska
  FC-AFC Rill-Shannon's Dark Del
  FC-AFC Warpath Tuff
    =AFC Acute Accent
    Bel-Aire Dam
    AFC Black Bandit
    FC Buck's Hobo
    NRFC '67-AFC Butte Blue Moon
    Calamity Jane of Rockmont
    FC-AFC Carbon Marker
    Coley's Grand Clipper
    Col-Tam's Stormy
    Connor's Hunter
    Del-Tone Mac's Belle
    Grant's Lady Bird
    Greenlief's Black Imp
    FC Harrowby Wheeler Dealer
    Montina Lady
    FC Mr. Mac's Billy Boy
    Nemo's Dell Again
    Netley Creek's Chicadee
    Rille Ann's Cole Buck Blazer
    Rille Ann's Mickey
    Ripco's Repeater
    FC Riskin

  Warpath Just in Case

Del-Tone Lad
—Muffet's Tuffet

Del-Tone Sam
—FC Beautywood's Tingler

Dessa's Little Tar Baby*
—AFC Pat's Penny Jo

Diablo De Norte
—FC-AFC Deerwood Shantoo

Diamond Jig
—FC-AFC Copper City Buck
  =Buckskin Torquin

Di Mondi's Danny
—Brandywine Star

Dolobran's Smoke Tail
—FC-AFC Bean Ball
  FC-AFC Frances Fishtail
  AFC Smoke Tail's Chico
    =Miss Fortune

Duke of Ashton
—AFC Cha Cha Dancer
  =AFC Bomar's Blackfoot Wog
  Country's Delight Caesar
  FC My Rebel
  AFC Squire of Reo Raj

Duke of Erin-Go-Bra Carnmoney
—AFC Jingo Jo's Duckmaster

Dunvegan Jock
—FC-AFC Hundred Proof Tad

Dutchmoor's Black Mood*
—AFC Andy Black of Chestnut Hill
  Ebony Mood's Bingo
    =Belle Shain's Steamboat Man
    Knots
    FC-AFC Randy Mayhall of Tina
    Tina's Black Chip

Dutchmoor's Etaoin Shrdlu
—Sauk Trail Black Mouse
  Sauk Trail Black Pepper
    =Kennon's Jockeaux
    Muscle's Jet Jock

Dutchmoor's Pooh Bear
—FC Jamie's Little Tigger
  FC Mr. Lucky of Oak Hill
  FC Royl Jay

Duxbak Scooter*
—Deadly Dudley's Duxbak Coot
  Duxbak Black Oak
  Fieldmarshall Heinz Guderian
  FC Harrowby Wheeler Dealer
  Kracken of Timber Town
  FC Minot's Magic Marker
  Time of Frontier
    =FC Bel-Aire Lucky Boy
    Bellatrix of Hickory Glen
    Chief Cody of Le-Mar
    Lil's Lucky Linda
    Paha's Pow on Top
    FC Patsy's Thunderchief

241

River Oaks Black Frost
FC-AFC River Oaks Rascal
Tiger's Lucky Buck

Duxcross Chemo
—AFC The Ballad of Tealbrook
The Bamboo Bandit

Dyke
—Colonel Smokey Squirrel
=Choppy Babe

Ebbanee's Ricochet*
—FC Invail's Cavalier Carom
FC Sheba's Westmoor Cleopatra
=Jingo Jo's Duckmaster
Masai of Aberdeen

Ebony Buck of Chandler
—AFC Mysaks Major Buck

Ebony's Jet Rebel
—Whittaker's Firefly

Ebony Mood's Bingo*
—Belle Shain's Steamboat Man
FC-AFC Randy Mayhall of Tina
Tina's Black Chip

Faro's Trey of Spades
—Faro's Mathew

Fenbroke's Beau
—AFC Polaris Luke

Flashes Black Drake
—April Fool's Yellow Jacket
=FC-AFC Baird's Centerville Sam
Blackfoot Lobo
Butte King of the Road

Floodbay's Baron O' Glengarven*
—Shar-Loy's Miss Midnight

Gadwall's Thunder
—Shantoo Tar Buck

Galleywind Swift
—Chauncey of Ellenwood

Galleywood Gunner
—FC Carnation Butterboy

Gee Baby*
—Mike's Lizzie Odom
=Pam's Black Splash

Geechee*
—Easy Does It of Valhalla
Geechee's Buck
Geechee's Daniel Dexter
Lulake's Rickie
Robinhood's Geechee Junior
Valhalla Bonefish Sam

Gerwin's Chocolate Cake
—AFC Oscar's Petite Lightning

Git 'N' Go Ace
—Roxie of Mercer Lake
=Happy's Twinkle

Glengarven's Kim
—FC-AFC Glengarven's Mik
FC Sheba's Westmoor Contessa

=FC Randy Dandy of Holly Hill
Sport of Upland Farm

Glengarven's Mik*
—Sport of Upland Farm

Glenhead Zuider
—FC-AFC Sazerac Mac

Glen-Water Fever Pitch
—FC Carnmoney Billy Jo
=FC Mr. Mac's Billy Boy

Glor-Loral Watch My Smoke
—FC-AFC Little Miss Samantha
FC-AFC Shadow of Rocky Lane
Shag of Shanty Bay

Grand Street Duck
—FC-AFC Midge of Greenwod
=Wildhearted Dinah

Great Lakes Duke
—Frosty Fortune of Flosum

Green Timbers' Shamus
—Chuck of Craigend Rock

Guy's Bitterroot Lucky*
—FC Bel-Aire Lucky Boy
Bitterroot's Taurus
Bruce's Happy Warrior
Happy Hollow's El Champ
Hi-M's Jake the Giant Killer
Lil's Lucky Linda
Lucky's Bitterroot Shasta
AFC Lucky's Lady in Red
Lucky's Shasta Beau
Tiger's Lucky Buck
Washington's Tizzy Lizzy

Gypsy Rose Satan
—Dutch's Black Lucifer

Hap
—FC-AFC Bair's Sambo
=FC Hank's Spook
Luke of Patty Jimsue

Happy Playboy*
—Happy Playboy's Pearl
=Mike of Burrview Acres

Hauser's Last Chance
—Bridget's Black Cargo

Highlander's Bojangles
—Mi-Cris Drambuie
FC Mi-Cris of Hayden
NRFC '71 Mi-Cris Sailor
FC Willowmount El Diablo
=River Road Bippy

Hiwood John
—Electricity of Audlon
FC-AFC Hiwinds of South Bay
=Chauncey of Ellenwood

Hiwood Stormy of Alaska*
—Coley's Grand Clipper

Homestead's Beau Jingles
—Jingles' Bitter Trace

Hoppy of Jefferson Lane
—Wayside Black Buster

Hoss Wright of Ponderosa
—Highlander's Dame Sally

Huracan of Vulcan Crest
—Brandi of Cayne

Hyde's Black Splash
—AFC Toni's Tar

Innycot Sailor
—Crozier's Firebrand

Ironwood Latigo
—FC-AFC Monster Mike

Jagersbo Claim Jumper
—FC-AFC White's Mar-Ke-Tam Nerro

Jet of Zenith
—FC Canuck-Crest Cutty Sark
Canuck-Crest Sally
AFC Potomac Buddy
=Abenaki's Sagamore
Chipsal John Henry
Imperial Crest Maggie
Miss Fortune

Jet Skipper
—Deadly Dudley's Deke

Jetstone Muscles of Claymar*
—Claymar's Crash Diver
Kennon's Jockeaux
Lincoln of Bel Air
Muscles Jet Jock
=Coll-A-Dene's Perky

Jigaboo of Mountaindale
—FC Cascade Charade

Joy's Coal Dust*
—FC-AFC Dusty's Doctari

Jupiter of Stony Knoll
—FC-AFC Jupiter's Hi-Laurel

Katy's Boy
—Donald Grunts Ray

Kellog's Cork of Lost River
—Kentuckian
=Dutch's Black Lucifer

Kewanee's Yogi
—Dixieland Joe

Killand's King Cole
—FC-AFC J. & L.'s Spooky

Kim O' Sage*
—Sage Brandy of Sunny Slope

King Cole of Menomin*
—FC Caliph Obsidian Hobii
FC Julie Cole of Menomin
=Coll-A-Dene's Kelly

Kingdale's Decoy
—Grand Admiral Raeder

King Donald D.
—Orion of River Park

Koskinen's Colonel
—Gentleman Jiggs
Koskinen's Pyewacket

Koskinen's Dirk
—FC-AFC Hoss of Palm Grove

Koskinen's Geronimo
—Koskinen's Pyewacket

Kranwood's Charlie of Falcona
—Conquistador of Fortune
=Conquistador of Fortune
Jingles' Bitter Trace (twice)

Labcroft Timmy of Blackbrook
—FC Hermitage Hill Drake
Paddler of Wintergreen

Larry's Lasser*
—FC Lasser's Captain Hook
FC V and C Chip
=Tarrnof of V & C Chip

La Sage's Neb
—Neb's Midnight Rebel
=FC-AFC Marelvan Mike of
Twin Oaks

La Sage's Smokey
—FC Counter Smoke
FC Cream Sity Coed
FC-AFC Sand Gold Kim
=AFC Creole Carpetbagger
Deelite's Mr. Bones
FC-NARFC '71 Dee's Dandy
Dude
AFC Geechee
Hal's Chula Prieta
J.A.M.'s Steamin' Demon
Jac-Lor Blarney Stone
Jac-Lor Rebellion
Jac-Lor's Laja
FC-AFC Misty of Otter Creek
Neb's Midnight Rebel
AFC Penny of Evergreen
Quien Sabe's Black Ace
FC-AFC Reimrock's Duke of
Orleans
FC-AFC Sage Joker
FC Sage's Saskeram Pete
FC-AFC Shamrock Acres Drake
FC Sindbad IV
Wallace's Playboy's Topsy Tar
FC Zipper Dee Do

Lee Labs Jimi
—FC Choc of San Juan

Legs of Wake
—FC Brazil's Black Jaguar

Lignite's Old Yeller
—Goose Spooker

Li'l Nick of Brignall
—Mondor's Jet

Liseter Timber
—FC-AFC Sam Frizel of Glenspey
=FC-AFC Samson's George of
Glenspey

Lord Beaver of Cork
—Harrowby Dandy

Lord Bomar*
—AFC Bomar's Blackfoot Wog
Bomar's Chris
Country's Delight Caesar
FC-AFC Radar Rip
FC Sauk Trail Senator
=Champagne El Toro

MacGene's Fall Guy
—Pixie IV
Ripshin Rooster

MacGene's Ripco Zipper
—Lady VI

Macopin Huron
—FC Jo Do's Jet Fire

Mac's Black Beau
—Dutch's Black Lucifer

Macushla of Rockmont
—NRFC '67-AFC Butte Blue Moon
Calamity Jane of Rockmont
Greenlief's Black Imp
=FC-AFC Baird's Centerville Sam
Blackfoot Lobo
Butte King of the Road
Rille Ann's Burr

Mainliner Mike
—FC Camliag Pramero
FC-AFC Hairspring Trigger
FC Nodrog Nike
FC-AFC Nodrog Penny
=Bow-Mar Black Brandy
AFC Brandy of Cortez
Cloud Burst
King Kong II
Nodrog Pixie
FC-AFC Nodrog Punkie
Rebcha's Super Duper
Skookum Bingo
FC Skookum Dale's Nike Mark X
FC-AFC Tigathoe's Mainliner
Mariah

Mainliner Mike II
—FC-AFC Tigathoe's Mainliner Mariah

Mallard of Devil's Garden*
—Meto of Devil's Garden

Man of Night
—Mark V
FC-AFC Torque of Daingerfield

Marian's Timothy
—Spook of Marian's Tim
=Coley's Grand Clipper
FC-AFC Jupiter's Hi-Laurel
Whiskey Creek Blue Sahib

Mark Chidley Swift
—FC Jolor's Compobosso

Mark Duck's My Spud
—Mark Duck's Dago

Mark of Gloster*
—Ol' Yeller

Mark of Hidden Springs
—FC John's Minnie

Marshwise Snapshooter
—Regina Di Campi

=Cherokee Peace Pipe
Claymar's Academy Award
Gayfeathers Domino
FC Jamie's Little Tigger
FC-AFC Jet's Target of Claymar
FC-AFC Jetstone Muscles of
Claymar
John's Spike
FC Mr. Lucky of Oak Hill
FC Royl Jay
Stone Castle's Yellow Jacket
FC Van's Pride Ebony Shadow

Martens' Busy Digger
—FC-AFC Harang's Grumpy Express
=FC Sam of Dixie Rapids

Martens' Hi Style Buck
—FC Del-Tone Buck
=Belle Shain's Steamboat Man
Bigstone Black Longshot II
FC Blitz Von Mobile
Bodoro's Coaley
Buck of Woodlawn
FC Buck's Hobo
Carr-Lab Spirit
FC-AFC Cork of Evergreen
AFC Dawn of Aladon
Del-Tone Mac's Belle
FC-AFC Franklin's Tall Timber
Hi Go Niki
Jac-Lor's Laja
Lakeshore Cowie
Montina Lady
Re-Mar's Black Buck
Rille Ann's Cole Buck Blazer
Rille Ann's Mickey
Ringo From Happy Hollow
FC-AFC Rover of Ramsey Place
AFC Sir Caleb of Audlon
AFC Willow's Boe Longshot

Martens' Little Smoky
—FC-AFC Candlewood's Beau of
Beaumont
AFC Hunt's Cloud of Smoke
Hunt's Digger by Little Smoky
Hunt's Nipper of Little Smoky
Miss Nyx
AFC Nilo Brandy Cork
Remohcs Ebony Ace
Rocket of Flint
FC Smoky's Black Jet
Tealwood Tammy
=Buckskin Bullet
Cedarhaven J.B.
Mitch's Dandy Bouncer
Piegan's Cryseyde
Salt Valley Espresso
Shamrock Acres Lucky Lady
Shamrock Acres Modoc Painter
Shamrock Acres Nylic Ned
Shamrock Acres Winnie Pooh
Sills Black Bandit
Tar Dessa Comanche Mike
Tarrnof of V & C Chip
AFC Winroc's Ripper

Martens' Mister Nifty*
—FC-AFC Bigstone Flint
  Bigstone Hard's Happy
  J.A.M.'s Steamin' Demon
  FC Martens' Black Powder Kate
  Martens' Mister Lucky
  AFC Penny of Evergreen
  FC-NARFC '72 River Oaks Corky
    =FC Copy Cat Del Norte
    Corky's Ramblin Riley
    Ducky O'Cedar
    Evergreen Binx
    FC Flint's Nifty Arrow
    FC-AFC Martens' Castaway
    Ripple River
    River Oaks Black Frost
    River Oaks Cream Cadet
    FC-AFC River Oaks Rascal
    River Oaks Rowdy Bear
    AFC Togom's Tiger of Abilena
    Wingford's Big Flint Stone
    FC Your Shot Minnesota Fats

Martens' Scrubby Giant*
—Black Nig Prince
  Igo Licorice Split To
  Martens' Mr. Stubbs
    =Cimaroc Coon Willie

Mawod's Shorty
—Dairy Hill's Top Banana

Meatball of District Ten
—Bomber II

Medlin's Cork of Grapevine
—Mark of Gloster
  FC Medlin's Otto of Toothacres
  FC Medlin's Texas Ruff
  Medlin's Texas Trooper
  FC Medlin's Tiny Boom
    =Gee Baby
    Medlin's Gay Teal of Castawac
    Ol' Yeller

Medlin's Texas Jack-Tar
—AFC Bayou Beau
    =Johnny's High Yellow

Michael of Pepin View
—FC-AFC Duke of Crookston

Mi-Cris Drambuie
—River Road Bippy

Middlespunk Scamper
—Claymar's Academy Award
  Warpath Cowboy Joe
  Warpath Kitty
  FC-AFC Warpath Rip

Mike of Swinomish
—AFC Caesar of Swinomish

Mike of Lake View
—Hey You of Lake View

Mister Jones of Niskayuna
—Sad Sam Jones
    =Jones' Daddy Wags

Mister Zan Sun
—FC Dink's Ginger Guiness Stout

Mitch of Bitterroot*
—Cedarhaven J. B.
  Mitch's Dandy Bouncer

Mixed Up Morty
—Morty's Ebony Magic

Moby Dick*
—Tom's Thadius

Mycur Bimbo
—AFC Waccamaw's Tinker

My Jet of Spook
—Smokey of Jetcin
  Spook of Jetcin

My Rebel*
—FC Copy Cat Del Norte
  Gahonk's Traveller
  Gahonk's Tyendinaga Totom
  FC-AFC Martens' Castaway
  FC-AFC Muktar of Offershire
  Pam's Black Spark
    =Muffet's Tuffet
    Thunder of Rebel's Gypsy

Namahbin of Oakridge
—John Henry of Oakridge
  AFC Timcin's Black Domino

Nascopie Dark Detroyer
—FC Country Club's El-Cid
    =AFC Geechee
    John Henry of Oakridge
    AFC Timcin's Black Domino

Nascopie of Highland Park
—Hielan Havoc

Nassau*
—Cimaroc Coon Willie
  FC Nassau's Nar of Minnewaska

Nethercroft Nemo of Nascopie*
—Nemo's Dell-Gin
  FC-AFC Nemo's Spyder of
    Round Valley

Netley Creek's Sugar
—Ravenhills Lucky Lady
    =FC-AFC Air Express
    Orion's Lady Dart
    Sassy Sioux of Tukwila
    AFC Wanapum Dart's Dandy
    Wanapum Sheba

Nicholas of The Navasot
—AFC Lady's Brazos Pete

Nic-O-Bet's Treveilyr Thunder
—Alpaugh's Whistlin Jim

Night Cap Again
—Happy's Twinkle
    =FC Carnation Rainstar
    Ern-Bar's Andy of Anzac
    FC-AFC Ern-Bar's Twinkle Boots
    Telstar of Zenith
    Twinkle's Mandy
    Twink's Tinker Bell

Nilo Captain's Courageous
—Glen's Lady's Casper

Nilo Smoky's Ace of Spades
—FC-AFC Shawnee Ace of Spades

Nilo Smoky's Black Powder
 —Buckskin Bullet

Nodak Ar-Dee
 —FC V-Jay's Black Paddle
  =AFC Caesar of Swinomish

Nodak Boots
 —FC Double Play of Audlon
  Ebony Major Sassy Miss
  Frankie of Rivernook
  FC-AFC Rosehill's Little Dutch Boots
   =Allo Dere Louise
    Bumble Buzz of Bee Sting
    Carnmoney Spud
    Dove of Little Dutch Boots
    Geechee's Buck
    Lad Crowder's Ranger
    Lakeshore Cowie
    Lulake's Rickie
    Muse's Bonnie Girl
    FC Nassau

Nodak Never Again
 —Sand Gold Venus

Nodak's Surprise
 —Chain's Princess Pet

Nodrog Nike*
 —King Kong II
  Skookum Bingo
  FC Skookum Dale's Nike Mark X

Nyrobie Playboy
 —Miss Fortune

Oakview's Mill Pond Duster
 —FC I Love Lucy of Audlon

Odessa's King
 —FC Cedar Haven Matador
  FC-AFC Dessa Rae
  Panther of the Coeur D'Alene's
   =FC-AFC Dessa's Black Angel
    FC Dessa's Little Tar Baby
    Dessa Sweet
    Panther Baby
    FC Swing Tarzan Swing
    FC Tar Dessa Venture
    Tyker Baby

One-Dollar Bill
 —FC-AFC Black Rocky

Othello of Parsonage Point
 —Zoe of Sandy Port

Otter O'Vyrnwy
 —AFC Cherokee Chief V
  Pin Oaks Little Otter
   =Cherokee Peace Pipe
    Gayfeathers Domino
    FC-AFC Hundred Proof Tad

Paha Sapa Chief II
 —Ace-Hi Indian Magic
  FC Attawan Pucka Sahib
  FC-AFC Carr-Lab Penrod
  FC Chief Black Feather
  AFC Jilly Girl

John's Spike
Lakenham Paha Sun Dance
Mystery Icabod
FC Paha Sapa Jack
Paha Sapa Jay
Paha Sapa Medicine Man
FC-AFC Paha Sapa Warpaint
FC-AFC Paha Sapa Warpath
FC-AFC Paha's Pow Wow
NARFC '65-FC Rebel Chief of Heber
FC-AFC Serrana Sootana of Genesee
Spring Farms Lucky
NRFC '68-NARFC '67 & '68
 Super Chief
Trappers Paha Cork

  =FC-AFC Air Express
   FC-AFC Balsom's Snooper
    Honker
   AFC Bayou Beau
   Beavercrest Goin' Gus
   AFC Bellota Cacahuete
   FC-AFC Black Rocky
   Bruce's Happy Warrior
   Carr-Lab Spirit
   Cascade's Rodney St. Clair
   Centennial Cric
   AFC Cha Cha Dancer
   Cherokee Chief V
   Chief Cody of Le-Mar
   Chief Consultation South Bay
   Chief Storm Cloud
   AFC Chipsal John Henry
   FC Cody of Wanapum
   AFC Copper Cities Colliery Cal
   FC-AFC Dairy Hill's
    Michikiniquia
   Dairy Hill's Wampum
   Desert Gypsy II
   Dixieland Coot's Tiger Baby
   Fieldmarshall Heinz Guderian
   High Brass Sassy
   High Low Jick
   Hi-Line King Pepper
   Imperial Crest Maggie
   FC-AFC Keg of Black Powder
   Little Billy Jo
   FC-AFC Magic Marker of
    Timber Town
   Orion's Lady Dart
   AFC Paha Sapa Hardcase
   FC-AFC Paha Sapa Warpath II
   Paha's Pow on Tap
   FC Patsy's Thunderchief
   Piegan's Cryseyde
   Pin Oaks Little Otter
   Pocatello Chief
   AFC Renegade Pepe
   Rockbend's Kamakura
   FC Round Valley's Lucky Tigger
   Royal Oaks Havoc's Haze
   AFC Royal Oaks Jill of Burgundy
   FC-AFC Samson's George of
    Glenspey
   Sassy Sioux of Tukwila
   Seymour's Black Diamond
   Seymour's Hot Line Pepper
   Shamrock Acres Lucky Lady

246

Shamrock Acres Modoc
  Painter
Shamrock Acres Nylic Ned
Shamrock Acres Super Drive
Shamrock Acres Superstition
FC Shamrock Acres Super Value
Shamrock Acres Winnie Pooh
Shantoo Tar Buck
Shar-Loy's Miss Midnight
AFC Sir Caleb of Audlon
Spring Farm's Smokey
AFC Wanapum Dart's Dandy
Wanapum Lucky Yo Yo
Wanapum Sheba
Warpath Cowboy Joe
Warpath Kitty
FC-AFC Warpath Rip
Washington's Tizzy Lizzy

Paha-Sapa Hardcase*
—Paha Sapa Pride of Casey

Paha Sapa Jet Stream
—Warpath Cowboy Joe
  FC-AFC Warpath Rip

Paha Sapa War Cloud
—Paha Sapa Medicine Man

Paha Sapa Warpath*
—FC-AFC Paha Sapa Warpath II
Paha's Pow Wow*
—Paha's Pow on Tap

Parky*
—Nefertiti

Patch of Bonniehurst
—FC-AFC Sir Knight Falcon
  =Bow-Mar Black Brandy
  Giljo's Nikki of Bow-Mar
  Nodrog Pixie
  FC-AFC Nodrog Punkie

Pebble's Rowdy Rebel
—Dyna-Mite-Win

Pecan Island Clipper
—Taffy of Janie Lane

Pee Cee Dee's Rowdy of Bardonda
—FC-AFC Molybru Butch of Barmond

Pepper's Jiggs
—FC-AFC Ivy Pat
  AFC King Tut V
  Masai of Aberdeen
  AFC Parky
  Pepper's Omega
  FC-AFC Velvet's Jezebel
  =FC Ace of Southwood
  AFC Brandy of Cortez
  AFC Chuk Chukar Chuk
  FC Cody of Wanapum
  Knight Train
  FC Larry's Lasser
  FC-AFC Muktar of Offershire
  Nefertiti
  Netley Creek's Black Brute
  Polaris Peter
  Ravenhill's Lucky Lady
  Rowdy's Sean of the Corkies

Wanapum Lucky Yo Yo
Wild Joker of Napi

Peppi of Lakewood
—Lakeland Tiger of Bruce

Peter-Dee of Hawkhome
—Broadmoor Rex

Playboy's Black Cloud
—Sam of Arrowhead Lake

Pokey of Sourdough
—FC-AFC Sandy of Sourdough
  =Champagne El Toro

Pomme De Terre Pete
—Lakeside Dean's Shadow
  =FC Nilo Brian Boru
  Nilo Gypsy
  FC Nilo Staindrop Charger
  Time of Frontier

Portneuf Valley Duke*
—Inashotte Dee Chuggy

Prince of Rapids Hollow
—FC Black Duke of Sherwood

Prince William of Erie
—FC-AFC Fisherman Bill of Delaware
  =Scioto Black Libby
  Seymour's Black Diamond

Problem Boy Duke of Wake
—FC-AFC Black Michael O'Shea
  Problem Boy's Dinny

Quien Sabe
—Quien Sabe's Black Ace

Raglando Rodarball
—Blackfoot Lobo

Ralston of Shamrock Acres
—Tycoon of Ralston Valley
  =Brock's Lively Lark

Ralston's Valley Floyd
—Amber's Dandy Beau

Ravenhill's Bass
—Netley Creek's Black Brute

Raven Mike of Stonegate
—Great Smoke Cloud
  Skookum Redwing
  Yaz Razzamatazz

Raven of Tredinnock
—Raven's Gingerbread Girl

Rebel Chief of Heber*
—AFC Paha Sapa Hardcase
  =Paha Sapa Pride of Casey

Rhett of Coldwater II
—FC-AFC Coldwater's Brendan
  =Brant of Blenheim

Rice's Busy Gamekeeper
—Onyx Greatford Pride
  =Silver Squire

Ricky's Buck
—FC Blitz Von Mobile

247

Ridgewood All Is Jake
—Beau Gentry

Ridgewood Playboy
—AFC Creole Carpetbagger
FC-NARFC '71 Dee's Dandy Dude
AFC Geechee
Hal's Chula Prieta
Jac-Lor Blarney Stone
Jac-Lor Rebellion
FC-AFC Misty of Otter Creek
FC-AFC Reimroc's Duke of Orleans
FC-AFC Shamrock Acres Drake
FC Sindbad IV
Wallace's Playboy's Topsy Tar
FC Zipper Dee Do
=Beau Gentry
Easy Does It of Valhalla
Geechee's Buck
Geechee's Daniel Dexter
Lulake's Ricky
Moon Rocket of Zenith
Robinhood's Geechee Junior
Sam of Arrowhead Lake
FC-AFC Tigathoe's Mainliner
Mariah
Valhalla Bonefish Sam

Riefler's Dutch
—Gee Baby
=Mike's Lizzie Odom

Rimrock Ringo
—Rimrock Roscoe

Ripco's Peter Pan
—AFC Acute Accent
FC-AFC Mackenzie's Ripco Mac
FC-AFC Mackenzie's Ripco Tar
Ripco's Repeater
NRFC '64- AFC Ripco's V. C. Morgan
=Angelique
Beaver State Hope
Breckonhill Erin's Kelli
FC-AFC Breckonhill's Sean
O'Moore
Centennial Chukaluk
AFC Dent's Midnight Rick
Goose Spooker
Lady VI
FC Larry's Lasser
Luke of Patty Jimsue
AFC Paha Sapa Hardcase
Pixie IV
Ripshin Rooster
Tyker's Fleck of Cork

Ripco's Western Blend
—FC Larry's Lasser
=FC Lasser's Captain Hook
FC V and C Chip

Rip's Smokey Duke
—Conty's Black Chip

Rip Van Winkle III
—Bar Me None
FC Dave's Demetrius

Riskin*
—Canuck-Crest Gallant
Pipers Highland Drummer

River Oaks Corky*
—Corky's Ramblin Riley
Ripple River
River Oaks Black Frost
River Oaks Cream Cadet
FC-AFC River Oaks Rascal
River Oaks Rowdy Bear
AFC Togom's Tiger of Abilena

Robbet's Black Hope
—FC-AFC Billy Pawlesta
AFC Gwen's Ringtail Velvet
AFC Gwen's Trouble
FC-AFC Petite Rouge
=FC-AFC Bob's Black Rebel
Lady's Brazos Pete
Little Billy Jo

Robbets Coaldust
—Medlin's Gay Teal of Castawac
=Gee Baby

Robinson's Blackbird
—Scioto Black Libby

Rocky Road of Zenith*
—Moon Rocket of Zenith

Rocket of Flint
—FC-AFC Orion's Sirius

Rod Iron of Chalet
—AFC Black Chief of Nakomis

Roman's Tar Boy
—Cinder of Cole

Rowdy Dow of Minyok
—Spirit's Black Pepper
=FC-AFC Harang's Grumpy
Express

Royal of Garfield
—Dajo's Black Velvet
J's Big Water Buck
FC Martens' Mister Nifty
FC Martens' Stormy
=FC-AFC Bigstone Flint
Bigstone Black Longshot II
Bigstone Hard's Happy
FC-AFC Cimaroc Tang
Geechee's Daniel Dexter
Igo Licorice Split To
J.A.M.'s Steamin' Demon
FC Martens' Black Powder Kate
Martens' Mister Lucky
Mar-Ten's Moneymaker
FC-AFC Orion's Sirius
AFC Penny of Evergreen
FC-NARFC'72 River Oaks Corky
NRFC '72-AFC Royal's
Moose's Moe
Sam of Arrowhead Lake
Wayside Black Buster

Royal's Moose
—NRFC '72-AFC Royal's Moose's Moe

Royal's Moose's Moe*
—Moose's Louise

Roy's Rowdy
—Rowdy's Sean of the Corkies
=AFC Andy Black of Chestnut Hill
FC-AFC Camliag Pramero
FC Cascade Charade
Dajo's Black Velvet
Del-Tone Rex
FC-AFC Flood Bay Boomerang
FC-AFC Floodbay's Baron O'Glengarven
FC-AFC Hairspring Trigger
J's Big Water Buck
FC Martens' Mister Nifty
FC Martens' Stormy
FC Nodrog Nike
FC-AFC Nodrog Penny
AFC Shamrock Acres Gun Away
FC Troublemaker of Audlon II

Rupert White Bear
—Coll-A-Dene's Perky

Sad Sam Jones*
—Jones' Daddy Wags

Sage Joker*
—Rockbend's Magic Marker

Sage Rider
—Sage Rambler

Sage of Sanfray
—Deelite's Mr. Bones
FC-AFC Sage Joker
FC Sage's Saskeram Pete
=Rockbend's Magic Marker

Salt Valley Ottie
—FC-AFC Dobe's Desdemona
Salt Valley Epaminondas
=Bar Me None
FC Dave's Demetrius

Salty of Sugar Valley
—Invail's Medicine Man
=Mi-Cris Drambuie
Mi-Cris of Hayden
NRFC '71 Mi-Cris Sailor
FC Peg of Turkey Run
FC Willowmount El Diablo

Sam Frizel of Glenspey*
—FC-AFC Samson's George of Glenspey
=Evergreen Binx
Salt Valley Espresso

Sam of Hunter Mountain
—Sam's Thunder Cloud

Sam Sloan Creek
—FC-AFC Ottley's Jazzbo

Samson's George of Glenspey*
—Evergreen Binx
Salt Valley Espresso

Satan of Yellowstone
—Mountain View's Buff

Shamrock Acres Gun Away*
—Black Irish Kelly

FC Carbo Computer
Invail's Gunner
Just Samson

Shamrock Acres Jim Dandy
—Brock's Lively Lark
AFC Ralston Valley Dandy Jake
=Amber's Dandy Beau
J. J.'s Lady Ebony
Tycoon of Ralston Valley

Shamrock Acres Super Drive
—Aquarian Lady O' The Autumn Moon

Shane of Shannon Hills
—Silver Squire

Shoremeadow Barnacle Bill
—Shoremeadow Challenge

Singing Woods War Cloud
—FC-AFC Balsom's Snooper Honker
Chief Storm Cloud
Desert Gypsy II

Sir Buck of Belle Isle
—Land O' Lakes Sunburst

Sir Knight Falcon*
—Bow-Mar Black Brandy
Giljo's Nikki of Bow-Mar
Nodrog Pixie
FC-AFC Nodrog Punkie

Skeeter of Upland Farm
—Brother Lem of Upland Farm
Cousin Jack of Upland Farm
=Sport of Upland Farm

Skipper of the Rapids
—FC Sam of Dixie Rapids

Skyline Black Panther
—Boise's Black Bart

Slo Poke Smokey of Dairy Hill
—FC-AFC Dairy Hill's Mike
=Dairy Hill's Night Watch
Dairy Hill's Planters Punch
Dairy Hill's Toddy Tot
Grand Admiral Raeder
FC-AFC Joy's Coal Dust

Smoky Le Blanc
—FC-AFC Bob's Black Rebel

Snake River George
—AFC Black "R" of Birch

Spirit Lake Smokey
—Jackson's Ripsnorter

Spirit of Bear River
—AFC Portneuf Valley Duke
=Inashotte Dee Chuggy

Spook of Manhattan
—FC-NARFC '66 Captain of Lomac
=Yogi II

Spring Farms Lucky*
—FC Cody of Wanapum
Pocatello Chief
FC Round Valley's Lucky Tigger
Spring Farms Smokey
Wanapum Lucky Yo Yo

Sprucelane's Chippewa Chief
—Abenaki's Sagamore
  AFC Chipsal John Henry
  Imperial Crest Maggie

Squire of Reo Raj*
—Yankee Black Power

Staindrop Talent
—Nilo Gypsy
  FC Nilo Staindrop Charger
  FC Nilo Brian Boru

Stan's Licorice Ladd
—Martin's Scokim

Star of South Shaughnessy
—Brant of Blenheim

Stillwater's Royal Rick
—AFC Dent's Midnight Rick
  FC Moby Dick
  FC Sassy Sioux of Willow Creek
    =Tom's Thadius

St. Louie's Trouble of Audlon
—FC-AFC Candlewood's Little Lou
  Blackberry Brandy V

Stonegate's Brazen Beau
—FC-AFC Stonegate's Arrow
    =Great Smoke Cloud
    Netley Creek's Chicadee
    Skookum Redwing
    Yaz Razzmatazz

Stone Castle Jack
—Claymar's Academy Award
  FC-AFC Jetstone Muscles of Claymar
  FC-AFC Jet's Target of Claymar
  Stone Castle Yellow Jacket
  FC Van's Pride Ebony Shadow
    =Claymar's Crash Diver
    Kennon's Jockeaux
    Lincoln of Bel Air
    Muscles Jet Jock
    Remohcs Ebony Ace

Stonegate's Knight of Roslyn
—FC Win-Toba's Black High Point

Stormalong A' Go Go
—Connor's Hunter

Stormy of Spirit Lake Gal
—Boatswain's Stormy Spirit
  Nascopie Cinder of Lucifer
  FC-AFC Sauk Trail Deepwell "Doc"

Straw Hollow's Ceb
—Straw Hollow's Rowdy Crusader

Sun Beau of Franklin
—FC Sherwood's Maid Marion

Super Chief*
—FC-AFC Air Express
  Chief Cody of Le-Mar
  Chief Consultation South Bay
  FC-AFC Dairy Hill's Michikiniquia
  Dairy Hill's Wampum
  Orion's Lady Dart
  FC Patsy's Thunderchief

Piegan's Cryseyde
Royal Oaks Havoc's Haze
AFC Royal Oaks Jill of Burgundy
Sassy Sioux of Tukwila
Seymour's Hot Line Pepper
Shamrock Acres Lucky Lady
Shamrock Acres Modoc Painter
Shamrock Acres Nylic Ned
Shamrock Acres Super Drive
Shamrock Acres Superstition
FC Shamrock Acres Super Value
Shamrock Acres Winnie Pooh
AFC Wanapum Dart's Dandy
Wanapum Sheba
    =Aquarian Lady O' The August
      Moon
    Bitterroot's Taurus
    Happy Hollow's El Champo

Syldonnel's Douk
—Seafield Chief

Tabak
—FC-AFC Pirate's Gold

Tanker of Los Altos Hills
—St. Hubert of Tewkesbury Knob

Tar Baby's Little Sweet Stuff
—FC-AFC Dessa's Black Angel
  FC Dessa's Little Tar Baby
  Dessa Sweet
  FC Gun Thunder Oly
  High Low Jick
  Panther Baby
  FC Swing Tarzan Swing
  Syldonnel's Captain Jack
  FC Tar Dessa Venture
  Tyker Baby
    =Angelique
    Beaver State Hope
    AFC Pat's Penny Jo
    FC Sweet William II
    Tar Dessa's Comanche Mike
    FC Toni's Blaine Child
    Tyker's Fleck of Cork
    Tyker's Lucky Penny
    Wandarin Heights Venture

Taliaferro's Tracer*
—Shannon's Terror

Tarblood Buffalo Chief
—FC-AFC Tarblood of Absaraka
    =AFC Beavercrest Sassy Sioux
    Dukw-Trax Mandegho
    Paha Sapa Jay
    FC-AFC Serrana Sootana of
      Genesee
    AFC Timberlake Flying Muffin

Tarblood of Absaraka*
—AFC Beavercrest Sassy Sioux
  Dukw-Trax Mandegho
  AFC Timberlake Flying Muffin
    =Archie the Cockroach
    Martin's Scokim

Tar Dessa Venture*
—Tar Dessa Comanche Mike
  Wandarin Heights Venture

Tar of Pintail
—J. J.'s Lady Ebony

Tar of Rock Montana
—Butte King of the Road

Techako's Ranger
—Leroy III

Teddy Bear
—FC-AFC Duke of Teddy Bear

Timber Shed Totem of Nascopie II
—FC Nethercroft Nemo of Nascopie
=Nascopie Cinder of Lucifer
Nemo's Dell-Gin
FC-AFC Nemo's Spyder of
Round Valley

Tim Dugan of Ogden
—AFC Targhee Sam

Tony's Black Cork
—FC-AFC Alamo Black Jack

Tornado of Vulcan Crest
—Lady of Wake
=AFC Lucky's Lady in Red

Tugney of Oakview
—FC-AFC Sir Mike of Orchardview
=FC I Love Lucy of Audlon

Tuxedo of Green Point
—Sam of Marlboro Country

Tyker Baby*
—Angelique
Beaver State Hope
FC Sweet William II
Tyker's Fleck of Cork
Tyker's Lucky Penny
=Ripple River

V & C Chip
—Tarrnof of V & C Chip

Valentine's Cork
—Allo Dere Louise
Dove of Little Dutch Boots

Van Wagner's Kernel
—AFC Irwin's Toby

Wacap's Geritol
—Wacap's Windy

Warpath Tuff*
—Connor's Hunter
Warpath Just in Case

Wasatch Renegade
—FC-AFC Keg of Black Powder
AFC Renegade Pepe

Washek's Diamond Duke
—Eggers Royal Blue

Washington's Tater Tate
—Belle Ringer

Whincovert Tango
—Cha-Cha-Cha of District Ten

Whygin Cork's Coot*
—Dixieland Coot's Tiger Baby

Whygin The Tarboy
—Whygin Wellmet Angus

Wingfords Water Witcher
—McKemie's Pola

Winter's Shadow
—Kootenai Buck

Yankee Clipper of Reo-Raj
—FC My Rebel
AFC Squire of Reo-Raj
=FC Anzac of Zenith
Belle Ringer
Bodoro's Coaley
Brother Lem of Upland Farm
FC Copy Cat Del Norte
Cousin Jack of Upland Farm
AFC Dawn of Aladon
NARFC '64 Dutchmoor's Black
Mood
Gahonk's Traveller
Gahonk's Tyendinaga Totom
FC-AFC Glengarven's Mik
Hi Go Niki
AFC Huck's Pride of Riverside
FC-AFC Martens' Castaway
Mar-Ten's Moneymaker
Mi-Cris Drambuie
Mi-Cris of Hayden
FC-AFC Muktar of Offershire
Old Vav
Pam's Black Splash
Re-Mar's Black Buck
FC-AFC Rocky Road of Zenith
FC-AFC Rover of Ramsey Place
FC Sheba's Westmoor Contessa
Yankee Black Power

Yankee Joe
—AFC Huck's Pride of Riverside

Zip of Geneva Lake*
—AFC White River Duke

LABRADOR DAMS

Ace-Hi Tammi
—Ace-Hi Indian Magic

Ace's Sheba of Ardyn
—FC Sheba's Westmoor Cleopatra
FC Sheba's Westmoor Contessa

Acute Accent*
—Angelique
Beaver State Hope

Aldice of Avandale
—El Negro Sam

Amber of White Grass
—Amber's Dandy Beau

Ardyn's Mercy Bound
—Ardyn's Black Bart

Ariadne of Greersliegh
—Onyx Greatford Pride

Arkansas Lady
—Choppy Babe

Arroyo Seco Cindy
—Arroyo Seco Rocket
Crook's Jolly Roger

Avalanche Mitzie
—McClintock's Ebony Belle

Ballybrook Lil
—Wingover Cherokee Chief

Bart's Jeri of Stonesthrow
—FC Cinder Feller of Stonesthrow

Bar-Jon Bell
—Harrowby Dandy

Bay City Katie Jane
—FC-AFC Cougar's Rocket
Meto of Devil's Garden
=Gunner of Gunthunder
FC-AFC Luka of Casey's Rocket
Rip Von Black Winkle

Bay City Zany Jane
=AFC Copper Cities Colliery Cal

Beaumark's Lady Tamee
—FC-AFC Bob's Black Rebel

Beautywood's Lady Fair
—Shoremeadow Challenge
Spook of Marian's Tim
=FC-AFC Jupiter's Hi-Laurel
Whiskey Creek Blue Sahib

Beautywood's Rebel Queen
—AFC Camliag Pramero
FC-AFC Hairspring Trigger
FC Nodrog Nike
FC-AFC Nodrog Penny
=Bow-Mar Black Beauty
AFC Brandy of Cortez
Cloud Burst
King Kong II
Nodrog Pixie
FC-AFC Nodrog Punkie
Rebcha's Super Duper
Skookum Bingo
FC Skookum Dale's Nike Mark X

Beautywood's Sugar Pill
—FC Beautywood's Tingler

Beavercrest Starlet
—AFC Beavercrest Sassy Sioux

Beavercrest Warpath
—Rimrock Roscoe

Belle High
—Beavercrest Goin' Gus
Inashotte Dee Chuggy

Belle of Curles Neck
—Raven's Gingerbread Girl

Belle of Sunset
—Black Sorcerer of Sunset
=AFC Chuk Chukar Chuk

Belle of Upland Farm
—Brother Lem of Upland Farm
Cousin Jack of Upland Farm

Bianca
—FC Hank's Spook

Big Mountain Yip
—FC-AFC Copper City Buck
=Buckskin Torquin

Big Oaks Dianne Gold of Ibaden
—FC-AFC Pirate's Gold

Bigstone Belle
—Bigstone Black Longshot II

Bigstone Black Liberty
—FC Your Shot Minnesota Fats

Bigstone Jumper
—FC Howie's Happy Hunter
FC Knight's Noel

Bigstone Lady B
—Ebony Mood's Bingo
=Belle Shain's Steamboat Man
FC-AFC Randy Mayhall of Tina
Tina's Black Chip

Bigstone Molly Dee
—Geechee's Daniel Dexter

Birdie's Misty
—Gaylab Gabriel
Gaylab's Shamus
FC-AFC Pelican Lake Peggy
Rocky's Dartega
=Great Smoke Cloud
Jo-Anne's Black Blade
Martens' Mister Stubbs
Skookum Bingo
FC Skookum Dale's Nike Mark X
Skookum Redwing

Bit O' Ginger
—FC Harrowby Wheeler Dealer
Nemo's Dell-Gin

Black Beauty of Random Lake
—FC-AFC Misty of Otter Creek

Black Belle of Mylla
—Bayou Pirate
=FC Buck's Hobo

Black Brant's Marilyn M.
—Zoe of Sandy Port

Black Brook's Bartered Bride
—FC-AFC Tigathoe's Mainliner Mariah

Black Bunny of Lakewood
—Moon Rocket of Zenith

Black Diamond Liz
—AFC Cha Cha Dancer
=Belle Ringer
AFC Bomar's Blackfoot Wog
Country's Delight Caesar
Pixie IV
Ripshin Rooster

Black Dixie Princess
—Sam's Thunder Cloud

Black Duchess of Palm Dessert
—Mondor's Jet

252

Black Lou of Strahenweis
—AFC Black "R" of Birch

Black Queen IX
—FC-AFC Mackenzie's Ripco Mac

Black Witch of Sunset
—AFC Chuk Chukar Chuk

Blitz of Round Valley
—FC-AFC Nemo's Spyder of
Round Valley
FC Round Valley's Lucky Tigger

Blue Lady
—AFC Huck's Pride of Riverside

Blue River Genie III
—Warpath Kitty

Bob's Miss Zipper
—Dukw-Trax Mandegho

Bonnie Jay of Krisday
—FC-AFC Balsom's Mandy
Kip's Front Page Banner

Bonnie Star of Netley
—FC-AFC Brandy Spirit of Netley
=AFC Simmer's Shot of Brandy

Bonython Copper
—Buck of Whittington

Breezeway's Tiny Lady
—FC-AFC Duke of Crookston

Buckeye Black Princess
—Scioto Black Libby

Buck's Dolly
—Claymar's Crash Diver

Camelot
—Knots

Canuck-Crest Packwood Peggy
—Pipers Highland Drummer

Canuck-Crest Sally*
—Abenaki's Sagamore
AFC Chipsal John Henry
Imperial Crest Maggie

Canuck-Crest Tami O'Churchlee
—FC Canuck-Crest Cutty Sark
Canuck-Crest Gallant
Canuck-Crest Sally
FC-AFC Magic Marker of
Timber Town
=Abenaki's Sagamore
AFC Chipsal John Henry
Imperial Crest Maggie
Pipers Highland Drummer

Canvasback Dee
—Gahonk's Traveller
Gahonk's Tyendinaga Totom

Carefree Lass
—FC-AFC Sazerac Mac

Carnation Raven
—FC Carnation Butterboy

Carnmoney Boots
—Carnmoney Spud
=Ahab's Emancipator
FC-AFC Ray's Rascal

Carnmoney Moira
—FC Duxbak Scooter
=Deadly Dudley's Duxbak Coot
Dixieland Joe
Duxbak Black Oak
Fieldmarshall Heinz Guderian
Happy Playboy's Pearl
FC Harrowby Wheeler Dealer
Kracken of Timber Town
FC Minot's Magic Marker
Time of Frontier

Carnmoney Penny Dhu
—Carnmoney Magnum

Carr-Lab Babe
—Dairy Hill's Toddy Tot
=Dairy Hill's Mad Hatter
FC-AFC Dairy Hill's
Michikiniquia
Dairy Hill's Wampum

Carr-Lab Jill
—FC-AFC Dairy Hill's Night Watch

Carr-Lab Spirit
—Hi-M's Jake the Giant Killer

Castlemore Sheila of Cordova
—FC-AFC Carnmoney Brigadier
=Wildhearted Dinah

Cathy-Chris Black Bess
—FC-AFC White's Mar-Ke-Tam Nerro

Cathy-Chris' Yellow Sue
—FC-AFC Doctor Pepper of Le-Mar
Mel's Yuletide Honey
Snoopy of Dickenson

Cedar Creek
—Quien Sabe's Black Ace

Cedar Ridge Jodi
—Pocatello Chief

Champagne Cassie
—Champagne El Toro

Chats Mandy
—FC Salt Valley Epaminondas

Chere Te Negresse
—River Road Bippy

Cheyenne's Lady
—Gentleman Jiggs

Chipaking Chick
—Cirrus Sea Serpent

Chiro's Lady Bee
—AFC Taliaferro's Tracer

Cimaroc Blond Bomber
—Cimaroc Coon Willie

Cimaroc Lady
—FC-AFC Cimaroc Tang

Cimaroc Lady Jean
—Bumble Buzz of Bee Sting

253

Lad Crowder's Ranger
Muse's Bonnie Girl
FC Nassau
=FC Nassau's Nar of Minnewaska
Cimaroc Coon Willie

Cinder Gal of Seneca
—FC-AFC Radar Rip

Cinder Toni of Sunnymede
—Targhee Sam

Cindy Lou Daglo
—Dyna-Mite-Win

Cindy of Bardonda
—Seafield Chief

Coll-A-Dene's Rockette Dee
—Coll-A-Dene's Perky

Cork's Tar Baby
—Alpaugh's Whistlin Jim

Cormat's Pam
—FC-AFC Stonegate's Arrow
=Netley Creek's Chicadee
FC Win-Toba's Black High Point

Corona's Miss Consistency
—Tar Dessa's Comanche Mike

Could Be's Miss Erable
—Seymour's Hot Line Pepper
Shamrock Acres Nylic Ned
Shamrock Acres Super Drive
Shamrock Acres Superstition
=Aquarian Lady O' The Autumn
Moon

Countess of Sheridain
—AFC Polaris Luke

Country Club's Little Bullet
—Syldonnel's Captain Jack
=FC-AFC Molybru Butch of
Barmond
Seafield Chief

Country Club's Little Deb
—FC-NARFC '66 Captain of Lomac
=Yogi II

Cowman's Ramah of Mishi Kamar
—Brant of Blenheim

Cowman's Stylish Girl
—FC Country Club's El-Cid

Cream City Clipper
—FC Cream City Coed
=NRFC '70-AFC Creole Sister
Deelite's Mr. Bones
Miss Jan's Dobie
Neb's Midnight Rebel
Quien Sabe's Black Ace
FC-AFC Sage Joker
FC Sage's Saskeram Pete

Cricket Diana
—River Road Reho

Cricket of Ralston Valley
—Warpath Just in Case

Cristy
—Bomar's Chris
=Champagne El Toro

Crystodigin Martin
—FC-AFC Orion's Sirius

Cuzz's Corky
—FC-AFC Petite Rouge
=FC-AFC Bob's Black Rebel
Lady's Brazos Pete

Dairy Hill's Flame's Fury
—FC-AFC Dairy Hill's Mike
=Dairy Hill's Night Watch
Dairy Hill's Planters Punch
Dairy Hill's Toddy Tot
FC-AFC Joy's Coal Dust

Dairy Hill's Toddy Tot
—Dairy Hill's Mad Hatter
FC-AFC Dairy Hill's Michikiniquia
Dairy Hill's Wampum

Danny's Joy of Tealbrook
—AFC The Ballad of Tealbrook
The Bamboo Bandit

Dart of Netley Creek
—FC-AFC Air Express
Orion's Lady Dart
Sassy Sioux of Tukwila
AFC Wanapum Dart's Dandy
Wanapum Sheba
=Netley Creek's Black Brute
Ravenhill's Lucky Lady

Dee Dee Baby
—Mike's Lizzie Odom
=Pam's Black Splash

Delia Dancer
—Ringo From Happy Hollow

Delta's Queen Bee
—Belle Shain's Steamboat Man

Del-Tone Colvinette
—Netley Creek's Chickadee

Denna
—Gueydan of Beaumark

Dessa Baby
—FC Toni's Blaine Child

Dessa Rae*
—FC-AFC Dessa's Black Angel
FC Dessa's Little Tar Baby
Dessa Sweet
Panther Baby
FC Swing Tarzan Swing
FC Tar Dessa Venture
Tyker Baby
=Angelique
Beaver State Hope
AFC Pat's Penny Jo
FC Sweet William II
FC Toni's Blaine Child
Tyker's Fleck of Cork
Tyker's Lucky Penny
Wandarin Heights Venture

Dick's Black Scamp
—FC-AFC Bigstone Flint
  FC Martens' Black Powder Kate
    =Ducky O'Cedar
    FC Flint's Nifty Arrow
    Wingford's Big Flint Stone
    FC Your Shot Minnesota Fats

Dinah of the Reward
—Kracken of Timber Town

Dixie Bell
—Mark V
  FC-AFC Torque of Daingerfield

Dixie Bingo
—AFC Chap

Dolly of Audlon
—Paha's Pow on Tap

Don's Ginny Soo
—Bigstone Hard's Happy
  FC-NARFC '72 River Oaks Corky
  Willow's Boe Long Shot
    =Corky's Ramblin Riley
    Ripple River
    River Oaks Black Frost
    River Oaks Cream Cadette
    FC-AFC River Oaks Rascal
    River Oaks Rowdy Bear
    AFC Togom's Tiger of Abilena

Don's Princess Peg
—Johnny's High Yellow

Dory II
—AFC Andy Black of Chestnut Hill

Duchess of Jolor
—Frosty Fortune of Flosum

Duchess of Miller's Haven
—FC My Rebel
  AFC Squire of Reo Raj
    =FC Copy Cat Del Norte
    Gahonk's Traveller
    Gahonk's Tyendinaga Totom
    FC-AFC Martens' Castaway
    FC-AFC Muktar of Offershire
    Pam's Black Splash
    Yankee Black Power

Duchess of Rankin
—Shar-Loy's Miss Midnight

Duchess of Rock
—Mar-Ten's Moneymaker

Duckmaster Teal
—AFC Jingo Jo's Duckmaster

Duckwind Dark Dawn
—Grand Admiral Raeder

Duckworth's Black Mandy
—Morty's Ebony Magic

Duke's Sheba
—Moose's Louise

Dulcie
—FC-AFC Duke of Teddy Bear

Duxbak Betty
—Happy Playboy's Pearl

Duxbak Cindy
—Dixieland Joe

Duxbak's Patsy Del Norte
—Chief Cody of Le-Mar
  FC Patsy's Thunderchief

Duxbak Queen
—Duxbak Black Oak

Duxbak Vronce
—FC Sweet William II

Dykes Potlach
—Centennial Chukaluk

Eason's Nikie
—FC Dink's Ginger Guiness Stout

Ebbanee's War Dancer
—FC-AFC Ebbanee's Ricochet
  =FC Invail's Cavalier Carom
  FC Sheba's Westmoor Cleopatra

Eby of Beaver Creek
—FC Lakenham Paha Sun Dance
  =Cascade's Rodney St. Clair
  Centennial Cric

Eee Gee's Nell
—Black Nig Prince

Erin O'Moore
—Breckonhill Erin's Kelli
  FC-AFC Breckonhill's Sean O'Moore
    =Ardyn's Black Bart
    Breckonhill Erin's Kelli

Evangeline Tar Baby
—Paha Sapa Pride of Casey

Evelyn's Diana
—Egger's Royal Blue

Faindi Kalp Asswad
—FC-AFC Sir Knight Falcon
  =Giljo's Nikki of Bow-Mar
  Nodrog Pixie
  FC-AFC Nodrog Punkie

Faro's Molly
—Faro's Mathew

Faro's Princess Christine
—Chuck of Craigend Rock

Fishers Babe
—Hey You of Lake View

Flash of Glenspey
—FC-AFC Sam Frizel of Glenspey
  =FC-AFC Samson's George of
    Glenspey

Flicker of Timber Town
—Sad Sam Jones
  =Jones' Daddy Wags

Franklin's Gold Charm
—FC-AFC Franklin's Tall Timber

Friday at Waxahachie Creek
—Ol' Yeller

Frisky Lou
—Dilly Be Wise

Gal
—FC-AFC Hoss of Palm Grove

Gale of Cedar Creek
—Quien Sabe's Black Ace

Gambler's Lady
—FC-AFC Fisherman Bill of Delaware
=Seymour's Black Diamond

Gambler's Rosie
—Seymour's Black Diamond

Garnet of Coeur D'Alene
—Kootenai Buck

Gee Gee
—Sandy of Sourdough
=Champagne El Toro

Gerwin's Petite Viking
—AFC Oscar's Petite Lightning

Gina
—AFC Black Jake of Devon
=AFC Hawk Hill's Sam of Devon

Glengarven's Black Bess
—FC-AFC Rill Shannon's Dark Del
=Del-Tone Mac's Belle
FC Mr. Mac's Billy Boy

Glengarven's Black Shadow
—FC-AFC Floodbay's Baron O'Glen-
garven
FC-AFC Flood Bay Boomerang
=Shar-Loy's Miss Midnight

Glengarven's Dainty Dell
—FC Randy Dandy of Holly Hill

Glen's Lady of the Mountains
—Glen's Lady's Casper
Lakeside Dean's Shadow

Glen-Water Fal-Lal
—Ebony Major Sassy Miss
Frankie of Rivernook
=Lady of Wake
FC-AFC Little Miss Samantha
FC-AFC Reimrock's Duke of
Orleans
FC-AFC Shadow of Rocky Lane
Shag of Shanty Bay
Wallace's Playboy's Topsy Tar

Glen-Water Fan Fare
—FC Del-Tone Buck
=FC-AFC Bigstone Flint
Bodoro's Coaley
Buck of Woodlawn
FC Buck's Hobo
Carr-Lab Spirit
FC-AFC Cork of Evergreen
AFC Dawn of Aladon
Del-Tone Mac's Belle
FC-AFC Franklin's Tall Timber
Geechee's Buck
Hi Go Niki
Jac-Lor's Laja
Lakeshore Cowie

Lulake's Rickie
FC Martens' Black Powder Kate
Montina Lady
Re-Mar's Black Buck
Rille Ann's Cole Buck Blazer
Rille Ann's Mickey
Ringo From Happy Hollow
FC-AFC Rover of Ramsey Place
AFC Sir Caleb of Audlon
AFC Willow's Boe Longshot

Glen-Water Fury
—Del-Tone Rex
=Warpath Cowboy Joe
Warpath Kitty
FC-AFC Warpath Rip

Golden Miss Muffet
—AFC Mysaks Major Buck

Gordon's Black Babe
—FC-AFC Glengarven's Mik
=Sport of Upland Farm

Grace-Art's Bouncing Baby
—John Henry of Oakridge
AFC Timcin's Black Domino

Grace-Art's Smart Lady
—AFC Geechee
=Easy Does It of Valhalla
Geechee's Buck
Geechee's Daniel Dexter
Lulake's Rickie
Robinhood's Geechee Junior
Valhalla Bonefish Sam

Grace-Art's Winalot
—Dairy Hill's Top Banana

Grady's Shadee Ladee*
—FC-NARFC '71 Dee's Dandy Dude
FC Zipper Dee Do
=Koskinen's Pyewacket
Moon Rocket of Zenith

Gramp's Joy
—Whittaker's Firefly

Greenlief's Black Imp*
—Butte King of the Road

Green Ridge Sally
—Bel-Aire Dam
AFC Black Bandit
FC-AFC Carbon Marker

Gun Thunder's Shadee Ladee
—Koskinen's Pyewacket

Gwen's Missie
—AFC Gwen's Ringtail Velvet
AFC Gwen's Trouble

Gypsy Queen of Random Lake
—Sand Gold Venus

Gypsy's Gun Ho
—Deadly Dudley's Deke

Halroy's Christmas Carol
—Tyker's Lucky Penny
=Ripple River

Happy of Broadway
—AFC White River Duke

Happy Rajah of Jumpsville
—Miss Nyx

Happy's Twinkle*
—FC Carnation Rainstar
  Ern-Bar's Andy of Anzac
  FC-AFC Ern-Bar's Twinkle Boots
  Telstar of Zenith
  Twinkle's Mandy
  Twink's Tinker Bell

Hasley's Midnight Star
—FC-AFC Monster Mike

Henry's Charm
—FC-AFC Baird's Centerville Sam

Her Majesty Pat
—Mountain View's Buff

Hetero Pam of Southlands
—Robinhood's Geechee Junior

High Brass Bama
—High Brass Sassy

Homestead's Dolly
—Conquistador of Fortune

Homestead's Sweet Pixie
—Jingles' Bitter Trace

Honor of Cluterol
—Jones' Daddy Wags

Howmor's Dark Gypsy
—FC Jamie's Little Tigger
  FC Mr. Lucky of Oak Hill
  FC Royl Jay

Hull's Oma
—AFC Kim O'Sage
  =Bumble Buzz of Bee Sting
  Lad Crowder's Ranger
  Muse's Bonnie Girl
  FC Nassau
  Sage Brandy of Sunny Slope

Hunt's Charming Annabelle
—AFC Hunt's Cloud of Smoke
  Hunt's Digger By Little Smoky
  Hunt's Nipper of Little Smoky
  FC Smoky's Black Jet
  =Cedarhaven J. B.
  Mitch's Dandy Bouncer
  Piegan's Cryseyde
  Sills' Black Bandit

Hylands Black Rex
—Lisa's Pet

Ike's Blue Lady
—Rocket of Frontier

Invail's Anise of South Bay
—FC Peg of Turkey Run
  =High Brass Sassy

Iowa Black Nipper
—FC-AFC Black Rocky
  Lincoln of Bel Air

Ironwood Cherokee Chica
—FC-AFC Carr-Lab Penrod
  FC Chief Black Feather
  FC-AFC Paha Sapa Warpaint
  Spring Farms Lucky
  FC-AFC Paha's Pow Wow
  NRFC '68-NARFC '67 & 68
  Super Chief
  =FC-AFC Air Express
  AFC Bellota Cacahuete
  Carr-Lab Spirit
  Chief Cody of Le-Mar
  Chief Consultation South Bay
  FC Cody of Wanapum
  FC-AFC Dairy Hill's
    Michikiniquia
  Dairy Hill's Wampum
  High Brass Sassy
  FC-AFC Magic Marker of
    Timber Town
  Orion's Lady Dart
  Paha's Pow on Tap
  FC Patsy's Thunderchief
  Piegan's Cryseyde
  Pocatello Chief
  Rockbend's Kamakura
  FC Round Valley's Lucky Tigger
  Royal Oaks Havoc's Haze
  AFC Royal Oaks Jill of Burgundy
  Sassy Sioux of Tukwila
  Seymour's Hot Line Pepper
  Shamrock Acres Lucky Lady
  Shamrock Acres Modoc Painter
  Shamrock Acres Nylic Ned
  Shamrock Acres Super Drive
  Shamrock Acres Superstition
  FC Shamrock Acres Super Value
  Shamrock Acres Winnie Pooh
  Spring Farms Smokey
  AFC Wanapum Dart's Dandy
  Wanapum Lucky Yo Yo
  Wanapum Sheba

Ivanhoe Sally
—Spirit's Black Pepper
  =FC-AFC Harang's Grumpy
  Express

Jac-Lor Miss Cindy
—Jac-Lor Blarney Stone
  FC-AFC Cork of Evergreen
  AFC Creole Carpetbagger
  Hal's Chula Prieta
  Jac-Lor's Laja
  Jac-Lor Rebellion
  =AFC Hunt's Cloud of Smoke
  Hunt's Digger by Little Smoky
  Hunt's Nipper of Little Smoky
  FC Smoky's Black Jet

Jacona of Indian Spring
—Coley's Grand Clipper

Jacona the Lark
—Hielan Havoc

Ja Dar's Miss Kim
—FC-NARFC '70 Andy's Partner Pete

Jemima's Blue Maxine
—Taffy of Janie Lane

Jerry
—FC-AFC Dessa Rae
=FC-AFC Dessa's Black Angel
FC Dessa's Little Tar Baby
Dessa Sweet
Panther Baby
FC Swing Tarzan Swing
FC Tar Dessa Venture
Tyker Baby

Jet Firefly of Dacity
—Claymar's Academy Award
FC-AFC Jetstone Muscles of Claymar
FC-AFC Jet's Target of Claymar
FC Van's Pride Ebony Shadow
=Claymar's Crash Diver
Kennon's Jockeaux
Lincoln of Bel Air
Muscles Jet Jock
Remohcs Ebony Ace

Jethaven Black Lucky
—AFC Bayou Beau
=Johnny's High Yellow

Jet Noir La Petite
—FC Buck's Hobo

Jet of Clear Lake
—Boise's Black Bart

Jet of Hart
—Mystery Icabod

Jet Star of Audlon
—AFC Sir Caleb of Audlon

Jet's Tammy
—NARFC '64 Dutchmoor's Black Mood
=AFC Andy Black of Chestnut Hill
Ebony Mood's Bingo
FC Jamie's Little Tigger
FC Mr. Lucky of Oak Hill
FC Royl Jay
Sauk Trail Black Mouse
Sauk Trail Black Pepper

Jezebel of Normandy
—FC Anzac of Zenith
Belle Ringer
FC-AFC Grady's Shadee Ladee
FC-AFC Rocky Road of Zenith
=FC Carnation Rainstar
FC-NARFC '71 Dee's Dandy
Dude
Ern-Bar's Andy of Anzac
FC-AFC Ern-Bar's Twinkle
Boots
Moon Rocket of Zenith
Sills' Black Bandit
Telstar of Zenith
FC Toni's Blaine Child
Twinkle's Mandy
Wild Joker of Napi
FC Zipper Dee Do

Jibodad Topsy
—AFC Gung-Ho of Granton
=Brant of Blenheim

Jibodad Velvet
—FC-AFC Ivy Pat
AFC Parky
Pepper's Omega
FC-AFC Velvet's Jezebel
=Chain's Princess Pet
Nefertiti
Polaris Peter
Rowdy's Sean of The Corkies
FC-AFC Sauk Trail Deepwell
"Doc"
FC Sauk Trail Senator

Jilly Girl*
—Fieldmarshall Heinz Guderian
Washington's Tizzy Lizzy
=FC Patsy's Thunderchief
Tiger's Lucky Buck

Jilly's Tiger Lil
—FC Bel-Aire Lucky Boy
Lil's Lucky Linda
Tiger's Lucky Buck

Jinjo Black's Jet Jewel
—FC Caliph Obsidian Hobii
FC Julie Cole of Menomin
=Coll-A-Dene's Kelly

Jo-Ann of Avandale II
—AFC Waccamaw's Tinker

John's Bridgit
—Bridgit's Black Cargo

Jumper of Spring Valley
—Geechee's Buck
Lulake's Rickie

Juste's Velvet Mist
—Aquarian Lady O' The Autumn Moon

Kara
—Chief Consultation South Bay

Kashpureff Lady Fats
—St. Hubert of Tewkesbury Knob

Keith's Brandy
—AFC Nilo Brandy Cork

Kelly of Country Acres
—McKemie's Pola

Kemper's Sassy Sue
—Lake Ripley Pooka
FC Michelle
=Leroy III
FC-AFC Ray's Rascal

Kim of Brimherst
—AFC Irwin's Toby

Kristan's Liz of Timber Town
—Storm's Ebony Echo

Labcroft Darling Zahm's Peggy
—FC Brazil's Black Jaguar

La Belle
—FC Choc of San Juan

La Chatelaine De La Meute
—Knight Train

258

La-Dee of River Lake
—FC-AFC Black Jet XVI
  Broadmoor Rex

Lady Blackduck
—Bigstone Count Black Rip

Lady Carbon Daglo
—AFC Gimp of Lakin

Lady Charkey of Evergreen
—Jackson's Ripsnorter

Lady Gretchen of Buffalo
—FC-AFC Tarblood of Absaraka
  =AFC Beavercrest Sassy Sioux
  Dukw-Trax Mandegho
  Paha Sapa Jay
  FC-AFC Serrana Sootana of
    Genesee
  AFC Timberlake Flying Muffin

Lady Jane XI
—AFC Bomar's Blackfoot Wog
  Country's Delight Caesar

Lady of Ahab
—FC-AFC Shawnee Ace of Spades

Lady of Allan-A-Dale
—NRFC '70-AFC Creole Sister

Lady of Wake*
—AFC Lucky's Lady in Red

Lady Roxanne of Muldoon
—FC-AFC Hiwood Stormy of Alaska
  =Coley's Grand Clipper

Lady Schrintza
—Yankee Black Power

Lady's Pie Doe
—Kennon's Jockeaux
  Muscles Jet Jock

Lakeshore Jody
—Lakeshore Cowie

Lakewood Resolution
—Montina Lady
  =AFC Lakeland Tiger of Bruce

Last Chance Spice Queen
—Zip of Geneva Lake
  =AFC White River Duke

Lilli of Corfu
—Nefertiti

Little Doll Face of Audlon
—FC I Love Lucy of Audlon

Little Smoky Lewbonnie
—Sills Black Bandit

Lockerbie Bally
—Brandywine Star

Lokate of High Point
—Chips of Birchwood

Long Lake Duchess
—FC-AFC Smokey of Park Avenue

Longshot's Rebel Rouser
—Old Vav

Lucifer's Lady*
—FC V-Jay's Black Paddle

Luka of Casey's Rocket*
—Peigan's Bolle Blake

MacGene's Tinker Bell
—AFC Dent's Midnight Rick

MacKenzie's Di Dee Dee
—FC Sassy Sioux of Willow Creek

Mac's Black Dawn
—Kentuckian
  =Dutch's Black Lucifer

Madam Hepzibah Hoo Ha
—Orion of River Park

Magi Gal of Christ Lac
—Bigstone Prairie Wind

Maiden Margaret
—Miss Fortune

Mandy of Jet
—Yogi II

Margie's Sugar Lady
—Buckskin Bullet

Mark's Jigger of Joy
—Rille Ann's Burr

Mark's Mate of Jolor
—FC Jolor's Compobosso

Mark's Mondak Penny
—FC Paha Sapa Jack

Mark's Koko Lady
—AFC Lady's Brazos Pete

Marlab's Gypsy
—AFC Shamrock Acres Gun Away
  =Black Irish Kelly
  Captain's Mist
  FC Carbo Computer
  Invail's Gunner
  Just Samson

Martens' Black Badger
—FC Martens' Mister Nifty
  FC Martens' Stormy
  =FC-AFC Bigstone Flint
  Bigstone Hard's Happy
  J.A.M.'s Steamin' Demon
  FC Martens' Black Powder Kate
  Martens' Mister Lucky
  AFC Penny of Evergreen
  FC-NARFC '72 River Oaks
    Corky

Martens' Black Doll
—Martens' Mister Lucky
  =FC Copy Cat Del Norte
  FC-AFC Martens' Castaway

Martens' Black Dot
—FC Bigstone Scout
  =FC Your Shot Minnesota Fats

Martens' Black Tagg
—Igo Licorice Split To
  =Cimaroc Coon Willie

Martens' Jumper
—FC Invail's Cavalier Carom
Invail's Medicine Man
=Peg of Turkey Run

Martens' Lady Jane
—Dajo's Black Velvet
J's Big Water Buck
=Bigstone Black Longshot II
FC-AFC Cimaroc Tang
Harrowby Dandy
Igo Licorice Split To
Mar-Ten's Moneymaker
FC-AFC Orion's Sirius
NRFC '72-AFC Royal's
Mooses's Moe
Wayside Black Buster

Martens' Little Bullet
—NRFC '65 Martens' Little Smoky
FC Martens' Scrubby Giant
=Black Nig Prince
FC-AFC Candlewood's
Beau of Beaumont
AFC Hunt's Cloud of Smoke
Hunt's Digger by Little Smoky
Hunt's Nipper of Little Smoky
Igo Licorice Split To
FC Lakenham Paha Sun Dance
Mark of Gloster
Martens' Mister Lucky
FC Martens' Mister Nifty
Martens' Mister Stubbs
FC Martens' Stormy
FC Medlin's Otto of Toothacres
FC Medlin's Texas Ruff
Medlin's Texas Trooper
FC Medlin's Tiny Boom
Miss Nyx
AFC Nilo Brandy Cork
Remohcs Ebony Ace
Rocket of Frontier
FC Smokey's Black Jet
Tealwood Tammy

Martens' Little Rocket
—Wayside Black Buster

Martens' Little Susie
—FC Copy Cat Del Norte
FC-AFC Martens' Castaway

Marv's Sussie
—Chauncey of Ellenwood

Masai's Star
—FC-AFC Coldwater's Brendan

Matilda II
—Little Billie Jo

Mawood Funf
—Ahab's Emancipator

Medlin's Cricket
—FC Medlin's Otto of Toothacres
FC Medlin's Texas Ruff
Medlin's Texas Trooper
FC Medlin's Tiny Boom
=AFC Bayou Beau
Gee Baby

Medlin's Texas Happy Time
—Medlin's Gay Teal of Castawac

Melissa of Oakridge
—Coll-A-Dene's Kelly
=Coll-A-Dene's Perky

Merry-Go-Round Tradewinds
—Electricity of Audlon
FC-AFC Hiwinds of South Bay
=Chauncey of Ellenwood

Michelle
—Leroy III

Mi-Cris Black Lady
—NRFC '71 Mi-Cris Sailor

Midge of Barbie Town
—Highlander's Dame Sally

Midge of Greenwood*
—Wildhearted Dinah

Midnight Chuckar
—AFC Bellota Cacahuete

Midnight Star of Ruslyn
—Spring Farms Smokey

Mike's Lizzie Odom*
—Pam's Black Splash

Mike's Nancy
—Sam of Marlboro Country

Millham Mist
—Land O' Lakes Sunburst

Miller's Susie Q
—Lady of Wake
=AFC Lucky's Lady in Red

Miss Behavior
—Happy's Twinkle
=FC Carnation Rainstar
Ern-Bar's Andy of Anzac
FC-AFC Ern-Bar's Twinkle Boots
Telstar of Zenith
Twinkle's Mandy
Twink's Tinker Bell

Miss Chief Cherokee
—Carr-Lab Spirit
=Hi-M's Jake the Giant Killer

Miss Chief Cinder
—FC Hermitage Hill Drake
Paddler of Wintergreen

Miss Debit of Shady Valley
—Paha Sapa Medicine Man

Miss Fiddlesticks
—FC-AFC Ray's Rascal

Miss Rusty Jig a Boo
—AFC Columbine Loran

Miss Tehama Tar
—FC-AFC Dusty's Doctari
Lucky's Bitterroot Shasta
Lucky's Shasta Beau

Missy of Big Bend
—AFC Pat's Penny Jo

Mistress of Sterling
—Goose Spooker

Misty Gem
—FC-AFC Mackenzie's Ripco Tar

Misty Velvet
—Whygin Wellmet Angus

Montana Sue
—Miss Jan's Dobie

Moody's Dell
—Corky's Ramblin Riley
River Oaks Rowdy Bear

Moon Shine Bobdee
—Buckskin Torquin

Morgan's Anne
—FC Larry's Lasser
=FC Lasser's Captain Hook
FC V and C Chip

Mountain Crest's Black Velvet
—Archie the Cockroach

Nascopie Little Aggie
—Nascopie Cinder of Lucifer

Naughty Mary of Audlon
—FC-AFC Candlewood's Beau of
Beaumont

Navajo Toni of Sunnymede
—FC Moby Dick
AFC Toni's Tar
=FC-AFC Lord Bomar
AFC Targhee Sam
Tom's Thadius

Neb's Deb
—FC-AFC Marelvan Mike of Twin Oaks

Nelgard's Counter Point
—FC Counter Smoke
FC-AFC Sand Gold Kim
=AFC Creole Carpet Bagger
FC-NARFC '71 Dee's Dandy
Dude
AFC Geechee
Hal's Chula Prieta
Jac-Lor Blarney Stone
Jac-Lor Rebellion
FC-AFC Misty of Otter Creek
FC-AFC Reimrock's
Duke of Orleans
FC-AFC Shamrock Acres Drake
FC Sindbad IV
Wallace's Playboy's Topsy Tar
FC Zipper Dee Do

Nelson's Vulcan Wind
—Brandi of Cayne

Nicoll's Blackie
—Nicoll's Comeback

Nilo Ida's Pretender
—Nilo Gypsy
FC Nilo Staindrop Charger
Time of Frontier

Nilo Lulubelle
—Yaz Razzmatazz

Nilo Pete's Ida
—FC Nilo Brian Boru
=Buckskin Bullet

Nilo Smoky's Cassandra
—Colonel Smokey Squirrel
=Choppy Babe

Nilo Solo's Margie
—Peter of Gaymark

Nilo Storm's Peggy
—FC John's Minnie

Nimrod's Wendy of Windy Main
—FC Nethercroft Nemo of Nascopie
=FC-AFC Nemo's Spyder of
Round Valley

Nodak Miss Que
—FC-AFC J. & L.'s Spooky
FC Nassau's Nar of Minnewaska

Nodak Tar Pride
—Smokey of Jetcin
Spook of Jetcin
=Dairy Hill's Planters Punch
Leroy III

Nodrog Penny*
—Bow-Mar Black Brandy
Nodrog Pixie
FC-AFC Nodrog Punkie
Rebcha's Super Duper

Nyssa's Tanagra of Zenith
—AFC Timberlake Flying Muffin

Odell's Nancy II
—FC Sindbad IV

Opal of Ramapo Valley
—Striper of Ramapo Valley
=Spring Farms Smokey

O'Torq's Kimberly
—AFC Togom's Tiger of Abilena
=Boatswain's Stormy Spirit

Ottertail Penny
—AFC Mallard of Devil's Garden
=Meto of Devil's Garden

Our Lady Midnight
—FC-AFC Alamo Black Jack

Pacific Mo Kee
—FC-AFC Luka of Casey's Rocket
Rip Von Black Winkle
=Piegan's Bolle Blake

Paha Sapa Belle
—FC-AFC Paha Sapa Warpath
=FC-AFC Paha Sapa Warpath II

Paha Sapa Rapid Water
—FC Riskin
=Canuck-Crest Gallant
Morty's Ebony Magic
Pipers Highland Drummer

Paha Sapa Wacincala
—Dakota Jake
  FC-AFC Warpath Tuff
    =Archie the Cockroach
    Connor's Hunter
    Warpath Just in Case

Pareenca Apache Tear
—Donald Grunts Ray

Patty Jimsue
—Luke of Patty Jimsue

Pat's Error Mitzie
—Mark of Gloster
  =Ol' Yeller

Pawlesta Fleetfoot of Audlon
—FC Double Play of Audlon

Peep of Beau
—Cha-Cha-Cha of District Ten

Peg's Blackfoot Queen
—FC-AFC Lord Bomar
  =AFC Bomar's Blackfoot Wog
  Bomar's Chris
  Country's Delight Caesar
  FC-AFC Radar Rip
  FC Sauk Trail Senator

Pelican Lake Biddy
—Martens' Mister Stubbs

Pelican Lake Peggy*
—Jo-Anne's Black Blade
  FC Pelican Lake Boo Boo

Penny Girl
—FC Attawan Pucka Sahib
  AFC Jilly Girl
  NARFC '65-FC Rebel Chief of Heber
  Trappers Paha Cork
    =AFC Cha Cha Dancer
    Fieldmarshall Heinz Guderian
    FC-AFC Muktar of Offershire
    AFC Paha Sapa Hardcase
    Washington's Tizzy Lizzy

Penny Girl II
—Dick's Black Duke

Penny of Delta
—Netley Creek's Black Brute

Penny of Evergreen*
—Evergreen Binx
  Salt Valley Espresso

Pen Pep Dolly
—FC-AFC Muktar of Offershire

Peppy of Lopez
—NRFC '65-AFC Ripco's VC Morgan
  =FC Larry's Lasser

Personality Plus
—Black Irish Kelly
  FC Carbo Computer
  Just Samson

Peterson's Pretty Penny
—Tom's Thadius

Pickrel's Ebony Babe
—FC-NARFC '69 Guy's Bitterroot
  Lucky
  FC-AFC Mitch of Bitterroot
    =FC Bel-Aire Lucky Boy
    Bitterroot's Taurus
    Bruce's Happy Warrior
    Cedarhaven J.B.
    Happy Hollow's El Champo
    Hi-M's Jake the Giant Killer
    Lil's Lucky Linda
    Lucky's Bitterroot Shasta
    AFC Lucky's Lady in Red
    Lucky's Shasta Beau
    Mitch's Dandy Bouncer
    Polaris Peter
    Tiger's Lucky Buck
    Washington's Tizzy Lizzy

Pierre's Kit of Garfield
—FC Ace of Garfield
  =FC Ace of Southwood
  Dajo's Black Velvet
  J's Big Water Buck
  FC Martens' Mister Nifty
  FC Martens' Stormy

Polly of Arroyo
—Col-Tam's Stormy

Pontchippi Matrix
—Shannon's Terror

Pre-Don Jacky
—J.A.M.'s Steamin' Demon
  AFC Penny of Evergreen
  =Evergreen Binx
  Salt Valley Espresso

Pretty Nifty
—Gee Baby
  =Mike's Lizzie Odom (twice)

Pride's Black Duchess
—FC Cedar Haven Matador
  Panther of the Coeur D'Alene's

Prim Pat of Ralston Valley
—Tycoon of Ralston Valley

Princess Nickawampus
—Rowdy's Sean of the Corkies

Princess of New Hope
—AFC Black Chief of Nakomis

Princess Pat X
—Midnight in the Bighorns

Princess Patricia Stieg
—FC-AFC Frances Fishtail

Princess Patsy La Coquette
—Conty's Black Chip

Princess Sootana of Buffalo
—FC-AFC Serrana Sootana of Genesee

  Paha Sapa Jay
    =Bruce's Happy Warrior

Purty Sure Judy
—Roxie of Mercer Lake
  =Git 'N' Go Ace

Queen Ace
—FC Ace High Scamp of Windsweep
Ace Hi Indian Magic
=Hermitage Hill Timberdoodle

Queen Eby of Lakenham
—Cascade's Rodney St. Clair
Centennial Cric
=Centennial Chukaluk
FC-AFC Rodney's Mr. M. L.
Coon

Queen of Dotken
—FC-AFC Hundred Proof Tad

Queen of High Tide
—FC Black Duke of Sherwood

Queen of Opal's Black Pepper
—FC-AFC Rodney's Mr. M. L. Coon

Queen of Valentine
—Beavercrest Black Tartar II
=Pocatello Chief

Queen of The Valley
—Hi-Line King Pepper

Queen's Folly
—Blackfoot Lobo

Ralston Valley's Kitty
—J.J.'s Lady Ebony

Ralston Valley's Lady Luck
Brock's Lively Lark

Random Molly
—FC Ace of Southwood
=Rille Ann's Burr

Random Rapscallion
—FC-AFC River Oaks Rascal
River Oaks Black Frost

Random Shot
—Deadly Dudley's Duxbak Coot
AFC King Tut V
FC Minot's Magic Marker
=FC Ace of Southwood
FC-AFC River Oaks Rascal

Ravencamp Black Heel
—Neb's Midnight Rebel

Ravenhills Char
—Ravenhills Lucky Lady

Rebel's Gypsy
—Thunder of Rebel's Gypsy

Rebel's Miss Muffet
—Muffet's Tuffet

Redd
—FC-AFC Balsom's Snooper Honker
Chief Storm Cloud
Desert Gypsy II

Red Lady's Cinderella
—FC-AFC Sir Mike of Orchardview

Regina Di Campi*
—John's Spike

Renegade Sioux
—AFC Cherokee Chief V

Pin Oaks Little Otter
=Cherokee Peace Pipe
Gayfeathers Domino
FC-AFC Hundred Proof Tad

Rexana
—Sage Rambler

Rille Ann's Lady
—Grant's Lady Bird
Rille Ann's Cole Buck Blazer
Rille Ann's Mickey

Rill Shannon's Dark Del*
—FC Mr. Mac's Billy Boy
Del-Tone Mac's Belle
=Corky's Ramblin Riley
River Oaks Rowdy Bear

Rimrock Briquet
—Van's Bomber

Ripco's Lady Jo
—FC Lasser's Captain Hook

Ripco's Lady Pam
—AFC Paha Sapa Hardcase
=Paha Sapa Pride of Casey

Ripco's Little Bit of Cork
—Tyker's Fleck of Cork

Rockbend's Redhead
—Rockbend's Kamakura
Rockbend's Magic Marker

Rolida's Ebony Angel
—Rolida's Stubby Bandit

Roman's Second Lady
—Cinder of Cole

Rosehill's Little Dutch Boots*
—Allo Dere Louise
Dove of Little Dutch Boots

Royal Lady in Black
—Sam of Arrowhead Lake

Royal Oaks September Song
—Bitterroot's Taurus
Happy Hollow's El Champo

Ruby's Jet
—Bar Me None
FC Dave's Demetrius

Runaway's Sacagewea
—Rincon Valley Jet

Rushmore's Black Shaw
—FC King Cole of Menomin
=FC Caliph Obsidian Hobii
FC Julie Cole of Menomin

Samantha of San Rafael
—AFC Copper Cities Colliery Cal

Sandy's Black Mahria
—River Oaks Cream Cadette
=Invail's Gunner

Sandy of Danville
—Sherwood's Maid Marion

Sauk Trail Black Pine
—Sauk Trail Black Mouse
Sauk Trail Black Pepper

Sauk Trail Black Starlight
—Whiskey Creek Blue Sahib

Sauk Trail Velvet Cougar
—FC-AFC Sauk Trail Deepwell "Doc"
FC Sauk Trail Senator

Seco Cindy
—Crook's Jolly Roger

Shadow of Dakota
—FC-AFC Paha Sapa Warpath II

Shady Bingo II
—AFC Caesar of Swinomish
=FC-AFC Bair's Sambo II

Shady Dutchess of Duluth
—Lakeland Tiger of Bruce

Shady Haven Farm Lady
—FC-AFC Bean Ball
AFC Smoke Tail's Chico
=Miss Fortune

Shady Haven Farm Smudge
—Zip of Geneva Lake
=White River Duke

Shamrock Acres Belle Aire
—FC-AFC Candlewood's Little Lou

Shamrock Acres Black Button
—Tealwood Tammy

Shamrock Acres Kerry Dancer
—Coll-A-Dene's Squire

Shamrock Acres P.D.Q.
—AFC Winroc's Ripper

Shamrock Acres Simmer Down*
—AFC Simmer's Shot of Brandy
=Sage Brandy of Sunny Slope
Tarnoff of V & C Chip

Shamrock Acres Smoky Cinder
—Shamrock Acres Lucky Lady
Shamrock Acres Modoc Painter
Shamrock Acres Winnie Pooh

Shamrock Acres Whygin Tardy
—AFC Royal Oaks Jill of Burgundy
Royal Oaks Havoc's Haze
=Bitterroot's Taurus
Happy Hollow's El Champo

Shamrock A of Ralston Valley
—FC-AFC Shamrock Acres Drake
FC Shamrock Acres Super Value

Sharmain's Black Ghost
—FC Jo Do's Jet Fire

Shasta Stormy
—FC-AFC Lucifer's Lady
=FC V-Jay's Black Paddle

Shay's Black Beauty
—AFC Button Boots

Sheena V
—Masai of Aberdeen

Sheer Delite
—Deelite's Mr. Bones

FC-AFC Sage Joker
FC Sage's Saskeram Pete
=Rockbend's Magic Marker

Shining Black Dixie
—FC Sam of Dixie Rapids

Shining Jackie
—FC-AFC Harangs Grumpy Express
=FC Sam of Dixie Rapids

Shirley's Bea
—Mark Duck's Dago

Shoe's Del-Tone Femme
—AFC Acute Accent
Ripco's Repeater
=Angelique
Beaver State Hope

Silent Susie
—FC V and C Chip
=Tarnoff of V & C Chip

Sills Little Smokey Lewbonnie
—Cedarhaven J. B.
=Sills Black Bandit

Simmers Shot of Brandy*
—Sage Brandy of Sunny Slope

Siskiyou Chain
—Chain's Princess Pet

Sister Kate of Upland Farm
—Sport of Upland Farm

Skip to My Lou
—Aerco's Bit O' Honey

Skookum Scooter
—Great Smoke Cloud
Skookum Bingo
FC Skookum Dale's Nike Mark X
Skookum Redwing

Smith's Cindy Lou
—FC-AFC Jupiter's Hi-Laurel
=Boise's Black Bart

Smokey Flame
—FC-AFC Joy's Coal Dust
=FC-AFC Dusty's Doctari

Smokey's Black Chrystal
—Tarrnof of V & C Chip

Smoky's Gal Tammy
—FC-AFC Black Michael O'Shea
Problem Boy's Dinny

Smokey's Miss Tremendous
—Piegan's Criseyde

Soot's Shadow of Genesee
—Bruce's Happy Warrior

Spade O'Cedar
—Ducky O'Cedar
FC Flint's Nifty Arrow

Sparkle Plenty of Whitmore
—April Fool's Yellow Jacket
=Butte King of the Road

Spirit Lake Gal
—NRFC '72-AFC Royal's Moose's Moe
=Boatswain's Stormy Spirit
Moose's Louise
Nascopie Cinder of Lucifer
FC-AFC Sauk Trail Deepwell
"Doc"

Springer's Cleo
—FC-AFC Beau of Blair House
Gunner of Gunthunder

Sprite of Ralston Valley
—AFC Ralston Valley Dandy Jake

Sprucelane's Ember
—FC Win-Toba's Black High Point

Stardust's Sheba
—Blackberry Brandy

Star Fire of Audlon
—Dixieland Coot's Tiger Baby

Stillwaters Lady Jeep
—Stillwaters Carry Back
=AFC Dent's Midnight Rick
FC Moby Dick
FC Sassy Sioux of Willow Creek

Stone Castle Gypsy
—Stone Castle Yellow Jacket

Stormalong A' Go-Go
—Connor's Hunter

Stormy Cindy
—Regina Di Campi
=John's Spike

Stormy's Black Cinderalla
—Shantoo Tar Buck

Stormy Snowy
—AFC Potomac Buddy
=Miss Fortune

Straw Hollow's Plover
—Straw Hollow's Rowdy Crusader

Sugar Plum's Tar Baby
—Cherokee Peace Pipe
Gayfeathers Domino

Sugar Sweet
—High Low Jick

Sumi No Kodomo
—Giljo's Nikki of Bow-Mar

Suzie
—FC Happy Play Boy
=Happy Playboy's Pearl

Suzie Q
—Mike of Burrview Acres

Swinomish Shady Teena
—FC-AFC Bair's Sambo II
=Luke of Patty Jimsue

Syldonnel's Dixie
—FC-AFC Molybru Butch of Barmond

Tad's Cork of Laketree
—FC Gun Thunder Oly

Tammy of Shannon Hills
—Silver Squire

Tam O'Shanter of Craignook
—FC-AFC Col-Tam of Craignook
=Col-Tam's Stormy

Tarbaby's Mistake
—FC-AFC Shadow of Provincetown

Tarb of Argyll
—Martin's Scokim

Techacko's Cinder
—Dairy Hill's Planters Punch

Telaka's Mist
—Captain's Miss

Tempa Jigg of Moore Hill
—AFC Brandy of Cortez

That's Mandy
—FC-AFC Dobe's Desdemona
Salt Valley Epaminondas

The Contesse
—Buck of Woodlawn
=AFC Huck's Pride of Riverside

The Duchess of Rosehill
—FC-AFC Rosehill's Little Dutch Boots
=Allo Dere Louise
Carnmoney Spud
Dove of Little Dutch Boots

Thunder Chief's Shiri
—FC-AFC Samson's George of Glenspey
=Evergreen Binx
Salt Valley Espresso

Thunder Cloud's Shadow
—FC-AFC Midge of Greenwood
=Wildhearted Dinah

Timcin's Queen of Spades
—Beau Gentry

Tina of Grey Summit
—Cloud Burst
FC-AFC Randy Mayhall of Tina
Tina's Black Chip

Tina Rose
—FC-AFC Ottley's Jazzbo

Tioga's Tabatha
—Invail's Gunner

Toni of Wanapum
—FC Cody of Wanapum
Wanapum Lucky Yo Yo
Wild Joker of Napi

Topsy Turvy Tar Baby
—FC-AFC Little Miss Samantha
FC-AFC Reimroc's Duke of Orleans
FC-AFC Shadow of Rockylane
Shag of Shanty Bay
Wallace's Playboy's Topsy Tar
=Sam of Arrowhead Lake

Toto of Audlon
—FC-AFC Billy Pawlesta
=FC Double Play of Audlon
Little Billy Joe

Trouble's Double of Audlon
—FC Troublemaker of Audlon II
=Bellatrix of Hickory Glen
Blackberry Brandy V
FC-AFC Candlewood's
Little Lou

Tweet's Taffy
—FC-AFC Tweet's Bebe

Twink of Belle Isle
—FC Mi-Cris of Hayden
Mi-Cris Drambuie
=Canuck-Crest Cutty Sark
Canuck-Crest Gallant
Canuck-Crest Sally
FC-AFC Magic Marker of
Timber Town
River Road Bippy

Twin Lakes Lady
—AFC Portneuf Valley Duke
=Inashotte Dee Chuggy

Tyker's Lucky Penny*
—Ripple River

Typhoon of Audlon
—Bellatrix of Hickory Glen

Uneva Drake's Lucky Lady
—FC-AFC Keg of Black Powder
AFC Renegade Pepe

Valgaard Lady of Shady Lane
—Bodoro's Coaley
AFC Dawn of Aladon
Hi Go Niki
Re-Mar's Black Buck
FC-AFC Rover of Ramsey Place

Valhalla Trooper's Persimmon
—Easy Does It of Valhalla
Valhalla Bonefish Sam

Van's Pride Ebony Shadow*
—Remohcs Ebony Ace
=Tar Dessa Comanche Mike

Velvet's Jezebel*
—Polaris Peter

Viewpoint Black Jodi
—FC Blitz Von Mobile

Wacap's Breeze
—Wacap's Windy

Walt's Honey Bee
—King Kong II

Wandarin Heights Shannon
—Black Susan of Polhemus
Bomber II
Pat of Orchard Glen

Wandarin Heights Williwaw
—Wandarin Heights Venture

Washington's Tootie Kazootie
—Pixie IV
Ripshin Rooster

Wellwatt Pitch Patty's Julie
—Hermitage Hill Timberdoodle

West Island Hortense
—FC Cascade Charade

Whisk of Gin
—Lady VI

Whygin Dark Ace
—NRFC '66 & '69 Whygin Cork's Coot
=Dixieland Coot's Tiger Baby

Whygin Gentle Julia of Avec
—AFC Shamrock Acres Simmer Down
=Brock's Lively Lark
AFC Ralston Valley Dandy Jake
AFC Simmer's Shot of Brandy
AFC Winroc's Ripper

Willowmount Honey Bunny
—FC Willowmount El Diablo

Willow's Red River Belle
—Crozier's Firebrand

Winds Way Babs of Houqua
—AFC Hawk Hill's Sam of Devon

Wingford's Dinah Soar
—Wingford's Big Flint Stone

Wondawhere You Are
—FC Danny's Cole Black Slate

GOLDEN SIRES

Amanda's Shades of Gold
—Sun Dance's Babe

Bang Away's Hay Bailer
—FC-AFC Ripp 'N Ready

Beckwith's Tallyho
—Honor's Darado of Spindrift

Bishops Golden Pet
—FC-AFC Clickety Click

Briggs Lake Mac
—Briggs Lake Golden Boy

Charlie Brown II
—Sir Michael Robert

Chief Oshkosh of Stilrovin
—AFC Chief Sands

Elkdale's Davy Jones
—Tink's Ben of Pennywise

Golden Duke of Trey-C
—FC-AFC Ronakers Novato Cain
=Brackenhollow's Sungold Rock

Goldenloe's Aces High
—Gigi's Golden Prince

Golden Rocket VI
—FC-AFC Sungold Sprite
FC-AFC Golden Rocket's Missile
Golden Rocket's Raincheck
Golden Rocket's Ruff Boy

Gunnerman's Coin of Copper
—Angus of Stilrovin
  Stilrovin Clipper Delane II
  FC-AFC Tioga Joe
  Sabe Lo Todo of Stilrovin
    =AFC Chief Sands
  Duke of Handjem
  King Kinike of Handjem
  Kinike Chancellor
  AFC Kinike Coquette

Harbor City Shadrach
—FC Macopin Maximum

High Farms Band's Clarion
—AFC Riverview's Chickasaw Thistle

Holway Leo
—FC-AFC Moll-Leo Cayenne
  Moll-Leo Ginger Snap
    =Jolly Again of Ouilmette
  Molly's Cayson Bear
  Sir Michael Robert
  Willhaggin's Ready Poacher

Holway Stubblesdown Jolly
—Jolly Again of Ouilmette
  =Bonnie Brooks Barney
  Bonnie Brooks Copper
  Bonnie Brooks Danny
  AFC Bonnie Brooks Elmer
  Bonnie Brooks Mike
  FC Bonnie Brooks Tuff & A Half

Jolly Again of Ouilmette*
—Bonnie Brooks Barney
  Bonnie Brooks Copper
  Bonnie Brooks Danny
  AFC Bonnie Brooks Elmer
  Bonnie Brooks Mike
  FC Bonnie Brooks Tuff & A Half

Little Joe of Tigathoe
—J's Teeko of Tigathoe
  =Tink's Ben of Pennywise

Lord Buff
—Jacqueline of Robin Way

Lucky Star Duke
—Dutch's Red

Major Drum
—Tigathoe's Chickasaw

Michael O'Destiny
—Destiny's Ready Ripple
  AFC Ready of Sacramento
    =Willhaggin's Ready Poacher

Moll-Leo Cayenne*
—Molly's Cayson Bear

Nickolas of Logan's End
—Tigathoe's Teetotaler
    =Jacqueline of Robin Way
    FC-AFC Ronaker's Novato Cain
    Tink's Ben of Pennywise

Poika of Handjem
—Duke of Handjem
  Kinike Chancellor
  AFC Kinike Coquette
  King Kinike of Handjem
  Northbreak's Panacea

Ready of Sacramento*
—Willhaggins Ready Poacher

Rip of Wildwood
—Sunburst Miss Polaris

Sherrydain Tag
—Brackenhollow's Sungold Rock
  FC-AFC Misty's Sungold Lad
    =AFC Sungold Sprite

Stilrovin Bear Cat
—FC-AFC Stilrovin Tuppee Tee
    =Angus of Stilrovin
    Stilrovin Clipper Delane II
    Tigathoe's Teetotaler

Swanson's Fella
—Mr. Nugget of Redmond

Thornwood's Rayo-De-Oro
—FC-AFC Gerry's Kaiwa of Rosamond

Tigathoe's Brass Blade
—Cazador's Hermanita

Widgeon's Dusty Traveler
—Marshall's Texas Duke

GOLDEN DAMS

Bonnie Brooks Honey
—Bonnie Brooks Copper
  Bonnie Brooks Danny

Bonny Lucy Loch
—FC-AFC Golden Rocket's Missile

Bracken Hollow Sherry
—FC-AFC Sungold Sprite

Diane O'Destiny
—Destiny's Ready Ripple
  AFC Ready of Sacramento
    =Willhaggin's Ready Poacher

Duke's Orofina
—Brackenhollow's Sungold Rock

Echo of Sands
—AFC Chief Sands

Featherquest Golden Quill
—FC Macopin Marimum

Golden Dipper
—Sunburst Miss Polaris

Golden Girl of Gigi
—Gigi's Golden Prince

Golden Purdue
—Sun Dance's Babe

Golden Scotch
—Mr. Nugget of Redmond

Golden Surprise for Xmas
—Cazador's Hermanita

Goldie of Tamarack
—FC-AFC Ripp 'N Ready

Gunnerman's Copper Penny
—Jolly Again of Ouilmette
=Bonnie Brooks Barney
Bonnie Brooks Copper
Bonnie Brooks Danny
AFC Bonnie Brooks Elmer
Bonnie Brooks Mike
FC Bonnie Brooks Tuff & A Half

Honor's Chances Are
—Honor's Darado of Spindrift

Indian Knoll's Memengwa
—Bonnie Brooks Mike

Joaquin's Dixie Lee
—Jacqueline of Robin Way

Jolly's Justi-Nuff
—Dutch's Red
FC-AFC Gerry's Kaiwa of Rosamond

J's Kate
—FC-AFC Ronakers Novato Cain

Luke's Golden Misty
—Misty's Sungold Lad

Metolius Miss
—Golden Rocket's Raincheck
Golden Rocket's Ruff Boy

Moll-Leo Ginger Snap*
—Willhaggins Ready Poacher

Molly of Crooked River
—FC-AFC Moll-Leo Cayenne
Moll-Leo Ginger Snap
Molly's Cayson Bear
=Molly's Cayson Bear
Willhaggin's Ready Poacher

Nancy's Golden Dawn
—Bonnie Brooks Barney
AFC Bonnie Brooks Elmer
FC Bonnie Brooks Tuff & A Half

Pink Lady of Audlon
—FC-AFC Stilrovin Tuppee Tee
=Angus of Stilrovin
Stilrovin Clipper Delane II
Tigathoe's Teetotaler

Princess Grace Ann
—Marshall's Texas Duke

Princess Kilroy
—J's Teeko of Tigathoe

Rushmore's Little Miss Muffet
—Briggs Lake Golden Boy

Shenandoah of Stilrovin
—Duke of Handjem
Kinike Chancellor
AFC Kinike Coquette
King Kinike of Handjem

Stilrovin Kathy-K
—Angus of Stilrovin
Sabe Lo Todo of Stilrovin
=AFC Chief Sands
Duke of Handjem
Kinike Chancellor

Stilrovin Tuppee Tee*
—Tigathoe's Teetotaler

Stilrovin Whitey Barker
—Stilrovin Clipper Delane II

Tansy of High Farms
—AFC Riverview's Chickasaw Thistle
Tigathoe's Chickasaw

Tigerdale's Bonnie Meg
—FC-AFC Tioga Joe

Tigerdale's Tinkerbelle
—Tink's Ben of Pennywise

Tink of Golden Anno Nuevo
—Sir Michael Robert

Wayfarer's Annette
—FC-AFC Clickety Click

Wildwing Abby
—Northbreak's Panacea

CHESAPEAKE BAY SIRES

Atom Bob
—Bob's Aleutian Trojan
The Big Fellow
=Kimkay Target
FC-AFC Koolwaters Colt of
Tri Crown

Baron's Tule Tiger*
—FC-AFC Tiger's Cub
Tiger's Texas Tiger
=Aubrae's Sand Turk
FC Cub's Kobi King

Beewacker's Chester
—Meg's Tammy O'Hara
=FC-AFC Mount Joy's Bit O'
Ginger
Mount Joy's Mickey Finn

Bomarc of South Bay
—FC-AFC Koolwater's Colt of Tri-
crown
=Baronland's Alaska Bob

Chesanoma's Louis
—FC-AFC Chesanoma's Kodiak

Chesaried Donachie Topper
—Aubrae's Sand Turk

Hector
—AFC Copper Topper Der Wunderbar

Honker of Mount Joy
—Mount Joy's Dilwyne Jez O'Meg

J. J.'s Coca Cola
—J. J.'s Hy-Wyne Willows

Meg's O'Timothy
—Mount Joy's Mickey Finn
FC-AFC Mount Joy's Bit O'Ginger

Mount Joy's Mallard
—FC-AFC Mount Joy's Louistoo
=Andy's Bullheaded Bulldozer
FC-AFC Chesanoma's Kodiak

Nancy's Cocoa Boy
—Stratte's Norske

Nelgard's Baron
—FC-AFC Baron's Tule Tiger

—FC-AFC Chesanoma's Kodiak
FC-AFC Tiger's Cub

Odessa Creek Benny
—Andy's Bullheaded Bulldozer

Rocky View's Radar Duke
—Baronland's Alaska Bob
Rocky of Cal-Peake

The Big Fellow*
—Kimkay Target

Tiger's Cub*
—FC Cub's Kobi King

CHESAPEAKE BAY DAMS

Aleutian Duchess
—Bob's Aleutian Trojan
=FC-AFC Koolwaters Colt of
Tri Crown

Bonnie La Bonita
—AFC Copper Topper Der Wunderbar

Chesareid April Echo
—FC Cub's Kobi King

Chopper's Bobbie
—Kimkay Target

Dinie's Miss Priss
=FC-AFC Chesanoma's Kodiak

Dyna of the Willows
—J. J.'s Hy-Wyne Willows

Frosty Milady
—FC-AFC Mount Joy's Louistoo
=FC-AFC Mount Joy's Bit
O'Ginger
Mount Joy's Dilwyne Jez O'Meg
Mount Joy's Micky Finn

Frosty's Bold Gypsy
—Aubrae's Sand Turk

Joanie Teal
—FC-AFC Baron's Tule Tiger
=FC-AFC Tiger's Cub

Meg O' My Heart
—Meg's Tammy O'Hara

=FC-AFC Mount Joy's Bit
O' Ginger
Mount Joy's Micky Finn

Mount Joy's Joy
—Andy's Bullheaded Bulldozer

Mount Joy's Jug Ears
—FC-AFC Mount Joy's Bit O' Ginger
Mount Joy's Dilwyne Jez O'Meg
Mount Joy's Micky Finn
=Andy's Bullheaded Bulldozer

Mystic Amber of Agassiz
—Rocky of Cal-Peake

Napolitano's Lady Bug
—FC-AFC Tiger's Cub
Tiger's Texas Tiger
=FC Cub's Kobi King

Silence of Goff's Market
—Stratte's Norske

South Bay Belinda B
—Baronland's Alaska Bob

Welcome of the Willows
—FC-AFC Koolwater's Colt of
Tri Crown

Wisconong Champagne Lady
—The Big Fellow
=Kimkay Target

FLAT COAT SIRES

Brancroft Dandy
—Copper Caliph of Mantayo

Halstock Javelin
—Wyndham's Wingover Brunhild

Stolford's Whinchat
—Stolford Black Queen
=Wyndham's Wingover Brunhild

Westerner
—Mantayo Ramblin' Wreck

FLAT COAT DAMS

Claverdon Duchess
—Copper Caliph of Mantayo
Mantayo's Ramblin Wreck

Stolford Black Queen*
—Wyndham's Wingover Brunhild

Stolford Hartshorn Memory
—Stolford Black Queen
=Wyndham's Wingover Brunhild

PART IV

JUDGES

of

OPEN ALL-AGE STAKES

and

AMATEUR ALL-AGE STAKES

1967 - 1972

JUDGES
OF
OPEN ALL-AGE STAKES
AND
AMATEUR ALL-AGE STAKES
1967 - 1972
PREFACE and COMMENTARY

In the following summary there are shown the number of Open All-Age Stakes and of Amateur All-Age Stakes judged by each person who has been active in this area during the years 1967-1972. With respect to these persons, we have also shown where applicable, the number of stakes in each category judged prior to the period reviewed, and the life-time totals.

The information set forth for the current period was compiled from Retriever Field Trial News, which, in turn obtained its information from the Trial Catalogues. Names have been checked where possible against the judges' list published annually by the American Kennel Club. However some errors may still be included due to last minute changes in judges which have not been reflected in the catalogues, and confusions resulting from failure in some catalogues to give the full names of judges. For example, the listing "Dr. Richard Ellis" leaves in the air whether the person referred to is Dr. Richard L. Ellis, or Dr. Richard A. Ellis, both of whom are active judges.

Further, the compilation is historical in approach and includes the record of all the subject judges, regardless of whether at the end of 1972 some are no longer active due to death, retirement, loss of eligibility or no longer in Amateur status. Persons desiring to determine current activity of judges are referred to the judges' list published annually by the American Kennel Club.

Prior judging records of persons who judged during the period reviewed were taken from the 1962-1966 Edition of the Labrador Retriever Club Book, and from the 1962-1966 Edition of The Handbook of Amateur Retriever Trials.

It is interesting to note that during the six year period, a total of 577 individuals are recorded as having judged one or more Open All-Age Stakes, or Amateur All-Age Stakes, or both. Of these, 244 appear as having judged one or more stakes prior to 1967, and of these 117 were already "Senior" judges with 8 or more points and 69 went on to become "Senior" judges after January 1, 1967. The remaining 333 individuals, judged for the first time subsequent to January 1967 — an average of 55 new judges a year for the six year period — Again of these new judges, 16 have now acquired "Senior" status. The aggregate of new "Senior" judges created during the period reviewed is thus 85, or an average of 14 per year. It is a matter of conjecture whether this rate of increase is adequate when there is taken into consideration the number of judges becoming inactive each year coupled with the ever increasing number of stakes to be judged.

Among the judges who were active during this period, the following have judged, during their lifetime the greatest number of Open and Amateur All-Age Stakes.

Name	No. Judged	Name	No. Judged
Dale Lundstrom	108	Herbert Fleishhacker, Jr.	65
J. W. McAssey	104	Robert D. Brown	63
Dr. George H. Gardner	97	Guy P. Burnett	60
Dr. John C. Lundy	96	E. C. Christiansen	60
Donald L. Burnett	90	W. J. Salomonsen	60
A. Wells Wilbor	87	John A. Love, Jr.	59
John Romadka	82	A. W. Agnew	55
Ernest J. Goppert, Jr.	76	James F. Stillwell	55
George D. Alt	73	Richard H. Hecker	53
Dr. Gene B. Starkloff	71	Harold Mack, Jr.	51
Hugh Adams	67	Paul Provenzano	50
Andrieus A. Jones	65		

The persons who judged the most Open and Amateur All-Age Stakes during the period, 1967-1972 were:

Name	No. Judged	Name	No. Judged
Donald L. Burnett	44	A. W. Agnew	22
Dale Lundstrom	43	Warren W. Carity	22
J. W. McAssey	39	Dr. R. C. Greenleaf	22
E. J. Goppert, Jr.	35	James V. Mediate	22
Paul Provenzano	33	A. Wells Wilbor	22
A. Nelson Sills	33	Charles R. York	22
Dr. Gene B. Starkloff	30	William K. Chilcott	21
Sid H. Eliason, Jr.	24	W. L. Malcolm	21
Richard H. Johnson	24	Mrs. S. Alan Williams	21
Howard T. Jones	24	Tom S. Bomford	20
Dr. John C. Lundy	24	Andrieus A. Jones	20
Gus F. Rathert	24	S. Alan Williams	20
Robert D. Brown	23	Dr. Robert D. Wood	20

JUDGES OF OPEN AND AMATEUR ALL-AGE STAKES

ACTIVE IN 1967 - 1972 PERIOD

NOTE: Numbers marked * include a National or National Amateur Championship Stake, as the case may be, judged during the 1967 - 1972 period.

	OPEN			AMATEUR			
	Prior to 1967	from 1967	Total	Prior to 1967	from 1967	Total	Grand Total
Ackles, Robert		1	1		1	1	2
Adams, Hugh	25	10	35	23	9*	32	67
Adams, Robert A.		1	1		1	1	2
Agnew, A. W.	18	10	28	15	12*	27	55
Ahlgren, Gary		2	2				2
Allen, Carl F.		5	5		6	6	11
Alpaugh, George L.		1	1		2	2	3
Alsaker, Harry G.	5	2	7	4	1	5	12
Alt, George D.	45	3	48	22	3	25	73
Anderson, Eugene L.	1	4	5	4	3	7	12
Anderson, Ken M.		5	5	2	5	7	12
Anderson, Richard					1	1	1
Andrews, Donald E.	1	2	3		6	6	9
Arnold, Fred J.		1	1		1	1	2
Aston, Dr. James W., Jr.					1	1	1
Aylstock, Frank		1	1		1	1	2
Bacus, Pat		1	1				1
Bader, Don					1	1	1
Baker, Dr. Ben B.	3	12	15	3	10	13	28
Baker, M. M.					1	1	1
Barnes, Daniel S.		3	3				3
Barratt, J. Steve				1	1	2	2
Barrett, Bob		1	1		1	1	2
Bateman, R. O.	6	4	10	6	9	15	25
Bauer, Al		1	1				1
Belmont, August	14	10	24	7	4	11	35
Bernard, Dr. William		1	1		1	1	2
Bernstein Jerome D.	3	2	5	2	2	4	9
Bicknell, Guthrie	22	1	23	22	1	23	46
Bierschied, Charles		1	1		1	1	2
Bisso, Robert J.		4	4		1	1	5
Blair, John R.		2	2				2

	OPEN			AMATEUR			
	Prior to 1967	from 1967	Total	Prior to 1967	from 1967	Total	Grand Total
Blazier, Elton	7	1	8	5	1	6	14
Blue, Robert		3	3		3	3	6
Blume, Les					1	1	1
Bly, Ray E.		2	2		4	4	6
Boatright, Joseph		1	1				1
Boehler, Orlie J.		1	1		1	1	2
Boelz, Dale					2	2	2
Boese, Henry		1	1				1
Boettcher, Jack		1	1				1
Bogrett, Jere W.	2	5	7	2	8	10	17
Bomford, Tom S.	3	10	13		10	10	23
Bonham, James					1	1	1
Borden, Richard D.		4	4		1	1	5
Bowen, William E.		1	1		2	2	3
Boyer, John L.		2	2		3	3	5
Bozone, Jesse		1	1				1
Bray, Mrs. George					1	1	1
Brewer, Delmar E.	2	1	3	2	2	4	7
Brewer, Oscar S.		2	2		5	5	7
Brice, Richard B.		1	1		1	1	2
Brinkman, Dr. Roy J.		2	2				2
Bronner, Henry A.		1	1				1
Broussard, Lee C.	3	5*	8	4	7	11	19
Broussard, Marjorie					2	2	2
Brown, Alanson C. III		1	1				1
Brown, Edward H.	10	8*	18	11	9*	20	38
Brown, Dr. Irwin S.	11	1	12	4	4	8	20
Brown, Robert D.	22	11	33	18	12	30	63
Browning, James D.					5	5	5
Bruch, E. P., Jr.	12		12	13	1	14	26
Bruns, Jack		2	2				2
Bryant, William		1	1				1
Bump, Glenn B.	12	7	19	10	6	16	35
Bunn, Charles E.		1	1		9	9	10
Burnett, Bruce		1	1				1
Burnett, Donald L.	24	29	53	22	15	37	90
Burnett, Guy P.	27	6	33	26	2	28	61
Burrill, Larry L.		4	4	4	5*	9	13
Buskoviak, I. J.	3	2	5	12	5	17	22
Buss, Dr. Irven		2	2		3	3	5
Butkovich, Anton B.		1	1		1	1	2
Buxton, Wilford J.					1	1	1
Camp, Frank L., Jr.	3	7	10	1	7	8	18
Carey, Mrs. W. B.		1	1				1
Carity, Warren W.	9	15*	24	11	7*	18	42
Carpenter, Kensyle L.	1	2	3		2	2	5
Carpenter, Mrs. Kensyle L.		1	1				1
Carraway, W. C.	4	4	8	2	4	6	14
Carrier, Les		1	1				1
Carrion, Walter J.		2	2		1	1	3
Case, Edward G.		1	1		1	1	2
Casey, James L.	6		6	6	1	7	13
Chance, Robert G.		1	1				1
Chandler, William A.		2	2		6	6	8
Chatelain, Felix					2	2	2
Cherry, Guy H., Jr.	10	2	12	10	1	11	23

	OPEN			AMATEUR			
	Prior to 1967	from 1967	Total	Prior to 1967	from 1967	Total	Grand Total
Chilcott, W. K.		10	10		11	11	21
Childress, Robert		1	1				1
Christensen, E. C.	24	8	32	18	10	28	60
Christenson, J. G.	1	1	2	2		2	4
Christiansen, Christian W.	2	8	10	4	6	10	20
Christiansen, Mrs. Christian W.				1	2	3	3
Christopher, Clifford	4	1	5	3	4	7	12
Clucas, Don		1	1		1	1	2
Coburn, Guy		1	1		1	1	2
Cockerell, Dr. S. F.	2	1	3	2	3	5	8
Cohn, Eugene M.	7	3	10	5		5	15
Coletti, Barry		3	3		2	2	5
Columbo, James C.	15	2	17	12	5	17	34
Colwill, Robert W.		1	1		1	1	2
Common, Miles E.	3	5	8	1	6	7	15
Compton, Owen G.	7	4	11	10	2	12	23
Connor, William D.		3	3		1	1	4
Copeland, William H.	4	2	6	4	4	8	14
Cornish, A. T.		2	2	1	6	7	9
Corona, Eugene A.					2	2	2
Correll, James					1	1	1
Cosner, Harry W.		3	3		4	4	7
Couch, Kenneth	1	2	3	2		2	5
Craig, C. A., II		4	4	1	4	5	9
Crain, Earl					1	1	1
Cramond, Pat		2	2				2
Cross, John R.					3	3	3
Crow, David					1	1	1
Culbertson, James		1	1				1
Cullen, Edward		2	2				2
Daley, William M.					2	2	2
Dashnaw, Dr. F. A.	9	4	13	9	4	13	26
Dean, Stuart M.	1		1	1	1	2	3
Deering, Rudy R.		2	2	1	3	4	6
Dega, Hugh					1	1	1
Dengal, Ron					1	1	1
Des Jardin, Donald		2	2		4	4	6
De Zurik, Donald					2	2	2
Dillon, William W., III		1	1		1	1	2
Doar, Bachman		1	1		1	1	2
Dobesh, Rupert A.	1	6	7	1	4	5	12
Doherty, James J.		1	1		3	3	4
Donnelly, Alvah		1	1		1	1	2
Dugan, Larry					1	1	1
Dyrenforth L. Y.					1	1	1
Ebeling, Arthur		1	1		1	1	2
Eckis, Robert E.	1	1	2	1	1	2	4
Eddy, Garrett					1	1	1
Effinger, Robert T., Jr.	3	2	5	1		1	6
Eggers Harold		1	1				1
Egly, Albert		1	1	2	3	5	6
Eliason, Sid. H., Jr.	12	12*	24	10	12	22	46
Elkins, Henry	2	1	3	1	2	3	6
Ellis, Dr. Richard A.	5	3	8	8	6	14	22
Ellis, Dr. Richard L.	7	7*	14	8	8	16	30
Emerson, John		1	1				1

	OPEN			AMATEUR			
	Prior to 1967	from 1967	Total	Prior to 1967	from 1967	Total	Grand Total
Erwin, Arnold		1	1				1
Evans, Harvey M.	7	1	8	6	2	8	16
Evans, Ted		1	1		1	1	2
Faddis, Wayne	16	7	23	17	11	28	51
Fajen, T. E., Jr.	9	9*	18	9	5	14	32
Fajen, Mrs. T. E., Jr.	4	1	5		4	4	9
Faue, Wilfred F.	5		5	2	1	3	8
Ferguson, Joseph V.		2	2		2	2	4
Fertitta, Dr. Julian J.		3	3		1	1	4
Files, Robert A.		2	2		3	3	5
Filson, Dr. Malcolm M.	10	9	19	5	7	12	31
Fiorella, Anthoni		1	1				1
Fischer, C. Alan	11	6	17	9	4	13	30
Flannery, Michael R.	1	11	12		6	6	18
Flashman, Dr. Forrest L.	22	4	26	15	3	18	44
Flath, H. Albert	3		3	3	4	7	10
Fleischmann, Mrs. Helen		4	4		1	1	5
Fleishhacker, Herbert, Jr.	35	4	39	23	3	26	65
Fletcher, Dr. Frank L.	13	6	19	11	6	17	36
Floberg, Leonard P.	1	2	3		1	1	4
Fotheringham, John T.		4	4		4	4	8
Franconi, James					1	1	1
Frank, Armin C., Jr.		3	3		3	3	6
Fraser, Robert		1	1		1	1	2
Frazer, W. Clayton		1	1				1
Fredricksen, John		2	2				2
Fruen, Donald					1	1	1
Frye, Stephen F.		2	2				2
Gacek, Stan		1	1		1	1	2
Gardner, Dr. George H.	55	5	60	34	3	37	97
Gardner, Jack	2	1	3	2	2	4	7
Gardner, Dr. Richard G.	3	9	12	2	9*	11	23
Gardner, Stephen V.	2	1	3	3	2	5	8
Garvey, Judge Richard J.					1	1	1
Gelardi, Sal					1	1	1
Gerding, Stanley F.	6		6	3	1	4	10
Gesner, Edwin E.	2	3	5	2	5	7	12
Gillespie, W. H.					1	1	1
Goans, Dale					1	1	1
Gomolchak, Leo					1	1	1
Goodrich, Raymond H.		1	1		2	2	3
Goodwin, Dana B.	4	1	5	4	1	5	10
Goppert, Ernest J., Jr.	20	20	40	21	15	36	76
Gott, Edwin H., Jr.					2	2	2
Gourley, Jack		1	1		2	2	3
Graham, James		1	1		1	1	2
Gray, George J.		2	2		3	3	5
Greene, Philip E. N., Jr.		1	1	3		3	4
Greenleaf, Dr. Richard C.	5	7	12	5	15*	20	32
Greve, Neil					1	1	1
Grunwald, Byron B.	15	7	22	10	9	19	41
Grunwald, Mrs. Byron B.					1	1	1
Guss, James		1	1				1
Haas, Jack L.				2	1	3	3
Hallberg, Wallace C.	15	9	24	9	6	15	39
Hamilton, George W.	16	1	17	17		17	34

| | OPEN | | | AMATEUR | | | |
	Prior to 1967	from 1967	Total	Prior to 1967	from 1967	Total	Grand Total
Hanna, Dr. James C.	4	2	6	6		6	12
Hannon, Ross					1	1	1
Hansen, George M., III		7	7		8	8	15
Harang, Jack W.					1	1	1
Harris, Weldon		3	3	1	5	6	9
Harrison, Timothy A.	2	1	3	2	2	4	7
Harvey, Dr. Charles B.		1	1				1
Hasell, Louis D., Jr.					1	1	1
Haskell, Lewis, III		2	2		2	2	4
Hatler, Patrick		3	3		2	2	5
Hays, Charles A.		1	1		1	1	2
Hecker, Richard H.	19	14	33	15	5	20	53
Heins, Richard		2	2				2
Heller, Mrs. Walter S.	10	3	13	8	8	16	29
Hempel, John P.		3	3		1	1	4
Henderson, Dr. J. W.	6	8*	14	9	8	17	31
Henderson, John		1	1				1
Heneghan, James J.	11	2	13	9	6	15	28
Herlin, C. P.		2	2		1	1	3
Hill, Eugene H.	1	3	4	1	4	5	9
Hilton, Frank H.	1	1	2		3	3	5
Hirt, Leland	1	5	6	5	5	10	16
Hoffman, Dr. M. D.		5	5		11	11	16
Hogan, William		1	1		2	2	3
Hogue, Jack		2	2		2	2	4
Hogue, Mrs. Jack					1	1	1
Horel, Dr. Tom		1	1		2	2	3
Horn, Richard L.		3	3		2	2	5
Horn, William		2	2		2	2	4
Horton, John					1	1	1
Hottel, Ted R.		2	2				2
Houston, Orlando					1	1	1
Howard, James H.		1	1				1
Howard, Robert E.		8	8		4	4	12
Hronis, Gust	2	5	7	1	5	6	13
Hronis, Mrs. Gust		6	6	1	7	8	14
Huleen, Dr. John		1	1		2	2	3
Hunt, Clifford J.	2	3	5	2	5	7	12
Hutchinson, Dr. Roy		3	3	1	5	6	9
Hutt, Donald	4	9	13		6	6	19
Hyatt, Robert		1	1		1	1	2
Imlar, John A.		1	1				1
Jackson, James B.	10	6*	16	5	5	10	26
Jacobs, Howard					1	1	1
Jarvis, Lloyd	3	1	4	2	2	4	8
Jenkins, Dr. John		1	1		1	1	2
Johnson, Gilbert		1	1				1
Johnson, Margie D.					1	1	1
Johnson, Rense R., Jr.		1	1		3	3	4
Johnson, Richard H.	8	13*	21	7	11	18	39
Johnson, Roger		1	1				1
Johnson, Wayne		1	1		1	1	2
Johnson, Willard C.	1	4	5	1	4	5	10
Jones, Andrieus A.	27	14	41	18	6*	24	65
Jones, Dan J.		4	4		2	2	6
Jones, Howard T.	1	13	14		11	11	25

	OPEN			AMATEUR			
	Prior to 1967	from 1967	Total	Prior to 1967	from 1967	Total	Grand Total
Kane, Bernard F.		1	1				1
Keady, Mrs. Edward		1	1		1	1	2
Keltgen, Dr. Victor B.	3		3	4	1	5	8
Kennon, Robert F., Jr.		1	1		2	2	3
Kerns, Richard		1	1				1
Kesky, Dr. G. Richard					1	1	1
Kiernan, Dr. Paul C.	8	6	14	6	11*	17	31
Kilbourn, Fred					1	1	1
Kincaid, Darrel D.		5	5		4	4	9
King, Jack					1	1	1
Kitchen, Earl F.	2	2	4	2	9	11	15
Klaren, Hugh I.	16	9	25	14	10*	24	49
Klicker, Elaine L.		1	1				1
Kloepfer, Roy		1	1				1
Knez, Fred L.		2	2				2
Knight, Lyle	1	1	2				2
Knox, Robert		2	2			1	3
Koch, Dr. Joe L.		2	2	1		1	3
Krauth, Norman				2		2	2
La Bud Leonard L.				1		1	1
Ladwig, Robert		1	1	3		3	4
Lambert, Richard				2	1	3	3
Lane, Joseph					1	1	1
Larson, Robert		1	1		1	1	2
Last, William C.		2	2				2
Laughlin, William K.	18	2	20	16	2	18	38
Le Clerc, Maurice J.	4	1	5	6	1	7	12
Lee, Richard		1	1				1
Leineke, Ron					3	3	3
Leonard, James R.		3	3		1	1	4
Lewis, Mrs. Reginald M.		4	4	2	6	8	12
Lezina, Raymond		2	2		1	1	3
Lindemere, Gordon	2	1	3	2		2	5
Lockwood, William F.					1	1	1
Lohr, Calvin E.		2	2	2		2	4
Long, Fred F.					1	1	1
Love, John A., Jr.	22	10	32	21	6*	27	59
Lowder, B. G.	1	1	2				2
Lucas, Robert		1	1				1
Lucas, Thomas J.				2	1	3	3
Lundstrom, Dale	35	26*	61	30	18	48	109
Lundy, Dr. John C.	38	14*	52	34	10	44	96
Mack, Harold, Jr.	16	10*	26	19	6	25	51
MacKay, Sandy F.	9	6	15	9	4	13	28
MacMillan, Philip		1	1				1
Madsen, Jack		2	2		2	2	4
Maeck, William		3	3				3
Magnusson, Roger N.		2	2		3	3	5
Mahan, Wayne E.	7	3	10		2	2	12
Mahoney, Daniel		2	2				2
Malcolm, W. L.	3	9	12	5	12	17	29
Mann, Don		1	1				
Mann, Robert W.					1	1	1
Marth, James K.		9	9		3	3	12
Martin, Charles					1	1	1
Martin, Daniel Wayne	2	4	6	1	1	2	8

| | OPEN | | | AMATEUR | | | |
	Prior to 1967	from 1967	Total	Prior to 1967	from 1967	Total	Grand Total
Martin, John					3	3	3
Martin, John M.		1	1		1	1	2
Mason, Austin B., Jr.	12	2	14	4	2	6	20
Matthews, Orus J., Jr.					2	2	2
Mayfield, Ross		1	1				1
McAssey, J. W.	36	20	56	29	19*	48	104
McClellan, P. G.	1		1		1	1	2
McClintock, Michael E.	1	3	4			2	6
McGraw, Everett R.	2	10	12	1	7	8	20
McGrew, H. C.	1		1	2	1	3	4
McInnis, Hugh, Jr.	1	8	9		10	10	19
McMahan, C. A.	5	5	10	7	2	9	19
McNaughton, William		2	2				2
McPhail, Marian	3	2	5		1	1	6
McWhorter, R. M.	4		4	4	4	8	12
Mediate, James V.	5	11	16	7	11	18	34
Melchiors, Jerry					3	3	3
Mensie, Vern A.					1	1	1
Mesch, Robert		4	4		3	3	7
Metz, Dr. Francis					2	2	2
Meyer, D. K.		1	1				1
Meyer, Wally					4	4	4
Michael, Charles E.		1	1				1
Michael, David		2	2		1	1	3
Mickey, William S.					1	1	1
Miller, Dr. Carroll S.		2	2		1	1	3
Miller, Frank W.	1	4	5	2	3	5	10
Miller, G. Glenn		7	7		7	7	14
Miller, Henry R., Jr.		1	1		1	1	2
Milliken, Dudley, Jr.					1	1	1
Mitchell, Andrew	2	1	3	2	3	5	8
Mitchell, Jack F.	5	2	7	7	2	9	16
Mitchell, Jesse J.		10	10		5	5	15
Mizen, Anthony J.		1	1				1
Mondor, Ernest		1	1		1	1	2
Montgomery, John T.		1	1		1	1	2
Moody, Mrs. Edna		1	1				1
Moody, Kenneth					1	1	1
Moore, Eugene R.	2	3	5	1	3	4	9
Moore, Winston H.	18	2	20	18	2	20	40
Moran, Dr. Frank S.					1	1	1
Morar, Jon W.					1	1	1
Morgan, Dr. John					1	1	1
Mortensen, C. W.	17	1	18	15		15	33
Moss, Gordon	10	3	13	7	2	9	22
Mullahey, Joseph A.		2	2		2	2	4
Mullen, J. Robert	12	1	13	10	2	12	25
Munroe, Scott		2	2		2	2	4
Murff, William					1	1	1
Murphy, Jack C.		5	5		1	1	6
Murray, Blaine		1	1		2	2	3
Nash, John F.	21	2	23	14	3	17	40
Nelson, Kenneth P.	5	1	6	4	2	6	12
Nelson, Niles		1	1		1	1	2
New, Cecil A., Jr.		1	1	5	1	6	7
Nicholson, James					1	1	1

	OPEN			AMATEUR			
	Prior to 1967	from 1967	Total	Prior to 1967	from 1967	Total	Grand Total
Norwood, Dr. Lyle		1	1				1
Nygaard, Wayne		1	1		2	2	3
Odell, Richard		3	3		2	2	5
Offerdahl, Ray		1	1		2	2	3
Olinger, Gordon B.		1	1	1	1	2	3
Olsen, S. L.	4	1	5		5	5	10
Olson, Dr. Duane					1	1	1
Olson, James R.		1	1		1	1	2
Olson, Dr. O. Charles	8	1	9	6	1	7	16
Orowitz, Milton D.	12	8	20	11	8*	19	39
Osborn, Ralph L.		5	5		6	6	11
Ott, Jack D.		1	1		1	1	2
Palmore, John S.					1	1	1
Parker, Dr. Clark					1	1	1
Parker, Dr. Dean	20	3	23	16	2	18	41
Partridge, Dr. Francis W.		1	1		3	3	4
Pasley, L. E.	1	3	4	1	5	6	10
Patopea, Rudy		1	1		3	3	4
Patrick, Joseph E.	2	1	3		3	3	6
Peltzer, Dr. Wesley E.	1	6	7	1	6	7	14
Pennington, Thomas		1	1		2	2	3
Pentheny, Hedley					1	1	1
Peterson, Lester		2	2		1	1	3
Pettijohn, James A.		1	1				1
Pierce, Dr. E. E.	4	3	7	4	4*	8	15
Pilar, Joseph M.		1	1		2	2	3
Poer, John		1	1				1
Poole, Robert N.	3	1	4	2	1	3	7
Poppendorf, Eugene					1	1	1
Pound, Perry E.	5	9	14	8	10	18	32
Pratt, Howard M.	3	3	6	3	5	8	14
Preston, John M.	2	1	3	3	1	4	7
Prindle, Clayton	1	10	11		3	3	14
Provenzano, Paul J.	9	13	22	8	20	28	50
Pruitt, Andrew D.	4	5	9	1	4	5	14
Puchner, Irving A.	18	1	19	16	1	17	36
Quinn, Courtney C.	12		12	6	1	7	19
Rabeler, H. J.		1	1		1	1	2
Rathert, Gus F.	5	15*	20	6	9	15	35
Rautiainen, Jack					1	1	1
Ray, Robert B., Jr.	16	6	22	13	9	22	44
Reames, Thomas J.	11	10	21	18	5	23	44
Reath, Mrs. B. Brannan, II	20	3	23	16	3	19	42
Reeve, Richard	10	8	18	7	5	12	30
Reid, W. Irwin		1	1				1
Rentz, J. F.	1	8	9		8	8	17
Reppert, Dr. Lawrence B.	1	5	6	1	5	6	12
Rice, Carroll A.		2	2	2	7*	9	11
Rice, Donald					1	1	1
Richards, Jerry		1	1		1	1	2
Richardson, Don		1	1				1
Richardson, E. W., Jr.					1	1	1
Rickard, Tom		1	1		2	2	3
Rieman, Keith	1	2	3	1	4	5	8
Rietz, Dr. Dan		1	1				1
Robinson, A. James	9	4	13	4	3	7	20

	OPEN			AMATEUR			
	Prior to 1967	from 1967	Total	Prior to 1967	from 1967	Total	Grand Total
Rockenbach, Roy		1	1		1	1	2
Rogers, Andy		1	1		1	1	2
Rohr, Norvin		1	1	1	3	4	5
Romadka, John	45	4	49	32	1	33	82
Romano, Noxie, M., Jr.	3	8	11	5	6	11	22
Rose, Frank, Jr.		1	1				1
Ross, Jerry		1	1		7	7	8
Roughen, John P.		2	2	1	1	2	4
Rovelstad, Robert		3	3				3
Rubel, Stanley J.		2	2	2	1	3	5
Ruffalo, Carl		2	2		7	7	9
Ryan, Dr. A. L.	7	4	11	8	2	10	21
Ryan, Robert W.		1	1	1	1	2	3
Sabbag, Dr. William					1	1	1
Sabban, Dr. Robert					1	1	1
Saffell, Elmer B.	1	3	4		3	3	7
Safranek, C. H.					1	1	1
Salomonsen, William J.	29	4	33	21	6	27	60
Sampson, Richard		1	1		3	3	4
Sandahl, Robert		1	1				1
Sant, Richard C.		1	1		1	1	2
Saunders, Wilbur					1	1	1
Saunders, Mrs. Wilbur		1	1				1
Savell, Clifford W.	2	5	7	4	3	7	14
Scharf, Les		1	1				1
Scheihing, Glenn P.		1	1		5	5	6
Scherer, Walter K.					2	2	2
Schmitt, Dr. Daryl P.	9	3	12	6	5	11	23
Schroeder, William F.	10	2	12	8	3	11	23
Seese, Gordon					1	1	1
Segal, N. Jack		1	1		2	2	3
Seguin, Mark		1	1				1
Sellen, John					1	1	1
Sessa, Ronald					1	1	1
Shaver, Dr. Robert		2	2		2	2	4
Shaw, Eugene E.	3	6	9		6	6	15
Shea, S. C.	11	7	18	6	5*	11	29
Shearer, B. F., Jr.	1	7	8	1	7	8	16
Shenar, John G.					1	1	1
Shidler, Harold	18	5	23	13	2	15	38
Shoemaker, J. Blaine		4	4		2	2	6
Shoemaker, Mrs. Paul	4	9	13	3	9	12	25
Sills, A. Nelson	7	20*	27	7	13	20	47
Simmons, Charles C.	7	1	8	7	2	9	17
Simonds, Marshall	2	10*	12	2	4	6	18
Skinner, George W.	6	6	12	4	7	11	23
Smith, Donald C.		1	1				1
Smith, Gary C.		1	1		1	1	2
Smith, Jaye		1	1				1
Smith, Orville P.		1	1		2	2	3
Smith, Ralph M.		6	6	1	4	5	11
Snoeyenbos, Louis J.		3	3		10	10	13
Sodorf, Cleon					1	1	1
Somerheiser, W. F.		1	1				1
Sparks, Robert	1	2	3	1	3	4	7
Spiker, Tom		1	1				1

	OPEN			AMATEUR			
	Prior to 1967	from 1967	Total	Prior to 1967	from 1967	Total	Grand Total
Springer, Ross		4	4	1	1	2	6
Sproston, Dr. E. Hugh					1	1	1
Starkloff, Dr. Gene B.	25	15*	40	16	15	31	71
Starkloff, Mrs. Gene B.	3		3	5	2	7	10
Stauffer, Robert		1	1				1
Stebbins, George W.	12	9	21	17	9	26	47
Steffanich, Stanley, Jr.	14	1	15	6	1	7	22
Stevens, Charles C. B.	2	1	3	1	2	3	6
Stevens, Mrs. Charles C. B.		3	3	1	3	4	7
Stewart, John					1	1	1
Stickney, Don		2	2		1	1	3
Stillwell, James F.	24	5	29	20	6	26	55
Stokes, Lloyd	1		1	1	1	2	3
Stone, Angus		1	1		1	1	2
Stritz, Rudy		1	1		1	1	2
Stroh, Peter	7	1	8	8		8	16
Stroud, Dr. Morris W., III		1	1				1
Stubblefield, Robert A.	2	1	3	2	1	3	6
Sutherland, Glen P.		1	1	1		1	2
Sveinson, Gordon		1	1				1
Swingle, Clinton D.		1	1		2	2	3
Tarrant, William		1	1				1
Tautfest, Eugene		1	1		1	1	2
Taylor, John E.		2	2		1	1	3
Tennant, Clifton J.	2	8	10	3	5	8	18
Tennant, S. G. B.	6	10	16	5	6	11	27
Thill, Herman		1	1				1
Thomas, Eugene		4	4		1	1	5
Thomas, Dr. Miles E.	3	9	12	3	9	12	24
Thompson, Charles C.		1	1	1	1	2	3
Thompson, Jay C.		2	2		2	2	4
Thompson, Steve		2	2		2	2	4
Thrane, George	2	7	9		3	3	12
Thurlow, Clearice		1	1		1	1	2
Tibbets, Raymond K.		1	1		1	1	2
Tigerman, Merle H.	2	1	3	3	2	5	8
Treadwell, Tim, III				1	1	2	2
Trimble, Tiff		1	1				1
Trzepacz, John		5	5		3	3	8
Tudor, Dr. John M.		1	1		2	2	3
Tunnel, Curtis		2	2		1	1	3
Turner, Stan O.		4	4		2	2	6
Tyler, Clarence W.	5	8	13	4	1	5	18
Van Bloom, John	8	6	14	5	4	9	23
Vandersluis, Dr. Robert W.		4	4		1	1	5
Vasselais, Mrs. Roger	1		1		1	1	2
Venerable, James		3	3		1	1	4
Venerable, Mrs. James		2	2		2	2	4
Versteeg, Dr. Charles N.	17	6	23	14	3	17	40
Vezey, Dr. Stanley A.				1	1	2	2
Vilagi, Sig E.		6	6		7	7	13
Voorhees, Charles K.		1	1		1	2	3
Walker, Jack T.		1	1		1	1	2
Walker, Mrs. Jack T.		1	1				1
Walsh, Thomas F.		1	1	1	1	2	3
Ware, Forest		1	1				1

281

	OPEN			AMATEUR			
	Prior to 1967	from 1967	Total	Prior to 1967	from 1967	Total	Grand Total
Warmoth, Gay		1	1		1	1	2
Watt, Rolland G.	12	1	13	13	1	14	27
Weber, Vernon	5	6	11	4	10	14	25
Wedin, Jim					1	1	1
Weiss, Donald P.		5	5	1	6	7	12
Welchi, John R.	1	4	5	1	3	4	9
Wever, James M.		2	2				2
Weyerhauser, Charles L.		1	1		3	3	4
White, Belton		2	2				2
White, John F.		1	1		2	2	3
White, Robert A.		1	1	1		1	2
Whitehill, Jeffrey W.		2	2	3	2	5	7
Whitson, D. B.		2	2				2
Wilbor, A. Wells	42	12	54	23	10*	33	87
Wiley, J. Guy		2	2		1	1	3
Wilkinson, Robert G.					1	1	1
Williams, Dr. M. F.	1	2	3	1	1	2	5
Williams, S. Alan	17	9*	26	10	11	21	47
Williams, Mrs. S. Alan	1	16	17	5	5	10	27
Williams, Ron T.		1	1				1
Williams, Vic					1	1	1
Williamson, Charles	1	3	4		4	4	8
Willis, Dr. Leon T.		1	1		1	1	2
Willis, Marshall	1	1	2	1		1	3
Willow, Robert		2	2		2	2	4
Wilson, George A.		1	1				1
Wilson, Henry R.	2	2	4	4	4	8	12
Wilson, William G.		1	1		1	1	2
Winburn, Dr. James R.	1	7	8		2	2	10
Wolfe, Harold R.		1	1		4	4	5
Wolfe, Robert N.	14	12	26	9	8	17	43
Wood, Richard L.				1	1	2	2
Wood, Dr. Robert D.	9	2	11	2	10	12	23
Wright, J. Douglas, Jr.					4	4	4
York, Charles R.	8	12*	20	5	10	15	35
Zimmerman, Dr. B. H.	6	1	7	5	2	7	14
Zinschlag, David	1	8	9		6	6	15
Zuchman, Mitchell N.		1	1				1
Zurcher, Dale A.	1	4	5		2	2	7

PART V

THE DOUBLE HEADERS

THE DOUBLE HEADERS

Organized in 1960 and dedicated to the support and best interests of the retriever game, The Double Headers is composed of members, all amateur handlers who have with the same dog, which the handler must have owned at the time, won both the Open and Amateur All-Age Stakes in the same AKC licensed or member club all-breed retriever trial.

Persons who have won Double Headers have increased since the date of the inception of The Double Headers' Club from 13 to 51, of which 44 can be considered as current members, with 15 new persons qualifying for membership during the 1967-1972 period.

At the end of 1972, Michael R. Flannery and River Oaks Corky with six double headers surpassed the record of five held for eleven years by Richard H. Hecker and Dolobran's Smoke Tail.

Mr. R. H. Hecker, one of the original prime movers of The Double Headers, has contributed the following foreword to this Part III:

FOREWORD

Our membership grows slowly but pridefully. In our first year, 1960, with only 13 charter members, we took both the National Amateur and the National, the latter with the only amateur trained dog as yet to do so. Since then we have added over 30 new members, captured 8 out of 12 National Amateur titles, and August Belmont and Don Weiss assisted Cotton and the Shoe by breaking in on the Berger-Walters-Riser monopoly of 7 National crowns in 11 years.

Augie really performed the hat trick. While serving as National Secretary, Field Trial Chairman, and head of most of the committees, he found time to pick up two consecutive National Amateur wins in 1967-68, then tacked on the National Championship to earn the only solid gold Double Header pin thus far issued. More are available for any of our amateurs who can come up with a dog like Soupy.

It is fitting that a do-it-yourself group of this stature continue to boost the retriever sport in all ways possible, and in particular by carrying on with the Open and Amateur record books. Thank you, August Belmont and John McAssey.

THE DOUBLE HEADERS

* Not currently an active member

Owner-Handler — Trial	Dog
R. O. Bateman AAA 9/67	Col-Tam of Craignook
August Belmont SAG 8/68; NAT AM 6/68 and NAT 11/68; DEL 10/72	Super Chief
Charles J. Bierschied RKM 8/65	Duke of Teddy Bear
Ray E. Bly SAM 3/69	Serrana Sootana of Genesee
Jere W. Bogrett BHB 6/72	Rodney's Mr. M. L. Coon
Richard D. Borden MNS 9/69; MNS 5/70	Smokey of Park Avenue
*James W. Bryan, Jr. PUG 8/57	Jibodad Dandy
Glenn B. Bump SRZ 2/61	Carr-Lab Hilltop
Charles E. Bunn, Jr. MTA 10/70	Sandy of Sourdough
Guy P. Burnett IDA 4/54; SPO 5/56; MON 9/56	Bitterroot Chinkee
Guy P. Burnett MON 9/68	Guy's Bitterroot Lucky
Wilford R. Buxton MOV 9/72	Nodrog Punkie
Kensyle L. Carpenter TAC 8/63	Tar Baby's Little Sweet Stuff
James L. Casey SCA 9/64; CSC 10/64	Cougar's Rocket
Dr. F. A. Dashnaw LAS 2/60	Meg's Pattie O'Rourke
Rudy R. Deering PUG 8/65; PUG 4/66	Captain of Lomac
*George L. Dukek WIL 8/58; NWR 4/59	Bracken's High Flyer
Sid H. Eliason, Jr. ACC 6/59; GSL 8/63	Salt Valley Ottie
Mrs. T. E. Fajen, Jr. MNS 9/63	Brandy Spirit of Netley
Michael R. Flannery MIL 6/69; MII 8/69; NFL 11/70 and MOB 3/71; FTP 6/71; ALK 8/72	River Oaks Corky
Mrs. E. C. Fleischmann SNA 5/64; SAG 9/66	Mount Joy's Louistoo
Leonard P. Floberg HEL 9/70	Clickety Click
W. H. Gillespie MIT 8/69	Pelican Lake Peggy
Raymond H. Goodrich SAG 7/71	Ray's Rascal
*James S. Guss WIS 9/63	Ebony's Jet Rebel
Richard H. Hecker SHE 8/57; MON 9/57; CNB 5/59; MNS 5/59; HEL 9/61	Dolobran's Smoke Tail
Richard H. Hecker GSL 5/60	Princess Patricia Stieg
Richard H. Hecker SCA 3/61; SHA 9/62	Frances Fishtail

Mrs. Walter S. Heller PUG 4/65	Baron's Tule Tiger
Andrieus A. Jones RED 7/61	Dairy Hill's Night Cap
Mrs. Albert P. Loening COL 9/63	Jet of Zenith
John W. Martin OHV 10/71	Orion's Sirius
John W. McAssey CNB 5/58	Mainliner Mike
*Cliff W. Mortensen TRI 6/53	Rip's Bingo
*Mrs. C. W. Mortensen DUL 8/63	Bingo's Ringo
*Ray E. Olson WMO 5/60; GSL 8/62	Avalanche Burnt Sage
Dr. Dean Parker SAM 3/63	MacKenzie's Clear Pitch
Dr. Wesley E. Peltzer GSL 8/66	Chesanoma's Kodiak
*Robert J. Pepper WMO 5/62; WMO 9/62	Pepper's Jiggs
Perry E. Pound SHE 9/65	Sir Knight Falcon
Gus F. Rathert LAS 2/65; NCA 3/67	Rebel Chief of Heber
Gus W. Riefler, Jr. NTX 10/60	Riefler's Dutch
*Edwin Salvino ORE 4/52; NWR 4/52	Ardyn's Ace of Merwalfin
*Edwin Salvino NWR 4/65	Ace's Shed of Ardyn
Harold Shidler SAG 3/56	Hal's Spi-Wise Zeke
Louis J. Snoeyenbos NOI 9/63	Del-Tone Colvin
Edward R. Spaulding SCA 9/56	Manzanal Nimbus
S. G. Borden Tennant NTX 10/65	Teal Timmy of Glado
George E. Thrane CHE 5/64	Camliag's Pramero
Roger Vasselais WOL 9/65	Glengarven's Mik
Roger Vasselais MNS 6/66; SWA 11/66	Sir Mike of Orchard View
Rolland G. Watt IDA 8/59	Queenie of Redding
Dr. Ronald T. Williams NCA 3/60	Manzanal Clover
Donald P. Weiss NTX 10/69	Creole Sister

Super Chief
August Belmont
National Amateur Champion of 1967 and 1968
National Champion of 1968

Ardyn's Ace of Merwalfin — Eddie Salvino

First Double Header — First Amateur Field Trial Champion

National Champion of 1960

Dolobran's Smoke Tail — Richard Hecker

Bracken's High Flyer
George Dukek
National Amateur Champion of 1959

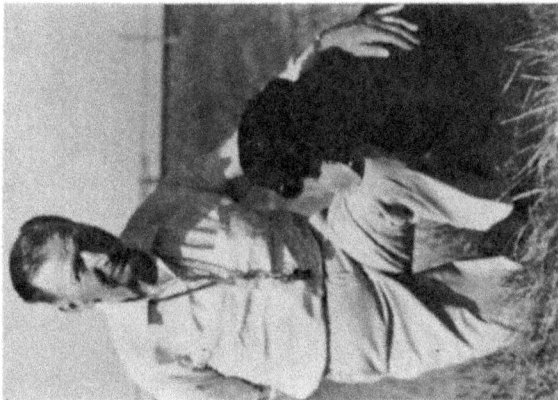

Del-Tone Colvin
Louis Snoeyenbos
National Champion of 1961 and 1963

Creole Sister
Don Weiss
National Champion of 1970

Pepper's Jiggs

Robert Pepper

National Amateur Champion of 1963

Carr-Lab Hilltop

Glenn Bump

National Amateur Champion of 1962

Queenie of Redding

Rolland Watt

National Amateur Champion of 1960

Guy's Bitterroot Lucky
Guy Burnett
National Amateur Champion of 1969

Captain of Lomac
Rudy Deering
National Amateur Champion of 1966
Canadian National Champion of 1966

Rebel Chief of Heber
Gus Rathert
National Amateur Champion of 1965

Tar Baby's Little Sweet Stuff
Ken Carpenter
Canadian National Champion of
1963 and 1965

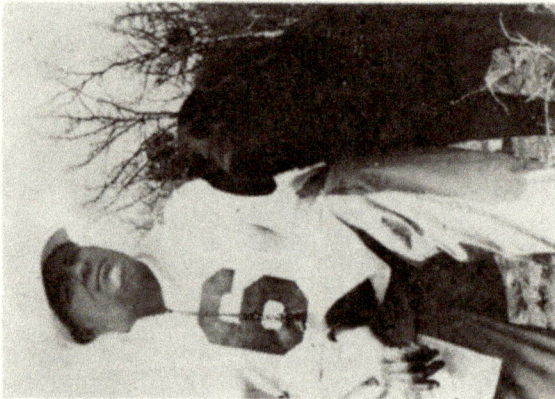

Hal's Spi-Wise Zeke
Hal Shidler
National Derby Champion of 1952

River Oaks Corky
Mike Flannery
National Amateur Champion of 1972
Canadian National Champion of 1971

Col-Tam of Craignook
Toby Bateman
National Derby Champion of 1962

Jet of Zenith
Mrs. Albert Loening
National Derby Champion of 1960

Meg's Pattie O'Rourke
Dr. Fred Dashnaw
National Derby Champion of 1958

Ray's Rascal
Ray Goodrich
National Derby Champion of 1969

Rip's Bingo
Cliff Mortensen

Mainliner Mike
J. W. McAssey

Salt Valley Ottie
Sid Eliason

Princess Patricia Stieg
Richard Hecker

Frances Fishtail
Richard Hecker

Dairy Hill's Night Cap
A. A. Jones

MacKenzie's Clear Pitch
Dr. Dean Parker

Ace's Shed of Ardyn
Eddie Salvino

Bingo's Ringo
Mrs. Cliff Mortensen

Brandy Spirit of Netley
Mrs. Theodore Fajen

Mount Joy's Louistoo
Mrs. E. C. Fleischmann

Camliag's Pramero
George Thrane

Cougar's Rocket
James L. Casey

Baron's Tule Tiger
Mrs. Walter Heller

Duke of Teddy Bear
Charles Bierschied

Sir Knight Falcon
Perry Pound

Glengarven's Mik
Roger Vasselais

Sir Mike of Orchardview
Roger Vasselais

Chesanoma's Kodiak
Dr. W. E. Peltzer

Nodrog Penny
Gordon Olinger

Serrana Sootana of Genesee
Ray Bly

Misty's Sungold Lad
Mrs. Jay Walker

Pelican Lake Peggy
Scottie Gillespie

Smokey of Park Avenue
Dick Borden

Clickety Click
Leonard Floberg

Sandy of Sourdough
Charles E. Bunn, Jr.

Orion's Sirius
John Martin

Nodrog Punkie

Bill Buxton

Rodney's Mister M. L. Coon

Jere Bogrett